THE NEO-ARAMAIC
ORAL HERITAGE OF
THE JEWS OF ZAKHO

The Neo-Aramaic Oral Heritage of the Jews of Zakho

Oz Aloni

https://www.openbookpublishers.com

© 2022 Oz Aloni.

This work is licensed under an Attribution-NonCommercial 4.0 International (CC BY-NC 4.0). This license allows you to share, copy, distribute and transmit the text; to adapt the text for non-commercial purposes providing attribution is made to the authors (but not in any way that suggests that they endorse you or your use of the work). Attribution should include the following information:

Oz Aloni, *The Neo-Aramaic Oral Heritage of the Jews of Zakho*. Cambridge Semitic Languages and Cultures 11. Cambridge, UK: Open Book Publishers, 2022, https://doi.org/10.11647/OBP.0272

Copyright and permissions for the reuse of many of the images included in this publication differ from the above. Copyright and permissions information for images is provided separately in the List of Illustrations.

In order to access detailed and updated information on the license, please visit, https://doi.org/10.11647/OBP.0272#copyright

Further details about CC BY-NC licenses are available at, https://creativecommons.org/licenses/by-nc/4.0/

All external links were active at the time of publication unless otherwise stated and have been archived via the Internet Archive Wayback Machine at https://archive.org/web

Updated digital material and resources associated with this volume are available at https://doi.org/10.11647/OBP.0272#resources

Every effort has been made to identify and contact copyright holders and any omission or error will be corrected if notification is made to the publisher.

Semitic Languages and Cultures 11.

ISSN (print): 2632-6906
ISSN (digital): 2632-6914

ISBN Paperback: 9781800643024
ISBN Hardback: 9781800643031
ISBN Digital (PDF): 9781800643048
DOI: 10.11647/OBP.0272

 This book is published with the support of the Martin Buber Society of Fellows at the Hebrew University of Jerusalem.

Cover images: The Abbasid Bridge in northern Iraq, photograph taken by Al Orfali, reproduced with permission, https://www.shutterstock.com/image-photo/abbasid-bridge-northern-iraq-1272853660

Cover design: Anna Gatti

CONTENTS

Acknowledgements xi

Introduction 1

    1.0.   The Jewish Community of Zakho 2

    2.0.   North-Eastern Neo-Aramaic (NENA) 9

    3.0.   The Study of Folklore 18

        3.1.   Jakobson and Bogatyrev's 'Folklore as a Special Form of Creation' 18

        3.2.   The Inherent Injustice of Analysis 21

        3.3.   The Study of Folklore as the Rejection of Folklore 22

    4.0.   The Database of Jewish NENA Recordings 23

    5.0.   Note on Transcriptions and Translations 24

    6.0.   Outline of the Book 26

Chapter 1: Proverbs 29

    1.0.   Paremiography: Published Collections of Zakho Proverbs 30

    2.0.   A Misleading Conception 34

    3.0.   Defining Proverbs 36

    4.0.   Image, Message, Formula, and Proverb Synonymy 41

    5.0.   'External' and 'Internal' Grammar and Structure 44

6.0.	Internal Structure	44
6.1.	Conditional Sentences	46
6.2.	Single Clause with Initial Noun	47
6.3.	Initial Noun or Pronominal Head with Relative Clause	48
6.4.	Two Independent Juxtaposed Clauses	49
6.5.	Parallelism	50
6.6.	Semantic Field of the Proverb's Image	51
6.7.	Rhyme	56
6.8.	Metre	57
6.9.	Alliteration	58
6.10.	None of the Features Listed Above	59
7.0.	Folkloristic Structure	59
8.0.	Proverbs in Behavioural or Interactional Contexts vs Proverbs in Narratives	64
9.0.	Seitel's Social Use of a Metaphor	65
10.0.	Arora's 'Perception of Proverbiality'	68
10.1.	Out-of-contextness	70
10.2.	Traditionality	70
10.3.	Currency	71
10.4.	Repetition	72
10.5.	Grammatical and Syntactic Features	72
10.6.	Metaphor	73

10.7.	Paradox and Irony	73
10.8.	Lexical Markers	74
10.9.	Prosodic Markers	74
11.0.	Deictic and Anaphoric Usage	75
12.0.	The Creative Process and the Proverb-reality Cycle	75
13.0.	Context Situations	78
14.0.	The Proverbs	82
15.0.	Appendix: Additional Proverbs (with No Glossing or Context Situation)	157

Chapter 2: Enriched biblical narratives 169

1.0.	The Enriched Biblical Narrative	169
2.0.	Related Genres	170
	2.1. Synchronically Related Genres	172
	2.2. Diachronically Related Genres	178
	2.3. The Christian *Durekṭa*	182
3.0.	Thematology	183
	3.1. The Motif as a Fundamental Concept in Folkloristics	184
	3.2. Thematology: The Concepts	187
4.0.	Transposed Motifemes	193
	4.1. Manners of Transposition	194
5.0.	Motifemes in Samra's Story	197

5.1.	Naomi and Elimelech's Wealth, the Charity of Naomi (14)–(35)	197
5.2.	Ruth and Orṭa are the Daughters of Meʾohav (40)	201
5.3.	Naomi's House Remains as She Left It (48)	202
5.4.	At the Synagogue (56)–(62)	203
5.5.	Boaz's Death and Elishay's Birth (64)–(83)	206
5.6.	Elishay Suspects His Wife of Unfaithfulness (85)–(89)	209
5.7.	David's Anointment (90)–(119)	215
5.8.	*Guri Kunzəri* (128)–(131), (179)–(181)	217
5.9.	The Seven Stones (147)–(150), (162)–(164)	220
5.10.	The Battle against Goliath (151)–(166)	222
5.11.	Goliath's Sword and ʾEliya Ḥəttè and His Condition (167)–(178)	224
5.12.	Saul's Illness (183)–(184)	228
5.13.	Jonathan's Friendship with David (185)–(190)	230
5.14.	King Saul's Sword and the Angel (191)–(193)	234
5.15.	King Saul's Promise (194)	235
5.16.	The Cave of Elijah the Prophet (195)–(200)	235
5.17.	Gila of Haifa (201)–(231)	236
5.18.	David Finds King Saul Asleep (233)–(234)	240

	5.19.	King Saul and Raḥela the Fortune-teller (235)–(242) 241
	6.0.	Conclusion 243
	7.0.	The NENA Text and Its Translation 244

Chapter 3: A Folktale 281

	1.0.	The Folktales of the Jews of Zakho 281
	2.0.	'The King and the Wazir': Synopsis 282
	3.0.	The Motif of Gender Transformation 284
	4.0.	*Baxtox ḥakoma-la* 'your wife is a king': Gender Boundaries and Perplexity 290
	5.0.	'The King and the Wazir': The Text 296

Closing Remarks 313

References 317

Index 343

ACKNOWLEDGEMENTS

First, I wish to thank the Neo-Aramaic speakers whose words are transcribed in this book: Samra Zaqen ז"ל, and, יבלח"א, Batia Aloni, and Ḥabuba Messusani. Thank you for the many hours of recording sessions, of which the Neo-Aramaic texts contained in this book represent a mere fraction.

I also thank the Neo-Aramaic speakers whose words do not appear here, but who were recorded for the Jewish NENA database: Mordechai ʿAdiqa, Esther ʾAlfiyye, Ḥakham Zekharya Barashi ז"ל, Ahuva Baruch, Naʿim Be-Khavod, Khatun Ben-ʾAbu, Zakiyya Ben-Naḥum (née Cohen Shammo) ז"ל, Shmuʾel Ben-Yosef, Murdakh Cohen Shammo ז"ל, ʾItzik Cohen, ʿAziz Cohen Shammo ז"ל, Moshe Cohen ז"ל, Aharon Cohen ז"ל, Ḥakham Eliyahu Ḥoja ז"ל, Carmela Krupnik (née Baruch) ז"ל, Zehava Mizraḥi, Naftali Mizraḥi, Shabbetai Nissim ז"ל and his wife Zəlfe (Zilpah) ז"ל, ʿEzra Polo ז"ל, Boʿaz Sandu, ʿAzar Sasson ז"ל, Salḥa Shazo, Varda Shilo, ʾAḥiyya Shiloni, Ḥaya Kheriya Vardi, Menashe Zaqen, Moti Zaqen, Yosi Zaqen, and Yitzḥak Zizi—thank you for your willingness to be recorded, patience, and hospitality, and for enriching my knowledge of the Neo-Aramaic language and culture.

This book is based on a PhD thesis submitted to the University of Cambridge in July 2018. I wish to thank my PhD supervisor, Prof. Geoffrey Khan, for his guidance and help throughout my time as his student, as well as thereafter. It was Prof. Khan who first encouraged me to start recording Jewish Neo-Aramaic speakers. I thank him also for that.

I thank the Cambridge Overseas Trust for generously awarding me the grant that allowed me to study at Cambridge at PhD level.

I thank the examiners of the PhD thesis, Prof. Alessandro Mengozzi and Dr Aaron Hornkohl, for providing many helpful comments.

I thank the Golden Web Foundation for generously awarding me the grant that allowed me to study at Cambridge at MPhil level.

I wish to thank Prof. Edit Doron ז"ל, who opened the doors of Neo-Aramaic and general linguistics for me. Prof. Doron also provided me with a scholarship for the study of Neo-Aramaic during the summer of 2009. I thank her for that as well.

I thank Prof. Yona Sabar for his advices, as well as for his invaluable reference works whose contribution to every page of this book is evident.

I thank Prof. Eran Cohen, who first taught me Neo-Aramaic grammar.

Prof. Galit Hasan-Rokem and Dr Dorota Molin read the manuscript carefully and provided many valuable comments. I thank them for that.

I thank Dr Yoel Perez and Dr Zadok Alon for their helpful comments on ch. 3.

The support of Prof. Harry Fox, Dr Daniel Weiss, Simon McKibbin, and my uncle, Dr Zadok Alon, has been invaluable. I thank them.

Dr Timothy Curnow and Dr Aaron Hornkohl offered many style corrections. I thank them for that.

Naturally, the responsibility for all errors in this book is mine.

I am grateful to the Martin Buber Society of Fellows at the Hebrew University of Jerusalem for its support in the publication of this book.

Last but not least, I wish to express my deepest gratitude to my mother, Batia Aloni. Without her extensive help in finding and interviewing Neo-Aramaic speakers, and deciphering obscure parts in their recordings, my research would have been impossible.

INTRODUCTION

This book deals with three genres of the oral heritage of the Neo-Aramaic-speaking Jewish community of Zakho, Kurdistan. During the past three decades, there has been a renewed interest in research on Neo-Aramaic, and a substantial increase has been seen in the amount of research. However, the contemporary study of North-Eastern Neo-Aramaic (NENA) has focused almost exclusively on aspects of the language, such as phonology, morphology, sentence-level syntax, lexicography, dialectology, diachronic development, and language contact. Content-based aspects of the study of the language and its cultures, such as folkloristic analysis, narrative structure, discourse structure, and phraseology, have been almost completely neglected. This book is but a first step in an attempt to fill this gap in NENA scholarship.

This Introduction begins by providing some background on the Jewish community of Zakho, before looking at the language spoken in that community, NENA, and previous research on it. There follows a brief discussion of the study of folklore, and then a description of the audio-recorded database upon which this book is based. The Introduction ends with an outline of the structure of the book, after an explanation of the system of transcription and translation of the NENA texts used here.

1.0. The Jewish Community of Zakho[1]

The town of Zakho is located in the northern tip of Iraqi Kurdistan, approximately ten kilometres south of the Turkish border and thirty kilometres east of the Syrian border. It is surrounded by high mountains. All roads leading to Zakho, including the main road from Mosul, go through rough mountain passes. The oldest part of Zakho, which includes *maḥallət huzaye* 'the neighbourhood of the Jews' is an island in the centre of the River Khabur, which flows through the town (for the geography of Zakho, see Gavish 2004, 21–26; 2010, 13–14).

It appears that the Jewish community of Zakho is old, though there are few documents which provide historical information about it. The oldest historical sources which attest the presence of Jews in Zakho are letters, the earliest of which date to the 18th century. These often contain Halakhic questions about various topics directed to rabbis of other cities (responsa): marital contracts, legal disputes, and familial affairs (Ben-Yaacob 1981, 58–62; Gavish 2004, 27–30; 2010, 15). Some of these letters contain requests for help from neighbouring communities after disasters, e.g., the famine of 1880 and the wave of persecutions of 1892.

Jewish travellers arrived in Kurdistan as early as medieval times—Benjamin of Tudela and Petaḥyah of Regensburg in the 12th century and Yehudah Al-Ḥarizi in the 13th century (Brauer

---

[1] For more about the history and culture of the Jews of Zakho and Kurdistan, see Brauer (1947; 1993); Ben-Yaacob (1981); Gavish (2004; 2010); Zaken (2007); Aloni (2014a).

1947, 17–20; 1993, 38–40). However, Jewish travellers first arrived in Zakho only in the 19th century (Ben-Yaacob 1981, 58–62). The first Jewish traveller to mention Zakho is Rabbi David D'Beth Hillel, who visited the town in 1827 and found approximately six hundred Jewish families living there. He describes the old synagogue and some Jewish customs unique to the community of Zakho, which he finds similar to customs described in ancient history books (Fischel 1939, 124). Based on that similarity, he concludes that the Jews of Zakho are descendants of the ten lost tribes of Israel. Israël Joseph Benjamin ('Benjamin the Second') arrived in Zakho in 1848 and found two hundred Jewish families there. He recounts that the chief rabbi of the town, Rabbi Eliyahu, asked for his advice in the matter of an *'aguna* woman[2]; contrary to Benjamin's advice, the rabbi released her from the bonds of her marriage (Benjamin 1859, 24).

According to the mnemohistory of the Jews of Kurdistan, they are descendants of the ten Israelite tribes exiled by Shalmaneser V, king of Assyria, as recounted in the Hebrew Bible: "In the ninth year of Hoshea, the king of Assyria captured Samaria. He deported the Israelites to Assyria and settled them in Halah, at the [River] Habor, at the River Gozan, and in the towns of Media" (2 Kgs 17.6; NJPS [1999] English translation).[3] 'Habor' is

---

[2] A married woman whose husband is missing but is still considered married according to Jewish law, and is thus unable to remarry.

[3] For a comprehensive study of the history of quests to locate the Ten Tribes, see Ben-Dor Benite (2009). For an analysis of the role of the Ten Tribes in Jewish folk-narratives recorded at the Israel Folktale Archives Named in Honor of Dov Noy (IFA), University of Haifa, see Stein (2015).

generally thought to be Zakho's River Khabur.⁴ According to Ben-Yaacob, it is possible that the Sambation (sometimes spelled Sabation), mentioned in the rabbinic literature as the frontier of the realm of the ten tribes, may be the Great Zab, another river of Kurdistan (Ben-Yaacob 1981, 12).⁵ Nachmanides identifies the Sambation as the River Gozan (in his commentary on Deut. 32.26). In many old and modern documents, the Jews of Kurdistan call themselves *ha-ʾovdim bə-ʾereṣ ʾaššur* 'those who are lost in the land of Assyria', an expression taken from Isaiah's prophecy of redemption "And it shall come to pass in that day, that a great horn shall be sounded; and they shall come that were lost in the land of Assyria, and they that were dispersed in the land of Egypt; and they shall worship the Lord in the holy mountain, in Jerusalem" (Isa. 27.13; JPS [1917] English translation, with some modification).

In the middle of the 19th century, Zakho became the chief spiritual centre for the Jews of Kurdistan (Gavish 2004, 50–56; 2010, 44–50), and many sources refer to it as *yerušalayim de-kurdistan* 'the Jerusalem of Kurdistan', since it became a centre of training for *ḥaxamim* 'rabbis', *mohalim* 'circumcisers', and *šoḥaṭim* '(kosher) slaughterers'.

The rabbis of Zakho were considered an important authority throughout the entire region. Its Great Synagogue could hold

---

⁴ A tributary of the Tigris. A separate river which bears the same name is a tributary of the Euphrates.
⁵ About the Sambation in Jewish literature see Werses (1986) and Stein Kokin (2013).

up to three thousand people. Another synagogue, which also contained a *bet midraš* 'study hall' and a *ḥeder* 'children's school', could hold up to one thousand people. The historian Walter Fischel, who visited Kurdistan twice during the 1930s, copied a Hebrew inscription from a wall of the Great Synagogue (Fischel 1939, 124; see also Ben-Yaacob 1981, 61; Gavish 2004, 161; 2010, 162).

אשרי אדם שומע לי לשקוד על דלתותי יום יום לשמור מזוזות פתחי כי
מוצאי מצא חיים ויפק רצון מה'. שנת ה'ת'ק'נ'ח ליצירה לפ"ק שנת ארבע
למלכות עלי כאן בג יר"ה.

> Happy is the man that hearkens to me, watching daily at my gates, waiting at the posts of my doors, for he who finds me finds life, and obtains favour of the Lord,[6] year 5568 of the creation [=the year 1798 CE], year 4 of the kingship of ʿAli Khan Bag YRH [=may his glory be exalted].

The Jews of Kurdistan immigrated to Israel in their entirety in two waves during the first half of the 20th century.[7]

Those in the first wave, during the 1920s and 1930s, immigrated mainly for religious reasons: coming to the Holy Land. Some social and political factors were also involved: World War I and its severe consequences; the British mandate over Iraq and Palestine; the deterioration in personal security of the Jews of

---

[6] Prov. 8.34–35 (JPS 1917), English translation, with some modification.

[7] There is evidence for the immigration of Jews to pre-state Israel even before this. Mann (1931–1935, I:488) has found a letter sent from the village of Sundur to Jerusalem in the early 18th century, which shows that individuals, at least, had immigrated by then (see Hopkins 1993, 51; Gavish 2004, 147; 2010, 150–51).

Kurdistan; and the decline in their economic status (see Zaken 2007). Migration during this period was undertaken on the initiative of individual immigrants. The immigrants arrived as small groups of families and individuals, sometimes youths without their parents, usually in caravans through Lebanon, and in many cases without the required migration certificates from the Iraqi authorities. They settled mainly in Jerusalem, in the 'Kurdish' neighbourhood. Their community was the first community of Jewish immigrants from Islamic countries in Jerusalem. In fact, it would be more precise to speak of several communities, since in general each group of immigrants from a particular town or village in Kurdistan established an independent community in Jerusalem, with its own synagogue and communal institutions. These communities occasionally sent emissaries to their home towns in Kurdistan with the aim of recruiting funds and more newcomers.

The second wave of migration commenced in March 1950, two years after the establishment of the State of Israel. The Iraqi government, as part of its efforts to deal with increasing internal instability, passed a law entitled 'Supplement to Ordinance Cancelling Iraqi Nationality', which stipulated that "the Council of Ministers may cancel the Iraqi nationality of the Iraqi Jew who willingly desires to leave Iraq" (Law No. 1 of 1950, *Official Gazette of Iraq*, 9 March 1950; see http://www.justiceforjews.com/iraq.html). One year later, the 'Law for the Supervision and Administration of the Property of Jews who have Forfeited Iraqi Nationality' was passed (Law No. 5 of 1951, *Official Gazette of Iraq*, 10 March 1951; see http://www.justiceforjews.com/iraq.html), under which all Jewish properties were confiscated and they were all expelled (Tsimhoni 1989). Within two years almost all of the Jews of Iraq, including almost all of the Jews of Iraqi Kurdistan, had immigrated to Israel (Gavish 2004, 300; 2010, 316–317). Most of these immigrants, who were referred to by the immigrants of the first wave as *ha-ʿolim ha-ḥadašim* 'the newcomers', remained for some time in the *maʿabarot* 'absorption camps', then were settled in the Katamonim neighbourhood in Jerusalem and in Maʿoz Tsion outside Jerusalem. The new reality brought about an unprecedented intergenerational gap between parents and children within the community.[8] Unlike the immigrants of the first wave, the 'new' immigrants were able to take advantage of the young state's modern education system, which naturally afforded them many advantages, but which was also guided by a 'melting pot' policy, one of the goals of which was the blurring of immigrants' communal identities.

The historical social and geographic conditions of the Jews of Kurdistan influenced the character and development of their NENA literature (see Sabar 1982a; 1982c; Aloni 2014a, 21–84). The isolation of each of the Jewish communities in Kurdistan, spread across the many towns and villages of this rugged mountainous land, which remained largely unpenetrated by foreign

---

[8] For the changes in the social structure of the community, see Gavish (2004, 300–19; 2010, 316–36). The internal division of the community into 'new' and 'old' immigrants has an interesting linguistic consequence: Sabar (1975) describes the NENA of the 'old' immigrants as surprisingly conservative and as less influenced by Modern Hebrew in its lexicon, phonology, and syntax. Sabar explains this as a result of the less extensive assimilation of the 'old' immigrants into Israeli society.

cultures or armies up until the 20th century, enabled the Jewish communities of the region to preserve very old traditions (see ch. 2, fn. 6). The social structure, as well as the material culture, which very much resembled those known to us from classical rabbinic literature, contributed to this preservation as well. Ancient literary and exegetical genres, such as Aggadic Midrashim and epic songs about biblical themes, which embellish the original narrative with Aggadic traditions, continued to be created and performed in the Jewish communities of Kurdistan in modern times (see ch. 2).

A simple division of the literary heritage of the Jews of Kurdistan into oral and written literature will not prove accurate, since most of this literature, including some of what now forms its written portion, has been passed down orally and bears distinctive features of oral transmission. Thus, for instance, the Jewish NENA Bible translations published by Sabar (1983; 1988; 1990; 1993; 1995a; 2006; 2014), were committed to writing by *ḥaxamim* of the community only in 20th-century Israel at the request of scholars. On the other hand, the Midrashim for the three portions of the Pentateuch, *Va-Yeḥi*, *Be-Šalaḥ*, and *Yitro*, also published by Sabar (1985; see also 2009), were committed to writing nearer to the time of their creation, being found in manuscripts from the 17th century; but they are also based upon traditions which were transmitted orally. Nonetheless, it will prove useful to distinguish between literature that has been preserved in manuscripts, which is literature of a religious character, and literature that is preserved only orally to this day.

2.0. North-Eastern Neo-Aramaic (NENA)

The Aramaic language is—or more accurately, the Aramaic languages are—one of the longest-lived, continuously spoken and documented living language groups, and one of the oldest languages spoken today.[9] The oldest Aramaic documents still extant date back to the 9th century BCE. Aramaic, initially the language of the Aramaean tribes in modern-day Syria, gained historical prominence after it was adopted as the administrative language of the Neo-Assyrian empire, together with the Assyrians' own language—Akkadian—in the 8th century BCE. It retained this status in subsequent empires, the Neo-Babylonian and the Persian Achaemenid empires. It seems that this unlikely historical occurrence—the adoption of a local language as the administrative language of what was the largest and strongest empire at the time—was due to the relative simplicity of the Aramaic writing system, compared to the Akkadian one.[10] Aramaic became the lingua franca of the ancient Near East. Most of the Aramaic texts in the Hebrew Bible, written in what is usually called Biblical Aramaic,[11] belong to this period of the language's history: Imperial Aramaic.

---

[9] The leading contender for the title of the oldest living language is Coptic, a descendant of Ancient Egyptian.

[10] Akkadian cuneiform included thousands of signs, and many years of training were required to master it.

[11] Biblical Aramaic is the language of most of the book of Daniel, a large part of Ezra, one verse in Jeremiah (10.11), and two words in Genesis (37.47).

The diffusion of Aramaic across a very large territory, from Egypt in the west to India in the east, brought about dialectal diversification and fragmentation of the previously more uniform language. The division between Eastern and Western Aramaic dialects became the most decisive one. But processes of change were not consistent within the boundaries of each geographic region: independent dialects spoken by different ethnic and religious groups that lived in the same geographic regions came into being. The results of these dialectal diversification processes, which began in the 3rd century BCE, are reflected in the present-day Neo-Aramaic dialectological map.

The term 'Neo-Aramaic' covers all of the Aramaic dialects spoken today. The earliest written attestation of these dialects is five hundred years old.[12] Neo-Aramaic is divided into four groups of dialects: North-Eastern Neo-Aramaic (NENA),[13] the group which includes all of the dialects of the Jews of Kurdistan; Western Neo-Aramaic,[14] spoken by Christians and Muslims in the vil-

---

[12] There is evidence for the existence of Neo-Aramaic dialects long before that. For example, an Arabic list of medicines dated to the beginning of the 11th century specifies the names of these medicines in other languages, and one of them very much resembles NENA (see Khan 2007a, 11). On the gap in documentation between late antiquity and the early modern period, and on the earliest documented sentence in Neo-Aramaic (16th century), see Hopkins (2000).

[13] According to Khan (2011, 708), this term was coined by Robert Hoberman (1988; 1989).

[14] For grammar and texts, see Arnold (1989–1991).

lages Maʿlula Bakhʿa and Jubbʿadin in the Anti-Lebanon Mountains north of Damascus; Ṭuroyo and Mlaḥso,[15] two closely related Aramaic languages, each of which has several dialects and which are spoken by Christians in the region of Ṭur ʿAbdin, in the Mardin Province of south-east Turkey; and Neo-Mandaic,[16] spoken by Mandaeans in the city of Ahwaz (in south-west Iran) and its environs.

NENA, spoken by Jews and Christians, originally in the wide area east of the River Tigris in Kurdistan, presents an exceptionally high degree of linguistic diversity. Scholars identify some 150 separate NENA dialects (Khan 2011, 709). Almost every village or small rural settlement in the vast mountainous tracts of Kurdistan had its own distinct dialect. Thus, for instance, the Jewish dialect of Aradhin was spoken by only four families, about thirty people, prior to their immigration to Israel (Mutzafi 2002a). The differences between several of the dialects are so significant that no mutual intelligibility is possible. The mountainous topography of Kurdistan, the scarcity of paved roads, and the sporadic character of human settlement in the region have all contributed to the emergence of this exceptional linguistic diversity.

As would be expected, geographical obstacles, such as the Tigris and the Great Zab rivers, are indeed important linguistic boundaries on the dialect map. Surprisingly, however, these geographical factors are not the only factors in determining dialect

---

[15] For grammar and texts, see Jastrow (1992).
[16] For grammar and texts, see Häberl (2009); for studies of Neo-Mandaic lexicon, see Mutzafi (2014).

cleavage. One of the most fundamental subgroupings within the NENA dialects is based on religious affiliation: the Jewish dialects differ from the neighbouring Christian dialects (Khan 2011, 709; 2007a, 6).[17] It was often the case that in a single town or village, the two communities, Jewish and Christian, spoke NENA dialects that were mutually unintelligible; this is the case, for example, in the towns of Urmi, Sanandaj, and Sulemaniyya.[18] Furthermore, the Jewish dialects of settlements remote from each other present familial resemblance. The dialect cleavage between Jewish and Christian NENA would seem to have been brought about by different histories of internal migration between the two religious communities (Khan 2007a, 6).

---

[17] The differences are particularly great east of the Great Zab river, i.e., in the Trans-Zab dialects.

[18] For comparisons between Jewish and Christian dialects, see Khan (2008b, 16), who discusses Jewish Amediya, Betanure, and Nerwa, in contrast with Christian Barwar; and also Mutzafi (2008a, 10), who contrasts Jewish Betanure with Christian Bishmiyaye. The differences between the Jewish and the Christian dialects of Zakho were not as extreme, though clearly there were two separate dialects (see Sabar 2002a, 4). For grammatical descriptions of the Christian dialect of Zakho, see Hoberman (1993); Mole (2002). For texts in the Christian dialects of Zakho and Dihok (Dohok), see Sabar (1995b). According to Mole (2002, iv–v, ix), the Chaldean community of Zakho was, up to the 1960s, relatively small. Immigration from surrounding villages, which were destroyed by the Iraqi government in 1976–1977, as well as a second wave of displacement in the late 1980s, led to the growth of that community, and brought about a diversification in the Neo-Aramaic dialects spoken by Christians in Zakho. The Christian dialect of Zakho is, therefore, not a homogenous dialect, and findings or data of different researchers (e.g., Hoberman and Mole) may consequently diverge.

The many Jewish NENA dialects can be divided into subgroups. The primary division is into three subgroups.

1. The first subgroup of Jewish NENA dialects is the *lišana deni* 'our language' subgroup. This includes the dialects of Zakho (Cohen 2012), Amadiya (Greenblatt 2010), Dohok, Barashe, Betanure (Mutzafi 2008a), Shukho, ʿAṛodan (Mutzafi 2002a),[19] ʾAtrush, Kara, and Nerwa, on the Iraqi side of the border; and two dialects—Challa (Fassberg 2010) and Gzira (Nakano 1970; 1973)—on the Turkish side of the border (Khan 2007a; Mutzafi 2008a; Fassberg 2010).

2. The second subgroup is spoken in the east of the NENA region, across the Great Zab, and is called the Trans-Zab subgroup by Mutzafi (2008b). This subgroup includes the dialects of Salamas (Duval 1883; Gottheil 1893), Urmi (Khan 2008a), Saqqəz (Israeli 1997; 2003; 2014), Sanandaj (Khan 2009), and Kerend (Hopkins 2002) in Iranian Kurdistan; and the dialects of Sulemaniyya and Ḥalabja (Khan 2004), Rustaqa (Khan 2002), Koy Sanjaq (Mutzafi 2004a), Ruwanduz, and Arbil (Khan 1999) in Iraqi Kurdistan.

3. The third subgroup consists of the dialects of Barzan (Mutzafi 2002b; 2004b).

Scholars believe that at the present state of research the drawing of a thorough and accurate dialectological map of NENA would be premature (Mutzafi 2008b, 409–10).

---

[19] This is the name of the village used by its Jewish inhabitants; its non-Jewish inhabitants call it ʾAraḍin.

The term 'Neo-Aramaic' brings to mind the idea of consecutive historical stages, with the Neo-Aramaic languages following historically on from previous Aramaic languages. However, this is not necessarily the case. It needs to be emphasised that all NENA dialects—indeed, all Neo-Aramaic dialects—have considerable historical depth, and that they are not direct descendants of any of the literary Eastern Aramaic dialects—Jewish Babylonian Aramaic, Syriac, and Mandaic—recorded in writing. The Neo-Aramaic dialects descend from ancient dialects that were spoken concurrently with the literary dialects, with only the latter being richly documented, thanks to the mostly religious corpora written therein. One of the indications of the ancient roots of Neo-Aramaic is the presence of Akkadian loanwords—predominantly names of agricultural tools and activities—which are found in Neo-Aramaic, but not in classical literary Aramaic. We must thus infer that the modern dialects are not identical with the classical dialects: the influences that they absorbed from Akkadian at the time when it was still spoken were distinct (Khan 2007a, 2, 11).

Over the past three decades there has been substantial growth in the linguistic scholarship of Neo-Aramaic. Many books and research papers have been published, among them dictionaries, grammatical descriptions, comparative studies, and theoretical investigations. Linguists have found a variety of important phenomena in Neo-Aramaic. Here four of these will be mentioned:

1. Partial ergativity (Khan 2007b; 2017; Doron and Khan 2010; 2012; Coghill 2016; Noorlander 2021). NENA

dialects exhibit ergativity.[20] Ergativity is defined as a grammatical system which exhibits syntactic or morphological treatment of the sentence subject in sentences employing an intransitive verb identical to that of the sentence object in sentences employing a transitive verb—treatment which is distinct from that of the subject of the transitive verb. Various subgroups of NENA dialects show different degrees of ergativity, but none of them is fully ergative: ergativity is restricted to defined areas of the verbal system (e.g., it is found in past tense only, or only with verbs of a certain lexical aspect). Comparing the distribution of ergativity in NENA subgroups reveals a tendency to gradual grammatical change: the transition to a nominative-accusative system (a system which distinguishes the treatment of subjects and objects regardless of the transitivity or intransitivity of the verb), which is more common cross-linguistically. Neo-Aramaic is the only Semitic language that presents ergativity, and the influence of Kurdish, an ergative language, has surely contributed to the introduction of ergativity into NENA. However, this is not a simple case of areal influence, since the seeds of ergativity are to be found already in ancient forms of Aramaic (Khan 2007a: 14). It appears that this feature of the language, which existed in an undeveloped form, became fully manifested in the 'sympathetic' environment of the Kurdish language.

---

[20] As do Ṭuroyo and Mlaḥso.

2. Language contact (Kapeliuk 2011). Until the emigration of its minorities, Kurdistan was a unique laboratory for research into the horizontal, contemporaneous, relations between languages. In a single geographic region, simultaneously and for extended periods of history, many dialects of languages that are members of separate families were spoken: Aramaic (North-Western Semitic), Kurdish (Indo-Iranian), Turkish and Azeri (South-Western Turkic), and Arabic (Central Semitic). The investigation of the mutual influences between these languages is a fertile ground for interesting conclusions (Khan 2005; 2007a, 15; Haig and Khan 2018).

3. Processes of change in the Semitic family. NENA attracts the attention of Semitists for what it may tell us about ancient Semitic languages. The study of NENA within the framework of historical Semitic linguistics enables a deeper and fuller understanding of long-term processes of change in the Semitic languages. It also helps in producing a fuller picture of the linguistic situation of the Semitic languages in antiquity (Khan 2005). Research can trace processes involving the full manifestation of phenomena which had already appeared embryonically in the ancient languages (e.g., the phonemicisation of the two sets of allophones of the *bgdkpt* consonants; Khan 2005, 84–87), as well as processes whose complete life cycles have occurred within the chronological boundaries of Neo-Aramaic. Processes of the latter type are especially surprising, since they sometimes repeat similar processes that occurred in the

ancient languages, with no apparent causal connection: what might be called the recycling of linguistic phenomena (e.g., the unification of the phonemes /x/ and /ġ/, newly formed by the split of *bgdkpt*, with the phonemes /ḥ/ and /ʿ/, respectively, similar to the merger which took place in ancient North-Western Semitic languages; Khan 2005, 87–93). This brings to mind concealed linguistic DNA, hereditarily passing from one temporally distant language to another within the same family.

4. Historical dialectology. The dialectological picture that NENA presents has challenged the picture of linguistic reality painted by linguists of previous generations: a picture of monolithic languages, devoid of significant dialectological diversity, with clear and defined boundaries. The overwhelming dialectological diversity within NENA has led scholars to speculate that the dialect picture in antiquity may have been equally diverse. This assumption aids in the understanding of many details in classical texts.[21]

---

[21] For instance, it is possible to explain differences between the three main reading traditions of Biblical Hebrew—the Tiberian, Palestinian, and Babylonian traditions—as reflecting dialect differences. It is possible to explain the (rare) divergence in several cases between the Tiberian vocalisation and the consonantal text in similar fashion.

3.0. The Study of Folklore

An important part of the present study centres around folkloric texts. This section, then, offers a brief discussion of the preliminaries of the discipline of folkloristics.

3.1. Jakobson and Bogatyrev's 'Folklore as a Special Form of Creation'

Given that this study analyses verbally performed items of folklore, a question arises: is there anything that marks off folk-texts and distinguishes them from other forms of verbal or literary expression? That is, is there anything that justifies treating items of folklore as belonging to an independent category, deserving of its own research methodologies? The answer to that question, according to the article 'Folklore as a Special Form of Creation' by Roman Jakobson and Petr Bogatyrev (1980 [1929])—regarded by many as the founding manifesto of modern folkloristics—is, of course, yes. Folklore is indeed a special, unique, form of human creativity, and it cannot be categorised as any other form of artistic creativity. Its nature is particularly dissimilar from written literature, since in folkloristic creativity an inherent component is what Jakobson and Bogatyrev (1980 [1929], 7) term the "preventive censure of the community." "An item of folklore per se begins its existence only after it has been adopted by a given community, and only in those of its aspects which the community has accepted" (Jakobson and Bogatyrev 1980 [1929], 4–5). Society is the preserving medium of the folkloric work of art, and the survival of a given work depends on its further transmission: "in folklore only those forms are retained which hold a functional value for the given community" (Jakobson and Bogatyrev 1980 [1929], 6).

According to Jakobson and Bogatyrev the relationship between a potential item of folklore, one which exists as knowledge common to many members of a community, and any actual, concrete, individual performance, is parallel to that between the two Saussurean concepts of *langue* and *parole*:

> In folklore the relationship between the work of art on the one hand, and its objectivization—i.e., the so-called variants of this work as performed by different individuals—on the other, is completely analogous to the relationship between *langue* and *parole*. Like *langue*, the folkloric work is extra-personal and leads only a potential existence; it is only a complex of particular norms and impulses, a canvas of actual tradition, to which the performers impart life through the embellishments of their individual creativity, just as the producers of *parole* do with respect to *langue*. (Jakobson and Bogatyrev 1980 [1929], 9)

The difference between oral and written literature is particularly salient when comparing the potential survival and longevity of the two: as opposed to folklore, a written literary work "retains its potential existence" (Jakobson and Bogatyrev 1980 [1929], 6). It can be revived and become influential once again after long periods, even centuries, of complete disregard and neglect by society. Its survival, or at least its potential survival, is not dependent upon intergenerational transmission or acceptance.

> In the field of folklore the possibility of reactivating poetic facts is significantly smaller. If the bearers of a given poetic tradition should die out, this tradition can no longer be resuscitated, while in literature phenomena which are a

hundred or even several hundred years old may revive and become productive once again! (Jakobson and Bogatyrev 1980 [1929], 7)

Despite the methodological separation between oral and written literature which the authors draw, an interesting form of relation between the two is possible, a reciprocal relation between folklore and written literature—the 'recycling' of folklore. Despite their categorical differentiation, their separate functions in culture, and their different paths of development, artistic literary works and folkloristic works may influence one another and may constitute the raw material of one another. The authors address this type of relation in discussing Pushkin's poem 'The Hussar', commenting that it is "a characteristic example of the way in which art forms change their functions in passing from folklore to literature and, vice versa, from literature to folklore" (Jakobson and Bogatyrev (1980 [1929]: 13–14). Pushkin based his poem on a popular folktale, but reworked it into a highly sophisticated and ironic poem, whose folksiness serves as an artistic device. The poem later reverted back to the realm of folklore, becoming part of a popular piece of Russian folk theatre.[22]

The close association between the inception of the theoretical framework of folkloristics and that of linguistics is notable throughout the article, both of whose authors are indeed famous for their contributions to linguistics: using key concepts of theoretical linguistics, the authors claim that the adaptation of an

---

[22] For a similar case of the relationship between NENA oral and written literature, the book *Toqpo šel Yosef* (Farḥi 1867) and the story of Joseph and his brothers, see Aloni (2014a, 27–30; 2014b, 339).

item of folklore by a society, and subsequent changes that the item of folklore undergoes, are parallel to processes of grammaticalisation and other innovative transformations in language. An incidental variation of a linguistic generalised principle—a lapsus or an element of personal style—cannot be considered a part of a language's grammar, unless it is gradually accepted into the general system. A *parole* incident, a personal performance, will remain defined as such unless it is integrated into the *langue*. This can happen only if the coincidental change matches the internal rules of development of the language.[23]

3.2. The Inherent Injustice of Analysis

Analysis of a verbal item of folklore, or of any item of folklore, almost always consists of analysis of a recorded, transcribed, written, concrete performance of that item, a performance that is but one of many possible performances of it. Analysis detaches the item of folklore from its broader original context. Any particular performance of an item of folklore emerges organically from the context in which it is performed—complex contexts many of whose constituent factors are normally disregarded and discarded in documentation and analysis. An actual performance is

---

[23] Naturally, almost a century after its publication, Jakobson and Bogatyrev's article has been followed by numerous important discussions and theoretical formulations regarding folkloristics and its object of study, which are beyond the scope of the present book. See, for instance, Finnegan (1977); Ben-Amos (1982); Bendix (1997); Shuman and Hasan-Rokem (2012); Honko (2013); Noyes (2016).

specially crafted by the performer (and by the environment—audience reactions, for instance), consciously and unconsciously, to match particular aspects of the situation: the event, the day, the place, and so on. A given analysis must disregard a substantial portion of these aspects of the particular situation. It is this necessary disregarding, partially intentional and partially arising from ignorance, that creates an injustice towards the item of folklore being analysed, the inherent injustice in any analysis.[24] It is brought about by the distinction between a concrete performance of an item of folklore and its abstract, potential, 'dematerialised', existence, common to many members of the community—a distinction which is so fundamental to the study of folklore.

3.3. The Study of Folklore as the Rejection of Folklore

Ironically, the inception of the study of folklore is linked to the rejection of folklore itself. The rise of folkloristics as a discipline occurred simultaneously with, and was driven by, the major forces and processes of change of Western modernity. One component of the cultural changes brought about by modernity was a rejection of the 'traditional'. Folklore, tagged as traditional, was rejected as being a feature of non-progressive cultures and societies, the opposite of how modern society perceived itself. The flourishing in Europe of the documentation, collection, and study

---

[24] This inherent injustice brings to mind the inherent injustice of the law pointed out by scholars of jurisprudence: the law must always ignore many of the relevant details of a given incident, many of the variables of a complex realistic occurrence, in order to be able to make effective generalisations (see Cover 1993).

of the folklore of various cultures during the 19th and early 20th centuries may thus be explained as an assertion, and a reinforced self-recognition, of the progress of modern society. Folklore was showcased as signifying precisely what modern society is not (Bendix and Hasan-Rokem 2012, 2; see also Bauman and Briggs 2003).

4.0. The Database of Jewish NENA Recordings

All of the NENA material contained in this book is drawn from a database of audio recordings of native speakers of Jewish NENA, members of the Zakho community, now living mainly in Jerusalem.[25] I have collected the recordings over the past eleven years by means of fieldwork, with the project commencing in April 2010. Thirty-three speakers[26] have been recorded for the database, which now comprises approximately 150 hours of audio recordings. Various spoken genres are represented in the database: enriched biblical stories, epic songs, different types of folktales, moralistic stories, fairy tales, jokes, proverbs and parables, food recipes, personal memoirs, poetry, mnemohistory, and conversations of various types.

---

[25] Twenty of the recorded speakers were born in Zakho; nine were born in Jerusalem into Zakho families; and four were born in Barashe, Challa, Kara, and Sandu, respectively.

[26] Thirteen women, twenty men.

It was Prof. Geoffrey Khan who first encouraged me to start recording speakers for this project in 2010, stressing the importance of the documentation and study of the NENA dialects.[27]

On a personal note, the contribution of the thirty-three women and men whom I have recorded, and in whose homes I have spent numerous hours—their contribution to my study, to my knowledge, and indeed to my life, has been invaluable. When I started my fieldwork, I set out to find informants, but what I have found was wonderful people.

5.0. Note on Transcriptions and Translations

The transcription system used throughout this book for the NENA texts is the one used by Prof. Geoffrey Khan in his NENA grammars (see, for instance, Khan 1999; 2004; 2008a; 2009). In addition to the standard Semitic consonant and vowel signs, intonation signs are employed: a superscript vertical line (*a'*) indicates an intonation unit boundary; a grave accent (*à*) indicates the main nuclear stress in an intonation unit; and acute accents (*á*) indicate non-nuclear word stresses in an intonation unit. Usually, vowels in stressed syllables are long and vowels in unstressed syllables are short; long vowels in unstressed syllables are marked with a macron (*ā*) and short vowels in stressed syllables are

---

[27] See Khan (2007a, 1): "The description of these dialects is of immense importance for Semitic philology. The dialects exhibit linguistic developments that are not only interesting in their own right but also present illuminating parallels to developments in earlier Semitic."

marked with a breve (ă).²⁸ Hyphens are used in the following cases: between the g-~k-,²⁹ b-~p-,³⁰ and qam- prefixes and their qaṭel verb base; before cliticised copulas -ile~-le -ila~-la -ilu~-lu; after the cliticised prepositions l-, b-, bəd-, ta-, etc.; after the conjunction u- 'and'; after the cliticised relative particle dəd-; before or after other cliticised elements: be- 'household of', la- 'no, not' -ši 'also', etc. Words or phrases in Modern Hebrew are written between superscript capital H letters (ᴴ...ᴴ).³¹

Morpheme-by-morpheme glossed NENA texts are provided in ch. 1, §14.0, and ch. 3, §4.0.

English translations are as literal as possible; tenses are kept as in the NENA text, at the expense of standard English style.³² An example of a particularly difficult word to translate is the word hə̀nna. The literal meaning of hə̀nna is 'this' or 'this thing'. Pragmatically it has several functions: a substitute for a word that the speaker is unable to remember (sometimes the speaker will add the forgotten word immediately thereafter); an

---

²⁸ This is also true for vowels whom the speaker chose to pronounce particularly long or short in their connected speech for various reasons (i.e., non-phonemically).
²⁹ Also with a prosthetic vowel: gə-.
³⁰ The hyphen is kept when the verbal prefixes g-~k- and b-~p- are assimilated to the subsequent consonant, e.g., q-qàbəl, p-pàyəš.
³¹ In some cases it is difficult to decide whether a phrase is a loan from Modern Hebrew or whether it is a loan from an older layer made prior to immigration to Israel.
³² For a study of Jewish Zakho NENA narrative syntax, see Cohen (2012, 237–357).

anaphoric pronoun referring back to an object or a concept mentioned earlier; an abbreviation replacing an idea that all participants know it refers to; and as a euphemistic substitute for words that the speaker wishes to avoid saying. The word *hə̀nna* is translated as italicised '*this*' throughout the English translations.

6.0. Outline of the Book

The three chapters of this book explore three genres[33] of the rich oral heritage of the Jews of Zakho: proverbs, enriched biblical narratives, and folktales. The three genres chosen for this book, or rather the analysed units of each of these genres, progress so to speak from the smallest unit, that of the proverb, to the larger unit of the motifeme, and then to the largest unit of a complete folktale.[34]

The first chapter deals with an important member of the family of gnomic genres: the proverb. The chapter provides contextualisation within the framework of paremiology, the study of proverbs. It suggests that what is lacking in the existing documentation and analysis of Jewish NENA proverbs (and indeed, in those of other languages as well) is a key factor in the understanding of the phenomenon of the proverb: the performative

---

[33] For the centrality of genre as a category in the study of folklore, see Ben-Amos (1969; 1976a; 1976b); Seitel (1999).

[34] Indeed, these three units are of different analytical statuses: the proverb and the folktale are both genres recognised by the community of speakers as such (i.e., emic genres; see the discussion in ch. 2, §3.1), whereas the unit of the motifeme is an analytical unit derived from a theoretical methodology (about the unit of the motifeme see ch. 2, §§3.2.2, 4.0).

context. The chapter presents a new collection of Jewish Zakho NENA proverbs.

The topic of the second chapter is the genre of enriched biblical narratives. The chapter proposes a tool for analysis of such narratives: the concept of the transposed motifeme. In order to achieve an understanding of this term, the chapter gives background for the concepts of motif and motifeme in the study of folklore. It describes the methodological approach in which the concept of motifeme is used: thematology. The chapter examines one example of an enriched biblical narrative, the narrative of Ruth and Naomi and King David as told by Samra Zaqen, and demonstrates an analysis of it using the concept of the transposed motifeme.[35]

At the centre of the third chapter is a folktale, 'The King and the Wazir' as told by Ḥabuba Messusani. This folktale is a rather unusual one, since it is built around a relatively uncommon motif in folk-literature, the motif of magical gender transformation. The chapter contextualises this motif in the scholarship of folk-literature, and proposes a reading of the folktale.[36]

The book ends with some Closing Remarks.

---

[35] The recording of the narrative recounted by Samra Zaken is available for listening at https://nena.ames.cam.ac.uk/dialects/78/.
[36] The recording of the folktale told by Ḥabuba Messusani is available for listening at https://nena.ames.cam.ac.uk/dialects/78/.

CHAPTER 1: PROVERBS

The so-called gnomic genres of oral culture are a group of genres which share the common feature of brevity. Proverbs, proverbial phrases, idioms, riddles, jokes, aphorisms, Wellerisms, and slogans are several important members of the group. The study of this group of oral genres is situated on the border between several disciplines: folkloristics, linguistics, anthropology, and literary theory. It seems that the gnomic genres are important not only to the cultural competence of a member of a community, but also to the linguistic competence of a speaker of a language: the Russian scholar Grigorii L'vovich Permiakov concluded as the result of an experiment that there is a "paremiological minimum" of 300 gnomic texts (Permiakov 1985), which "native as well as foreign speakers […] need to know […] in order to communicate effectively in that language" (Mieder 1997, 405). This chapter is dedicated to a prominent member of the group of gnomic genres: the proverb.

The study of proverbs and proverbial phrases can generally be divided into two realms: paremiography, which is the collection, compilation, and lexicography of proverbs; and paremiology, which is the theoretical study of proverbs and proverb usage. This chapter will begin with an overview of the existing paremiographical collections of Jewish Zakho NENA proverbs (§1.0), and will then discuss some paremiological issues exemplified by Zakho proverbs (§§2.0–13.0). The remainder of the chapter consists of proverbs collected in my own fieldwork (§§14.0–15.0).

1.0. Paremiography: Published Collections of Zakho Proverbs

Four collections of Jewish Zakho NENA proverbs have been published so far: Pesaḥ Bar-Adon (1930), Yosef Yo'el Rivlin (1945; 1946), Judah Benzion Segal (1955), and Yona Sabar (1978). Together they comprise approximately 400 proverbs.[1]

Each of these collections utilises a different lexicographical system. In the early days of Jewish Neo-Aramaic scholarship, Bar-Adon (1930, 12) published, a short collection of seven proverbs, which he had heard from Ḥakham Baruch. Bar-Adon quotes the Neo-Aramaic proverb in vocalised Hebrew script, gives its literal[2] translation in Hebrew, and adds a comment about its "intention," sometimes including linguistic remarks. For example:

> 1. *šuləd ʾozili xurasi, ləbbi k-čahe g-nexi ʾizasi*
> '[In Hebrew:] A work done for me by my friends, my heart gets tired [but] my hands rest.'
> The intention: When one's work is done by others, one cannot be sure whether the workers are doing the work decently, and so one's heart is not at ease, as opposed to one's hands, which are at rest. Or: The heart gets tired when work is performed by friends and the heart itself does nothing. (Bar-Adon 1930, 12)[3]

---

[1] A few proverbs occur in more than one collection.

[2] On the difficulties that the term 'literal meaning' entails, see Searle (1979).

[3] His footnotes have been omitted. The Neo-Aramaic in the examples cited in this section is transcribed according to the transcription system used throughout this book, which involves some modification of the

Rivlin lists the 108[4] proverbs of his collection in alphabetical order. They are transcribed in vocalised Hebrew script. For each proverb, there is a literal[5] Hebrew translation, after which he gives a short explanation of the meaning or intention of the proverb. For example:

> 32. *ʾan peši tre, peši ṭlaha*
> (If today there are two, tomorrow there will be three.)
> Meaning if a man and a woman marry, children will follow; or if two people join together loyally, their partnership will grow and more people will join. (Rivlin 1945, 213)

In some instances, when a proverb alludes to a narrative that is necessary to understand it, Rivlin adds the narrative as well.[6] For example:

> 95. *xa ʾena ʾəl səlqa u-xa ʾena ʾəl kotəlka.*
> (One eye towards the beet and one eye towards the dumpling.)
> A tale: They served a man some beet, which was very good and sweet, and also a meat dumpling. He did not know which he should choose. As a result, other people ate them both, and he was left with neither. (Rivlin 1945, 213)[7]

---

forms given by the original authors. The translation from Hebrew is mine.

[4] Rivlin (1945, 207) states that this is "a selection from one thousand proverbs in the language of Targum [=NENA]" which are in use by the Jews of Kurdistan.

[5] See fn. 2 above.

[6] On proverbs that represent or summarise narratives, see §8.0 below.

[7] This is reminiscent of Buridan's ass.

Rivlin acknowledged the value of his collection of proverbs for linguistic research. At the time of its publication, there was hardly any published material in the Jewish Zakho dialect, or in any other Jewish Neo-Aramaic dialect. However, he proclaimed that his motivation in publishing these proverbs was to

> open a window which will allow us to observe the spirit of this Jewish tribe, which is almost lost in the land of Assyria,[8] and also to observe the spirit of the environment in which they live, their manner, and their wisdom and morals. (Rivlin 1945, 208; my translation)

Segal divides the 143 proverbs in his collection into thirty-three semantic categories, such as ambition, authority, boasting, and boldness. The proverbs are given in a detailed phonetic transcription (which does not correspond to the modern standard for transcribing Neo-Aramaic). Each proverb is translated literally[9] into English. Linguistic comments, mainly etymological, are given for each proverb, and reference is also made to other paremiographical collections. For many of the proverbs, a concise remark about meaning is given. For example:

> [Category:] Ambition
> 1. súse gə-mná'le u-sariṭlána-ši g-márəm ʾáqle
>
> (sariṭlána Syr[iac] rarely for ܣܪܝܛܠܐ, Payne Smith, Thesaurus, s.v.; ši, Kurd[ish]; aqle, perhaps from argle, Syr[iac] ܐܪܓܠ, rather than from Syr[iac] ܠܘܐ 'twist'.
>
> 'The horse is being shod, and the crab also lifts its foot.' (Rivlin, No. 84: 'The water-reptile(?) lifts its foot, and says, Shoe me.' Maclean No. 58: 'They came to shoe the mule,

---

[8] This is an allusion to Isa. 27.13 (my footnote).
[9] See fn. 2 above.

and the frog put out his foot too.' Maclean, however, explains the proverb: If one man gets a present everyone else expects one too.). (Segal 1955, 254)

Segal's principal informants in compiling the collection were Ḥakham Mordekhai ʿAlwani and Ḥakham Ḥabib ʿAlwani (Segal 1955, 253).[10] It seems that one of Segal's goals was to contextualise the proverbs that he collected with other collections of Aramaic, Kurdish, and Middle Eastern proverbs, and point out linguistic issues that emerge from these proverbs.

The aim of Sabar's collection is not only to document NENA proverbs, but to document all proverbs that were used by the Jewish community of Zakho, regardless of the language in which they were framed. Two-thirds of his 153 proverbs are indeed in Zakho's Jewish NENA. However, the criterion for this collection is not language-based, but community-based, and it documents the lexicon of proverbs shared by the community. Sabar lists proverbs in the three languages commonly spoken by the members of the Jewish community of Zakho—NENA, Kurdish, and Arabic—as well as giving one proverb in the Christian NENA dialect of Zakho (Sabar 1978, 221, no. 16), and one proverb which is partially in Turkish (Sabar 1978, 226, no. 81). According to Sabar, in addition to multiple loanwords from old layers of Hebrew, Kurdish, Persian, Arabic, and Turkish, a salient feature of Jewish Neo-Aramaic speech is its colouring "with numerous proverbs in the languages of their neighbouring ethnic groups," which the Jews "naturally incorporated into Neo-Aramaic speech" (Sabar 1978, 215). Sabar notes that the reasons for not

---

[10] Ḥakham Ḥabib ʿAlwani was the author's grandfather.

translating "foreign" proverbs into NENA may have been in order to enhance the authenticity of folk-narratives of the foreign milieu, or to preserve the proverb's specific "literary form, such as rhyme, play on words, rhythm, metre, and other prosodic features, which would be lost in translation" (Sabar 1978, 218).[11]

Sabar gives the transcribed proverb, its translation into English, a reference to other paremiographical collections, including the Zakho collections discussed above, and an explanation of the meaning of the proverb or any linguistic issues that emerge from it. For example:

> 77. *kepa l-duke yaqura.* 'A stone is heavy in its (original) place.' A person is respected only as long as he is in his own community, Cf. Segal, 34; Maclean (1895), 122; Socin (1882), p. 119, r (vars.); Tikriti, 783; Yahuda, Y. B., 643 (vars.). (Sabar 1978, 226)

Sabar (1978, 232) also gives an index of 'subjects'; for example, the proverb given above appears under 'Honor and Shame' (Sabar 1978, 232).

2.0. A Misleading Conception

It is common to see proverbs as traditional sayings expressing a general truth, tokens of folk-wisdom formulated and polished into pithy, gnomic sentences. The most important and meaningful constituent of a proverb, according to this common view, is

---

[11] In my opinion, the use of a foreign language may also serve as a marker of proverbiality by increasing out-of-contextness. On out-of-contextness as an important feature of proverbs, see this chapter's discussions in §§3.0 and 10.1 below.

its content, which is identical with its wise or moralistic message. A more literary-oriented approach might also be interested in the literary mechanisms (figurative language, prosody, intertextuality, etc.) that the proverb utilises in order to effectively convey its message. But even then, the assumption is that the important part of the proverb is the meaning contained therein, its semantics. This conception is very much based on the classical idea of the proverb as a moralistic-didactic literary product. It is strengthened by the way proverbs are collected, presented, and traditionally studied in classical and other ancient proverb anthologies.

This conception of the proverb is a misleading one in so far as it concerns the linguistic and folkloristic documentation, study, and analysis of proverbs. It may result in neglecting three central elements of the phenomenon of the proverb. Firstly, an extensive set of proverbs and proverbial phrases—those which do not match the view of the proverb as incapsulating 'traditional wisdom' or having moralistic or didactic value—is left out, despite being a part of the oral culture of a community. This may be termed the *lexicographical gap*, since it is a shortcoming in the completeness of the paremiographical collection. Secondly, the functional and pragmatic value of proverbs is ignored. The social-behavioural and linguistic circumstances in which a certain proverb may or may not be used and the ends that the utterance of a proverb aims to achieve either in the social sphere or in the discourse are key elements of proverb competence. Ignoring them results in what may be termed the *pragmatic gap*. And thirdly, the fact that the meaning of a proverb is not determined solely by its internal constituents, but to a very large extent by its discursive environment—that is, the fact that a proverb's meaning is context-dependent—is often forgotten. This results in a *semantic gap*, since the portion of the meaning of a proverb which lies outside the boundaries of its sentence is missed.

The importance of context parameters for the study of folklore performance in general has long been recognised. It was expressed succinctly by the functionalist anthropologist Malinowski (1926, 24, quoted in Bascom 1954, 335): "The text, of course, is extremely important, but without the context it remains lifeless." Equally relevant are the words of the folklorist Alan Dundes:

> Functional data must, therefore, be recorded when the item is collected. An item once removed from its social context and published in this way deprives the scientific folklorist of an opportunity to understand why the particular item was used in the particular situation to meet a particular need. (Dundes 1965, 279, in his introduction to a reprint of Bascom 1954)

In the collection of proverbs contained in this chapter, an attempt has been made to overcome these three gaps—the lexicographical, the pragmatic, and the semantic: the first gap, by broadening the scope of what would be considered a proverb, and the latter two by giving context situations for each proverb.[12]

3.0. Defining Proverbs

Despite their very wide distribution in all registers of language, and the ease with which we intuitively recognise proverbs when

---

[12] See §13.0 below.

encountering them, it is not at all trivial to define what one is. In fact, some paremiologists have believed that it is impossible to do so. Perhaps the most influential book in modern paremiology begins with the following statement:

> The definition of a proverb is too difficult to repay the undertaking. An incommunicable quality tells us this sentence is proverbial and that one is not. Hence no definition will enable us to identify positively a sentence as proverbial. (Taylor 1985, originally published in 1962, quoted in Dundes 1981, 44)

The author, Archer Taylor, "remarked that in a way his whole book constituted a definition of the proverb" (Dundes 1981, 44).

Another influential scholar, Bartlett Jere Whiting, writes:

> To offer a brief yet workable definition of a proverb, especially with the proverbial phrase included, is well nigh impossible. Happily no definition is really necessary, since all of us know what a proverb is. (Whiting 1952, 331, quoted in Dundes 1981, 44)

Despite these sceptical remarks concerning the possibility and (lack of) necessity of such a definition, many scholars have offered their views on this question, either in works dedicated wholly to the theoretical quest for a definition, or as tentative theoretical premises in works dealing with other paremiological issues. In what follows, three of these definitions are given, and attention is drawn to certain aspects of these definitions.

A short definition is given by Peter Seitel, in an article which will be further discussed below (see §9.0 below):

> Proverbs [...] may be provisionally defined as short, traditional, 'out-of-context', statements used to further some social end. (Seitel 1969, 145)

This definition raises a few questions. What is the nature and degree of the 'out-of-contextness' of proverbs? How do they relate then to the discursive, linguistic, social, or behavioural contexts in which they occur? What is the meaning of "traditional" in that respect, and why should proverbs be regarded as such? How does the utterance of a proverb "further some social end," and what type of ends does it further?

Galit Hasan-Rokem defines proverbs as a genre of folk-literature, among the genres that have been termed gnomic or minor:

> The most common of these genres is the proverb, which may be defined as a genre of folk literature which presents a specifically structured poetical summary referring to collective experience. The proverb is used in recurring situations by the members of an ethnic group to interpret a behavioural or interactional situation, usually one which is a source of conflict or scepticism. (Hasan-Rokem 1982a, 11)

In the spirit of the aforementioned (see above, Introduction, §3.0) programmatic article by Jakobson and Bogatyrev (1980 [1929]), Hasan-Rokem introduces into the discussion the element of collective experience. The proverb is a mediator between communal experience and communal poetics, and the private, personal usage of it within personal experience. Hasan-Rokem points out several features that underlie the phenomenon of the proverb. Firstly, by referring a situation to the community's values and transferring it to a conceptual level, the proverb restores equilibrium to the situation. Secondly, a proverb, once used, creates a collocation, a link, between the situation at hand and a chain of past situations that the same proverb may apply to. Hasan-Rokem terms this "the paradigmatic aspect of proverb usage" ('paradigmatic' here in the Saussurean sense of the term). When proverbs are used within a narrative, it is this usage that creates intertextuality, a relationship with other narratives and situations in which the same proverb may appear. And thirdly, the ability of the individual to properly use a proverb in acceptable, "correct," contexts is "the syntagmatic aspect" (again in the Saussurean sense). Hasan-Rokem terms this ability "proverb competence."[13]

These two definitions by Seitel and Hasan-Rokem emphasise the function of proverbs. They attach more importance for the understanding of what a proverb is to its relationship with its context (social, behavioural, discursive, and narrative contexts) than to the qualities of the particular sentence or phrase which happens to be that proverb. They maintain that what determines whether we deem an utterance a proverb or not are chiefly parameters *external* to that utterance.[14]

---

[13] See §5.0 below. 'Competence' here is as used by Chomsky; Hasan-Rokem (1982a, 11) refers to Chomsky (1965, 4).

[14] This is not to say that Hasan-Rokem or Seitel dismiss or ignore the *internal* parameters of the structure of the proverb. Hasan-Rokem speaks of three levels of the proverb: the use, the function, and the structure (see in particular Hasan-Rokem 1982a, 18–53; see also Hasan-Rokem 1993, where both the context and poetics of the proverbs are analysed). For Seitel's (1969) argument, the concept of metaphor, which pertains

Alan Dundes, on the other hand, offers a different view. His approach to the question of what a proverb is relies on observing its internal structure. "The critical question is thus not what a proverb does, but what a proverb is" (Dundes 1981, 45). Thus he offers the following definition, which involves the linguistic concepts of topic and comment:[15]

> [T]he proverb appears to be a traditional propositional statement consisting of at least one descriptive element, a descriptive element consisting of a topic and a comment. (Dundes 1981, 60)

The attempt to define the proverb intrinsically, avoiding dependence on external factors, is appealing. Dundes's definition, however, has a point of weakness: it may be applicable to many utterances, even those which are clearly not proverbs. It does not indicate what is not a proverb. As Arora (1994, 10) puts it, "Dundes' topic/comment analysis is likewise applicable to any number of ordinary, 'made-up' utterances." The only thing that differentiates 'ordinary utterances' from proverbs under this definition is the concept of traditionality.[16] We shall return to Dundes's approach in §7.0 below.

To conclude this section on definitions, here are two final short, informal definitions, which may be regarded as proverbs in their own right. Cervantes stated that proverbs are "short sen-

---

to *internal* structure, is crucial. On internal and external parameters see §5.0 below.

[15] These are particularly associated with the functional sentence perspective of the Prague School.

[16] For a discussion of the concept of traditionality, see below, §10.0, specifically the features discussed in §§10.2–3.

tences drawn from long experience" (quoted by Dundes 1981, 61). And Lord John Russell defined the proverb as "one man's wit and all man's wisdom" (Taylor 1981, 3). Taylor, using an altered formulation of this definition as the title for an article, states that this definition underwent a process of proverbial change, and is now remembered as giving prominence to wisdom rather than wit: "the wisdom of many and the wit of one" (Taylor (1981, 3–4).

4.0. Image, Message, Formula, and Proverb Synonymy

The Finnish folklorist and paremiologist Matti Kuusi, distinguishes between three components of the proverb: the proverb's image, its message, and its formula (Kuusi 1966; Dundes 1981, 46–47). The proverb's image is its semantic content considered independently from its pragmatic function as a proverb. The proverb's message is usually not expressed explicitly in its semantic content, and is related to its pragmatic function. The proverb's formula is its syntactic or logical structure.

Some formulas recur in the proverbial lexicon independently of the proverb's image or message. This can be better understood with an example:

> *be-kálo šˀəšlu,* ' *be-xə́tna lá rˀəšlu.* '
> '[In] the house of the bride they are [already] rejoicing, [but in] the house of the bridegroom they have not [yet] felt [anything].' (proverb no. (6) in the present collection[17])

This proverb's image is related to a wedding: one family is already celebrating their daughter's engagement while the other family has not even heard about it.[18] The message of the proverb, made explicit, is 'one party is ahead of the other in a shared venture; one of the parties may even not express agreement to the initiative'. The formula of this proverb, two independent clauses of which the second is negative, recurs in other proverbs:

> *dərmán šəzáne ˀiz,* ' *dərmán ṣríʿe lès.* '
> 'There is a cure for the mad, [but] there is no cure for the crazed.' (proverb no. (10) in the present collection)
>
> *yóma gnèle,* ' *qáza u-bála là-gnelu.* '
> 'The day ended, [but its] troubles did not end.' (proverb no. (16) in the present collection)

The division between the three components of the proverb has relevance to a phenomenon that may be termed 'proverb synonymy'. Synonymy between proverbs may occur in either the images or the messages of the proverbs. Image synonymy is similitude of the images expressed in the proverbs, whereas message synonymy occurs when different proverbs with dissimilar images

---

[17] The proverbs are given in §§14.0–15.0. The proverbs in §14.0 are given morpheme-by-morpheme glosses, and a context situation is provided for each.

[18] On the procedure for betrothals and weddings in the Jewish community of Zakho, see Aloni (2014a, 88–101).

convey a similar message and are used to further a similar end. Take, for example:

> šàqfaˈ la mšápya ʾəl šàqfa,ˈ lá-k-tafqa ʾə̀bba.ˈ
> '[If] a piece did not resemble a[nother] piece, it would not have met it.' (proverb no. (72) in the present collection)

The message of this proverb is that 'the two parties are together, or are collaborating on some ill endeavour, only because there is something similar in their characters, or because of the implicit agreement of the less guilty party'. It is synonymous with the message of the following proverb, though their images are very different:

> čūčə́ksa kfə́lla zarzúra u-tróhun fayyàre
> 'A bird was the surety of a starling and both of them can fly.' (proverb no. (72) in Rivlin 1946, 211; my translation)

The message is also the same in:

> sawóna qrə̀ṣle,ˈ sotə́nta hnèle-la.ˈ
> 'The old man pinched [and] the old woman enjoyed it.' (proverb no. (58) in the present collection)

Since synonymous proverbs are usually synonymous only in one of the three components, they always present a degree of contrast. The choice between different synonymous proverbs, in the same situation, may emphasise different aspects of that situation, and by that offer different interpretations of the same situation.

5.0. 'External' and 'Internal' Grammar and Structure

When considering the grammar and structure of proverbs and proverb usage, the discussion may be divided into two interrelated aspects: the 'external' and the 'internal'. Given that the term 'grammar' refers to a set of implicit rules which govern the correct use of a linguistic item, and that the term 'structure' refers to the manifestation of these rules in any particular occurrence as well as to the relationships between the various constituents of that structure, 'external' refers here to the relationship of a proverb with its surrounding linguistic environment (its co-text) and with its non-linguistic circumstances (its context); 'internal' refers to the structure, content, and grammatical phenomena within the sentence(s) or phrase(s) that constitutes the proverb itself. The 'structure' here includes linguistic-grammatical and poetic features (such as syntactic structure, selection of lexical items, prosody, etc.), as well as internal 'folkloristic structure' (on folkloristic structure, see §7.0 below).

The following five sections consider several approaches to both the internal and the external analysis of the grammar and structure of proverbs.

6.0. Internal Structure

Looked at in terms of their internal linguistic features, Jewish Zakho proverbs appear in various forms. They consist of a variety of syntactic structures: they may be comprised of one sentence or more, or they may not be a complete sentence at all; they may employ various types of subordinate clauses. They may use special, poetic, or rare lexical items, or may use everyday or even vulgar language. They may utilise various topoi and images from various semantic fields. They may or may not be in metre, may rhyme or not, may use alliteration or other types of sound play, or may use puns. It would seem that there are no particular grammatical or poetic constraints on, or prerequisites for, a sentence or a phrase in order that it should be a proverb. To put it differently, there are no absolute grammatical or linguistic parameters according to which the interpretation of an utterance in natural speech as a proverb by the listeners is predictable (on the perceptibility of proverbiality, see §10.0 below).

However, it does seem that many Zakho proverbs do have one or more of a small set of characteristic grammatical features that may increase the likelihood of an utterance being perceived as a proverb. Some of these features, though particularly common in proverbs, do not entail proverbial interpretation; they are common also in non-proverbial language. On the other hand, one of the features—the feature of 'two independent juxtaposed clauses' (§6.4)—does entail, or at least radically increase the likelihood of, proverbial interpretation. Examples of proverbs with each of these features are quite common among the proverbs in the published collections, as well as in those of the present collection.

The features which suggest a possible interpretation as a proverb may be grouped under three categories. There are four syntactic features: conditional sentences, single clauses with an initial noun, an initial noun or pronominal head with a relative clause, or two independent juxtaposed clauses; two semantic features: parallelism and particular semantic fields; and three prosodic features: rhyme, metre, and alliteration.

In what follows, each feature is demonstrated through several examples. In addition, those proverbs in the present collection as well as in previously published collections which possess the relevant feature are listed. Following sections exemplifying each feature, some examples of proverbs which do not possess any of these features are given.

6.1. Conditional Sentences

Some proverbs have the structure of a conditional sentence.[19]

> hákan soténi hawéwala ʾə̀škàsa,ˈ b-ṣarxáxwala màmo.ˈ
> 'If our grandmother had had testicles, we would have called her uncle.' (proverb no. (12) in the present collection)

Some conditional proverbs do not make the conditional marker *hakan* 'if' explicit.

> šàqfaˈ la mšápya ʾəl šàqfa,ˈ lá-k-tafqa ʾə̀bba.ˈ
> '[If] a piece did not resemble a[nother] piece, it would not have met it.' (proverb no. (72) in the present collection)

Conditional proverbs in the present collection: nos (12), (72), (84), (91).

---

[19] Hasan-Roken (1982b, 285) makes the following claim: "all proverbs have a common deep structure, which may be perceived and described as the logical structure of a conditional proposition. This assumption is based on the fact that all proverbs are universal generalisations, and never represent only a single instance" (my translation).

Conditional proverbs in the previously published collections:[20] R:18, R:19, R:20, R:28, R:31, R:33, R:34, R:35, R:36, R:38, R:96; SE:21, SE:28, SE:36, SE:38, SE:89, SE:94, SE:95, SE:115, SE:142; SA:2.

6.2. Single Clause with Initial Noun

In many cases the initial noun in a proverb is extraposed and thus topicalised.

> *dúnye qzàya-la*'
> 'The world is [only] a preparation. [Therefore everything should be taken easily].'[21] (proverb no. (78) in the present collection)
> *ʾə́zla dída g-mzabnále go-ṛáḅa šuqàne.*'
> 'She sells her yarn in many markets.' (proverb no. (98) in the present collection)
> *ʾarxe ʾarxəd ʾilaha-lu*
> 'Guests are guests of God.' (SA:5)

Initial noun proverbs in the present collection: nos (11), (17), (28), (32), (35), (42), (54), (56), (67), (68), (70), (73), (78), (79), (83), (88), (89), (93), (98), (105), (124), (127), (139), (141), (142), (144), (146), (157), (166), (172), (178), (181), (190).

---

[20] Throughout this chapter, in referring to individual proverbs from the previously published collections the following abbreviations are used: BA = Bar-Adon (1930); R = Rivlin (1945; 1946); SE = Segal (1955); SA = Sabar (1978). The number following the colon represents the number of the proverb in the respective collection.

[21] Several speakers offered the interpretation: 'The world should be managed [smoothly].'

Initial noun proverbs in the previously published collections: BA:1; R:75, R:76, R:77, R:87, R:89, R:105, R:108; SE:8, SE:10, SE:34, SE:39, SE40, SE:42, SE:43, SE:44, SE:49, SE:51, SE:52, SE:53, SE:55, SE:57, SE:60, SE:62, SE:68, SE:74, SE:75, SE:77, SE:90, SE:91, SE:92, SE:98, SE:101, SE:102, SE:103, SE:104, SE:107, SE:109, SE:112, SE:113, SE:117, SE:119, SE:120, SE:132, SE:135, SE:139, SE:143; SA:2, SA:17, SA:22, SA:27, SA:37, SA:41, SA:43, SA:44, SA:45, SA:58, SA:63, SA:69, SA:77, SA:100, SA:107, SA:116–124, SA:131, SA:142.

6.3. Initial Noun or Pronominal Head with Relative Clause

Some proverbs consist of an initial noun or pronominal head, followed by a relative clause.

> ʾíza dəd lébox nagzə̀tta nšùqla.'
> 'A hand that you cannot bite, [you should] kiss.' (proverb no. (2) in the present collection)
> kúd k-íʾe ṛàba' k-éxəl čùča.'
> 'He who knows much eats little.' (proverb no. (18) in the present collection)

Relative clause proverbs in the present collection: nos (2), (18), (19), (20), (21), (22), (23), (27), (29), (30), (33), (35), (36), (37), (40), (48), (50), (62), (64), (71), (76), (87), (142), (170), (184), (188), (189).

Relative clause proverbs in the previously published collections: BA:1; R:1, R:2, R:4, R:5, R:6, R:7, R:8, R:9, R:10, R:11, R:12, R:13, R:21, R:24, R:37, R:62, R:73, R:98, R:104; SE:9, SE:11, SE:12, SE:14, SE:23, SE:24, SE:32, SE:47, SE:63, SE:65,

SE:72, SE:76, SE:82, SE:86, SE:108, SE:110, SE:124, SE:127, SE:133, SE:136, SE:138; SA:6, SA:7, SA:8, SA:9, SA:10, SA:88, SA:89, SA:91, SA:136, SA:141.

6.4. Two Independent Juxtaposed Clauses

In some cases, a proverb is comprised of two (or more) syntactically independent juxtaposed clauses, with no conjunction or anaphoric pronoun in the latter.

núra xe qòqa,' tanésa xe nàša.'
'[Like] fire under a clay pot, a word under a person.' (proverb no. (55) in the present collection)

tóra g-nàpel,' sakíne g-zàḥfi.'
'The ox falls down, [and] the knives become abundant.' (proverb no. (15) in the present collection)

dərmán šəzáne ʾìz,' dərmán ṣríʿe lès.'
'There is a cure for the mad, [but] there is no cure for the crazed.' (proverb no. (10) in the present collection)

xá bàba' gə-mdábər ʾəsrà yalúnke,' ʾəsra yalúnke la-gə-mdábri xá bàba.'
'One father [can] support ten children, [but] ten children cannot support one father.' (proverb no. (39) in the present collection)

Many of these proverbs are also rhymed, or contain alliteration.

be-kálo šʾə́šlu,' be-xə́tna lá rʾə́šlu.'
'[In] the house of the bride they are [already] rejoicing, [but in] the house of the bridegroom they have not [yet] felt [anything].' (proverb no. (6) in the present collection)

lá ʾáw jàjik,' lá ʾáw žàḥḥar.'

'Not [of] that jajik [=herbal cheese], [and] not [of] that poison.' (proverb no. (44) in the present collection)

Juxtaposed clause proverbs in the present collection: nos (3), (6), (9), (10), (15), (16), (31), (34), (39), (43), (44), (49), (52), (55), (58), (59), (61), (66), (69), (74), (75), (80), (82), (85), (92), (96), (97), (109), (148), (153), (176), (189), (191).

Juxtaposed clause proverbs in the previously published collections: R:1; SE:41, SE:65, SE:73, SE:93, SE:141; SA:4, SA:10, SA:13, SA:18, SA:20, SA:21, SA:23, SA:28, SA:38, SA:42, SA:46, SA:48, SA:50, SA:68, SA:96, SA:137, SA:138, SA:144, SA:147.

6.5. Parallelism

Some proverbs exhibit overt semantic parallelism between two parts of the proverb.

> *xása g-ǝmra:' ʾaxòni,' xuzí xazyánnox wázir dùnye,' ʾaxóna g-èmer:' xàsi,' xuzí xazǝ́nnax xǝddámtǝd bàxti.'*
> 'The sister says: 'My brother, I wish I would see you [=that you would be] the wazir of the [entire] world.' The brother says: 'My sister, I wish I would see you [=that you would be] the servant-maid of my wife.' (proverb no. (3) in the present collection)
>
> *xá bàba' gǝ-mdábǝr ʾǝsrà yalúnke,' ʾǝsra yalúnke la-gǝ-mdábri xá bàba.'*
> 'One father can support ten children, [but] ten children cannot support one father.' (proverb no. (39) in the present collection)

Parallelism in proverbs in the present collection: nos (3), (6), (9), (10), (39), (42), (43), (44), (45), (48), (49), (55), (58), (61), (65),

(75), (80), (82), (85), (86), (96), (97), (109), (153), (163), (168), (176), (177), (189), (191).

Parallelism in proverbs in the previously published collections: BA:1, BA:2, BA:7; R:1, R:2, R:5, R:11, R:14, R:16, R:17, R:25, R:26, R:34, R:38, R:50, R:52, R:69, R:78, R:92, R:107; SE:11, SE:15, SE:17, SE:25, SE:26, SE:29, SE:37, SE:44, SE:46, SE:48, SE:50, SE:52, SE:56, SE:65, SE:70, SE:103, SE:104, SE:105, SE:111, SE:116, SE:122, SE:123, SE:125, SE:128, SE:131; SA:10, SA:13, SA:16, SA:21, SA:23, SA:38, SA:42, SA:147.

6.6. Semantic Field of the Proverb's Image

There are several particularly common semantic fields from which proverbs' images are drawn. It should be emphasised that the semantic field of the proverb's image does not determine other aspects of that proverb, that is, its message formula or its function.

6.6.1. Marriage

> *palgə̀d bártil,*' *hə̀nna-le.*'
> 'One half of the bride-price is henna.' (proverb no. (67) in the present collection)

Marriage image proverbs in the present collection: nos (6), (8), (23), (25), (42), (67), (87), (101), (117), (151), (153), (160), (169).

Marriage image proverbs in the previously published collections: R:8, R:16, R:20, R:34, R:63, R:65, R:76, R:77, R:81, R:101, R:106; SE:27, SE:107, SE:108, SE:110, SE:111, SE:112, SE:113, SE:114, SE:131.

6.6.2. Family

> *bróni u-bər-bróni u-ṭéʾni ʾə̀lli.*ˈ
> '[Behold, here are] my son and my son's son, [but yet] my load is upon me.' Or: 'My son and my son's son and my load are upon me.' (proverb no. (7) in the present collection)
> *kúd gáwər yə̀mman,*ˈ *b-ṣarxáxle bàbo.*ˈ *kúd gáwər sòtan,*ˈ *b-amráxle màmo.*ˈ
> 'Whoever marries our mother, we shall call him father. Whoever marries our grandmother, we shall call him uncle.'[22] (proverb no. (23) in the present collection)

Family image proverbs in the present collection: nos (3), (6), (7), (12), (23), (39), (42), (80), (112), (114), (117), (151), (153).

Family image proverbs in the previously published collections: R:10, R:21, R:32, R:36, R:53, R:101; SE:16, SE:17, SE:30, SE:31, SE:81, SE:113, SE:114, SE:121; SA:8, SA:82, SA:87, SA:88, SA:90, SA:105.

6.6.3. Men and Women

> *díwan baxtàsa,*ˈ *bə́š bassìma-le*ˈ *mən-díwan gùre.*ˈ
> 'Sitting with women is better than sitting with men.' (proverb no. (83) in the present collection)

Men and women image proverbs in the present collection: nos (12), (25), (58), (83), (86), (117), (151).

---

[22] Sabar (2002a, 210) notes that *màmo* is "used by young people addressing a paternal uncle or any old person." Each of the two sentences of this proverb can be used separately.

Men and women image proverbs in the previously published collections: BA:7; R:8, R:41, R:64, R:68, R:78; SE:10, SE:52, SE:53, SE:57, SE:106, SE:109, SE:110, SE:123.

6.6.4. Animals

Figures include donkeys, dogs, fish, foxes, mice, chickens, roosters, partridges, goats, crabs, lions, sheep, snakes, bulls, cows, calves, livestock in general, birds, horses, camels, ravens, doves, cats, ants, fleas, lice.

> ʾə́zza mgurwànta¹ k-šátya mən-réš ʾèna.¹
> 'The grimy goat drinks from the fountain-head.' (proverb no. (1) in the present collection)

Animal image proverbs in the present collection: nos (1), (4), (7), (15), (22), (24), (28), (29), (31), (32), (35), (41), (54), (56), (57), (66), (70), (73), (90), (93), (102), (139), (141), (143), (165), (183).

Animal image proverbs in the previously published collections: BA:4, BA:6; R:3, R:6, R:16, R:17, R:27, R:44, R:49, R:50, R:55, R:66, R:72, R:73, R:74, R:75, R:82, R:84, R:84, R:87, R:93, R:99, R:107, R:108; SE:1, SE:2, SE:3, SE:4, SE:6, SE:8, SE:22, SE:33, SE:40, SE:47, SE:48, SE:59, SE:60, SE:67, SE:68, SE:70, SE:71, SE:99, SE:101, SE:117, SE:120, SE:122, SE:130, SE:131, SE:138, SE:142; SA:21, SA:48, SA:52, SA:55, SA:68, SA:69, SA:70, SA:71, SA:72, SA:73, SA:75, SA:80, SA:84, SA:96, SA:99, SA:100, SA:103, SA:109.

6.6.5. Kitchen and Cooking

qóqa g-èmer¹ xési dèhwa-la,¹ ʾətrána [var: káfkir] g-èmer¹ ʾàtta mpə́qli mə́nnox.¹

'The clay pot says, "My bottom is made of gold"; the ladle says, "I just came out of there."' (proverb no. (61) in the present collection)

qə́zra dəd hawéba ṛába kabanìyat,¹ k-ə́sya yán malùxta¹ yán pàxta.¹

'A [pot of] cooked food that many cooks are involved in making turns out either [too] salty or [too] bland.' (proverb no. (64) in the present collection)

Kitchen cooking and food image proverbs in the present collection: nos (24), (41), (44), (48), (55), (61), (62), (64), (75), (120), (115), (138), (149), (150), (159), (171), (172), (175), (176), (189), (191).

Kitchen cooking and food image proverbs in the previously published collections: BA:4; R:103, R:104; SE:71, SE:75, SE:129, SE:135; SA:67, SA:137.

6.6.6. Vulgarity

Figures include genitalia, excrement, urine, flatulence, prostitution, promiscuity.

parṭə́ʾna màrre,¹ la-k-iʾen ma b-ózən bəd-ó miráta dìdi,¹ xmára màrre¹ ba-ʾána lá g-màḥkən.¹

'The flea said: "I do not know what to do about that good-for-nothing of mine [=my penis]", the donkey said: "I, then, shall not speak."' (proverb no. (66) in the present collection)

Vulgarity serves to increase the out-of-contextness of the proverb, its 'improper' images being sharply contrasted with the casual stream of discourse (see also §10.1 below).

Vulgarity image proverbs in the present collection: nos (12), (22), (30), (31), (40), (47), (50), (53), (58), (63), (66), (68), (69), (70), (84), (88), (96), (99), (103), (104), (105), (107), (111), (144), (151), (155), (156), (164), (182).

Vulgarity image proverbs in the previously published collections: R:50, R:62, R:70, R:80, R:94, R:102; SE:35, SE:38, SE:47, SE:58, SE:59, SE:67, SE:68, SE:100, SE:122, SE:123; SA:15, SA:24, SA:25, SA:48, SA:58, SA:74, SA:126, SA:129.

6.6.7. Death and the Dead

> mísa dóhun qam-qorìle, ʾál gan-ʿèzen,' ʾál gəhənàm,' lè-waju.'
> 'They have buried their dead, they do not care whether he goes to heaven or hell.' (proverb no. (51) in the present collection)

This does not include proverbs whose message refers to death or to the deceased but whose image does not, such as (in the present collection) proverbs nos (11), (193), and (194).

Death and the dead image proverbs in the present collection: nos (19), (25), (50), (51), (60), (125), (158), (183).

Death and the dead image proverbs in the previously published collections: BA:5; R:35, R:60, R:65, R:106, R:107; SE:5, SE:20, SE:21, SE:28, SE:30, SE:33, SE:58, SE:70, SE:82, SE:131; SA:8, SA:28, SA:44, SA:72, SA:73, SA:115.

6.7. Rhyme

Some proverbs rhyme.

> šúl ʾozíle xuràsi,' k-čáhe lóbbi u-g-néxi 'ìzasi.'
> 'Work done [for me] by my friends, my heart gets tired and my hands rest.' (proverb no. (71) in the present collection. Cf. BA:1)
>
> gwàra' stàra.'
> 'Marriage is a shelter.' (proverb no. (8) in the present collection)

Rhymed proverbs in the present collection: nos (6), (8), (9), (27), (29), (42), (45), (49), (52), (59), (60), (65), (68), (71), (75), (76), (77), (80), (82), (86), (87), (92), (95), (106), (108), (119), (126), (150), (151), (152), (159), (162), (176), (184), (190), (192), (193), (197).

Rhymed proverbs in the previously published collections: BA:1, BA:2, BA:3, BA:7; R:7, R:9, R:19, R:20, R:21, R:22, R:23, R:24, R:25, R:26, R:28, R:29, R:31, R:33, R:37, R:38, R:45, R:46, R:48, R:59, R:68, R:69, R:71, R:78, R:86, R:90, R:91, R:95, R:97; SE:22, SE:24, SE:47, SE:79, SE:81, SE:85, SE:88, SE:91, SE:103, SE:104, SE:108, SE:111, SE:118, SE:122, SE:123, SE:125, SE:129, SE:130, SE:132; SA:4, SA:6, SA:8, SA:16, SA:17, SA:20, SA:21, SA:23, SA:32, SA:37, SA:38, SA:68, SA:79, SA:81, SA:87, SA:92, SA:95, SA:102, SA:103, SA:105, SA:112, SA:116–124, SA:127, SA:129, SA:141, SA:150.

6.8. Metre

Some proverbs present an equal number of stresses in the two parts of the proverb, similar to the metre of biblical poetry.

> dréla máya bəd-tré šaqyàsa.'
> 'She poured water in both troughs.' (proverb no. (81) in the present collection)
> maríra xtàya,' xə́lya ʾəlàya.'
> 'Bitter below, sweet above.' (proverb no. (82) in the present collection)

Proverbs in metre in the present collection: nos (4), (6), (8), (13), (14), (15), (21), (29), (33), (34), (42), (44), (45), (52), (53), (55), (58), (59), (60), (65), (68), (71), (74), (75), (77), (81), (82), (85), (92), (96), (97), (101), (108), (109), (116), (119), (123), (139), (140), (143), (145), (147), (148), (150), (159), (168), (175), (177), (193), (197).

Proverbs in metre in the previously published collections: R:3, R:12, R:14, R:15, R:22, R:25, R:28, R:37, R:55, R:57, R:58, R:69, R:73, R:78, R:85, R:86, R:91, R:92, R:98, R:99, R:100; SE:11, SE:15, SE:16, SE:18, SE:19, SE:23, SE:25, SE:26, SE:29, SE:37, SE:41, SE:42, SE:46, SE:47, SE:48, SE:49, SE:50, SE:56, SE:59, SE:61, SE:79, SE:91, SE:105, SE:111, SE:122, SE:123, SE:125, SE:131, SE:132, SE:141; SA:4, SA:9, SA:17, SA:18, SA:21, SA:23, SA:28, SA:37, SA:46, SA:49, SA:53, SA:68, SA:79, SA:92, SA:102, SA:108, SA:112, SA:150.

6.9. Alliteration

Alliteration or other forms of sound play are common in proverbs.

> bróni u-bə́r-bróni u-ṭéʾni ʾə̀lli.'
> '[Behold, here are] my son and my son's son, [but yet] my load is upon me.' Or: 'My son and my son's son and my load are upon me.' (proverb no. (7) in the present collection)
> kúri u-kurə̀sti,' u-ṭéʾni ʾə̀lli.'
> '[Behold, here are] my young goat, and my young she-goat, [but yet] my load is upon me.' Or: 'My young goat and my young she-goat and my load are upon me.' (proverb no. (7) var. in the present collection)
> xmárta mpə́qlula xalawàsa.'
> 'The she-ass found relatives [lit. uncles].' (proverb no. (28) in the present collection)
> lá ʾáw jàjik,' lá ʾáw žə̀ḥḥar.'
> 'Not [of] that jajik [=herbal cheese], [and] not [of] that poison.' (proverb no. (44) in the present collection)

Proverbs with alliteration in the present collection: nos (2), (6), (7), (13), (28), (29), (44), (46), (47), (59), (60), (65), (72), (81), (82), (85), (92), (95), (96), (100), (101), (107), (108), (116), (119), (123), (126), (128), (133), (137), (140), (148), (150), (159), (161), (162), (163), (168), (184), (189), (191), (192), (193), (195), (197).

Proverbs with alliteration in the previously published collections: BA:7; R:7, R:10, R:12, R:14, R:18, R:19, R:46, R:57, R:63, R:79, R:83, R:87, R:92, R:99; SE:11, SE:29, SE:37, SE:40, SE:48, SE:49, SE:50, SE:52, SE:60, SE:80, SE:115, SE:116, SE:118,

SE:128, SE:131; SA:7, SA:10, SA:13 (quoted as 'variant'), SA:14, SA:17, SA:23, SA:30, SA:31, SA:40, SA:42, SA:49, SA:50, SA:53, SA:57, SA:102, SA:103, SA:113, SA:139.

6.10. None of the Features Listed Above

Some proverbs contain none of the aforementioned features.

> *xá lébe l-xà,' g-émer tré tré sáloxun 'əlli.'*
> 'One cannot overcome [even] one, [but] yet he says come unto me in pairs.' (proverb no. (38) in the present collection)
> *dámməd šə́mša g-nàpqa' 'éwa g-él kə̀sla' 'áp-awa g-ə́be šàxən.'*
> 'When the sun comes out [=appears], the cloud goes to her, it also wants to warm up.' (proverb no. (154) in the present collection)

Proverbs with none of the above features in the present collection: nos (26), (38), (94), (110), (113), (118), (121), (122), (129), (130), (131), (132), (134), (135), (154), (167), (173), (174), (179), (180), (185), (186), (187), (196).

Proverbs with none of the above features in previously published collections: R:39, R:40, R:42, R:43, R:47, R:51, R:54, R:56, R:61, R:67, R:88; SE:7, SE:45, SE:54, SE:64, SE:66, SE:69, SE:78, SE:83, SE:84, SE:87, SE:96, SE:97, SE:126, SE:134, SE:137, SE:140; SA:47, SA:56, SA:83, SA:85, SA:86, SA:106, SA:130, SA:133.

7.0. Folkloristic Structure

In his article 'On the Structure of the Proverb', Alan Dundes (1981) offers an approach towards the analysis of proverb structure different from the one taken in the previous section. Dundes still focuses on the internal structure of the proverb, but not on its linguistic structure. Rather than taking into account the proverb's grammatical elements, Dundes considers what he terms its 'folkloristic structure':

> To the extent that proverbs are composed of words, there would have to be linguistic structure involved. The question is rather whether there are underlying patterns of 'folkloristic structure' as opposed to 'linguistic structure' which may be isolated. (Dundes 1981, 46)

Dundes also detaches his analysis from the question of function:[23] "The critical question is thus not what a proverb does, but what a proverb is" (Dundes 1981, 45).[24]

As quoted above (§3.0), Dundes defines the proverb as "a traditional propositional statement consisting of at least one descriptive element, a descriptive element consisting of a topic and a comment" (Dundes 1981, 60). The terms 'subject' and 'predicate' are deliberately avoided here, since these syntactic elements do not always coincide with the topic-comment pair.

In the tradition of structuralism, a central concept in Dundes's analysis is contrast or opposition. When a proverb is comprised of more than one "descriptive element," the relation between these elements may be either oppositional or non-oppositional. An example given by Dundes for a non-oppositional "multi-descriptive element proverb" (Dundes 1981, 60)—that is,

---

[23] And, indeed, a given proverb from its context. See §13.0 below.
[24] This contrasts with the approach of Seitel, for example. See §9.0 below.

a proverb consisting of more than one descriptive element—is *like father, like son*. A Zakho example would be:

> *lá ʾáw jàjik,*¹ *lá ʾáw žàḥḥar.*¹
> 'Not [of] that jajik [=herbal cheese], [and] not [of] that poison.' (proverb no. (44) in the present collection)

Dundes's example for an oppositional multi-descriptive element proverb is *Man works from sun to sun but woman's work is never done*, where there are oppositions of man versus woman, and finite work versus infinite work. A corresponding Zakho example would be:

> *bába g-yáwəl ta-yalònke*¹ *kútru k-fàrḥi,*¹ *yálonke g-yáwi ta-babòhun*¹ *kútru g-bàxi,*¹
> '[When] a father gives to [=provides for] his children, both [sides] are happy, [when] children give to their father, both [sides] cry.' (proverb no. (80) in the present collection)

This distinction between oppositional and non-oppositional constitutes the primary division in Dundes's typology of multi-descriptive element proverbs. The oppositional or non-oppositional relation between the descriptive elements in a proverb is generated by different proportions of "identificational-contrastive" features (Dundes 1981, 52).[25] Some proverbs involve primarily contrastive features and are therefore clearly oppositional, while others involve identificational features and are non-oppositional. But many proverbs combine both identificational and contrastive features. Thus, the axis of oppositional-non-oppositional must be seen as a continuum (Dundes 1981, 59).

---

[25] The term is taken from linguist Kenneth Pike.

Proverbs achieve varying degrees of contrast or similarity by employing different combinations of contrast between their structural constituents. The strongest contrast is produced when both pairs of topics and the comments of the two descriptive elements are in opposition: *Last hired, first fired* (last ≠ first, hired ≠ fired). Similar examples exist in Zakho:

dərmán šəzáne ʾìz,' dərmán ṣríʿe lès.'
'There is a cure for the mad, [but] there is no cure for the crazed.' (proverb no. (10) in the present collection)
(cure for the mad ≠ cure for the crazed, there is a ≠ there is no)
mád mjomə́ʿlu bəd kočə̀ksa,' zə́llu bəd ʾətràna.'
'What they have saved with a spoon, they wasted with a ladle.' (proverb no. (48) in the present collection)
(saved ≠ wasted, spoon ≠ ladle)

A lesser contrast exists when only one pair of these components is in opposition: *Easy come, easy go* (easy = easy, come ≠ go). Zakho examples of this lesser degree of contrast include:

lá èwa' u-lá sə̀xwa,'
'Not [in] cloud and not [in] fine weather.' (proverb no. (45) in the present collection)
(not = not, cloud ≠ fine weather)
sawóna qrə̀ṣle,' sotə́nta hnèle-la,'
'The old man pinched [and] the old woman enjoyed it.' (proverb no. (58) in the present collection)
(old man ≠ old woman, to pinch parallels to enjoy)

Non-opposition will be produced when none of the components are in contrast: *Many men, many minds*. Zakho examples:

qə́mle čùka,' *bsə́mla dùka.*'
'Čuka got up, [and] the place become [more] pleasant.' (proverb no. (59) in the present collection)
ʾóz hawùsa,' *mándi b-ṃàya.*'
'Do an act of kindness, [and] throw [it] in the water.' (proverb no. (74) in the present collection)

For Dundes (1981, 54), "all proverbs are potentially propositions which compare and/or contrast." A high level of contrast or contradiction between the elements of the proverb is analogous, suggests Dundes, to the concept of complementary distribution in linguistic theory. For example, consider *When the cat's away, the mice will play* (Dundes 1981, 55). From the three sets of contrasting composites in this proverb—cat ≠ mice, one ≠ many, absence ≠ presence—there appears an image of two mutually exclusive situations: the presence of the cat versus the presence of the mice. These two situations can be said to be in complementary distribution, since when one is the case the other cannot be. Once again, an analogous example can be found in Zakho proverbs:

šùla' *ʾàrya-le,*' *g-náḥki ʾə̀lle,*' *k-páyəš ruvìka,*'
'Work is a lion. Only touch it [and] it becomes a fox.' (proverb no. (73) in the present collection)
(untouched [not commenced] work ≠ touched [commenced] work, lion ≠ fox)

The two situations—where one has not started work and it is as intimidating as a lion, and where one has started work and consequently it has shrunk to being a fox—are mutually exclusive, and may be described as being in complementary distribution.

On the basis of these principles Dundes offers several types of underlying 'folkloristic structure' of proverbs. These types, in addition to giving insights concerning the theory of the phenomenon of the proverb, may be used as a tool for the classification and lexicography of proverbs.

8.0. Proverbs in Behavioural or Interactional Contexts vs Proverbs in Narratives

A distinction should be made between proverbs used in social interaction and proverbs used within a narrative. Those two categories, however, overlap to a degree. Firstly, narratives in themselves can perform, and usually do perform, a function in social interaction. And secondly, the account of proverb used in social interaction—the context situations provided in the present proverb collection, for example—is always in the form of a narrative: the actual social happening has been narrativised.

Scholars have studied the use of proverbs within narratives, particularly folk-narratives,[26] as a special case of proverb usage, with its own unique additional characteristics:

> The use of a proverb within a folk narrative, stresses the paradigmatic, cultural aspect of the proverb. The proverb within the narrative creates an effect of intertextuality, a relationship between several texts. (Hasan-Rokem 1982a, 11)[27]

A special class of proverb consists of those proverbs which allude to particular narratives, usually narratives which are well-known

---

[26] A book dedicated to this topic is Hasan-Rokem (1982a).
[27] Hasan-Rokem refers here to Morawski (1970) and Abrahams and Babcock (1977).

to members of the community. A proverb of this type immediately brings to mind the associated narrative, and thus telling it in its entirety becomes unnecessary. The frequent use of a proverb of this kind separately from its narrative grants it a degree of independence, and it is possible that a member of the community could learn the correct usage, message, and social function of such a proverb without becoming aware of its narrative, although, naturally, knowing the narrative is a condition for a fuller understanding of it.

Several such narrative-dependent proverbs are recorded in the present collection: nos (70), (101), and (117). There are also examples in the previously published collections: R:3, R:4, R:5, R:6, R:9, R:10, R:20, R:37, R:41, R:43, R:59, R:82, R:85, R:95; SE:65; SA:12, SA:30.

9.0. Seitel's Social Use of a Metaphor

A model of analysing the elements of a proverb's utterance in relation to its extra-linguistic context was suggested by Peter Seitel (1969). Seitel divides each performance of a proverb into three components:

> 1. the 'social context': the various elements that constitute the relation between the speaker and the hearer of a proverb, the circumstantial relation between the addressee of the proverb and its addresser;
> 2. the 'imaginary situation': the constituents of the image expressed in the proverb itself and the nature of the relations between them;

> 3. the 'social situation': the situation in social interaction that the proverb is applied to, the social end that the proverb is intended to further.

This can be exemplified using the following Zakho proverb.

> *xmára k-íʾe ʾáxəl nàʿnaʿ?!*
> 'Does a donkey know to eat spearmint?!' (proverb no. (41) in the present collection)

This proverb was said by a grandmother to her grandson when the latter refused to eat a certain dish she had prepared for him. According to Seitel's terminology, the social context would be the familial relation between a grandmother and a grandson, with all that it entails (age, gender, traditional roles, generational gap, etc.); the imaginary situation would be the image expressed in the proverb itself, that is to say the donkey, the spearmint, and the relation between them, perhaps 'inability to eat', 'lack of appreciation', or 'ignorance of the quality of'; and the social situation to which the proverb is applied is the refusal of the grandson to eat the dish due to, in the grandmother's view, ignorance towards its quality or mere stubbornness. It is clear, and this is one of the central qualities of the phenomenon of the proverb, that there is an analogical relationship between the imaginary situation of the proverb and the social situation.

Another important part of Seitel's model is the concept of correlation. In our example, the grandson fills two roles: he takes part in both the social context—being a child, male, grandson, of a certain age, and so on—and also in the social situation—being the one that refuses stubbornly and ignorantly to eat. The mapping of one type of relation onto the other by means of applying a proverb is termed by Seitel 'correlation'.

Seitel proposes a simple and useful way of classifying types of correlation. A proverbial correlation may be either in the first, second, or third person, singular or plural. In our example, the correlation is that of second person singular. Had the grandmother directed the proverb to two of her grandchildren, the correlation would have been second person plural. Had the grandmother uttered the proverb while speaking to her daughter, the mother of the grandson, about the grandson's refusal, the correlation would have been third person singular.

As Seitel shows, the very same proverb may have different, and sometimes reversed, meanings when used in different correlations. Seitel states that, in the community whose proverbs are the subject of his study,[28] proverbs belonging to the type involving animals, when correlated with human beings in a first-person correlation, are always intended to justify one's own actions, whereas the same type of proverb, and indeed the same proverbs themselves, when in a second-person correlation, are intended as a negative appraisal of the addressee's actions. There seems to be a rule operating here, which can only be discovered by documenting and analysing the features of the context and the situation. It is a demonstration of the importance of the documentation of these features for the study of the phenomenon of the proverb in any given language community.

Seitel's approach is directed at answering a critical question:

---

[28] The Ibo people of Eastern Nigeria.

> Given that a person has memorized a certain number of proverb texts, by application of what set of rules does he speak them in a culturally appropriate manner and by what criteria does he judge the correctness of another's usage? (Seitel 1969, 144)

In Seitel's view, the answer to this question is to be found in these 'external' categories of function.

10.0. Arora's 'Perception of Proverbiality'

Unlike other scholars who have attempted to define the genre of proverbs, Shirley Arora, in her article 'The Perception of Proverbiality' (Arora 1994), does not try to find intrinsic features of the proverb by studying a particular corpus of actual proverbs, on the basis of which a definition may by formulated. In her view, the important question is not what a proverb is, but rather what leads listeners to identify a proverb when they encounter one. Arora distinguishes between two separate questions. The first question is, how does the researcher identify a proverb? That is, how does the researcher determine the category of their object of investigation, in which some phrases are included and some are not (Arora 1994, 4)?[29] The second, more fundamental, question is, how does a speaker of a particular language, within a particular oral culture, identify a proverb? How does the *speaker* assign the label 'proverb' correctly? From a descriptive point of view, this is a central question; as Arora (1994, 6) argues, "the success of a proverb performance as such must depend ultimately

---

[29] In the words of Seitel (1969, 144): "How does one recognize that which he is going to study?"

on the listener's ability to perceive that he or she is being addressed in traditional, i.e., proverbial, terms."

By applying the label 'proverb' to an utterance, the listener refers its content not to the authorship of the immediate speaker, but to the authority of communal tradition. This dissociation of the proverb from the individual speaker is an important factor in the performance of a proverb, and is one of the sources of its effectiveness in fulfilling its social function.

> What *is* significant, and essential to the success of any proverb performance, is evidence that the utterance in question was 'not made up' by the speaker; that it belongs to the category of 'they say,' not 'I say.' (Arora 1994, 8)
>
> The *listener* knows that the proverb used by the *speaker* was not made up by *that* person. It is a proverb from the cultural past whose voice speaks truth in traditional terms. It is the 'One,' the 'Elders,' or the 'They' in 'They say,' who direct. The proverb user is but the instrument through which the proverb speaks to the audience. (Arewa and Dundes 1964, 70, adapted by Arora 1994, 5, with Arora's adaptations in italics)

Thus the question of how a listener knows that a particular phrase is intended as a proverb arises. How does he or she know that it is expected of him or her to refer the saying to communal authorship?

Arora's claim is that a number of features increase the probability of a phrase being perceived as a proverb. Some of these features are independent of the 'genuineness' of the proverb: an 'artificial' newly composed proverb, in which these features are deliberately incorporated, may well be perceived as a genuine 'traditional' one; this is indeed shown to be the case by the results of an experiment reported in the article (Arora 1994, 13–23). These features, therefore, play a crucial role in the process of the acceptance or rejection of new proverbs in a particular community.[30]

Each of the nine features that Arora suggests increase the chance of a listener interpreting an utterance as a proverb are now discussed in turn.

10.1. Out-of-contextness

The out-of-context nature of proverbs, when used in a natural conversational context, is a feature noted by many paremiologists.[31] Here it is argued that the 'abruption' of the natural, well-contextualised, flow of conversation, is one of the markers that allow the listener to identify a proverb. This trait, naturally, can be observed by a listener or researcher only when proverbs occur within the framework of natural discourse.[32]

10.2. Traditionality

For a researcher, the traditionality of a proverb is in many cases a verifiable attribute (Arora 1994, 7). A proverb that is claimed to be 'traditional' by a community of speakers may be found either in historical documents of previous periods of the language or in more recent scholarly paremiographical collections.

---

[30] Arora, whose study is based on the identification of proverbs in Spanish by members of Spanish-speaking communities in Los Angeles, acknowledges that these features and the ranking of their relative prominence may differ in different languages.

[31] See, for instance, Seitel's definition quoted in §3.0 above.

[32] Hence the importance of providing context situations in a proverb collection; see §13.0 below.

This, however, cannot be applied to languages for which written sources are lacking. Neo-Aramaic, in this respect, presents in a challenging situation: there is relatively little historical documentation of Neo-Aramaic and its various dialects. However, other forms of older Aramaic are abundantly documented. A comparison between the corpus of Neo-Aramaic proverbs and the corpus of Talmudic Aramaic proverbs, for instance, may prove fruitful.[33] Furthermore, many Neo-Aramaic proverbs may have parallel proverbs attested in historical documents of other languages of the area (Hebrew, Kurdish, Persian, Turkish, or Arabic).

10.3. Currency

Taylor (1985, 3) defined the proverb as "a saying current among the folk." There is no doubt that general acceptance is an important, perhaps crucial, feature of a proverb. But what is the criterion for considering a proverb to be current? What is the 'critical mass' of currency? It seems that there is no clear answer for this.[34]

Determining the currency of a proverb becomes more problematic when investigating a language such as Jewish Neo-Aramaic, with a limited number of native speakers. If one wishes to capture the 'traditional' situation, one must assume that modern

---

[33] For examples of Jewish Zakho proverbs with Talmudic or Midrashic parallels, see proverbs nos (15), (39), (44), (52), (64), (77), (178) in the present collection.

[34] Arora (1994, 7): "but no one has suggested a means of identifying the point at which sufficient 'currency' has been attained to mark the magical transformation from non-proverb to proverb."

speakers' knowledge, judgement, and familiarity with the lexicon of proverbs represent those of the community of earlier period. However, this problem is solved if the subject of study is defined as the language as it is spoken today by its present community of speakers, and the oral culture of that community.

It should be borne in mind that *actual* traditionality and currency have little or no significance for the speaker and listener in a proverb performance situation. The speakers usually do not possess any factual knowledge about these variables. As Arora puts it, "from the ethnic point of view, age and currency are largely assumptions based on the attribution of these characteristics to the abstract category of 'proverbs'" (Arora 1994, 8).

10.4. Repetition

The fact that a particular phrase is repeated on more than one occasion by speakers is an indication that it is a proverb. It is not a sufficient one though, since it is also common for simple sentences to be repeated in conversation. Arora claims, however, that "more complex utterances are not as a rule repeated word for word on other occasions" (Arora 1994, 8).

10.5. Grammatical and Syntactic Features

Proverbs are likely to have some grammatical or syntactical features which both make the proverb "easier to remember and transmit" (Silverman-Weinreich 1981, 71, quoted in Arora 1994, 9–10), and "[intimate] to those who do not know it that it *is* a proverb" (Silverman-Weinreich 1981, 71, quoted in Arora 1994, 9–10). These features, however, are not in themselves sufficient for a definition of the genre, since they "would appear equally applicable to non-traditional, conversational utterances" (Arora 1994, 10; see §6.0 above for examples of this type of features).

10.6. Metaphor

When browsing through an existing collection of proverbs, labelled as such, we automatically interpret the proverbs' images as meant metaphorically: the label 'proverb' entails metaphorical interpretation.

In reality, however, the process is the opposite: the out-of-contextness of a statement "labels it as a metaphor, to be understood figuratively, and leads in turn to its identification as a proverb" (Arora 1994, 11). The metaphorical interpretation, triggered by the utterance's out-of-contextness, entails the labelling as 'proverb'. The metaphorical quality of a proverb is determined by its context. It "becomes metaphorical only within its context" (Arora 1994, 11). As a result, paremiographical collections which document only the proverbs, and isolate them from their original discursive context, lack something fundamental to the phenomenon of the proverb and its study (see §13 below).

10.7. Paradox and Irony

Proverbs may use features such as paradox or irony, or "sharp contrasts and surprising comparisons" (Arora 1994, 11, referring to the ideas of Silverman-Weinreich 1981, 77). These semantic features "add to the impression of an utterance as a polished artefact, rather than a casual statement" (Arora 1994, 12).³⁵ In doing so, "they contribute to the 'made-up/non-made-up' contrast" (Arora 1994, 12).

10.8. Lexical Markers

The use of archaic lexical items both "mark[s] an utterance as non-conversational" and "provide[s] added evidence to the listener that what he is hearing is an 'old' saying" (Arora 1994, 12). Along the same lines, Sabar (1978, 218 and fn. 18) claims that "proverbs may indicate various dialects or older strata and include archaic forms or words, some of them unknown or obsolete outside of the proverb. […] As any folk literature, proverbs, too, may preserve archaic words and forms."³⁶

10.9. Prosodic Markers

The use of certain prosodic (or as Arora terms them, phonic) markers can signal to a listener that an utterance is a proverb. For example, if an utterance involves rhyme, metre, or alliteration, it is more likely to be treated as a proverb.

> The existence or absence of metric substructure in a message is the quality first recognized in any communicative

---

³⁵ For a discussion from another angle of the proverb being 'a polished artefact', see §12.0 below.

³⁶ Sabar gives the following example (SA:150): *zálle xóla básər dòla.* 'The rope has followed the drum (or the bucket).' Sabar explains that the original meaning of the archaic word *dòla* 'bucket' was lost in Neo-Aramaic, and so the word is interpreted as its homonym, 'drum'; hence the different explanations of the proverb. See proverb no. (77) in the present collection.

event and hence serves as the primary and most inclusive attribute for the categorization of oral tradition.... The presence of such markers indicates 'a deliberate deviation from everyday speech'. (Ben-Amos 1976a, 228–29, quoted in Arora 1994, 13)

11.0. Deictic and Anaphoric Usage

A distinction may be made between the deictic and anaphoric usages of proverbs. Proverbs may be used deictically—that is, they may refer to persons, events, situations, or objects that are extra-linguistic, but still have relevance to the speaking event. Proverbs may also be used in reference to persons, events, situations, facts, and so on that were previously mentioned in the discourse—that is, anaphorically.

The anaphoric usage of proverbs is most evident when proverbs are employed in narrative, where it is clear that they refer to an intra-discursive element. The distinction between deictic and anaphoric proverb usage is not identical to that between behavioural and narrative usages. Deictic and anaphoric usages can each be found in both behavioural and narrative contexts.

12.0. The Creative Process and the Proverb-reality Cycle

In order to recognise a proverb as such, the addressee ought to identify in it a degree of creative reworking. The addressee must sense the trace of a creative process (see also §10.7 above). The creative formulation is what makes encountering an utterance of a proverb enjoyable, and appreciated as meaningful, and is ultimately responsible for the proverb's acceptance. The trace of creative work can take various forms: interesting prosody, rhyme, or metre, a surprising metaphor, or humour. Each of the features discussed in §§6.1–10 and 10.1–9 above may serve as a trace of creative processing, detectable by the listeners.

The various kinds of creative formulation are the result of the focusing of the creative effort on different stages of what is here termed the proverb-reality cycle:

> (a) a general, recurring situation in reality, or a general truth learned from experience (i.e., a 'type'[37] of reality, in terms of linguistic theory)
>
> ⇓
>
> (b) the formulation of a proverb, by way of abstraction, generalisation (the *poiesis* of the proverb, its creative processing)
>
> ⇓
>
> (c) the application of an existing proverb to a particular situation in reality (a 'token' of reality); the instantiation of the proverb

The creative effort may be concentrated in varying proportions in the three stages of this cycle, as well as in the transitional stages leading from one to the other. Focusing the creative effort

---

[37] As opposed to a 'token'. The relation in the pair type/token in this context is similar to the one in the Saussurean pair *langue/parole*.

in different stages produces different types of proverb. For example, consider the following two types of proverb.

1. Proverbs which are formulations of general truths with unique wording and rhyme, metre, or alliteration. These proverbs tend to be spoken when the situation depicted in them actually occurs, that is to say, they tend not to be used metaphorically. Examples would be:

pára xwàra' ta yóma kòma.'
'A white coin for a black day.' (proverb no. (65) in the present collection; also BA:2, SA:102)
This proverb may be said, for instance, when a small amount of money is saved, or when coins change hands.
palgə́d qaḥbùsa' mə́n nəxpùsa.'
'Half of the lewdness is caused by shyness.' (proverb no. (68) in the present collection)
This proverb may be said, for instance, when a shameful incident happens to someone who is considered too modest or self-righteous.

2. Proverbs which do not express in their image a general truth or a general statement. These are spoken in situations which are completely different from what is expressed in their image, and often in a very surprising way. An example would be:

ʾaqúbra lá g-yáʾəl go-nùqba,' g-máyʾəl kanúšta ʾə̀mme.'
'A mouse cannot enter the hole, [but yet it tries to] take a broom in with it.' (proverb no. (4) in the present collection)

This proverb is used to describe a person who commits himself or herself to a task beyond his or her powers, or to refer to a situation in which the resources are not sufficient to achieve a goal.

Another example would be:

kúd g-ə́be sàker,' lá-g-manelu kašîye.'
'Whoever wants to get drunk does not count the cups.'
(proverb no. (21) in the present collection)

This proverb is used when someone tries to save expenses after having already decided they want to achieve something, or to express the view that one should commit oneself wholeheartedly to what one is doing.

In a proverb of type (1), the focus of creativity would be in stage (b), the proverb's poetic formulation, and in the transitional stage leading to it, the identification of the recurring situation in reality. In a proverb of type (2), the focus of creativity would be stage (c), the application of the proverb in a surprising manner, in a situation which is seemingly unrelated to the proverb's image.

Even a trace of the focus of creativity in the proverb is sufficient to enable the proverb's acceptability, and its preservation in shared cultural memory.

13.0. Context Situations

In the present collection of proverbs, a context situation is provided for each proverb in §14.0, giving a situation in which a speaker may use the proverb naturally. There are two main reasons for providing these context situations.

1. The context situation is an example of the correct use of the proverb. It provides the information about proverb competence involved in the usage of that particular proverb—for instance, the correlations between the constituents of the proverbs and reality, the out-of-contextness of the proverb, and so on.[38]

2. A context situation is the most effective and accurate way of recording the message of the proverb. For many of the proverbs, the message—a principal part of the proverb's meaning—cannot be inferred from the proverb's image. It may be argued that the most important part of the meaning of the proverb lies outside of it.[39]

An example of the importance of context statements for the second reason, that they give an effective means for recording the message of the proverb, can be demonstrated with a proverb

---

[38] Hasan-Rokem (1982a, 16): "The different performances reveal the denotative and connotative variation of a proverb, in the same way as different performances reveal the semantic variation of a word."

[39] In discussing the understanding of proverbs, Hasan-Rokem (1982a, 15) notes that "in and of itself, the proverb is an inadequate source." The corpus of Aramaic proverbs recorded in the Talmud serves as an illustration of this. In many cases, the meaning of these proverbs is unclear, as is evident from opposing interpretations made by commentators. The reason is not necessarily that obscure words are used in the proverb. Rather, it is precisely because the meaning of the proverb lies primarily in its message, and in its social usage, both of which can be understood only if context is provided. When context is not recorded, the fragile meaning of the proverb is easily forgotten.

which appears in all four previously published collections (with slight variations):

déna l-gùre,¹ tálga l-ṭùre.¹

'Debt on men, snow on mountains.'[40]

Each collection gives a different explanation of the message of this proverb, and has a different understanding of the correlations between the metaphor's constituents and what they represent. Bar-Adon explains: "A man must not despair due to the load of his debt, like the eternal snow which the mountains carry patiently" (Bar-Adon 1930, 13; my translation). That is, the ability of mountains to steadily resist the weight of snow is correlated to men's perseverance. Rivlin explains: "Meaning, people will not give back what you lend them" (Rivlin 1946, 212; my translation). That is, the disposition of snow to melt is correlated with people's tendency not to pay back. Alternatively, snow as a common reality is correlated with people's indifference towards their debts. Segal explains: "Do not be afraid to incur debts; they will disappear like the winter snows" (Segal 1955, 268). That is, the snow's disposition to melt is correlated with a debt's tendency to eventually be settled. Finally, Sabar explains: "Just as it is natural for the lofty mountains to have snow on top, so it is for men to have debts. Don't be ashamed to borrow money!" (Sabar 1978, 223). That is, the naturalness of mountains carrying a heavy load of snow is correlated with the supposed naturalness of men to have debts.

---

[40] Sabar's (1978, 223) translation has been provided here. Interestingly, the second half (in SE:125: the first half) of the proverb appears in the Babylonian Talmud, Taʿanit 3b: תלגא לטורי.

In addition to offering different understandings of the message of this proverb and the function of the metaphor, the cited collections do not help us to establish the rules for the correct usage of this proverb, that is to say, in which social and discursive circumstances it may or may not be spoken.[41]

---

[41] A further example of the importance of context in proverb usage is seen in Dundes (1981, 51), where he comments on Sokolov's (1950, 285) statement that what distinguishes a proverb from a riddle in the case of a particular Russian sentence that can be used as both is intonation:

> Sokolov is incorrect, however, when he contends it is only by means of a single change of intonation that a proverb is transformed into a riddle. It is obviously not intonation per se which is the critical causal factor. Instead, it is the context in which the text is cited. [...] The context or rhetorical intention of the speaker determines the intonation pattern and the genre distinction.

14.0. The Proverbs

The proverbs and proverbial phrases in this collection were collected from various informants. All context situations, unless otherwise stated, are recorded from Batia Aloni. Each proverb is glossed,[42] translated,[43] and given a context situation.[44]

(1)   ʾə́zza mgurwànta\| k-šátya   mən-réš   ʾèna.\|
    goat.F grimy.F   IND-drink.IPFV.F from-head.GEN fountain/spring.F

'The grimy goat drinks from the fountain-head.'

Vars.: ʾə́zza mgurwànta\| g-éza ʾəl réš ʾèna.\|

'The grimy goat goes to the fountain-head.'

ʾə́zza mgurwànta\| k-šátya mən-réš xawòra.\|

'The grimy goat drinks from the river's head.'

yáʿel dmáxla kəslèni| jmádla mən-qàrsa| məndéli ʾə́lla laḥèfa| márra-li ʾo-laḥéfa dəd-máni-le dəd-màni-le?!| la-g-bànne!| lá-g-ban mkásyan ʾə̀bbe!| mə̀rri-la| hăwa páxe-paqə̀ž,| ʾə́zza	Yael spent the night with us, she was very cold [lit. she froze of cold], I covered her with a blanket [lit. I threw a blanket on her], she said to me, "This blanket—whose is it, whose is it?! I do not want it! I do not want to cover [myself] with it!" I told her, "Very well,

---

[42] The Leipzig Glossing Rules (https://www.eva.mpg.de/lingua/resources/glossing-rules.php) are used here. Abbreviations used are: ACC accusative, COP copula, DAT dative, DEM demonstrative, F feminine, FUT future, GEN genitive, IMP imperative, IND indicative, INF infinitive, IPFV imperfective, JUS jussive, M masculine, NEG negator, PAST past tense, PFV perfective, PFV_PTCP perfective participle, PL plural, POSS possessive, REL relative, S singular, VERB_N verbal noun, 1 first person, 2 second person, 3 third person.
[43] See note about translation in §5.0 of the Introduction.
[44] See §13.0 above.

mgurwànta' g-éza šátya mən-réš 'èna.' [you] fastidious half-wit [lit. bland-clean]! A grimy goat goes [and] drinks from the fountain-head."

(2) *'íza d-əd léb⁴⁵-ox nagz-ət-ta' nšùq-la.'*
hand.F of-GEN unable-2MS bite.IPFV-3MS-ACC.3FS kiss.IMP.2S-ACC.3FS

'A hand that you cannot bite, [you should] kiss.'

Var.: *'íz lébox nagzətta' nšùqla.'*

'Hand you cannot bite, kiss.' Cf. SE:72.

The connection between kissing and biting as opposite expressions of love and hate can be found in an interpretation of Gen. 33.4 in Midrash Genesis Rabbah 78.9 with regard to Jacob and Esau.

xa-báxta 'úzla gazənta 'el-'izàmsa' u-məḥkéla ma-'úzla u-mtoʿəlla b-rèša.' u-márra g-óbawa nasyáwa 'əmma,' márra lá-g-maxərwánne bés 'axòni,' 'íz lébox nagzətta' nšùqla.' u-məḥkéli 'əmma ḫàš.'

A [certain] woman complained [lit. made a complaint] about her sister-in-law, and told [her] what she had done and what trouble she caused her [lit. and played with her head]. And she said she had wanted to quarrel with her, [but] she said [to herself] "I should not destroy my brother's house, a hand which you cannot bite, kiss it. And I spoke with her well [=nicely]."

(3) *xása g-əmra:' 'axòn-i,' xuzí xazy-án-nox*
sister IND-say.IPFV.3FS brother-POSS.1S I_wish see.IPVF-1FS-ACC.2MS

wázir dùnye,' 'axóna g-èmer:' xàs-i,' xuzí
wazir.M.GEN world.F brother IND-say.IPFV.3MS sister-POSS.1S I_wish

xaz-ə́n-nax xəddámt-əd bàxt-i.'
see.IPFV-1MS-ACC.2FS servant_maid-GEN wife-POSS.1S

---

⁴⁵ A construction from older Aramaic *la 'it b-* 'there is not in-'.

'The sister says: "My brother, I wish I would see you [=that you would be] the wazir of the [entire] world." The brother says: "My sister, I wish I would see you [=that you would be] the servant-maid of my wife."'

Vars.: *xása g-ə̀mra:*¹ *ʾaxòni, xuzí xazyánnox wazìra,*¹ / *wázir màsa,*¹ / *ḥakóm dùnye,*¹ / *ḥakómət qàṣra,*¹ / *ḥakóma go qàṣra,*¹…*ʾaxóna g-èmer:*¹ *xàsi,*¹ *xuzí xazə́nnax gawésa qam bèsi.*¹

'The sister says: "My brother, I wish I would see you a wazir, / a wazir of a town, / the king of the world, / a king of a castle, / a king in a castle,…" The brother says: "My sister, I wish I would see you a beggar in front of my house."'

*ʾana-ṛába g-əbánne ʾaxóni bùxra,*¹ *kúllu šə́nne màd g-ṭalə́bwa mə́nni g-yawànwale,*¹ *u-hám pàre dámməd g-lazə́mwa.*¹ *roḥáyi ʾay-xlísa ṭàle wéla.* *dammə́d-gúrre ʾúzli ṭále u-tabáxte màd g-əbéwa,*¹ *u-hár g-ṭalə́bwa mə́nni maʾinánna báxte bəd-šúl bèsa*¹ *čŭkun-léba mnóšəd gyána ʾóza šùla.*¹ *básər kmá šə́nne*¹ *fhə̀mli mad-náše g-ə̀mri,*¹ *xása g-ə̀mra*¹ *ʾàxoni,*¹ *xuzí xazyánnox wázir dùnye,*¹ *ʾaxóna g-èmer:*¹ *xàsi,*¹ *xuzí xazə́nnax xədámtəd bàxti.*¹

I love my eldest [lit. firstborn] brother very much, throughout the years [lit. all of the years] whatever he asks me I give him, also money when he needed. My own dear soul [lit. sweet spirit/soul] was for him. When he married I did for him and for his wife whatever they wanted, and he always used to ask me to help his wife with the housework because she cannot do [this] work by herself. After a few years I understood what people say: The sister says 'My brother, I wish I would see you [=you would be] the wazir of the [entire] world. The brother says: "My sister, I wish I would see you [=you would be] the servant-maid of my wife."

(4) ʾaqúbra lá g-yáʾəl   go-nùqba,' g-máyʾəl
mouse.M NEG IND-enter.IPFV.3MS in-hole.M IND-insert.IPFV.3MS

kanúšta ʾə́mm-e.'
broom.F with-GEN.3MS

'A mouse does not [=cannot] enter the hole, [but yet it tries to] take a broom in with it.'

Var.: ʾaqúbra lébe yáʾel go-nùqba...

'A mouse cannot enter the hole...'

Cf. proverbs nos (38) and (140) below, which are synonyms.

xmàsi,' qam-ʿazmálan ta-pə̀sha,' ʾána mə́rri ta-xurà̀sti' ʾásya ʾəmmèni,' lə́bbi pə́šle ʾə́bba látla čù-xa,' góri pqèʾle,' mə̀rre-li,' ʾaqùbra,' lèbe yáʾel go-núqba,' g-máyʾəl kanúšta ʾə́mme.'	My mother-in-law invited us for Passover. I told my friend she should come with us, I felt sorry for her [lit. my heart started for her] [since] she does not have anyone [=any relatives]. My husband was not pleased [lit. exploded] [about this], he told me, a mouse, [even when] it cannot enter the hole, takes a broom with it.

(5) ʾəl réš yatùme' g-lépi garàʾe.'
on head.M.GEN orphan.M IND-learn.IPFV.3PL barber.MPL

'On the head of the orphan do the barbers learn.'

Var.: ʾəl réš yatùma' g-lépi ʾə́lle grà̀ʾa.'

'On the head of the orphan they learn to cut hair over it.'

damməd-škə́lli lépan mbàšlan,' g-əmbašlánwa matfunìyye[46] u-xamùṣta,[47] u-kúlla qazáne k-šaqlánwala ta-jiráne déni dəd-	When I started learning to cook, I used to cook *matfuniyye*[46] and *xamuṣta*,[47] and I used to take the whole pot to our neighbours who were poor and had many children [lit. a

---

[46] A tomato soup with meat dumplings.
[47] A sour soup with meat dumplings.

faqíre weàlu' u-ʾə́swalu xa-kəflə́təd yalùnke.' xmási mə̀rra,' ʾóṭo-hila dùnye,' ʾəl réš yatùma' g-lépi grà'a.' bălə-ʾáhat ʾúzlax mə̀ṣwa-šĭk.'

large family/household of children]. My mother-in-law said, "This is how the world is, on the head of the orphan they learn to cut hair, but you have also done a mitzvah [=a good deed]."

(6) *be-kálo š'ə́š-lu,' be-xə́tna lá r'ə́š-lu.*[148]
house.GEN-bride shake.PFV-3PL house.GEN-bridegroom NEG feel.PFV-3PL

'[In] the house of the bride they are [already] rejoicing, [but in] the house of the bridegroom they have not [yet] felt[48] [anything].'

jíran déni séla márra ta-yə́mmi sətùna,' mbàrəxli,' g-ə́bi mšádri góri háwe ᴴkónsulᴴ go-ʾamèrika.' yə́mmi mboqə̀ra,' máni mə̀rrelax?' mə̀rra,' čú-xa băle k-i̯'an' čŭkun ᴴkónsulᴴ híle sawòna,' u-lés čú-xa mux-gòri.' yə́mmi štə̀qla.' xaráe márra ta-bàbi,' be-kálo š'ə́šlu,' be-xə́tna lá r'ə́šlu.' básər kmá sabàsa,' jíran márra la-mšodə́rru gòri,' mšodə́rru gèr náša.'

Our neighbour came [and] said to my mother, "Sətuna, bless me, they want to send my husband to be a consul in America." My mother asked, "Who told you?" She said, "No one, but I know because the consul is an old man, and there is no one [suitable] like my husband." My mother remained silent. Afterwards she said to my father, "[In] the house of the bride they are [already] rejoicing, [but in] the house of the bridegroom they have not [yet] felt [anything]." After a few weeks, the neighbour said, "They did not send my husband, they sent another person."

---

[48] According to Sabar (2002a, 286), the meaning of this verb is 'to notice, wake up (as a result of noise, etc.)'. For NENA speakers in Israel, though, the fundamental meaning of *r'š* is 'to feel'. This is possibly due to the influence of the Modern Hebrew cognate *rgš*.

(7) brón-i   u-bər-brón-i   u-ṭé'n-i   'ə̀ll-i.'
son-POSS.1s and-son-GEN-son-POSS.1s and-load.M-POSS.1s on-1s

'[Behold, here are] my son and my son's son, [but yet] my load is upon me.'

Or: 'My son and my son's son and my load are upon me.'

Vars.: kúri u-kurə̀sti,' u-ṭé'ni 'ə̀lli.' / rəš-x̀àsi.'

'[Behold, here are] my young goat, and my young she-goat, [but yet] my load is upon me / on my back.'

Or: 'My young goat and my young she-goat and my load are upon me / on my back.'

Cf. proverb no. (180) below.

kúlla dúnye híla l-rèši.' bróni u-bər-bróni u-ṭé'ni 'ə̀lli.'	'The entire world is on my head. My son and the son of my son—and my load is on me.'
šul-'éza kúlle-ile 'ə̀lli,' hám 'axwási u-hám yalúnke dídi b-áse páshi 'ə̀mmi.' kúri u-kurə̀sti,' u-ṭé'ni 'ə̀lli.' gúlli mgombə́lli go-šùla.'	'The work of the holiday [=Passover] is on me. My siblings as well as my children will come to spend Passover with me. My young goat, and my young she-goat, [but yet] my load is upon me. I am completely immersed in work [lit. I am mixed and shaped into balls in work].'

(8) gwàra'   stàra.'
marriage [=marry.INF] cover.INF

'Marriage is a shelter.'

Var.: gwàra' stàra-le.'

'Marriage is a shelter.'

Cf. R:81, a synonym.

| dáde hàr g-əmráwa ṭaléni,' bráti bnása lázəm gòri,' gwàra' stàra-le.' | Dade always used to tell us: "My daughter, girls should get married, marriage is a shelter." |

(9) doḷàmand¹— bríxa háwe ˀə̀l-lox,¹ fàqqir¹—
   rich.M   blessed.MS be.IPFV.3MS on-2MS poor.MS

m-éka   wéle-lox.¹
from-where be.PFV.3MS-DAT.2MS

'[To the] rich [they say] may it be a blessing [lit. blessed] for you, [to the] poor [they say] where did you get it from [lit. from where is it to you]?'

Vars.: ˁàšir¹—bríxa háwe ˀə̀llox,¹ ˁàni¹—méka wéle-lox.¹

'Rich—may it be blessed for you, poor—where did you get it from?'

fàqqir¹ mèka-lox,¹ doḷàmand¹ brìxa ˀə́llox.¹

'Poor—where is it from? Rich—blessed upon you.'

Cf. R:94, SE:98, SE:99, SE:100.

šə́lo lúšle bádle xásta u-zə́lle l-knə̀šta.¹ kúllu qam-baqríle ˀe-bádle mèka-ila?¹ krə́ble u-márre qam-zonə́nna dúksət náḥum zangín zúnne bádle dìde.¹ ˀàya-ila,¹ ˁàni¹ mèka-lox,¹ ˁàšir¹ brìxa ˀə́llox.¹	Šəlo wore a new suit and went to synagogue. Everyone asked him: 'This suit where is it from?' He became angry and said: 'I bought it where Naḥum the rich had bought his suit.' That is, poor—where did you get it from, rich—[may it be] a blessing [lit. blessed] for you.'

(10) dərmán šəzáne ˀìz,¹ dərmán șríˁe lès.¹
    cure.M.GEN mad.PL there_is cure.M.GEN crazed.PL there_is_not

'There is a cure for the mad, [but] there is no cure for the crazed.'

ʾe-báxta léwa nàša,¹ čú-xa lébe ʾáwəz ʾə́mma,¹ šəzànta-la,¹ qə́mla ʾizámsa mə̀rra,¹ léwa šəzànta,¹ xúzi l-šizanùsa,¹ dərmán šəzáne ʾìz,¹ dərmán ṣríʿe lès.¹
That woman is not human, no one can get along [lit. do] with her, she is crazy. Her sister-in-law said [lit. rose and said], 'She is not mad, I wish she were mad [lit. may it be on madness]. There is a cure for the mad, but not for the crazed.'

(11) dùnye¹ lá-k-peša   ta čù-xa.¹
world.F NEG-IND-remain.IPFV.3FS for no_one

'The world will remain for no one.'

Var.: *dúnye la-péša ta-čù-xa.¹*

'The world will remain for no one.'

Cf. SA:45.

múrdax bər-yóna ʾúzle ṛàba bədxáye díde,¹ zúnne u-mzobbáne be-sawàsa,¹ bnéle go-yerušaláyim ṛàba,¹ u-palgə́d ᴴkvišímᴴ go-yerušaláyim ʾàwa bnéle,¹ u-ʿála ġáfle nə̀xle.¹ kúllu náše bhə̀tlu,¹ xá mə́rre ta-daw-xèt,¹ dùnye¹ lá-k-peša ta čù-xa.¹ ʾafə́llu ta-móše rabènu.¹
Murdakh the son of Yona did a lot in his life. He bought and sold houses, he built a lot in Jerusalem, and half of the roads in Jerusalem it was who built, and he passed away [lit. rested] suddenly. All the people were shocked, one said to the other, "The world does not remain to anyone", not even to Moses our Master.

(12) hákan soté-ni   hawé-wa-la   ʾəškàsa,¹
if   grandmother-POSS.1PL be.IPFV-PAST-DAT.3FS testicle.FPL
b-ṣarx-áx-wa-la   màmo.¹⁴⁹
FUT-call.IPFV-1PL-PAST-ACC.3FS uncle.M

---

[49] Sabar (2002a, 210) on *màmo*: "used by young people addressing a paternal uncle or any old person."

'If our grandmother had had testicles, we would have called her uncle.'⁴⁹

ʾamóyi màrre,' hắkan ʾozánwa ʾòṭo,' kazbə́nwa ṛàḅa.' báxte qam-jobàle,' šmèʾlan' šmèʾlan,' hắkan sóti hawéwala ʾəškàsa,' b-ṣarxáxwala màmo.'

My uncle said: "If I had done such and such [lit. like that], I would have profited a lot." His wife answered him: "So we heard, so we heard, if my grandmother had had testicles, we would have called her uncle."

(13) hắkan u-bàlkid' ḥawwəl-bàla.'
    if   and-maybe   trouble.F

'Maybes cause only trouble.'

wan-mfakóre hắkan ʾozánwa ʾòṭo,' bálkid ḅə́š-ṭov hòya,' u-hắkan ʾòṭo,' bálkid...' yə́mmi màrra' hắkan u-bàlkid' ḥáwwel-bàla.' lá-lazəm xášwat hắkan ʾòṭo' u-hắkan ʾòṭo.'

I was thinking if I had done so [lit. like this], maybe it would have been better, and if [I had done] so [lit. like this], maybe... My mother said: "If and maybe [cause only] trouble, you should not think if so and if so."

(14) huzáya g-nápəq   mən màḥkame,'
    jew.M IND-exit.IPFV.3MS from court.F

    ʿaqə́le   k-ése   b-rèš-e.'
    mind/intelligence.M-POSS.3MS IND-come.IPFV.3MS in-head.M-POSS.3MS

'[Only when] the Jew comes out of the court, does he gain back his wit.'

zə́lli ṭáʾyan šúla ta-ʿèšan.' sèli,' qam-baqríli kma-šoʾàle.' mən-šèṭan' pə́mmi ġlàqle' lá yʾéli maʾàmran.' mpə́qli u-mtoxmə́nni má-lazəm mjobànwa.' ʾə̀h!' huzáya g-nápəq mən-màḥkame,' ʿaqə́lle k-ése b-rèše.'

I went to look for a job [in order] to support myself. I came, they asked me a few questions. From Satan [=Satan made it so that], my mouth closed, I did not know what to say. I went out and thought about what I should have answered. Ah! The Jew goes out of the courthouse [and] his mind comes [back] to his head.

(15) tóra g-nàpel,' sakíne g-zàḥf-i.'
ox.M IND-fall.IPFV.3MS knife.PL IND-proliferate.IPFV-3PL

'The ox falls down, [and] the knives become abundant.'

Var.: tóra mpə̀lle,' sakíne zḥə̀flu.'

'The ox fell, knives became abundant.'

See: נפל תורא חדד לסכינא 'The ox fell—sharpen the knife' (BT[50] Shabbat 32a)[51]

| mpə́lle ganáwa go-bes-sáleḥ ʾàġa,' bése qam-sarə̀qle.' ʾàtta,' xá básər xá k-ési nàše,' g-ə́bbi páre dəd-doyə̀nnule.' la-wə́llule mohlə̀ta.' ʾàya-la,' tóra g-nàpel,' sakíne g-zàḥfi.' | A thief entered [lit. fell into] the house of Saleḥ Aġa, he 'cleaned out' his house. Now, one by one people come, they want the money they had lent him. They did not allow him a respite. That's it, the ox falls, the knives increase. |

(16) yóma gnè-le,' qáza u-bála là-gne-lu.'
day.M set.PFV-3MS trouble and-trouble NEG-set.PFV-3PL

'The day ended, [but its] troubles did not end.'

Var.: yóma g-gàne,' qáza u-bála là g-gáne.'

'The day ends, [but its] troubles do not end.'

Cf. SA:147. See also Sabar (2002a, 123), under g-n-y.

| ʾə́dyo šmḗʾli kma-dardubā́lă sélu ʾəl-náḥum ʿàrja,' yóma g-gàne,' qáza u-bála lá g-gāne.' | Today I have heard how many ailments came upon Naḥum the lame, the day ended [lit. set], [but] the troubles did not end [lit. set]. |

(17) képa ʾəl-dúk-e yaqùra.'
stone.M on-place-POSS.3MS heavy.M

---

[50] BT = Babylonian Talmud, Vilna edition.
[51] I thank Prof. Yoel Elitzur for this reference.

'A stone is heavy [when it is] in its place.'
Cf. SE:34, SA:77.

sámra márra ta-gòra,ˈ sa-šoqáxla zàxo,ˈ ʾáx ʾəl-dòhokˈ bắlkid ʾiláha ʾizéni marùxla,ˈ k-ʾan hám go-dòhokˈ jamáʿa b-dóqi qàdrox.ˈ mə̀rrə-laˈ ʾána lá g-šoqə́nna zàxo,ˈ lá g-šóqən jamáʿa dìdi,ˈ képa ʾəl-dúke yaqùra.ˈ

Samra said to her husband: Let's leave Zakho, [and] go to Dohok, maybe God will broaden our hands [= will make us prosper], I know that also in Dohok the community will respect you [lit. hold your honour]. He told her: I do not leave Zakho, I do not leave my community, a stone in its place is heavy.

(18) kúd   k-íʾe   ṛàḅaˈ k-éxəl   čùča.ˈ
whoever.GEN IND-know.IPFV.3MS much IND-eat.IPFV little

'He who knows much eats little.'

brat-ʾìyo,ˈ sqə́lta u-maʿaqùl íla,ˈ kúd séle ṭalə̀bla,ˈ lá ʾbèla.ˈ ʿaqə́lla là qṭéʾle ʾəl-čù-xa.ˈ là gúrra,ˈ pə́šla go-bés be-bàba,ˈ kúd k-íʾe ṛàḅaˈ k-éxəl čùča.ˈ

The daughter of ʾIyo is beautiful and noble, whoever came to ask for her hand, she did not want [him]. Her mind was not cut on anyone [= She was not satisfied with anyone]. She did not get married. She remained in the house of her father; whoever knows much eats little.

(19) kúd   g-èl,ˈ   mən kís   gyàn-e g-él.ˈ
whoever.GEN IND-go.IPFV.3MS from pocket.M REFL-3MS IND-go.IPFV.3MS

'He who passes away, it is from his own pocket that he loses.'

mzabnána dəd-dé dəkkána nàxle.ˈ yalúnke díde qam-zabníla dəkkànaˈ u-msofə́rru mən-màxxa.ˈ čú-xa lá k-taxə́rre u-lá g-matxə́rre ʾo-pappùka.ˈ ʾə̀h!ˈ kúd g-èl,ˈ mən-kís gyàne g-él.ˈ mġabíne ʾə̀lle.ˈ čú-xa mən-gébe lá xsə̀rre,ˈ ʾáwwa xsə̀rre.ˈ

The shopkeeper of that shop passed away [lit. rested]. His children sold the shop and travelled away from here. No one remembers nor mentions that poor soul. Ah! Whoever goes [= dies], goes at his own expense [lit. from his own pocket]. What a pity! [lit. pity/deprivation on him!] No one apart from him lost [or: lacked] anything, [it is only] he [who] lost [or: lacked].

(20) kúd   lá   zál-le   ʾəl ʾìz-e¹
whoever.GEN NEG walk/go.PFV-3ms on hand.F-POSS.3MS
lá-k-iʾe   lá   ʾàql-e.¹
NEG-IND-know.IPFV.3MS in-honour.M leg-POSS.3MS

'He who never walked on his hands does not understand how important his legs are.'

Vars.: kúd g-él ʾəl ʾizàse,¹ k-ṭʾe b-qádər ʾaqlàse.¹

'He who walks on his hands, knows how important his legs are.'

kúd g-él ʾəl ʾíze,¹ kṭʾe b-qádər ʾaqlàse.¹

'He who walks on his hands, knows how important his legs are.'

Cf. SE:18.

farrán déni wéale ʿayàn,¹ ṭlahá šabása qam-šeʾáxla mabóse l-bèsa,¹ ṛába mʿolʿəllan.¹ damməd-zə́llan básər ṭlahá šabása kəz-farràn,¹ yə́mmi màrra-le,¹ ᴴbarúx ha-šémᴴ ṭṛə̀slox,¹ u-ʾátta lá g-əmʿàzbax,¹ u-k-iʾáx qàdrox.¹ ʾáwa mjoyə̀ble,¹ kúd lá zə́lle ʾəl-ʾìze¹ lá-k-iʾe b-qádər ʾàqle.¹

Our baker was sick. For three Shabbats [or: weeks] we prepared [lit. whitewash/plastered[52]] the Shabbat food[53] at home, it was a nuisance [lit. we were very pestered]. When we went after three weeks to the baker, my mother told him, 'Thank God you became healthy, and now we shall not suffer, and we [now] know your worth [lit. honour].' He replied, 'Whoever [never] walked on his hands, does not know the honour [=importance] of his legs.'

---

[52] Whitewash or plaster was presumably used to insulate the pot in order to keep it hot.

[53] Jewish law forbids cooking on the Sabbath. The food for the Sabbath is cooked on Friday and left hot, using insulation or a small source of heat, for twenty-four hours.

(21) kúd   g-ɔ́be   sàker,'
    whoever.GEN IND-want.IPVF.3MS be_drunk.IPFV
    lá-g-mane-lu   kašìye.'
    NEG-IND-count.IPFV-ACC.3PL cup.PL

'Whoever wants to get drunk does not count the cups.'

Cf. SE:9, SE:11, which are synonyms.

g-ɔ́bən ṛàḅa lépen ṭárən ṭiyàra,' mə́rri ta-yə̀mmi,' hákan k-ṭarə́nna ṭiyára ʾəmmed-maʿáləm dídi saʿà-u-pálge,' lázəm yawə́nne xamšì rupíyye.' hákan k-ṭarə́nna palgə̀d-saʿà,' lázəm yawə́nne ʾarbì rupíyye.' bə́š-ṭov ṭáli kúd-yom lépen palgə̀d-saʿa,' bằle,' ṛàḅa páre lázem dàfʿən,' yə́mmi mə̀rra-li,' bròni,' kúd g-ɔ́be sàker,' lá-g-manelu kašìye.'

I would very much like to learn to fly aeroplanes. If I fly the aeroplane with my teacher [for] one and a half hour[s], I must pay [lit. give] him fifty rupees. If I fly it [for] half an hour, I must pay [lit. give] him forty rupees. It is better for me to learn each day [for] half an hour, but I must pay a lot of money. My mother said to me, "My son, whoever wishes to get drunk does not count the cups."

(22) xmára g-yasr-í-le   kəz-xmàra,' g-láep
    donkey.M IND-tie.IPFV-3PL-ACC.3MS chez-donkey.M IND-learn.IPFV.3MS
    mə̀nn-e.'
    from-3MS

'[When] you [lit. they] tie a donkey near a[nother] donkey, it learns from it.'

Vars.: xmára g-yasríle kəz-xmàra,' g-láep mə́nne fuʿàle.'

'[When] you [lit. they] tie a donkey near a[nother] donkey, it learns its ill deeds.'

xmára g-yasríle kəz-xmàra,' gə-mʿàrət.'

'[When] you [lit. they] tie a donkey near a[nother] donkey, it farts.'

xmára g-yasríle kəz-xmàra,' g-láep mʿárət muxwàse.'

'[When] you [lit. they] tie a donkey near a[nother] donkey, it learns to fart like him.'

Cf. R:99, SA:68, SA:99.

ʾaná tré yalònke,' mən-yóm ílu məǵzaz,' g-ózi ṛába pəʿəllòs.' ʾaw-zóra moláple ʾaw-ṛúwwa ʾáwəz ḥublotìyye.' g-nádi ʾàxxaˈ u-g-ṭóri ʾàxxa.' qam-mapqíla roḥàyan.' xmára g-yasríle kəz-xmàra,' g-láep mànne.'

These two children, since the day they are together, they make many mischievous actions. The little one taught the big [= older] one naughtiness. They jump here and break [things] there [lit. here]. And they took our soul out [= gave us a hard time]. [If] you tie a donkey near [another] donkey, it learns from it.

(23) kúd   gáwər   yə̀mm-an,'
whoever.GEN marry.IPFV.3MS mother-POSS.1PL

b-ṣarx-áx-le   bàbo.' kúd   gáwər
FUT-call/scream.IPFV-1PL-ACC.3MS dad   whoever.GEN marry.IPFV.3MS

sòt-an,'   b-amr-áx-le   màmo.[54]
grandmother-POSS.1PL FUT-call/say.IPFV-1PL-ACC.3MS uncle

'Whoever marries our mother, we shall call him father. Whoever marries our grandmother, we shall call him uncle.'[54]

Cf. SE:115. Note that each of the two sentences of this proverb can also be used separately.

dʾə́rri ʾəl-šúla básər ṭlahá yárxe dəd-wéwali go-ʾamèrika.

I returned to work after spending three months in America [lit. three months that I have

---

[54] See fn. 49 above.

mə̀rruli,' ^H*menahḗl*^H *dḗni ʾaw-ḃàš.*' *mə̀rri,*' *kúllu xà-ilu.*' *kúd gáwər yə̀mman,*' *b-ṣarxáxle bàbo.*' been in America]. They told me [that] they replaced our good manager. I said: 'They are all the same [lit. one]. Whoever marries our mother we shall call father.'

sélelan ḥázzan xása ta-knə̀šta,' *léwe mən-məllə́ta dèni,*' *băle-ṛába ḃaš hìle.*' *frə́ḥlan u-mə́rran xá ta-daw-xə̀t,*' *šud-lá-hawe mən-məllə́ta dèni,*' *kúd gáwər sòtan,*' *b-amráxle màmo.*' A new hazzan came [lit. came for us] to the synagogue, he is not from our people [=Kurdistani Jews], but he is very good. We were happy and we said one to the other, '[It is good even if] he should not be from our people, whoever marries our grandmother, we shall call uncle.'

(24) xá də́qn-e   q-qèza,'   ʾaw-xét   g-èmer'
one beard.F-POSS.3MS IND-burn.IPFV.3FS DEM.MS-other IND-say.IPFV.3MS

hál-li   qaqwán-i   mṭaw-ə̀n-na.'
give.IMP-DAT.1s partridge-POSS.1s roast.IPFV-1MS-ACC.3FS

'The beard of one is on fire, the other says: "Let me roast my partridge [over it]."'

Var.: *xá g-báxe də́qne ila bə-qyàza,*' *xóre g-émer hálli čígari maʿəlqə̀nna.*'

'One is crying his beard is on fire, his friend says, "Let me light my cigarette [with it]."'

Cf. SA:20, a variant; proverb no. (25) below, a synonym.

wan-gúlta mgumbálta go-šùli.¹ látli wáʿada xékan rèši.¹ mərjáne k-xázya ḥàli,¹ g-əmràli,¹ kappàrax,¹ dré ʾenáx ʾəl-bràti¹ híl ʾán ʾəl-ḥámmam u-daʾràn.¹ mə́rrila mərjàne,¹ qə́ṣṭəd ʾáw də́qne qèza,¹ ʾaw-xét g-emə̀rre¹ hálli qaqwáni mṭawə̀nna.¹

I am completely immersed and troubled [lit. mixed up and shaped into a ball] in my work. I have no time to scratch my head. Mərjane sees my situation, she tells me: "[I am] your expiation,[55] watch [lit. put your eye on] my daughter while [lit. until] I go to the bath and return." I told her: "Mərjane, [this is] the story of that one who [when] his beard is on fire, the other tells him, give me my partridge [and] I shall roast it."

(25) *xá wél-e qam-šnàqa,¹*
one COP-3MS[=be.PFV.3MS] in_front_of-hanging.VERB_N[=hang.INF]

báxt-e g-ə́mra,¹ hál-li
wife-POSS.3MS IND-say.IPFV.3FS give.IMP-DAT.1S

pàre,¹ ʾán ʾəl-ḥàmmam.¹
money[=coin.MPL] go.IPFV.1S to-bath.M

'One is about to be hanged, his wife says, "Give me money, I shall go to the bathhouse."'[56]

Var.: *xá wélu bə-šnáqa dìde,¹ báxte g-ə́mra,¹ hálli páre ta-ḥàmmam.¹*

'One is about to be hanged [lit. they are hanging him], his wife says, "Give me money for the bathhouse."'

---

[55] A form of address expressing affection.

[56] The reference is to the *miqve* 'ritual bath', where the wife bathes after her menstrual period in preparation for marital relations. The woman in the proverb does not understand the severity of the situation of her husband, and intends to prepare herself for him.

Cf. proverb no. (24) above.

yəmmi g-ə́ba šéʾa mabóse tré daqíqe qábəl šàbsa,ˈ séla brút jiráne ṭləbla mənna,ˈ maxwéli máṭo g-əmgámbeli[57] *kutèle.ˈ yəmmi mə̀rra,ˈ ʾàtta?!ˈ sáʿət xnáqət gəsəksa?ˈ xá wéle qamšnàqa,ˈ báxte g-ə̀mra,ˈ háli pàre,ˈ ʾán ʾəl-ḥàmmam.ˈ*

My mother wants [=is just about] to prepare [lit. whitewash/plaster[58]] the Shabbat food, two minutes before Shabbat [starts], the daughter of the neighbours came and asked her, "Show me how you shape into balls[57] the meat dumplings." My mother said, "Now?! At the time [of] the choking [=slaughtering?] of the [goat's] kid? One is about to be hanged, his wife says, give me money, [so that] I shall go to the bathhouse."

(26) xá də̀qn-e   k-ṭáʾən,ˈ   ʾaw-xét
one BEARD.F-POSS.3MS IND-carry.IPFV.3MS DEM.MS-other

k-čàhe.ˈ
IND-become_weary.IPFV.3MS

'One carries his own beard, [but] the other gets tired.'

Var.: *xá də́qne k-ṭaʾə̀nna* [ACC.3F],ˈ *ʾaw-xét k-čáhe mə̀nna.*ˈ

'One carries his own beard, [but] the other gets tired of it.'

Cf. proverb no. (180) below.

---

[57] See Sabar (2002a, 122), under *g-m-b-l*.
[58] See fns 52–53 above.

mə̀ryam,¹ g-máʾina yalúnke dída ṛábət ṛàba.¹ g-óza mád k-ṭàḷbi.¹ záʾo g-əmràla,¹ qáy k-čáhyat ʾóṭo ṛàba?¹ yalúnke dídax rùwwe-lu,¹ kúd-xa šud-ʾáwəz ta-bèse.¹ mjoyə́bla mə̀ryam,¹ háwwa kàssi wélax!¹ ʾáhat mà-wajax?¹ xá də̀qne k-ṭáʾən,¹ ʾaw-xét k-čàhe.¹

Məryam helps her children a great deal. She does whatever they ask for. Zaʾo tells her: 'Why do you tire yourself that way so much? Each one should make for his [own] home [= each child should take care of himself].' Məryam answered her: 'All right, my dear one you are, what's it to you [lit. you what is your concern]? One carries his own beard, [but] the other becomes tired.'

(27) *xábra   dəd-g-nápəq   mən-tré səppàsa,¹*
spoken_word.M REL-IND-go_out.IPFV.3MS from-two lip.FPL

g-závər-ra   kúll-a màsa.¹
IND-turn.IPFV.3MS-ACC.3FS all-3FS village.F

'Whatever goes out of the lips will circle the whole village.'

Vars.: *...g-závər go-kúlla màsa.¹*

'...in the whole village.'

...g-závər go-kúllu maswàsa.¹

'...in all of the villages.'

...g-závərru [ACC.3PL] kúllu maswàsa.¹

'...circle all of the villages.'

Cf. R:97, SA:141.

básso bax-dárwəš mə̀rrali, Basso the daughter of Darwəsh told me: "I want to tell you something, but a word under your slipper."⁵⁹ I told her: "See, my lips are closed, I know that a word that goes out of the two lips circles in the entire village."
g-ə́ban ʔamránnax xa-mə̀ndi,
*bălĕ-xábra xe-pelàvax.*⁵⁹
mə̀rrila, xzé səppási ílu ġlìqe,
k-ʔan xábra dəd-g-nápəq mən-tré səppàsa, g-závər go-kúlla màsa.

(28) *xmárta mpə́q-lu-la xalawàsa.*
donkey.F go_out.PFV-3PL-DAT.3FS uncle.PL

'[Suddenly] the she-ass found relatives [lit. uncles].'

ʔó yála ləple ʔə̀mmi, xà mə́skin wéle, kúllu g-maxéwale u-gaxkíwa ʔə̀lle, xa-yóme jgə̀rre, qə́mle ʔəl-gyàne, mxéle xa-yàla, qam-qaṭə́lle bəd-šarqìʕe. kúllu bhə̀tlu, mə̀rru, dúqle jurʕùta, čŭkŭn sawóye sèle. xmárta mpə́qlela xalawàsa. This boy learned [=went to school] with me, he was such a poor soul, they used to hit him and laugh at him. One day he became angry, braced himself [lit. rose on himself], hit one child, he killed him with slaps [=hit him hard]. Everyone was frightened [or: astonished], they said, "He became courageous [lit. he grabbed courage], because his grandfather came. The she-donkey found uncles."

(29) *xmára dəd kúš-li mə̀nn-e, šèṭan šud ráku ʔə́ll-e.*
donkey.M REL descend.PFV-1S from-3MS Satan let ride.IPFV.3MS on-3MS

'A donkey from which I have [already] dismounted, let [even] the devil ride it.'

Var.: *xmára dəd kúšli mə̀nne, šud šèṭan ráku ʔə́lle.*

'A donkey from which I have [already] dismounted, the devil should ride it!'

---

⁵⁹ See proverb no. (195) below.

Cf. proverb no. (164) below, which is a synonym.

xzéli brat-xáḥam ʾə́šḥaq go-šùqa.' *mə́rri-la xazále k-îʾat máni k-pálex mən-gébax go-farmašìyye? mə́rra-li xmára dəd-kúšli mə̀nne,*' *šud-šèṭaṇ ráku ʾólle, lá k-îʾan*' *u-là-waji.*'

I saw the daughter of Ḥakham ʾəšḥaq in the market. I told her: "Khazale, do you know who works instead of you [= who has the job you used to have] in the pharmacy?" She told me: "A donkey from which I have dismounted, let the devil ride it, I do not know and I do not care."

(30) *kúd-ʾət-le ḥə̀nna,*' *k-ṣáweʾ zə̀bb-e.*'
all.REL-there_is-DAT.3MS henna.F IND-dye.IPFV.3MS penis.M-POSS.3MS

'Whoever has henna, dyes his penis [as well].'

Vars.: ...*zə̀bbe šə́k k-ṣawéʾle.*'

'...dyes also his penis.'

...*šud ṣawéʾle zə̀bbe.*' '...may he dye his penis!'

yaʿaqúbe zúnne ta-gyáne xà pálṭo' *xáru bés bába*[60] *má sqə̀lta.*' *xaràe*' *xzéle go-dáy dəkkàna*' *ṣúdra sqə́lta ta-kalə̀bsa,*' *g-əmšápya ʾəl-day-pàlṭo.*' *wéala ṛába gə̀ran.*' *qam-zawə̀nna ta-kalə́bsa díde.*' *maʿalùm,*' *kúd ʾə́tle ḥə̀nna,*' *k-ṣáweʾ zə̀bbe.*'

Yaʿaqube bought himself [such] an overcoat, may its father's house be destroyed,[60] how beautiful [it is]! Afterwards he saw in that [same] shop a nice shirt for a she-dog, [which] resembles that overcoat. It was very expensive. He bought it for his dog. [It is] obvious, whoever has henna, dyes his penis [as well].

(31) *ksésa gə-mqòqya,*' *kír dikə́la g-nə̀pəl.*'
hen.F IND-cackle.IPFV.3FS penis.GEN rooster IND-fall.IPFV

'The hen cackles, [and] the penis of the rooster falls [off].'

---

[60] An expression of appreciation.

ḥắbo márra g-ə́ba msáfra ta-kúlle ʾèza.ˈ góra mə̀rreˈ ʾáp-ana wen-mnèkar.ˈ yə́mmi g-xə́kla u-mə̀rra,ˈ ksésa gə-mqòqya,ˈ kír dikə́la g-nàpəl.ˈ m̥áṭo msafrétun bəd-ʾez-zyàra?ˈ ʾéka b-ozétun pə̀sḥa?!ˈ

Ḥabo said she wants to travel [away] for the entire festival [of Passover]. Her husband said, "I am also eager [to go]." My mother laughed and said, "The hen cackles, [and] the penis of the rooster falls [off]. How will you travel during the festival of Passover? Where will you spend [lit. make, i.e., celebrate] Passover?!"

(32) kálba g-háwe kučə̀ka.ˈ
dog.M IND-give_birth.IPFV.3MS puppy.M.

'A dog sires puppies.'

séle-lan xa-jíran ràʿ,ˈ ṣaráxa u-mṣaʿràna,ˈ u-ʿášəq ḥə̀sse,ˈ škə́llan mbáqrax náše ʾə̀lle,ˈ màni-leˈ méka sèle.ˈ márru-lan ʾó bər-yáʿqov qadàrči-le.ˈ mbúrxa šə̀mmed xalàqa,ˈ ʾáy raʿúsa u-ʾáw ṣráxa u-ʾáw ḥə̀s ta-kùtru.ˈ kálba g-háwe kučə̀ka.ˈ

One bad neighbour came to [live next to] us, a screamer and a foul-mouth, and likes-his-own-voice. We started to ask people about him, who is he, where did he come from. They told us, "This is the son of Yaʿaqov Qadarči." Blessed be the name of the Creator! The [same] wickedness and the [same] screaming and the [same loud] voice to the both of them. A dog sires a puppy.

(33) kúd tákel ʾəl jiràn-e,
whoever.GEN rely.IPFV.3MS on neighbour-POSS.3MS

páyəš là ʿašáya.ˈ
remain.IPFV.3MS NEG dinner.F

'He who relies on his neighbour, remains without dinner.'

Var.: *kúd tákel ʾəl xuràse,ˈ b-dámex lá ʿašáya.ˈ*

'He who relies on his friends, will sleep without dinner.'

yə́mmi hàr g-əmráli.ˈ lazəm-yáʾat ta-gyànax.ˈ lá táklat ʾəl-čù-xa.ˈ

My mother always tells me: "You should know how to get along [lit. know for yourself].

| kúd tákel ʾəl jiràne,ˈ páyəš là ʿašáya.ˈ | Do not count on anyone. Whoever relies on his neighbour, stays without dinner." |

(34) xóla qṭèʾ-le,ˈ ṣíwe mborbə̀z-lu.ˈ
rope.M cut.PFV-3MS wood.MPL scatter.PFV-3PL

'The rope broke, [and] the sticks scattered.'

Cf. SA:144.

| zə́lli ʾəl-marimóe[61] kəz-xuràsti.ˈ bába u-yə́mma nə́xlu bxà yárxaˈ ṭalḅílan xàye.ˈ[62] bxéla u-mzorzə̀qla,ˈ mə́rra xóla qṭèʾle,ˈ ṣíwe mborbə̀zlu.ˈ ʾátta ʾaxawási b-ázi kúd-xa ʾəl-šùleˈ u-kúd-xa b-ʾùrxe,ˈ kúlleni mbàrbəzax.ˈ bés bábi u-yə́mmi xrùle.ˈ | I went to pay my condolences [lit. to the marimoe[61]] to [lit. at] my friend. Her father and her mother passed away [lit. rested] within one month— may they ask for life for us.[62] She cried and trembled. She said, "The rope snapped, the wood has scattered. Now my siblings will go each one to his work, each one in his way, all of us will scatter. The house of my father and mother has been destroyed." |

---

[61] The Jewish mourning period of seven days, the shivʿa.
[62] An expression said after mentioning the deceased.

xuzí⁶³ ʾəl-dán yomàsa,' dammǝd-bábi u-yə́mmi wéalu ṣàx,' u-kúd šàbsa,' u-kúd ʾèza,' kúlleni k-əsyáxwa kə̀slu.' kúlleni wéalan mə̀zġaz.' u-go-palgə́d šábsa kud-g-ezə́lwa l-šùqa,' yán ʾəl-xa-xəlmə̀ta dìde,' k-eséwa be-bàbi,' hár k-xazyáxwa xa-ʾaw-xèt.' mən-yóm nə̀xlu,' ṭalbíloxun xàye.¹⁶⁴ kúd xá hile-žġíla bəd-šoʾále dìde,' xóla qṭèʾle' u-ṣíwe mborbə̀zlu.'

I long for those days [lit. I wish/would that for those days],⁶³ when my father and my mother were alive, and each Shabbat, and each festival, we all used to come to their home [lit. chez them]. And on weekdays [lit. in the middle of the week], whoever went to the market, or to do some task of his, would come to the house of my father, [and so] we used to always see one another. Since the day they passed away [lit. rested]—may they ask life for you⁶⁴—each one is busy with his own things, the rope snapped and the wood has scattered.

(35) ksésa dəd gə-mràmda,'   b-réš   gyàn-a
hen.F REL IND-spread_dirt_by_digging.IPFV.3FS⁶⁵ in-head self-POSS.3FS

gə-mrámda.'
IND-spread_dirt_by_digging.IPFV.3FS

'A hen that spreads dirt, does so upon her own head.'

ʾə́ čàḥla,' kúlle yóma g-máḥkya ʾəl-nàše.' ʾó ʾóṭo-ile u-ʾé ʾúzla hádxa u-hàdxa.' ʾátta kúllu lébu daʾlìla.' ksés gə-mràmda,' b-réš gyàna gə-mrámda.'

That bimbo, all day long she speaks of people. This one is like that, and this one did such and such. Now nobody can stand her [lit. everybody is not able to see her]. A chicken that spreads dirt, does so upon her own head.

---

⁶³ See Sabar (2002a, 193), under כוזי.
⁶⁴ An expression said after mentioning the deceased.
⁶⁵ Apparently from the Arabic root *rml* 'to sprinkle with sand' (definition from Wehr and Cowan 1976, 360).

(36)   *kúd   réš-e   léwe   go qarqəšyàsa,*'
whoever.GEN head.M-POSS.3MS COP.NEG.3MS in tremor/quarrel.MPL

'ál   kəndàla.'
go.IPFV(.JUS.)3MS steep_slope.M

'Whoever is not engaged with the chaos of this world, is of no worth.'

Said by Ḥakham Zekharya, a well-known figure in the Zakho community in Jerusalem.

xáḥam zəxáya wéale maḥkyána u-ṛàba kèfči,' kúd-məndi g-maʿaləqwale mux-nùra,' u-hár g-eməṛwa,' kúd réše léwe go-qarqəšyàsa,' ʾál kəndàla.' u-ʾána g-óben náše dəd-réšu híle go-qarqəšyàsa.'	Ḥakham Zekharya was talkative and very joyful, anything would light him up like fire, and he always used to say, "Whoever's head is not [immersed] in tremors and quarrels, may he go to [=fall into] a steep slope, and I like people whose head is [immersed] in tremors and quarrels."

(37) *xolá kud ʾáwəz tərnìni,*[66] *lázəm [var: ʾána]*
is_it_so all.REL do.IPFV.3MS tərnini must/need [I]

ràqz-ən.'
dance.IPFV-1MS

'I am not obliged to dance for anyone who makes [= sings] *tərnìni*'.[66]

Var.: *xolá kud ʾámər/ʾámərri tərnìni,' ʾána b-ràqzən.*'

'Is it so that [for] anyone who tells/tells me *tərnìni*, I will dance?!'

Cf. proverb no. (137) below.

---

[66] Sabar (2002a, 313) on *tərnàna tərnìni*: "sound imitations of dance."

xurásti kúd-yoma g-əmrà-li sa-ʾáx kəz-dé qam-ʿazmàlan¹ sa-ʾáx kəz-dayá qam-ʿazmalan. mə́rri-la xolá kud-ʾámer tərnìni,¹ lázəm ràqzan.¹ xolá kud-ʿazə́mli lázəm ʾàn.¹

My friend tells me every day, "Let's go to [visit] this [person], she invited us, let's go to [visit] that [person], she invited us." I told her, "Is it so that [when] anyone says tərnini, I should dance? Is it so that [when] any-one invites me, I should go?"

See proverb no. (104) below for an additional relevant context.

(38) xá léb-e   l-xà,¹ g-émer   tré tré sá-loxun
one unable-3MS on-one IND-say.IPFV.3MS two two come.IMP-2PL

ʾə̀ll-i.¹
on-1s

'One cannot overcome [even] one, [but] yet he says come unto me in pairs.'

Cf. the synonymous R:47, SE:7, proverb no. (4) above and no. (140) below.

xazále brat-xáḥam šàlom¹ k-palxáwa kəz-xa-məšpáḥa dolamàn,¹ kúd-yom mə́n bə́noke híl lèle k-palxáwa.¹ bás yóm xušèba¹ lá-k-palxawa.¹ xà yóma,¹ mə́rra ta-yə̀mma,¹ jìran dəd-maʿalə̀mti¹ g-ə́ba pálxan kə́sla b-yóm xušèba,¹ má g-ə̀mrat ᴴʾìmaᴴ?¹ yə́mma mjoyə̀bla:¹ bràti,¹ xá lèbe l-xá,¹ g-émer tré tré sáloxun ʾə̀lli,¹ wat-qrə́fta mən-šúla dídax kəz-maʿalə̀mtax,¹ g-ə́bat pálxat xa-xə̀t dúka?!

Khazale the daughter of Ḥakham Shalom used to work for [lit. at] a [certain] rich family. She would work every day from morning until evening. Only on Sunday[s] did she not work. One day, she said to her mother, 'The neighbour of my boss wants me to work for [lit. at] her on Sunday[s]. What do you say, mother?' Her mother answered: 'My daughter, one is not able to overcome one [lit. one cannot on one], he says come to [fight] me in pairs [lit. two two come on me], you are wrenched from your work at your boss['s], [and] you want to work [at] another place?!'

(39) xá bàba' gə-mdábər ʾəsrà yalúnke,' ʾəsra yalúnke
one father IND-sustain.IPFV.3MS ten child.PL ten child.PL
la-gə-mdábri xá bàba.'
NEG-IND-sustain/support.IPFV.3PL one father

'One father can support ten children, [but] ten children cannot support one father.'

Cf. R:53 (where Rivlin gives a similar proverb in Arabic), SE:17, proverb no. (80) below. See רחמי דאבא אבני רחמי דבני אבני דהוו ליה 'The love of the father is for the sons, the love of the sons is for the sons they have' (BT Sota 49a); אב א' מפרנס עשרה בניו באהבה וברצון ועשרה בנים לא מפרנסים באהבה וברצון אב א' שלהם 'One father provides with love and willingly for ten sons but ten sons do not provide with love and willingly for their one father' (Horowitz 1649, 64a); אב אחד יכול לפרנס עשרה בנים ועשרה בנים אינם יכולים לפרנס אב אחד 'One father can provide for ten sons but ten sons cannot provide for one father' (Shapiro 1911, 20).

hamínko íle be-ḥàl,' lés xá yawə́lle xa-kočə́ksa maràqa,' ʾàya-íla,' xá bàba' gə-mdabér ʾəsra yalúnke,' ʾəsra yalúnke la-gə-mdábri xa-bàba.'	Haminko is in bad shape [=ill]. There is no one to give him [even] one spoon of soup, that is it [=that is what is referred to by], one father [can] support ten children, ten children cannot [lit. do not] support one father.

(40) kúd gə-mtáʿel b-əd-ʾəxre,' ríx
whoever.GEN IND-play.IPFV.3MS in-GEN-faeces.PL smell.M.GEN
ʾəxre k-ése mə̀nne.'
faeces.PL IND-come.IPFV.3MS from-3MS

'Whoever plays with faeces, smells like faeces.'

Var.: kúd gə-mtáʿel bəd-ʾəxre,' k-ése mən-ʾizase.'

'Whoever plays with faeces, the smell of faeces comes from his hands'.

Cf. SE:47.

xaḥam-náḥum hár g-èmer,ˈ ʾénox ʾəl-gyànox!ˈ hăkan-xzélox xurása ganàweˈ duglàneˈ šəxtàne,ˈ mənnox-šik b-áse ríx ganawúsa u-dùgle.ˈ kúd gə-mtáʿel bəd-ʾə̀xre,ˈ ríx ʾə́xre k-ése mə̀nne.ˈ	Ḥakham Naḥum always says, "Be careful [lit. (keep) your eye on yourself]! If you find [lit. saw] friends [who are] thieves, liars, dirty, also from you the smell of theft and lies will come. Whoever plays with faeces, the smell of faeces comes from him."

(41) xmára k-íʾe ʾáxəl nàʿnaʿ?!ˈ
donkey.M IND-know.IPFV.3MS eat.IPFV.3MS spearmint.F

'Does a donkey know to eat spearmint?!'

mbošə́lli xà xamúṣta,⁶⁷ xáru bés bàbeˈ⁶⁸ kma-bassə̀mta wéala.ˈ séla ḥabúba jíran dìdi,ˈ qam-ṭamʾála u-škə́lla maʿibàla,ˈ léba mə̀lxa,ˈ lazəm-hóya bə̀š xamúṣta.ˈ yəmmi šmeʾla u-mə́rra kappàrax ḥabúba,ˈ ᴴyófiᴴ-d⁶⁹ xamúṣta bráti mbošə̀lla,ˈ xmára k-íʾe ʾáxəl nàʿnaʿ?!ˈ frə́ḥli ràba.ˈ	I cooked such a xamúṣta⁶⁷ soup, may the house of its father be destroyed,⁶⁸ how good it was! Ḥabuba my neighbour came, tasted it, and started to scorn it, 'There is no salt in it, it should be more sour.' My mother heard and said: '[I am] your expiation⁷⁰ Ḥabuba, my daughter cooked a wonderful xamúṣta. Does a donkey know [how] to eat spearmint?!' I was very happy.

(42) káls-ox mən-súlta mèsi-la,ˈ
daughter_in_law-POSS.2MS from-dunghill.F bring.IMP.2MS-ACC.3FS

---

⁶⁷ A sour soup with meat dumplings.
⁶⁸ An expression of appreciation.
⁶⁹ The Hebrew noun *yofi* here takes the NENA genitive marker *-d*.
⁷⁰ A form of address expressing affection.

dúk-əd   bràt-ox¹   mbàni-la.¹
place.F-GEN daughter-POSS.2MS select.IMP-ACC.3FS

'Take you daughter-in-law from the dunghill, [but] the place of your [own] daughter [you should] select it well.'

mámo múrḍax mə́rre ta-bàbi,¹ bróni mpə́lle basər-brát ḥayíka garà'a,¹ g-óben 'án ṭalabáye dìda,¹⁷¹ lá-k-i'en mə́ṭo-híle bés-be-bàba,¹⁷² 'éma nàše-lu.¹ bábi mjoyìble¹ kálsox mən-súlta mèsi-la,¹ dúkəd bràtox¹ mbàni-la.¹ mə́rre ta-bàbi,¹ xàbrox híle 'əstázi.¹	Uncle Murdakh said to my father: "My son fell after the daughter of Ḥayika the barber [= he likes her], I would like to go to negotiate the marriage,⁷¹ I do not know what her family is like [lit. how the house of her father is],⁷² what [kind of] people they are." My father answered him: "Take your daughter-in-law from the dunghill, the place of your daughter select it well." He said to my father: "That is true [lit. (this) is your word], my teacher."

(43) *lá háw-ət   dùša¹   [var.: xə̀lya¹] lá meṣi-lox,¹*
NEG be.IPFV-2MS honey.M [var.: sweet.M] NEG suck.IPFV.3PL-ACC.3MS

lá háw-ət   dùša¹   márira lá reqì-lox.¹
NEG be.IPFV-2MS honey.M bitter.M NEG spit.IPFV.3PL-ACC.3MS

lá háw-ət   wìša¹   lá torì-lox.¹
NEG be.IPFV-2MS dry.M NEG break.IPFV.3PL-ACC.3MS

lá háw-ət   rakìxa¹ lá marčì-lox.¹
NEG be.IPFV-2MS soft.M NEG crush.3PL-ACC.3MS

'Do not be [too] sweet, so that they will not suck you.

Do not be [too] bitter, so that they will not spit you [out].

---

[71] For details about the process leading to a Zakho Jewish wedding, see Aloni (2014a, 85–101).

[72] The extended family household in Zakho, *be-* 'house of', and the changes it has undergone in Israel are discussed in Aloni (2014a, 85–88).

Do not be [too] dry, so that they will not break you.
Do not be [too] soft, so that they will not crush you.'

Cf.: אל תהי מתוק פן יבלעוך 'Do not be sweet lest they swallow you' (Arama 1573, 88b; my translation). See also additional references in Zlotnik Avida (1938, 53–54).

bròni' xzí ma-ksúle rambàm,' lazəm-hár ʾázət go-pàlga,' lá háwət ṛába xə̀lya' lá meṣeìlox,' lá háwət màrira' lá reqìlox.' lá háwət wìša' lá torìlox.' lá háwət rakìxa' lá marčìlox.'

My son, see what Maimonides wrote, one should always go in the middle [path]. Do not be too sweet, so that they do not suck you, do not be bitter so that they do not spit you [out], do not be dry so that they do not break you, do not be soft so that they do not crush you.

(44) lá ʾáw jàjik,' lá ʾáw žə̀ḥḥar.'
NEG DEM.M jajik.M NEG DEM.M poison.M

'Not [of] that *jajik*,[73] [and] not [of] that poison.'

Var.: lá ʾáw jàjik' bəd d-ʾáw žə̀ḥḥar.'

'Not [of] that jajik with that poison.'

Cf. אומרים לה לצרעה לא מדובשך ולא מעוקצך 'They say to the wasp: not of your honey and not of your sting' (Midrash Tanḥuma, Parashat Balak 6); משל אמרי ליה לצרעה לא מן דובשך ולא מן עוקצך 'A proverb: they say to the wasp: not of your honey and not of your sting' (Midrash Tanḥuma Buber edition, Parashat Balak 9; my translation). This is used as a proverb in Modern Hebrew as well.

---

[73] A dish made of yogurt or cream cheese with *parpaxìne* 'purslane'. Sabar (2002a, 126): "soft herbal cheese." See Shilo (1986, 49).

xurásti wə́lla-li maḥfúra rúwwa u-sqìla.' bale-kmá šəxtána wewàle,' roháyi mpə́qla híl qam-qalwànne.' xá šábsa plə́xli ʾə̀bbe.' ʾə̀h! lá ʾáw jàjik,' lá ʾáw žə̀ḥḥar.'

My friend gave me a large and beautiful carpet, but how dirty it was! My soul went out [=I had a hard time] until I cleaned it. One week I worked on [lit. in] it. Ah! Not [of] that jajik, nor [of] that poison.

(45) *lá ʾèwa' u-lá sə̀xwa.'*
  NEG cloud.M and-NEG fine_weather.M

'Not [in] cloud and not [in] fine weather.'

xurásti muxšə́mla⁷⁴ mən-gòra.' damməd-mṣolə̀ḥlu,' básər kma-yomàsa,' qam-baqrále gòra,' ʾíman g-ə́bet ʾáx be-bàbi.' mə́rre xá-yoma la-ʾéwa u-la sə̀xwa.' fhə́mla lá-g-be ʾə̀l' u-štə̀qla.'

My friend had a fight with her husband and went back to live with her parents for some time.⁷⁴ When they reconciled [with each other], after several days, she asked her husband, "When would you like us to go to the house of my father?" He said, "On a day [when there is] no cloud [and] no fine weather." She understood that he does not want to go and was silent.

(46) *lés mənn-ì' u-lés mənn-ì.'*
  there_is_not from-1s and-there_is_not from-1s

'There is no one like me, there is no one like me.'

Cf. R:91, proverb no. (103) below.

bax-mámo sótəd karmèla' q-qemáwa kùd yóm,' bázəl mbə̀noke,' k-kanšáwa kùlla maḥále,' u-g-zamràwa,' lés mənnì' u-lés mənnì.' u-xá-dora qam-baqrànna' qáy g-zámrat ʾe-

Bakh-Mamo [=Uncle's Wife] the grandmother of Carmela, used to get up every day at dawn, she would sweep the entire neighbourhood, and sing, "There is no one like me, and there is no one like me." And one time I asked her, "Why do you sing this song?" and she

---

⁷⁴ Sabar (2002a, 201) on *x-š-m*: "to feel alienated (daughter-in-law who after a quarrel goes back to live temporarily with her parents)."

zəmə̀rta,' u-mə̀rra-li' ma-léwa ʾòṭo?' ṭʾéli ṭʾèli' bə́š-ṭov mən-gyáni lá xzèli.¹⁷⁵ mə́rri-la bax-màmo' yə́mmi ʾə́tla ḥəkkòsa,' dammə́d-ʾiláha xlə́qle dùnye,' mə́rre ta-xa malʾàx,' ʾó képa háwe bəd-ʾizòx,' u-kúd k-xázət dəd-ʿaqə́lle lá qáṭəʾ ʾəl-gyàne,' mxíle ʾo-képa ʾəl-rèše.' ʾaw-màlʾax' híl ʾə́dyo híle ḥmìla' u-képa go-ʾìze.'

said to me, "What, is it not so? I searched [and] searched, [and] did not find [anyone] better than myself."⁷⁵ I told her, "Bakh-Mamo, my mother has a story, when God created the world, He said to one angel, 'Let this stone be in your hand, and whoever you see that is not satisfied with himself [lit. that his mind is not cut upon himself] strike his head with this stone [lit. hit this stone on his head].' This angel until today waits [or: stands] and the stone [is] in his hand."

See an additional context situation at proverb no. (103) below.

(47) la k-xárya ta la ʾàxla.'
NEG IND-DEFECATE.IPFV.3FS for NEG eat.IPFV.3FS

'She does not defecate so that she should not eat.'

Var.: la ʾáxla ta la xàrya.'

'She does not eat so that she should not defecate.'

ʾo-nàša' xa-qúruš⁷⁶ la-g-yáwəl ta-čù-xa.' čə̀nnika-le.' lá-k-xare tá lá ʾàxəl.' múx yə̀mme-ile' g-našṭáwa qàlma,' u-gəlda-dída gə-mzabnàwale.'⁷⁷ u-bàbe,' šásət ʾárbi hóya ʾə́lle,' lá g-yawə́lla ta-čù-xa.'⁷⁸

That person does not give [even] one quruš⁷⁶ to anyone. He is a miser. He does not shit so that he would not eat. He is like his mother, she would skin a louse and sell its skin.⁷⁷ And his father, [when] he has a forty [degree] fever, he would give it to no one.⁷⁸

---

⁷⁵ See proverb no. (106) below.

⁷⁶ Sabar (2002a, 283): "small Turkish coin." The reference here is probably to the *grush*, an old Israeli coin.

⁷⁷ See proverb no. (102) below.

⁷⁸ See proverb no. (91) below.

(48) *mád   mjomə́ʿ-lu   b-əd   kočəksa,¹ zə́l-le   b-əd*
what-REL collect.PFV-3PL in-GEN spoon.F   go.PFV-3S in-GEN

ʾətràna.¹
ladle.M

'What they have saved with a spoon, they wasted with a ladle.'

Cf. SA:137.

xa-náša ʾúzle gazə́da ʾəl-bàxte.¹ g-émer k-pálxən ràḅa¹ g-əmjámʿən dínar ta-dìnar¹ g-yáwən ta-báxti máʿaš kud-yàrxa.¹ básər xà yóma¹ g-ə́mra làtla páre,¹ látla bəd-má msòqa.¹ mád g-əmjámʿən bəd-kočəksa,¹ g-él bəd-ʾətràna.¹	One man complained [lit. made a complaint] about his wife. He says "I work a lot, I gather one dinar to the other [lit. dinar to dinar], I give my wife an allowance each month [or: the salary of each month]. After [only] one day she says she does not have money, she does not have with what to shop in the market. What I gather with a spoon, goes with a ladle.'
dámməd wéali zùrta,¹ láswa ṃáya go-yerušàlayim.¹ g-daryáxwa ṣàṭle,¹ ta-kúd čəppáksəd mə́tra k-košáwa go-dáy ṣàṭle.¹ ṃáya wéalu ráḅa gə̀ran.¹ xá-yoma séle ʾaxòni¹ mxéle pə́hna ʾəl-ṣàṭle¹ kúllu ṃáya bə̀zlu.¹ yə́mmi mə̀rra,¹ mád mjomə́ʿlan bəd-kočəksa,¹ zə́llu bəd-ʾətràna.¹	When I was young [lit. small], there was no water in Jerusalem. We used to put a bucket [out], so that every drop of rain goes down into that bucket. Water was very expensive/valuable. One day my brother came, he kicked [lit. gave a kick to] the bucket, all of the water spilled. My mother said, 'What we gathered with a spoon, went [away] with a ladle.'

(49) *mən núra dòhun¹ lá g-šàxn-ax,¹*
from fire.M GEN.3PL NEG IND-become_warm.IPFV-1PL

mən tə́nna dòhun¹ g-ʿàmy-ax.¹
from smoke.M GEN.3PL IND-become_blind.IPFV-1PL

'Their fire does not warm us, but their smoke blinds us.'

xurásti mə̀rra-li,¹ b-ásyan ʾəmmed-yalónke dìdi,¹ ʾáni mtáʿli ʾəmmed-brònax,¹ u-ʾáxnan b-yápyax káde⁷⁹ ta-ʾèza.¹ séla ʾáya u-kəflə̀ta,¹ ḥáram hakan-mtoʿəllu,¹ bắle ṣrə̀xlu¹ bxèlu¹ u-nṣélu xá ʾəmmed-daw-xèt.¹ kúlle ḥóš qam-šaxtenìle.¹ mə́rri-la xurà̀sti,¹ mən-núra dóxun là-šxənnan,¹ mən-tə́nna dóxun ʿmèlan.¹

My friend told me, "I will come with my children, they will play with your son, and we will bake *kade*⁷⁹ for the festival." She and her large family came [lit. she came, she and her large family], they did not play at all [lit. it is forbidden if they played], but they did scream, cry, and fight one with the other. They soiled the entire courtyard [=entrance room]. I told her, "My friend, we did not warm from your fire, [but] we did become blind from your smoke."

(50) *mís ṛába xepì-le¹ gə-mʿàrət.¹*
dead.MS.GEN much wash.IPFV.PL-ACC.3MS IND-fart.IPFV.3MS

'A corpse that you wash too much will break wind.'

Vars.: *mísa dəd [REL] ṛába xèpile¹ gə-mʿàrət.¹*

'A corpse that you wash too much will break wind.'

mísa dəd [REL] xépile ṛàba¹ gə-mʿàrət.¹

'A corpse that you wash too much will break wind.'

---

⁷⁹ Sabar (2002a, 180) on *kada*: "baked turnover stuffed with cheese." It is the customary dish for the festival of Shavuot. See Shilo (1986, 162).

bron-xalto-ʾə̀ster,' lə́ple najarùsa.' mə̀rre,' yə̀mmi,' g-lépen najarùsa,' b-ozə́nnax xazáne sqə̀lta.' məsséle ṣìwe' u-škólle ʾáwez xazàne.' băle-xolá qam-xalə̀ṣla,' xá yóma g-èmer' ʾó dárga léwe b̭àš,' mxalpə̀nne,' xá yóma g-èmer' ʾaqlás xazáne hílu plìme,' mxalpə̀nnu.' kúd yóm mboʿbə́ṣle ʾé xəzàne.' yə́mme pqèʾla.' mə́rra-le bròni,' mís ṛáb̭a xepìle' gə-mʿàrət.' k-mále mbaʿbəṣə́tta ʾé xazàne.'

The son of Aunt Esther studied carpentry. He said, 'My mother, I am studying carpentry, I will make for you a beautiful closet.' But has he indeed finished it? One day he says, 'This door is not good, I shall replace it', another [lit. one] day he says, 'The legs of the closet are crooked, I shall replace them.' Each day he messed with [lit. poked] that closet. His mother exploded [= was exhausted and impatient]. She told him, 'My son, a dead [person] that is washed [too] much, farts. Enough messing with [lit. poking] this closet.'

(51) (ʾáni) mísa dóhun qam-qorì-le, ʾál
they dead.MS GEN.3PL PAST-bury.3PL-ACC.3MS go.IPFV.3MS

gan-ʿèzen' ʾál gəhənnàm.' (lè-waj-u).'
Garden[-of]-Eden go.IPFV.3MS hell NEG-concern-POSS.3PL

'They have buried their dead, they do not care whether he goes to heaven or hell.'

Var.: mísa dóhun k-xèpile,' ʾál gan-ʿèzen' ʾál gəhənàm.'

'They have washed their dead, [they do not care whether] he goes to heaven or hell.'

xazále zə́lla l-šùqa,' zúnna ṛáb̭a xə̀dra.' mùrdax,' mšodə́rre žăgil díde u-bróne ṣàleḥ,' maʾinìla.' sélu drélu kúllu sállat qam-dárgət bèsa' u-zə̀llu.' séla xazàle,' ʾéna

Khazale went to the market, she bought a lot of vegetables. Murdakh sent his worker and his son Saleḥ to help her. They came [and] put all of the baskets near the door of the house and went [away]. Khazale came, her eyes became dark

*xsə̀qlu,*ˈ *xzéla kùlla xə́dra híla mburbázta go-ḥòš,*ˈ *qaṭwása gə-mtáʿli l-tàm.*ˈ *mə́rra ʾə̀h!*ˈ *ʾáni ʾùzlu šúlu,*ˈ *mísa dóhun qam-xèpile,*ˈ *ʾál gan-ʿèzen*ˈ *ʾál gəhənnám lè-waju.*ˈ [i.e., she was unpleasantly surprised by the sight], she saw that all of the vegetables were scattered in the courtyard, where cats play [lit. cats play there]. She said, 'Ah! They did their work, they have washed their dead [person], [if] he goes to heaven or to hell—they do not care.'

(52) *mbáqər kúll-a dùnye*ˈ *ʾóz ʿaqə́l-ox tə̀ne.*ˈ
 ask.IMP.2S all-3FS world.F do.IMP.2S mind/intellect-POSS.2MS alone

'Ask all of the world [= everyone], [but] act only according to your own opinion.'

Var.: *mbáqər kúlla dùnye*ˈ *ʾóz b-xábrox tə̀ne.*ˈ

'Ask all of the world [= everyone], [but] act only according to your own word.'

Cf. שיתין מליכין יהון לך ומליכות נפשך לא תשבוק 'You should have sixty advisors, but do not forsake the advice of yourself' (Ben Sira 1544, 15b).[80]

*mtoxmə́nni ṛába mà-ʾozán,*ˈ *yə́mmi mə̀rra-li,*ˈ *bràti,*ˈ *mbáqər kúlla dùnye*ˈ *ʾóz ʿaqə́llax tə̀ne.*ˈ I though hard [lit. much] [about] what I should do, my mother told me, 'My daughter, ask the entire world, do [what] your mind [says] alone.'

(53) *múx yatúma ʾə́t-le zə̀bba.*ˈ
 like orphan.M (REL) there_is-DAT.3MS penis.M

'Like an orphan who has a penis.'

Or: 'He has a penis like an orphan.'

Var.: *múx yatúma máre zə̀bba.*ˈ

'Like an orphan, owner of a penis.'

---

[80] Referred to by Weissberg (1900, 61).

ʾámti zúnna qundắre xàse,' séla kəslèni,' šʾə́šla gyána ta-max-uyálu ṭalèni,' yə́mmi mə́rra g-maxuyálan qundắre dìda,' múx yatúma ʾə́tle zə̀bba.'

My aunt bought new shoes, she came to us [= to our house], she shook herself [= behaved flauntingly] in order to show them to us, my mother said, "She shows us her shoes, like an orphan that has a penis."

gʾela bəd-ṭrambel dida mox yatúma máre zə̀bba.'

She was proud of her car like an orphan that has a penis.

(54) nahagóna zə́l-le ʾəl-mə̀lxa.'
large_calf/young_person.M go.PFV-3MS to-salt.M

'The calf went to [bring] salt.'

damməd-ʾaxóni mə́rre ta-yə́mmi dəd-xzélele šúla u-p-šákəl páləx tré šabása xèt,' yə́mmi mə̀rra' hàwwa! nahagóna zə́lle ʾəl-mə̀lxa. xázyax ʾila[ha]-ʿàyən.'

When my brother told my mother that he had found himself a job and that he would begin to work in two weeks, my mother said, "All right![81] The largish calf went for the salt. We shall see with the help of God [lit. may God help]."

séle xór ʾaxóni mboqə́rre ʾéka-le ʾaxòni.' yə́mmi mə̀rra' nahagóna zə́lle ʾəl-mə̀lxa. gxə̀kle.'

My brother's friend came and asked where my brother was. My mother said, "The largish calf went for the salt." He laughed.

See the additional context situation at proverb no. (133) below.

(55) núra xe qòqa,' tanésa xe nàša.'
fire.F under clay_pot.M word.F under person.M

'[Like] fire under a clay pot, a word under a person.'

brat-ʿáqo mpə́lla go-pə́mmed nàše.' kúlla mahále məhkéla ʾèlla.' qam-šaʿwəṭíla bəd-xábre

The daughter of ʿAqo fell into the mouth of people [= people started gossiping about her]. The entire neighbourhood

---

[81] Said dismissively.

dòhun.' 'ó márre zálla 'əmməd-dòha,' u-'ó márre dmáxla 'əmməd dawàha.' u-'áya pappùke,' báxta bắš wéla,' maḥkóyəd náše qam-makəmla b-'en-kùllu. núra xe qòqa,' tanésa xe nàša.'

spoke about her. They burnt her with their words. This [one] said she went with that [person] and this [one] says she slept with that [person]. And she, poor thing, she was a good woman, the speech [=gossiping] of people made her black in the eyes of everyone. Fire under the clay pot [is like] word[s] under a person.

(56) nunìsa' mən réš-a   k-xàrw-a.'
fish.F   from head-POSS.3FS IND-become_spoil.IPFV-3FS

'A fish [starts to] rot from its head.'

Cf. BA:4, SA:100.

čŭga lá-zonat go-dé dəkkàna.' mắre-dəkkána duglána u-ganàwa-le.' yalúnke dìde' u-žaġíle dìde' kúllu muxwàse,' ləplu mənne.' 'òṭo-ila,' nunìsa' mən-réša k-xàrwa.'

Never buy in that shop. The owner of the shop is a liar and a thief. His children and his workers are all like him, they learned from him. This is how it is, the fish spoils from its head.

(57) sí   xmàr-i'   'iláha 'əmm-ox.' hákan màr-i
go.IMP.2MS donkey-POSS.1s God with-2MS if   master-POSS.1s

háwe   'əmm-i,' 'iláha p-áwe   'ə́mmi.'
be.IPFV.3MS with-1s God FUT-be.IPFV.3MS with-1s

'Go, my donkey, may God be with you. If my master is with me, God will [also] be with me.'

bắno masséle xa-žáġil ta-fə́rna dìde.' hedi-hèdi' 'o-žáġil 'úzle kùlle mándi.' bắno wə́lle go-'íze kùlla fə́rna.' básər kma-wà'da,' bắno xzéle fə́rna là-k-kazba,' báxte mə̀rra-le,' bắno mə́rrox go-

Bəno brought a worker to his bakery. Gradually this worker did everything [in the bakery]. Bəno gave the entire bakery into his hand [=gave the supervision over to him]. After some time, Bəno saw that the bakery did not produce profit, his wife told him, "Bəno you

*ləbbox xarxáṣi šrèli,*¹ *šúli b-awə́zle ʾó žáġil,*¹ *sí xmàri*¹ *ʾiláha ʾə́mmox.*¹ *băle-léwa ʾòṭo,*¹ *hăkan màri háwe ʾə́mmi,*¹ *ʾilaha p-áwe ʾə́mmi.*¹ *hăkan háwət go-fə̀rna,*¹ *baṛáxa b-nápla go-fə̀rna.*¹

said in your heart [= to yourself] 'I have untied my sash, this worker will do my work. Go, my donkey, God be with you', but it is not so, if my master is with me, God will [also] be with me. If you were at the bakery, a blessing will fall into the bakery [= it will be prosperous]."

(58) *sawóna qrə̀ṣ-ḷe,*¹ *sotə́nta hnè-le-la.*¹
old_man pinch.PFV-3MS old_woman cause_pleasure.PFV-3MS-DAT.3FS

'The old man pinched [and] the old woman enjoyed it.'

Cf. R:72, SE:56, SA:139.

*yə́mməd bádre sèla,*¹ *xzéla néhra šwíqa u-bèsa mṭùrbəla.*¹ *séla bádre màrra-la,*¹ *séle sàleḥ,*¹ *mə́rre-li sa-mpóq xápča go-šə̀mša*¹ *b-áx šəmel-hằwa,*¹⁸² *xaráe máṣiḥax xòri.*¹ *ʾáp-ana šúqli néhri u-zə̀lli.*¹ *yə́mma mə́rra hằwwa bráti,*¹ *sawóna qrə̀ṣḷe,*¹ *sotə́nta hnèle-la.*¹

Badre's mother came, she saw [that] the laundry [was] left [unattended] and the house was a mess [lit. unorganised, cumbersome]. Badre came and said, "Saleḥ came, he said to me, 'Come out to the sun [for] a little [while], we shall go for a walk. After that we shall visit my friend.' So I left my laundry and went." Her mother said, "Very well, my daughter, the old man pinched [and] the old woman enjoyed [it]."

(59) *qə́m-le čùka,*¹ *bsə́m-la dùka.*¹
get_up.PFV-3MS Čuka.M become_pleasant.PFV-3FS place.F

'Čuka got up, [and] the place became [more] pleasant.'

Var.: *qə́mle čuka,*¹ *rúxla dùka.*¹

'Čuka got up, [and] the place became more spacious.'

---

[82] Apparently from Arabic *nšəm al-hawa* 'breath air'.

A small change that makes a difference for the better. Čuka was the *shamash* (custodian) of one of the synagogues of the Jewish-Kurdish community in Jerusalem.

Cf. SA:41.

séli máṣiḥan xàsi¹ u-ʾózan gazə́nta ʾəl-xmàsi.¹ jíran dìda¹ wéwala kə̀sla,¹ láswa-bi maḥkyánwa ʾəl-xmàsi.¹ dámməd zə́lla xurásta márri ta-xàsi¹ ʾằh!¹ qə́mle čùka,¹ bsə́mla dùka.¹ ʾátta ʾíbi maḥkyán u-ʾamránnax máʾiz ʾəl-lə̀bbi.¹

I came to visit my sister and to complain [lit. make complaint] about my mother-in-law. Her neighbour was there [lit. at her]. I could not speak about my mother-in-law. When her friend went [away], I said to my sister, 'Ah! Čuka got up, [and] the place became more pleasant. Now I can speak and tell you what is in my heart.'

(60) *qam-mayʾə́l-ən-ne   qam-mòsa,¹   ta yáʾel*
PAST-bring_in-1MS-ACC.3MS in_front_of-death.M for enter.IPFV.3MS

qam   šàsa.¹
in_front_of fever.F

'I brought him to death so that he will [agree to] enter the fever.'

séla bax-náḥum u-márra ta-yə̀mmi,¹ xzè¹ wan-bə-myàsa,¹ lébi ʾón xudáni bət-yalúnke dìdi,¹ lá-g-madwan ʾón šúl bèsi.¹ márri ta-nàḥum,¹ ʾíz xa-báxta maʾináli xága b-šabsá bəd-šúla yaqùra,¹ bəd-néhra u-spə̀nja,¹ b-yawáxla treṭláha lìre.¹ lá ʾbèle.¹ yə́mmi štə̀qla.¹ zə́llu tré yomàsa,¹ yə́mmi xzéla nàḥum,¹ mə̀rra-le,¹ nàḥum,¹

The wife of Naḥum came and said to my mother, "See, I am dying [=having a very hard time], I cannot take [lit. make] care of my children, I do not have enough time to do my housework, I said to Naḥum, there is a woman that would help me once a week with the hard [lit. heavy] work, with laundry, and with washing the floor, we shall give [=pay] her two [or] three lire. He did not agree [lit. want]." My mother remained silent. Two days passed [lit. went], my mother saw Naḥum, she told him,

šmòʾ¹ la-šamʾə́t xrìwa.¹⁸³ xzéli bàxtox,' ṛabə́d-ṛaba ʿayyàne-la.' lə́bba pə́šle xa-mə̀sta,¹⁸⁴ lázəm šaqléten xa-xə́ddamta maʾinála kùd-yom.' hákan là' ʾila-là-wəz…¹⁸⁵ náḥum pə́šle xà-ḷappa.¹⁸⁶ mə́rri ta-yə̀mmi,' ṣaḥḥə́tax bassə̀mta!' qam-mayʾəlátte qam-mòsa,' ta-yáʾəl qam-šàsa.' náḥum zə́lle l-bèse,' mə́rre ta-bàxte,' maʿlèš,' šqúlla ʾe-jìran,' šud-maʾinálax xá-ga b-šàbsa.'

"Nahum, hear [=listen], [may] you not hear [anything] bad.⁸³ I saw your wife, she is very-very ill. Her heart turned into a [single] hair⁸⁴ [=her heart shrank because of the hard work, she became sick], you must take [=hire] for her a housemaid that will help her every day. If not, God forbid [lit. may God not do (that)]…" Nahum turned into a [small] lump [=became scared].⁸⁶ I told my mother, "[May] your health/vigour be well/pleasant [=well done, bravo]! You have brought him into death so that he will enter the fever." Nahum went home, he said to his wife, "All right, take [=hire] this neighbour, may she help you once a week."

(61) qóqa g-èmer' xés-i dèhwa-la,' ʾətrána
clay_pot.M IND-say.IPFV.3MS under-1S gold.M-COP.3FS ladle.M

[var.: káfkir] g-èmer' ʾàtta mpə́q-li mə́nn-ox.'
[var.: large_spoon] IND-say.IPFV.3MS now go_out.PFV-3MS from-2MS

'The clay pot says, "My bottom is made of gold"; the ladle says, "I just came out of there."'

Cf. R:103.

---

⁸³ See proverb no. (129) below.
⁸⁴ See proverb no. (136) below.
⁸⁵ Contraction of ʾiláha lá ʾàwəz.
⁸⁶ See proverb no. (135) below.

brat-ṣə́mṣar mpoṣə́nna gyàna,¹ kma-ḅáš wéwala ˀəmmed-xədàmta.¹ xədámta g-xə́kla u-mə̀rra,¹ xuzí palgə́d madməhkélax wèwala,¹ ˀàtta mpə́qli mə́nnax.¹

The daughter of the real estate agent praised herself, how kind [lit. good] she was to [lit. with] her housemaid. The housemaid laughed and said, "I wish [even] a half of what she said were true [lit. has been], I just came out of you."

ḥabúba ˀúzla gazə́nta ˀəl-xmàsa,¹ damməd-wáx mahkòye¹ séla xmása u-škə́lla mpaṣóne gyàna.¹ lés go-kúlla mása xmása muxwàsi.¹ kmá g-əmˤazezánna kàlsi.¹ ḥabúba lxə̀šla,¹ ˀána k-î'an ˀéma déhwa ˀís xèsax.¹

Ḥabuba complained [lit. made a complaint] about her mother-in-law. While we were speaking, her mother-in-law came and started praising herself. "There is not a mother-in-law like myself in the entire village. How much I respect/pamper my daughter-in-law." Ḥabuba whispered, "I know which gold there is under you."

(62) *qóqa dəd k-torá-le kabanìye,¹*
clay_pot.M REL IND-break.IPFV.3FS-ACC.3MS cook.F

lá-k-ese hə̀s mə̀nn-e.¹
NEG-IND-come.IPFV.3MS sound.M from-3MS

'A clay pot that is broken by the cook does not make a sound.'

Vars.: *...čù-həs lá-k-ese mə́nne.¹*

'...no sound comes from it.'

...čəppèn la-k-ése mə́nne.¹

'...two drops [of sound] do not come from it.'

Cf. R:104, SE:121.

msofə́rri u-mṭéli ʾəl-dúksəd g-ebànwa,' ṭʾéli dúksa ta-maḥmelánne ṭrambél dìdi,' la-xzèli,' básri séle p̣óḷis ʾəmmed-ṭrambél dìde,' qam-maḥmə́lle dúkəd ^A mamnùʿ^A ḥíla,' mə́rri ta-gyàni, ʾó p̣óḷis g-áwəz mád g-ə̀be,' qə́qa dəd-k-torále kabanìye,' lá-k-ese ḥə̀s mə̀nne.' čúxxa lá g-əmə́rre xa-məndi.'

I travelled and arrived to the place I had wanted, I looked for a place to park [lit. make-stand] my car, I did not find [lit. see] one, after me came a policeman with his car, he parked it where [lit. in a place of] it is forbidden, I said to my-self, this policeman does what-ever he wants, a clay pot that the cook breaks, does not make a sound [lit. no sound comes from it]. No one tells him [or: can tell him] [=the police-man] anything.

(63) k-xáre má-d g-ə̀be,' g-ə́be
IND-defecate.IPFV.3MS what-REL IND-want.IPFV.3MS IND-want.IPFV.3MS

wìša,' g-ə́be miyàna.'
dry.M IND-want.IPFV.3MS liquid.M

'He defecates whatever he wants, [if] he wants dry [it is dry], [if] he wants liquid [it is liquid].'

Vars.: *hắkan g-ə́be k-xáre wìša,' hắkan g-ə́be k-xáre miyàna.'*

'If he wants he defecates dry, if he wants he defecates liq-uid.'...*rakìxa.*' '...soft.'

ʾo-nàša lébox mhémenət ʾə́lle ʾə́l čú mə̀ndi.' mád g-ə́be g-èmər.' hắkan g-ə́be k-xáre wìša' hắkan g-ə́be k-xáre miyàna.'

This person, you cannot be-lieve him about anything [lit. you cannot believe on him on anything]. He says whatever he wishes. If he wished he'd defecate dry [faeces], if he wished he'd defecate liquid [faeces].

(64) qə́zra dəd hawé-b-a ṛáḅa kabanìyat,'
cooked_food.F REL be.IPFV.3MS-in-3FS many cook.FPL

k-ə́sya yán malùxta' yán pàxta.'
IND-come.IPFV.3FS or salty.FS or bland.FS

'A [pot of] cooked food that many cooks are involved in making turns out either [too] salty or [too] bland.'

Cf. SE:135. Also compare: קדרא דבי שותפי לא חמימא ולא קרירא 'A pot of partners is neither hot nor cold' (BT 'Eruvin 3a).[87]

ta-teféllin dəd-bròni¹ kúd xá márre-li ma-'òn.¹ xa-márre 'òṭo¹ xa-márre 'òṭo.¹ mə̀rri-lu¹ qə́zra dəd-rába kabanìyat g-əmbašlìla,¹ g-dári 'ízu gàwa,¹ u-g-baxšìla,¹ g-nápqa yán pàxta yán malùxta.¹ šùqu-lan,¹ malušáxle bróni teféllin mȧṭod g-ə̀be.¹	For the *bar mitzvah* celebration [lit. *tefillin*] of my son, each one advised [lit. said] me what to do. One said [you should do] so and the other [lit. one] said [you should do] so. I told them, "A food that many cooks have cooked, put their hand in, and stirred, turns out either bland or [too] salty. Leave us, we shall wear [= put on] my son's *tefillin* [= celebrate my son's *bar mitzvah*] however he wishes."

(65) pára xwàra¹ ta yóma kòma.¹
coin.M white.M for day.M black.M

'A white coin for a black day.'

Cf. BA:2, SA:102.

'axóni g-émer ta-bràte,¹ ḥfə́zlu pàre¹ ta-hawélax xa-pára xwàra¹ ta-yóma kòma.¹	My brother [always] tells his daughter, "Save the money so that you will have one white coin for a black day."

(66) parṭə́'na mə̀r-re,¹   lá-k-i'en   ma b-ózən
flea.M   say.PFV-3MS NEG-IND-know.1MS what FUT-do.IPFV.1MS

bəd-ó   miráta   dìdi,¹ xmára mə̀r-re¹
in.GEN-this.M unclaimed_inheritance of-1S donkey.M say.PFV-3MS

---

[87] I thank my grandfather Ḥakham Ḥabib 'Alwan for this reference.

ba[88]-ʾána lá   g-màḥk-ən.¹
then[88]-I   NEG IND-speak.IPFV-1MS

'The flea said: "I do not know what to do with that good-for-nothing of mine [=my penis]," the donkey said: "I, then, shall not speak."'

Var.: parṭə́ʾna mə̀rre,¹ miráta dídi xə́lle lèbbi,¹...

'The flea said: "The good-for-nothing of mine ate my heart [=is causing me distress],..."'

Cf. SA:103.

ṣáleḥ bər-mə́ro mə́rre ta-ʾaxóne bùxra,¹ àh!¹ ʿjə́zli mən-màdrase!¹ lázəm ṛába lèpən,¹ látli wáʿda xápča mtàʿlən.¹ ʾaxóne dəd-g-láyəp páyəš ḥàkim¹ mə̀rre¹ ba[88]-ʾàna má b-ámrən,¹ látli wáʿda xékən rèši.¹ ʾàya-ila¹ parṭə́ʾna mə̀rre,¹ lá-k-iʾen ma b-ózən bəd-ó miráta dìdi,¹ xmára mə̀rre¹ ba[88]-ʾána lá g-màḥkən.¹

Ṣaleḥ the son of Məro said to his eldest brother: "Ah! I am tired of school! I must study a lot, I don't have time to play a little." His brother, who is studying to become a doctor, said: "Well, what will I say? I do not have time to scratch my head." That is it: The flea said, "I do not know what to do with that good-for-nothing of mine," the donkey said, "I, then, shall not speak."

(67) palg-əd ḅárṭil,¹   ḥə̀nna-le.¹
half-GEN bride_price.M henna.F-COP.3MS

'One half of the bride-price is henna.'

---

[88] Sabar (2002a, 103): "proclitic particle to indicate mild puzzlement, wonder, complain."

xurásti qam-ʿazmálan ʾáxlax ẓálaṭa.' márra ṭalèni,' ʾúzli xà ẓálaṭa,' xàru bès bàba ʾe-ẓàlaṭa.' sèlan,' xə̀llan,' kúlla ẓáḷaṭa wéala xàssa,' márrila xurásti,' ʾúzlax ẓáḷaṭa kúlla ṭárpəd xàssa,' palgíd bàrṭil,' hə̀nna-le.'

My friend invited us to eat a salad. She said to us, "I have made such a salad [lit. one salad], may the house of its father be destroyed,[89] that salad." We came, we ate, the entire salad was [made of] lettuce, I told her, "My friend, you have made a salad all of which is leaves of lettuce, one half of the bride price is henna."

(68) palg-ə́d qaḥbùsa'   mə́n nəxpùsa.'
half-GEN prostitution/adultery.F from shyness/modesty.F

'Half of the lewdness is caused by shyness.'

ʿáziz bər-jíran déni nàḥum,' yála yəkkàna-le,' yála ḅáš u-naxòpa-le.' yalúnkəd ḥára lóplu ṭálbi mə́nne šoʾàle,' ʾóz ʾò-məndi' hálli ʾò-məndi.' ʿáziz g-náxəp ʾámər làʾ,' làtli,' lébi ʾòzən.' bábe nàḥum' g-záde ʾə́lle ṛàḅa.' márre-le bròni,' dŕi bàlox,' palgə́d qaḥbùsa' mə́n nəxpùsa.' lóp már làʾ.'

'ʿAziz the son of our neighbour Naḥum is an only child, a good and shy child. The children of the neighbourhood learned to ask him for things, do that thing, give me that thing. ʿAziz is [too] shy to say, "No, I do not have [it], I cannot do [it]." His father Naḥum is very worried [lit. afraid] about him. He told him: "My son, pay attention, one half of lewdness is caused by shyness, learn to say no!"'

(69) šqə́l-la   mən šə̀rm-a' [var.: šə̀rma'] dré-la ʾəl
take.PFV-3FS from anus.F-POSS.3FS [var.: anus.F] put.PFV-3FS on

pàs-a.'   [var.: pàsa.']
face-POSS.3F.SG [var.: face.F]

'She took from her anus [and] put on her face.'

Var.: *šqə́lla mən šə̀rma' šəpla ʾəl pàsa.'*

---

[89] An expression of appreciation.

'She took from her anus [and] smeared on her face.'

See the context situation for proverb no. (111) below.

(70) šə́rm-əd   ʾiwánta glè-la.'
     anus/buttocks.F-GEN ewe.F be_exposed.PFV-3FS

'The ewe's buttocks are exposed.'

mad-hı́la ʾiwánta ʾəlı́sa dída hàr g-əmkásya šə̀rma' u-ʾə́zza dumə́ka dída daqíqa-le u-g-əmgámbel l-ʾèl,' damməd-ʾiwánta g-nádya dumə́ka dída g-yàsəq' u-k-xazı́la šə̀rma.' xá-yoma ʾiwánta ndéla ʾəl-jălal,' ʾəlı́sa dída rùmla.' ʾə́zza hmə́lla u-màrra,' ʾè!' šə́rməd ʾiwánta glèla!' gúmla lá-k-xaze ʿujjə́ksa dìde.'[90]

Because the ewe, tail fat always covers her buttocks, and the goat, her tail is thin and curls upwards, [so] when the ewe jumps, her tail goes up and her buttocks are visible [lit. they see her buttocks]. One day the ewe leaped over a brook, her tail fat went up. The goat stood and said, 'Huh! The buttocks of the ewe are exposed!' The camel does not see its [own] hump.[90]

(71) šúl   ʾozı́-le   xuràs-i,'
     work.M.GEN do/make.IPFV.PL-ACC.3MS friend.PL-POSS.1S

k-čáhe   lə́bb-i   u-g-néxi   ʾìzas-i.'
IND-get_tired.IPFV.3MS heart-POSS.1S and-IND-rest.IPFV.3PL hand.FPL-POSS.1S

'Work done [for me] by my friends, my heart gets tired and my hands rest.'

Var.: šúl ʾozı́le xuràsi,' k-čáhe lə́bbi u-là-g-nexi ʾìzasi.

'Work done [for me] by my friends, my heart gets tired and my hands do not rest.'

Cf. BA:1, SE:85, SA:127.

---

[90] See proverb no. (93) below.

kálsi séla maʾináli bed-šúl pə̀sha.' *kúd daqíqa qam-baqráli mắṭo ʾózan ʾó-məndi u-ʾò-məndi.*' *kúlle wáʿda ʾéni wéla bàsra.*' *ʾamránna má ʾòza.*' *bə̀š čhéli.*' *márri tagyàni,*' *šúl ʾozíle xuràsi,*' *k-čáhe lə́bbi u-g-néxi ʾìzasi.*'

My daughter-in-law came to help me with [lit. in] the [house]work of Passover. Every minute she asked me how to do [lit. should I do] this thing and this thing. The entire time my eye was after her [= I watched over her]. [In order to] tell her what to do. I became more tired [than I would have otherwise]. I said to myself, work done [for me] by my friends, my heart gets tired and my hands rest.

(72) *šàqfa*' *la mšápya*   *ʾəl šàqfa,*'
piece.F NEG resemble.IPFV.3FS to piece.F

lá-k-tafqa   *ʾə̀bb-a.*'
NEG-IND-meet/stumble_upon.IPFV.3FS in-3FS

'[If] a piece did not resemble a[nother] piece, it would not have met it.'

Vars.: *wàṣla*' *la mšápya ʾəl wàṣla,*' *lá-g-ʿalqa ʾə̀bba.*'

'[If] a piece would not resemble a piece, it would not stick to it.'

wàṣla' *la mšápya ʾəl wàṣla,*' *lá-g-ʿalqa ʾəl wàṣla.*'

'[If] a piece would not resemble a piece, it would not stick to a piece.'

Cf. R:72, SA:139.

hayíka bər-čúna ṛába čənnìka-le,' *kúllu k-ìʾi.*' *u-báxte*' *mbúrxa šə́mməd xaláqa*' *ʾáp-aya čənníke muxwàse.*' *šàqfa*' *lá mšápya ʾəl šàqfa,*' *lá-k-tafqa bəd-šàqfa.*'

Ḥayika the son of Čuna is very stingy, everyone knows. And his wife—blessed be the name of the Creator—also she is stingy like him. [If] a piece did not resemble a[nother] piece, it wouldn't meet [that] piece.

(73) šùla¹ ʾàrya-le,¹ g-náḥki ʾəlle,¹ k-páyəš
work.M lion.M-COP.3MS IND-touch.IPFV.3PL on-3MS IND-become.IPFV.3MS
ruvìka.¹
fox.M

'Work is a lion. Only touch it [and] it becomes a fox.'

Var.: šùla¹ mux-ʾàrya-le,¹...

'Work is like a lion...'

yʾə́lli l-bèsa¹ réši mborbə̀zle¹ u-ʾéni xšə̀klu.¹ mə́rri yə̀mmi,¹ ʾə́tli ràḅa šúla,¹ lá-k-iʾan má ʾòn¹ u-má lá ʾòzan,¹ ʾéka šàklan.¹ bràti,¹ šúla ʾàrya-le,¹ mánde ʾízax ʾəlle¹ páyəš ruvìka.¹

I entered home, my head became scattered [=I became weary and confused] and my eyes were darkened. I said, "My mother, I have much work, I do not know what I should do and what I should not do, where I should start from." "My daughter, work is a lion, throw your hand at it [=commence performing it], it becomes a fox."

(74) ʾóz hawùsa,¹ mándi b-m̩àya.¹
do.IMP.2S favour.F throw.IMP.2MS in-water.PL

'Do an act of kindness, [and] throw [it] in the water.

Var.: ʾóz hawùsa,¹ màrpe b-m̩áya.¹

'Do an act of kindness, [and] let [it] go in the water.'

Cf. SE:54, SA:37, proverbs nos (89) and (90) below. Also compare: 'Send your bread upon the water, for after many days you shall find it' (Qoh. 11.1).[91]

---

[91] About the Jewish tale-oicotype associated with this verse, see Noy (1971).

mən-dámməd wéali zùrta' yə́mmi qam-malpáli ʾón hawúsa ʾəmməd-nàše' u-lá ṭálban ču-məndi.' hár g-əmràli' ʾóz hawùsa,' mánde b-màya.'

Since I was little, my mother taught me to do people favour[s], and not to ask for anything [in return]. She always told me, do a favour, throw [it] into the water.

(75) *dmóx kpìna, qú swìʾa.'*
sleep.IMP.2S hungry.MS rise.IMP.2S satiated.MS

'Sleep hungry [and] rise full.'

Var.: *dmóx kpìna, qú šamìna.'*

'Sleep hungry [and] rise fat.'

ḥabúba mə̀rra-li:' bràti,' kúllu wéalu faqìr go-záxo,' bxá kóza qùṭma,' g-marwéwalu yalùnke,[92] *lá mux-ʾàxxa.' ʾə́swa lelawàsa,' lá-g-damxanwa mən-kə̀pna.' yə́mmi g-emràwa-li,' dmóx kpə̀nta,' qú swèʾta.' ʾóṭo g-zaġlàwali' ta-dàmxan.'*

Ḥabuba said to me: "My daughter, everyone was poor in Zakho, with one pile of ashes they would raise the children,[92] not like here. There were nights, I did not sleep out of hunger. My mother told me, sleep hungry, rise satiated. This is how she would tempt me to sleep."

(76) *dúkəd g-jàrya' k-pàrya.'*
place.GEN IND-flow.IPFV.3FS IND-be_abundant/overflow/heal.IPFV.3FS

'Where it flows, it heals.'

Var.: *dúkəd g-jàrya' k-pàsxa.'*

'Where it flows, it opens up.'

ḥále u-ʿáziz hay-xamšíʾ-šənne hilu-gwìre.' ḥáram hákan šméʾlan

Ḥale and ʿAziz have been married for fifty years. We have never heard [lit. it is forbidden

---

[92] See proverb no. (114) below.

*xa-čəppén mənnòhun.' hắle xa-bàxta-hila,' béʾta bắla pə̀mma,*¹⁹³ *u-ʿàziz-šik,' léwe mahkyàna.' ʾè šábsa,' yom-xušéba mbə̀noke,' šméʾlan čriqéne mən-besòhun.' nṣélu xà naṣúsa,' lá mhimə́nnan ʾanya-náše k-tʾi nási u-ṣárxi ʾòṭo.' hắle bxéla u-qtə́lla gyàna.' yə́mmi mə̀rra,' lá yʾélan ču̇́-məndi ʾəl-danya-nàše.' šáhude mə̀rre,' ʾána rʾə́šli xésa talə̀tta-la.*¹⁹⁴ *ʾéna wealu-ṣə̀ṛṛ.' ʾiláha-d-ʾúzle ʾe-pərṣə́nta psə̀xla,' dúkəd g-jàrya' k-pàrya.'*

if we heard] [even] a [single] sound [lit. a two-drops] from them. Ḥale is such a woman, an egg without a mouth,⁹³ and also ʿAziz is not talkative. This week, on Sunday morning, we heard shrieks from their house. They had such a fight, we could not believe that these people know how to fight and scream like that. Ḥale cried and killed herself [= was in great sorrow and distress]. My mother said, "We did not know anything about those people." Shahude said, "I felt that it is wet under her.⁹⁴ Her eyes were malicious. [Good that] God made [lit. God that made] this abscess open up, where it flows, it heals."

(77) *zə́l-le   xòla'   básər   dòla.'*
go.PFV-3MS rope.M after/behind drum/bucket.M

'The rope followed the bucket [or: drum⁹⁵].'

Cf. SE:79, SA:150. See also: הלך החבל אחר הדלי 'The rope followed the bucket' (Midrash Tanḥuma, Parashat Miqets 10).⁹⁶

---

⁹³ See proverb no. (100) below.
⁹⁴ See proverb no. (110) below.
⁹⁵ See Sabar (1978, 231).
⁹⁶ See also Midrash Tanḥuma, Parashet Va-Yyigash 5; Yalquṭ Šimʿoni, Parashat Va-Yyigash 150.

bər-amóyi zúnne bésa go-^(H(ʿen-ha(ʿemèq.^(II)97) ʾaxóni màrre,ˈ ba-ʾáp-ana b-án ʾəl-^(H(ʿen-ha(ʿemèq!^(H)) yámmi màrra,ˈ hắwwa bròni,ˈ sì!ˈ zálle xòlaˈ bássər dòla.ˈ

The son of my uncle bought a house in Eyn Ha-Emek.[97] My brother said, "Well, I also would go to Eyn Ha-Emek!" My mother said, "All right, my son, go! The rope went after the bucket."

(78) dúnye qzàya-la.ˈ

world.F prepare.VERB_N-COP.3FS

'The world is [only] a preparation. [Therefore everything should be taken easily].'[98]

Cf. SA:43, SA:44, SA:45.

krábli mən-gòri,ˈ zálli be-bàbi,ˈ bxéli u-márri ta-yàmmi,ˈ qáy šúqlax bábi magúrri ta-bər-ʾamòyi?ˈ g-mázəd ʾálli ràba šánne,ˈ u-ʿaqálle lé[w]e mux-ʿaqálli.ˈ náša ḅàš-ile,ˈ ḅále ʾána lá-qam-goranne mən-məhábbe.ˈ yámmi màrra,ˈ bràti,ˈ là-karbát,ˈ náša ḅàš-ile,ˈ maʿášlax ḅàš,ˈ u-naš-gyána dèni híle.ˈ dúnye qzàya-la.ˈ ʾátta b-asélax yalùnke,ˈ u-mkéfat ʾábbu,ˈ ʾiláha b-dáre ʾahava-šalóm benòxun.ˈ

I was angry with my husband, I went to the house of my father, I cried and said to my mother, 'Why did you let my father marry me to my cousin? He is many years older than I am [lit. he exceeds me many years], and his mind is not like my mind. He is a good man, but I did not marry him out of love.' My mother said, 'My daughter, do not be angry, he is a good man, and he is our relative [lit. he is people of ourselves]. The world is about managing it. Soon you will have children [lit. now children will come to you], and you will be happy with them, God will give [lit. put] love [and] peace between you [both].'

See also the context situation for proverb no. (82) below.

---

[97] A community settlement in the north of Israel, founded in 1944 by immigrants from Kurdistan.

[98] Several speakers offered the interpretation: 'The world should be managed [smoothly].'

(79) bés   ʾiláha ʾəmìra.ˈ
house.M.GEN God   be_built.PFV_PTCP.M
'The house of God is built.'

See ch. 2, §7.0, no. (156).

mə́rri ta-ṣàmṛa,ˈ bə̆ne u-bomaxét p-káwəš tàlga.ˈ čúxa lá-g-napəq mən-bèse.ˈ ʾátta g-én ʾəl-šùqa,ˈ g-ə́bat zonánnax xa-məndi?ˈ mə̀rra-li,ˈ lá bràti,ˈ ʾə́tli mád g-làzman,ˈ ʾə́tli ʾixàla,ˈ bés ʾiláha ʾmìra,ˈ u-mburáxtət ʾiláha hòyat.ˈ
I said to Samra, "Tomorrow and the following day it will snow [lit. snow will descend]. No one will go out of his house. I am going now to the market; would you like me to buy you anything?" She said to me, "I have what I need, I have food, the house of God is built, and be blessed by God [=may God bless you]."

(80) bába g-yáwəl   ta-yalònkeˈ kútru k-fàrḥ-i,ˈ
father IND-give.IPFV.3MS to-child.PL both IND-rejoice.IPFV.3PL

yálonke g-yáwi   ta-bab-òhunˈ kútru g-bàxi.ˈ
child.PL IND-give.IPFV.3PL to-father-POSS.3PL both IND-cry.IPFV.3PL

'[When] a father gives to [=provides for] his children, both [sides] are happy, [when] children give to their father, both [sides] cry.'

Cf. proverb no. (39) above.

ḥamínko bxéle u-mə̀rre,ˈ lá-g-ben čú-xa yawə́lli pàre,ˈ bába g-yáwəl ta-yalònkeˈ kútru k-fàrḥi,ˈ yálonke g-yáwi ta-babòhunˈ kútru g-bàxi.ˈ šud-čù-xa la-báxe.ˈ
Ḥaminko cried and said: "I do not want anyone to give me money, [when] a father gives to his children, both [sides] are happy, [when] children give to their father, both [sides] cry. May no one cry."

(81) dré-la   máya b-əd-tré šaqyàsa.ˈ
put.PFV-3FS water.PL in-GEN-two water_trough.FPL
'She poured water in both troughs.'

Cf. proverb no. (98) below, a synonym.

yəmmi mə́rra-li bràti' dóq rába qádər dína jíran dèni' yə́mməd ʾefrày im' u-qádər xátun yə́mməd ʿàziz.' ʾilá[h]a ʿáyən xá mən-yalúnke dóhun páyəš mázzal dìdax.' lázəm-dáryat máya bəd-tré šaqyàsa.'

My mother told me, "My daughter, hold much the honour of [= give much respect to] Dina, our neighbour, the mother of Ephraim, and the honour of Khatun, the mother of ʿAziz. God will help, one of their children will be your luck [= you will marry]. You should pour water in both troughs."

(82) marı́ra xtàya,' xə́lya ʾəlàya.'
bitter.M lower.M sweet.M high.M

'Bitter below, sweet above.'

zə́lli maṣihə́nna ḥabùba.' yʾéli ṛába ʿayàne-la. hı́la mṭaʾòne.' dámməd yʾə́lli, kéfa séle u-frə́hla ṛàba.' mə̀rra-li' bràti' ʾiláha mabhə́rra ʾəllàx,' mátod mobhə́rrax ʾə́lli yòmi.' mə́rri go-ləbbi,' ʾàya-la,' marı́ra xtàya,' xə́lya ʾəlàya.' ḥála marı̀ra-le' u-ʾáya xlìsa-la.' dúnye qzàya-la.'⁹⁹

I went to visit Ḥabuba. I knew that she was very ill. She is dying [lit. carrying]. When I entered, she became very happy. She told me, "My daughter, may God make it shine/bright upon you, like you have brightened my day upon me." I said in my heart, "That is it, bitter below, sweet above. Her situation is bitter and she is [= appears] sweet. The world is all about managing it."⁹⁹

(83) díwan baxtàsa,' bə̀š bassíma-le'
divan¹⁰⁰.M.GEN woman.PL more pleasant.M-COP.3MS

mən-díwan gùre.'
from-divan¹⁰⁰.M.GEN man.PL

'Sitting with women is better than sitting with men.'

Cf. SE:109, an antonym.

---

⁹⁹ See proverb no. (78) above.
¹⁰⁰ Or: drawing room, council, assembly.

dammǝd-ġárib *ʾóče* *k-eséwa* *kǝslèni,*ˈ *lá-g-yaʾǝlwa* *kǝs-bábi* *yátu ʾǝmmed-xaḥamìne,*ˈ *k-eséwa go-barbànke,*ˈ *g-yatúwa ʾǝmmed-baxtàsa,*ˈ *g-gaxǝ́kwa u-g-èmǝr,*ˈ *díwan baxtàsa,*ˈ *bǝ̀š bassíma-le*ˈ *mǝn-díwan gùre.*ˈ *u-lázǝm yaʾètun,*ˈ *dammǝd-baxtása g-màḥki*ˈ *gúre k-šàtqi.*ˈ[101] *ʾána p-šàtqan*ˈ *u-g-šanéwa mǝn-gǝ̀xka.*ˈ

Whenever Ġarib ʾOče came to us, he would not enter to my father [=my father's room] to sit with the Ḥakhamim, he used to come in the veranda, sit with the women, laugh and say, "A *divan* of women is more pleasant than a *divan* of men. And you should know, [that] when women speak men [should] remain silent.[101] I will remain silent and laugh my head off [lit. faint from laughter]."

(84) *hǎkan g-nàpel,*ˈ   *ʾaxl-í-wa*   *ʾǝ̀xre,*ˈ
  if   one_who_regrets.PL eat.IPFV-3PL-PAST faeces.PL

  lá-g-peš-i-wa   *ʾǝ́xre* *go-dùnye.*ˈ
  NEG-IND-remain.IPFV-3PL-PAST faeces.PL in-world.F

  'If those who regret ate faeces, there would be no faeces left in the world.'

*ndǝ́mli ṛába ʾǝl-pǝʿullós dǝd-ʾùzli,*ˈ *u-l-ᴴmaʿasímᴴ dǝd-là ʾúzli.*ˈ *túli u-ṣfǝ̀nni.*ˈ *yǝ́mmi mǝ̀rra-li,*ˈ *bràti*ˈ *hǎkan nadáme ʾaxlíwa ʾǝ̀xre,*ˈ *lá-g-pešiwa ʾǝ́xre go-dùnye.*ˈ

I regretted very much over the foolish deeds that I had done, and the deeds that I had not done. I sat and brooded. My mother told me: "My daughter, if those who regret ate shit, there would not remain any shit in the world."

(85) *ṭʾé-li* *raḥùqa,*ˈ *xzé-li* *qarìwa.*ˈ
  search.PFV-1s far.M   find/see.PFV-1s close.M

  'I searched far away [but] I found close by.'

---

[101] See proverb no. (86) below.

ʾaxón ḥabùba' ṭʾéle xa-brát ḥalál ta-g-áwər u-báne bèse,' msofə́rre l-mòṣol' msófərre l-bàġdad,' ču bráta lá-mpəlla go-lə̀bbe.' dʾə́rre l-zàxo,' go-ʾùrxa' xzéle xa-bráta spàhin' mùx šə́mšəd sèhra g-màbhəra.' škə́lle máḥke ʾə̀mma,' mpə́qla náša dìde' u-hám rwéla go-maḥàle díde.' ḥabúba mə̀rra,' ʾaxòni,' ṭʾélox raḥùqa' xzélox qarìwa.' ʾiláha mabhə́rra ʾə̀llox.'

The brother of Ḥabuba looked for a good girl [lit. daughter of kosher, i.e., of good family, qualities and reputation] to marry and build his house [with]. He travelled to Mosul, he travelled to Baghdad, no girl caught his attention [lit. fell in his heart]. He returned to Zakho, on the way he saw a fine girl, shining like the moonlight [lit. like the sun of the moon]. He started speaking with her, it turned out that she was [lit. she went out] a relative of his [lit. his people], and she also grew up in his neighbourhood. Ḥabuba said: "My brother, you searched far away, [but] found near. May God make [light] shine upon you."

(86) damm-əd-baxtása g-màḥk-i,' guráne k-šàtq-i.'
time-GEN-woman.PL IND-speak.IPFV-3PL man.PL IND-be_silent.IPFV-3PL

'When women speak, men are silent.'

See the context situation for proverb no. (83) above.

(87) kúd   lá   k-šáqəl   mən-mə̀llət-e,'
whoever.GEN NEG IND-take.IPFV.3MS from-ethnic_group.F-POSS.3MS

g-él   b-ʿə̀llət-e.'
IND-go.IPFV.3MS in-illness.F-POSS.3MS

'Whoever does not take [a wife] from his own ethnic group, goes [=dies] in his sickness.'

Cf. SE:24.

bər-ʾamóyi gúrre xá mən-náš ʾàxxa,ˈ roḥáye qam-mapqàla.ˈ ʾəl-kúd mándi g-nàṣi.ˈ yə́mme màrra-le,ˈ bròni,ˈ kúd lá k-šáqəl mən-məllə̀te,ˈ ʾila-lá-wəz g-él¹⁰² b-ʿəllə̀te.ˈ

The son of my uncle married one of the people of here [=Ashkenazim], she took his soul out of him [=she gave him a hard time]. They fight about everything. His mother told him, "My son, whoever does not take [a wife] from his own ethnic group, God forbid [lit. may God not make it], goes [=dies] in his sickness."

(88) kúd ʾéra pḷìma,ˈ ʾáxxa k-ṭàres.ˈ
all.REL penis.M crooked/twisted.M here IND-heal.IPFV.3MS

'Every crooked penis finds its cure here.'

Var.: …ʾáxxa k-páyəš ràsṭ.

'…becomes straight here.'

bés xáḥam wéale qam-šùqa.ˈ kùd g-ezálwa ʾəl-šùqa,ˈ bəd-ʾúrxe g-yaʾə́lwa bés be-xàḥam.ˈ bráte màrra,ˈ lá doqétun ʾə̀lli,ˈ kúd ʾéra pḷìma,ˈ ʾáxxa k-ṭàres.ˈ ʾána čhèli mən-dánya ʿlíqe u-flíte dəd-k-ési ʾàxxa.ˈ kúlle yòma xá g-yaʾəlˈ xá g-nàpəq.ˈ básar kma-šə̀nneˈ fḥámla ʾéma bésa b̭àš wéle,ˈ mùx bès ʾavrahám ʾavìnu wéwale,ˈ psíxa ʾəl-ʾarbá ʾalàle.ˈ xá g-yáʾəl bə-bxàya,ˈ dammədg-nàpəq

The house of the Ḥakham was near the market. Whoever went to the market would, on his way, enter the house of the Ḥakham [lit. the house of the household/family of the Ḥakham]. His [=the Ḥakham's] daughter said, "Do not hold [this] against me [lit. on me], every crooked penis finds its cure here. I am tired [lit. became tired] of these lowly people [lit. caught and dissolute]¹⁰³ who come here. All day long one enters [and] one goes out." After several years, she understood what a good house it was, it was like the house of Abraham Our Father, open to its four sides. One

---

¹⁰² Contraction of ʾiláha lá ʾàwəz.

¹⁰³ A collocation. The first word of the pair may also mean 'accidentally conceived'.

páse híla mpuršàqta,' xáḥam u-báxte k-šamʔíwa kùd-xa,' g-maʔiníwa kùd-xa,' u-kúd yʔə́lle l-tàm' mpə́qle mabṣùṭ.' mərádè ḥṣìle.'

would enter crying, when he would go out his face [was] smoothed, the Ḥakham and his wife used to listen to anyone, used to help anyone, and whoever entered there went out satisfied. His wishes fulfilled.

(89) *hawúsa là-ʔoz-ət ʔəmməd-huzáya.'*
favour.F NEG-do.IPFV-2MS with-jew.MS

'Do not do a favour for a Jew.'

Cf. proverb no. (74) above.

xzéli xa-šúla ḅáš ta-bər-xàlti,' mə́rri-le sì' škòl' hám p-kázbət páre ḅàš,' ham-mtàhnət.' ṛába náše g-əbíwa palxíwa go-dé dùksa.' bər-xálti zə̀lle,' škə́lle šùla,' plə́xle xá šàbsa' u-mə̀rre' ʔó léwe ṭàli,' səhràne¹⁰⁴-la' băle léwa ṭàli.' qə́mle u-qam-šawə́qla ʔe-dùksa,' gan-ʕézen wéla ṭàle!' xšúli ta-gyàni,' hawúsa là-ʔozət ʔəmməd-huzáya.'

I found a good job for my cousin, I told him, "Go, start [working there], you will earn good money, and enjoy it as well. Many people would have liked to work in this place." My cousin went, started working [lit. started the job], worked one week and said: "This is not for me, it is a *sehrane*¹⁰⁴ [=pleasant as a spring celebration], but it is not for me." He left [lit. he rose and left] that place. It was the Garden of Eden [=exceptionally good] for him! I thought to myself, "Do not do a favour for a Jew."

(90) *mándi láxm-ox reš-ṃàya,' bálkid xa-nunísa b-doqà-le.'¹⁰⁵*
throw.IMP.2MS bread.M-POSS.2MS on-water.PL maybe one-fish.F FUT-catch.IPFV.3FS-ACC.3MS

---

¹⁰⁴ A spring celebration. See ch. 3, fn. 39.
¹⁰⁵ I thank Prof. Yona Sabar for this proverb.

'Throw your bread over the water, maybe a fish will catch it.'[106]

Cf. SE:54, SA:37, proverb no. (74) above. See 'Send your bread upon the water, for after many days you shall find it' (Qoh. 11.1).

| dammǝd-ṱéli šùla,' ṭlǝ́bli mǝn-ʾǝstázi maʾǝ́nni.' mə̀rre-li:' mándi láxmox reš-màya,' bálkid xanunísa b-doqàle.' mšádǝr ksáwe ta-ṛába dukàne.' | When I was looking for a job, I asked my teacher to help me. He told me: "Throw your bread to [lit. on] the water, maybe a fish will grab it. Send letters to many places." |

(91) šásǝt ʾárbi hóya ʾǝl-le,' lá g-yawǝ́l-la
fever.F.GEN forty be.IPFV.3FS on-3MS NEG IND-give.IPFV.3MS-3FS
ta-čù-xa.'
to-any-one

'[Even if] he had fever of forty [degrees], he would give it to no one.'

See the context situation for proverb no. (47) above.

(92) hám zyàṛa' hám tǝjjàṛa.'
also visit.F also trade.F

'A visit, as well as a trading opportunity.'

| yǝ́mmi mə̀rra' b-án maṣihánna bǎ̀sso,' hila-ʿayyàne,' dammǝd-dáʾran mə̀nna,' b-yáʾlan be-xáham nàhum' u-p-šáqlan mǝ́nne ṭahún pə̀sra,' go-ʾúrxi zónan tré ṭlahá ʾawáye mǝn-šùqa,' bàš-ila?' maʿálum yǝ̀mmi,' ṣahǝ́tax | My mother said, "I shall go visit Bǎsso, she is ill, when I return from her, I will go [lit. enter] to Ḥakham Naḥum's house, and take from him the meat grinder, on my way I will buy two [or] three things from the market, isn't it [a] good [plan]?" "Of course, mother, well done [lit. may your |

---

[106] See above, fn. 91.

bassəma' hám *zyàṛa*' hám *təjjàṛa*.' health/vigour be well/pleasant], both a visit and a trading opportunity."

(93) *gúmla lá-k-xaze ʿujjə́ksa dìd-e.*'
camel.M NEG-IND-see.IPFV.3MS hump.F of-3MS

'The camel does not see its [own] hump.'

See the context situation for proverb no. (70) above.

(94) *ʾíz-ox mpə́l-la go-tér ʾilàha.*
hand.F-POSS.2MS fall.PFV-3FS into-sufficient God

'Your hand fell into the sufficient [=abundance] of God.'

Cf. proverb no. (112) below.

ʿáziz mə́rreli kmá g-əbéla məšpáḥa dèni.' *mə́rre ta-yóʾel gor-fàruḥ,*' *xə́tən xaḥam-ḥábib u-šətùna,*' *lá-k-iʾət ʾéma ᴴmazzálᴴ ʾə́tlox dəd-gúrrox brat-xáḥam ḥàbib,*' *ʾízox mpə́lla go-tér ʾilàha.*' 'ʿAziz told me how much he loves our family. He told Yoʾel the husband of Faruḥ, the son-in-law of Ḥakham Ḥabib and Sətuna, "You do not know what luck you have that you married the daughter of Ḥakham Ḥabib, your hand fell into the abundance of God."

(95) *rozána rozàna,*' *ʾíz-i péša dərmàna.*'
earthquake.F earthquake.F hand.F-POSS.1S become.IPFV.3FS cure.M

'Earthquake earthquake! My hand shall be the cure!'

Said by women after an earthquake, while putting their hands on the ground.

(96) *ʾixál-e pàrta,*' *ʿurṭyás-e prə̀zla.*'
food.M-POSS.3MS bran/sawdust.F fart.F.PL-POSS.3MS iron.M

'His food [is of] sawdust [but] his farts [are of] iron.'

Var.: ...*ʿurṭíse pòlaz.*'

'...his fart [is of] steel.'

jìran déni,' kmá wàʿda,' lá-k-palex,' látle šùla.' látle xá qúruš¹⁰⁷ máʿeš gyàne.' mə́rri-le mqálu ḥòš,' mqálu jaradòkat,' šqól tré ṭláha qrùše,' mdábər ḥàlox.' mjoyìble,' ʾána lá-gon ʾo-šùla,' lá-gə-mqalwən básər nàše.' xási mə́rra-li šùqle,' ʾó ʾixále pàrta-le,' ʿúrṭise prə̀zla.'	Our neighbour, for some time, has not been working, he does not have a job. He does not have even one *quruš*¹⁰⁷ to support himself. I told him, clean the courtyard, clean the stairs [=staircase] take [=earn] two [or] three *quruš*, sustain your situation [=earn a living, take care of yourself]. He answered: "I do not do these things, I do not clean after people." My sister told me: "Leave him, his food is sawdust [but] his farts are iron."

(97) ʾáhat m̭fàṣel,'   ʾáxnan b-lòš-ax.'
  you.MS cut_out.IMP.2S we   FUT-wear.IPFV-1PL

'You shall cut it [and] we shall wear it.'

Compare Sabar (1974, 330), nursery rhyme no. 3:

   xımyānox mfāṣıl uʾāhıt lōš [...]

   'May your father-in-law cut out (garments) for you to wear.'

In that case, however, the expression is used not as a proverb but rather literally.

sámra mə́rra ta-jìran dìda, šqól brat-xási ta-brónox,' sqə́lta u-ḅàṣ-ila.' mə̀rre-la,' mad-ʾámrat bax-ʾəstàzi,' ʾáhat m̭fàṣel,' ʾáxnan b-lòšax.'	Samra said to her neighbour, "Take the daughter of my sister for your son [=marry them], she is beautiful and good." He said to her, "Whatever you say, wife of my teacher. You will cut out, and we shall wear."

(98) ʾə́zla díd-a g-mzabná-le   go-ṛáḅa šuqà-ne.'
   yarn.M GEN-3FS IND-sell.IPFV.3FS-ACC.3MS in-many market.M-PL

---

¹⁰⁷ Sabar (2002a, 283): "small Turkish coin." The reference here is probably to the *grush*, an old Israeli coin.

'She sells her yarn in many markets.'

Cf. proverb no. (81) above, a synonym.

| xási márra b-ásya maʾinàli,' u-ṭálax-šik márra b-ásya maʾinàlax,' u-márra b-áza kəz-yə́mmi mbašlàla,' ʾána k-ṭʾan lá-g-oza mə́ndi mən-mə̀ndi,' bắle ʾə́zla dída g-mzabnále go-ráḅa šuqàne.' | My sister said that she would come [and] help me, and to you she also said that she would come [and] help you, and she said that she would go to my mother [and] cook for her, I know that she does not do a thing from a thing [=she won't do anything], yet she sells her yarn in many markets. |

(99) *béʾta nápla   mən šə̀rm-a,'   lá-k-tora.'*
   egg.F fall.IPFV.3FS from buttocks.F-POSS.3FS NEG-IND-break.IPFV.3FS

'[If] an egg falls from her buttocks it does not break.'

| ʾé báxta qómәd ṣiṭa-la,'[108] béʾta nápla mən šə̀rma,' lá-k-tora.' bắle-kása k-ṭʾa ráḅa ta-gyána.' | This woman is [of one] span's stature,[108] [If] an egg falls from her buttocks, it does not break. But her belly knows a lot for herself [=she is very cunning, her appearance is misleading]. |

(100) *béʾta bála   pə̀mma.'*
   egg.F without mouth.M

'An egg without a mouth.'

Cf. SA:31.

See the context situations for proverbs nos (76) above and (112) below.

(101) *gúr-rax   gúr-rax   barrәkyás-ax*
   get_married.PFV-3FS get_married.PFV-3FS kilim_rug.PL-POSS.3FS
   čə̀q-lu.'
   tear.PFV-3PL

---

[108] See proverb no. (116) below.

'You got married, you got married, your rugs have torn [because of the many suitors that stepped on them].'

ʾávro bə́ṭṭi g-əbéwa mzabə́nwa bèse.' ṛába náše sélu u-zə̀llu,' u-bèsa' lá zùnnu.' mə́rre ta-gyàne,' ʾə-mà-pəšla?' qə́sted xazàle pə́šla,' sélu ṛába ṭalaḅáye ṭàla' sélu u-zə́llu u-là-qam-gorila.' yə́mma mən-qaḥríta mə̀rra,' gúrrax gúrrax barakyásax čə́qlu.'

'ʾAvro Bəṭṭi wanted to sell his house. Many people came and went, and did not buy the house. He said to himself, "What's happened [lit. what did that become]? It is like the story of Khazale [lit. it has become Khazale's story], many suitors came for her, they came and went and did not marry her. Her mother out of her sorrow said, 'You got married, you got married, your rugs tore.'"

(102) *g-nášṭi qàlma' u-gə́lda díd-a gə-mzabnì-le.'*
IND-skin.IPFV.3PL louse.F and-skin.M of-3FS IND-sell.IPFV.3PL-ACC.3MS

'They skin a louse and sell its skin.'

Var.: *g-nášti bàqqa,' g-əmzábni gə́lda dìda.'*

'They skin a frog, [and] sell its skin.'

See the context situation for proverb no. (47) above.

(103) *g-jáyer mən šùrs-e.'*
IND-urinate.IPFV.3MS from navel.F-POSS.3MS

'He urinates through his navel [unlike all others].'

Var.: *mən šùrse g-jáyer.'*

'Through his navel he urinates.'

Cf. proverb no. (46) above.

ʾo-náša ṛába gèʾya-le,ˈ k-xášu gyáne ṛàba,ˈ k-xášu lés mànne,ˈ¹⁰⁹ léwe múx kùllu.ˈ g-jáyer mən šùrse.ˈ

This person is very haughty, he thinks highly of himself [lit. he thinks himself (too) much, i.e. he is full of himself], he thinks there is no one like him [lit. there is not of him],¹⁰⁹ he is not like everyone. He urinates from his navel.

(104) dré-le párra b-rèš-eˈ u-ʾéra go-šə̀rma.ˈ
put.PFV-3MS feather.M in-head.M-POSS.3MS and-penis.M in-anus.M

'He put a feather on his head and a penis in his anus.'

moʾə́nni ḥázqəl bəd-ṣabágəd bèse.ˈ séle ʾaxòne,ˈ ḥázqəl g-emə̀rre:ˈ xzí ʾéma šúla sqíla ʾúzle ʾò.ˈ ʾana-roḥáyi mpə́qla mən-čə̀hwa,ˈ g-xə́kli u-mə̀rri,ˈ hằwa,ˈ drí párra b-rèši.ˈ

I helped Ḥazqəl with painting his house. His brother came, Ḥazqəl told him: "See what a good [lit. beautiful, i.e., of good quality] job he made [lit. this (person) made]." I, my spirit went out [of me] [because] of exertion, I laughed and said, "Right, put a feather on my head."

bádre mə̀rra-li,ˈ šmòʾ,ˈ lá-šamʾat xrìwa,ˈ¹¹⁰ qam-ʿazmíli máḥkyan go-díwan gùre,ˈ muṛáḍi ḥṣə̀llu,ˈ ʾé ḍóṛa qamésa ʿzə́mlu báxta máḥkya ʾəmməd-ruwàne.ˈ msofə́rri l-ᴴtel-ʾavìvᴴˈ mṭèli,ˈ qam-matwíli go-qurnísəd sə̀dde ˈ kúllu guráne məḥkélu xá-basər daw-xèt,ˈ híl mṭéle ḍòṛiˈ yóma gnèleˈ náše kúllu mborbə̀zluˈ də́mmi bə̀zle.ˈ mə́rri-la xurà̀sti,ˈ

Badre told me, 'Listen, may you not hear evil,¹¹⁰ they invited me to speak in a divan [=assembly] of men, my wishes came true, this is the first time that they invite a woman to speak with the magnates. I travelled to Tel-Aviv, I arrived, they sat me in the corner of the stage, all of the men spoke one after the other, until my turn arrived, the day ended, all of the people scattered, my blood spilled [=I was shamed, humiliated].' I told her, 'My friend, my mother told me a long time ago, grab your honour with

---

¹⁰⁹ See proverb no. (46) above.
¹¹⁰ See proverb no. (129) below.

yə́mmi márra-li mən-zùna¹ dóq qádrax bəd-ʾizàxˈ u-lóp tagyànaxˈ xolá kúd ʾamə́r tərnìniˈ lázəm ràqzat,¹¹¹¹ xzé ma-séla b-rèšax,ˈ drélu pára b-rèšaxˈ u-ʾéra go-šə̀rmax.ˈ

your hand [= have dignity], and learn for yourself [= know how to take care of yourself, protect your interests], must you dance for whoever says tərnini?!¹¹¹ See what has happened to you [lit. see what came unto your head], they put a feather on your head and a penis in your anus.'

(105) ḥámmam g-maʿlə́q-le b-əd ʿurṭyàs-e.ˈ
 bath.M IND-set_fire.IPFV.3MS-ACC.3MS in-GEN fart.F.PL-POSS.3MS

'He heated the bath [water] with his farts.'

Cf. R:70, SA:58.

go-maḥále dèni,ˈ ʾə́swa xasotə̀nta,ˈ pappúke láswa-la má ʾaxlàwa.ˈ náše g-raḥmíwa ʾə̀lla,ˈ g-yawíwala pərtòxe.ˈ xà-dora,ˈ séle nəssìmo,ˈ xzéle ʾe-pappùke,ˈ mə̀rre,ˈ ʾátta há ʾahà máḥken ʾə́mməd naš-máḥkame u-maʾinìla.ˈ baser-tré ṭláha šabàsa,ˈ lá šméʾlu mə́nne čù-məndi,ˈ yə́mmi mə̀rra,ˈ ʾo-náša la-úzle čù-məndi,ˈ ḥámmam g-maʿlə́qle b-ʿurṭyàse.ˈ mə̀rwala baxmaṣlíaḥ.¹¹¹²

In our neighbourhood, there was one old woman, poor soul, she did not have what to eat. People use to take pity on her, they used to give her crumbs. Once, Nəssimo came, he saw that poor soul, [and] he said, "Now right away I will speak with the people of the government [= authorities] and they will help her." After two [or] three weeks, no one heard [lit. they did not hear] anything from him, my mother said, "That person did not do anything, he set fire to the bath with flatulence. The wife of Maṣliaḥ said so."¹¹²

---

¹¹¹ See proverb no. (37) above.
¹¹² See proverb no. (117) below.

(106) *ṭ'é-li   ṭ'è-li,ˈ   bə́š-ṭov mən gyáni lá xzè-li.ˈ*
search.PFV-1S search.PF-1S more-good from self-1S NEG see.PFV-1S

'I searched [and] searched [but] did not find [anyone] better than myself.'

Cf. SE:80.

See the context situation for proverb no. (46) above.

(107) *xáre   qàm-eˈ   xáre   bàsr-eˈ   xà*
defecate.IPFV.3S/PL in_front-3MS defecate.IPFV.3S/PL behind-3MS one

íla.ˈ
COP.3FS

'[Whether] you defecate in front of him [or] behind him, it is one [= it is the same for him].'

Var.: *xáre qàmeˈ xáre bàsreˈ lá g-mfàreq.ˈ*

'[Whether] you defecate in front of him [or] behind him, he does not distinguish.'

ʾo-náša be-ʿàṣel híle.ˈ lá-g-daʾəl mád g-ózi ṭàle.ˈ xáre qàmeˈ xáre bàsreˈ... — That person is ill-mannered. He is not able [or: does not want] to see what [people] do for him. You defecate in front of him, you defecate behind him...

(108) *kúd   ṣabòʾṭaˈ xá ṣanèʾta.ˈ*
all.REL finger.F one craft/skill.F

'Each finger, a skill.'

ʾe-bàxta,ˈ rába šàter-ila,ˈ xa-ʾéšet ḥàyil.ˈ kúd ṣabòʾṭaˈ xá ṣanèʾta-la.ˈ xuzí ʾaxòniˈ mgábe ta-gyáne xá muxwàsa.ˈ — That woman, she is very skilful/clever/strong, a woman of valour. Each finger, a skill. I wish, my brother would choose for himself one like her.

(109) *xa g-èmerˈ   xa gə-mtàrjəm.ˈ*
one IND-say.IPFV.3MS one IND-translate.IPFV.3MS

'One is talking, the other is translating.'

ʾanya-yalùnke,ˈ kùllu sélu ʾə́lli,ˈ mád g-ònˈ gə-mʿámri ʾə̀lli.ˈ xá g-èmerˈ xá gə-mtàrjəm.ˈ ʾiláha nàṭərru.ˈ ràweˈ u-parqìli.ˈ

These children, they all came upon me. Whatever I do, they boss me around. One says [and] the other [lit. one] translates. May God guard them. May they grow and let me be.

(110) xés-e   talə̀tta.ˈ
under-3MS wet.F

'Under him it is wet.'

See the context situation for proverb no. (76) above.

(111) lá   gə-mfárqa   ʾéra mən gizàra.ˈ
NEG IND-distiguish.IPFV.3FS penis.M from carrot.M

'She cannot distiguish between a penis and a carrot.'

brat-ʾàvroˈ xà behéma-la,ˈ lá k-iʾa ču-məndi,ˈ lá gə-mfárqa mə́di mən-mə̀ndi,ˈ ʾéra mən gizàra,ˈ bắle-yʾèla ta-gyána.ˈ pə́šla qìra,ˈ ṭpéla bəd-mənàššе,ˈ la-nxə̀pla,ˈ šqə́lla mən-šə̀rma,ˈ dréla l-pàsa,ˈ¹¹³ u-qam-jabrále gúrre ʾə̀mma.ˈ

The daughter of ʾAvro, she is so stupid/vulgar [lit. one beast she is], she does not know anything, she cannot tell one thing apart from the other, a penis from a carrot, but she knew for herself [=she knew how to manage well]. She made herself [as sticky] as tar, she glued [herself] to Mənašše, with no shame [lit. she was not shy], she took from her buttocks [and] put on her face,[113] and she forced him to marry her.

(112) mpə́l-la go-kás yə̀mm-a.ˈ
fall.PFV-3FS in-belly.F.GEN mother-POSS.3FS

'She fell into her mother's belly.'

Cf. proverb no. (94) above.

---

[113] See proverb no. (69) above.

šánne brat-ʾìyo¹ kmà ḅáš wèla¹ čəppén la-k-ése mə̀nna,¹ xa-béʾta bằla pə̀mma.¹¹⁴ ʾiláha mroḥə́mle ʾə̀lla,¹ mšodə́rre-la xa-bər-ḥalàl¹ u-qam-gawə̀rra.¹ yə́mme u-bábe hám g-əbíla ṛàḅəd ṛáḅa¹ u-gəmʿazəzìla,¹ mpálla go-kás yə̀mma.¹ mbúrxa xalàqa.¹

Šanneʾ the daughter of ʾIyo, how good she was! A drop does not come from her [=she is quiet, does not complain], an egg without a mouth.¹¹⁴ God had mercy on her, [and] sent her one good boy [lit. a son of kosher] and he married her. His mother and father also like her very very much [lit. much of much], and they pamper her, she fell into her mother's belly. Blessed is the Creator!

(113) mxə́-la pə̀hna ʾə́l-la.¹
strike.PFV-3FS kick.M on-3FS

'She struck a kick over her.'

šamúʾel u-ṣíyon jirànè wéalu,¹ lə̀plu mə́zġaz,¹ zə́llu l-ʿàskar mə̀zġaz,¹ kúd mándi g-ozíwa mə̀zġaz.¹ wéalu mux-jəmə̀ke.¹ zə́llu l-ᴴʾunivérsitaᴴ mə̀ġzaz,¹ bằle-šamúʾel wéwale bə̀š marekápa,¹ u-bə̀š ʿáqel.¹ lə́ple lə̀ple,¹ mxéle péhna ʾəl-ṣìyon¹ pə́šle ḥàkim.¹ ṣíyon-heš híle bə-lyàpa.¹

Šamuʾel and Ṣiyon were neighbours, they went to school [lit. studied] together, went to the army together, they used to do everything together. They were like twins. They went to university together, but Šamuʾel was more master-of-shoulder [=diligent and successful], and brighter. He studied [and] studied, he struck a kick over Ṣiyon, he became a doctor. Ṣiyon is still studying.

(114) b-xá kóza qùṭma,¹ g-marwé-wa-lu yalùnke.¹
in-one pile.M ash.M IND-raise.IPFV.3PL-PAST-ACC.3PL child.PL

'With one pile of ash they used to raise children.'

See the context situation for proverb no. (75) above.

(115) lá k-káweš mən-ṣàpya.¹
NEG IND-go_down.IPFV.3MS from-strainer.M

---

¹¹⁴ See proverb no. (100) above.

'He does not go down through the strainer.'

ʾo-náša lébi daʾlànne,' kma-ʿaqùša-le!' mád g-ṭálban mənne,' lá g-ewəz, g-ón là-g-on,' lá g-maḥṣəllu muṛàdi,' ʿaqùša-le,' lá k-káweš mən-ṣàpya.'

I cannot stand [lit. see] this person, how hard [lit. viscous; = stubborn, solemn] he is! Whatever I ask him, he would not do [it], whatever I do [lit. I do (and) I do not do], he does not fulfil my wishes, he is stubborn [lit. viscous], he does not go down through the strainer.

(116) qóməd   sìṭa'   u-kása   k-ìʾa.'
stature.M.GEN span[115].M and-belly.F IND-know.IPFV.3S

'He is as tall as a span but [lit. and] his belly knows [=he is cunning].'

See the context situation for proverb no. (99) above.

(117) mə̀r-wa-la   bax-maslíaḥ.'
say.PFV-PAST-3FS wife.GEN-Maṣliaḥ

'Said the wife of Maṣliaḥ.'

dámməd kurdináye dəd-záxo sélu l-əsraʾə̀l,' láswa šúla go-rušalàyim,' wé[w]alu ràba faqíre.' b-yom-xušéba gə-msafríwa ʾəl-maswása u-g-palxíwa go-daštàsa.' kúd-xa k-šaqə́lwa ʾə́mme làxma' u-xápča pexwárin ta-ʿàyəš.' xà-yoma' xa-náša məséle bắs' làxma.' láswale čú-məndi ʾəl-bèse.' škə́llu ʾàxli,' bax-maṣlíaḥ

When the Kurds [=Jews of Kurdistan] of Zakho came to Israel, there was not [any] work [=jobs] in Jerusalem, they were very poor. On Sunday[s] they used to travel to the villages and work in the fields. Each one used to take with him bread and some condiment to eat [lit. live (on)]. One day, one man brought only bread. He did not have anything at home. They started eating, the wife of Maṣliaḥ told him, "Do you

---

[115] That is, the distance measurement based on the distance between the thumb and the small finger of the human hand.

g-əmrále bás làxma ʾə́tlox?! have only bread?! Wait don't eat, I will send you right away [lit. now] some condiment." He waited and waited, the day ended. His friends told him, "The day ended, come, let's finish work." He told them, "But the wife of Maṣliaḥ said she would send me [some] condiment." From that day [on], they say, "Said the wife of Maṣliaḥ."

ḥmól lá-ʾaxlət ʾátta p-šadrànnox, xápča pexwàrin. ḥmálle lá-xəlle zawáʾta dìde. ḥmálle u-ḥmálle, yóma gnèle. xuráse mə̀rrule, yóma gnèle, sá xalṣàxle šúla. mə̀rrelu, bắle báx maṣlíaḥ mə́rrali mšadráli pexwàrin. mən-dáw yóma g-ə́mri mə̀rwala bax-maṣlíaḥ.

See also the context situation for proverb no. (105) above.

(118) *ʾén-a sé-la qam-gyàn-a.*
eye.F-POSS.3FS come.PFV-3FS in_front_of-self-POSS.3FS

'Her [own] eye came unto her.'

xurásti márra b-ásya kə́sli u-maʾinàli xápča. séla mqolə́pla tré zabàše, kmá ʾéna séla qam-gyàna. My friend said she would come to me and help me a little. She came [and] pilled two watermelons, how much her eye came to her! [= she was so proud of it!]

(119) *naxír-a naxír bəndàqa, səppás-a səppás*
nose.M-POSS.3FS nose.GEN hazelnut.F lip.PL-POSS.3FS lip.PL.GEN

waràqa, mbúrxa šə́mməd xalàqa.
paper.F blessed.MS name.GEN Creator

'Her nose is like a hazelnut, her lips are [thin] as paper, blessed be the name of the Creator!

Var.: *...pása pás waràqa,...*

'...her face is [smooth] as paper...'

Cf. Sabar (1974, 332), nursery rhyme no. 15, 'Rhymes of praise for baby girls'.

sélu ṭalabáye ta-brát ʾaxòniˈ u-zmə̀rru-laˈ naxíra naxír bəndàqa,ˈ səppása səppás waràqa,ˈ mbúrxa šə́mməd xalàqa.ˈ u-kúlleni mtohnèlan.ˈ

They came to ask for the hand of [lit. they came for the 'asking' of] my niece and they sang to her, "Her nose is like a hazelnut, her lips are [thin] as paper, blessed be the name of the Creator!" And all of us were happy.

(120) rə́zza k-ṭáʾən ṃàya.ˈ
rice.M IND-carry.IPFV.3MS water.PL

'Rice [can] take up water.'

ʿerán ṭlə́ble mə́nni máḥkiyan ʾə́mməd təlmída díde lišána dèni.ˈ mə́rri ta-təlmída ʾàse,ˈ máḥkiyax líšana dèni,ˈ mə́rre g-ə́bən ʾásən bále mésen ʾə́mmi tré xuràsiˈ maʿalèš?ˈ mə̀rri,ˈ ʾáse go-ʾèni,ˈ ṭláha ʾárxe u-xáʿ ʾárxa xà-ila,ˈ rə́zzi k-ṭáʾən ṃàya.ˈ

Eran asked me to speak with his student [some] lišana deni. I told the student to come, we shall speak [some] lišana deni, he said, "I want to come but I want to bring with me two [of] my friends, okay?" I said, "They should come upon my eyes [=by all means], three guests and one guest are the same, my rice [can] take up water."

(121) qam-mapqá-la mən-màʿne.ˈ
PASR-take_out.3FS-ACC.3FS from-meaning.F

'She took it out of meaning [=she exaggerated, she overdid it].'

Cf. Sabar (2002a, 222), under maʿne.

ʿzə́mlu xá zamàrtaˈ u-zmə́ra ṛába ṛàba ˈ u-lá fhə́mlan čù-məndi.ˈ mə́rri ta-xa-báxta dəd-wéala túta qàmi,ˈ qam-mapqála mən-máʿne ʾe-zamàrta.ˈ

They invited one singer, and she sang more and more, and we didn't understand anything. I told a woman who was sitting next to me, "she took it out of meaning, this singer. How much she sings, and how much she whines," no one enjoys [it].

(122) qam-mapqá-la   mən-naxìr-i.'
PAST-take_out.3FS-ACC.3FS from-nose.M-POSS.1S

'She took it out of my nose.'

xurásti márra b-ásya šaqláli bəd-trambél dìda,' la-ʾán go-dé šəmša,' ḥmə́lli ḥmə̀lli,' séla u-mə́rrali háwal b-áx zónax xamándi ṭàli' u-xárae b-áx ʾəl-xəlmə́ta dìdax,' qam-maʿaṭəlàli' u-ʾé maʿarúf dída qam-mapqála mən-naxìri.'

My friend said she would come and take me in her car, so I should not walk in that sun. I waited [and] waited, she came and told me, "First we shall go buy something for me, and afterwards we shall go to your task." She delayed me, and this favour of hers, she took it out of my nose.

wéali l-bèsa,' škə́lli ʾáxlan u-séla xási qam-lazləzàli,' qam-mapqále ʾixála mən-naxìri.'

I was at home, I started eating and my sister came [and] hurried me, she took the food out of my nose.

(123) ʾúz-la   là-ʾuz-la.'
do.PFV-3FS NEG-do.PFV-3FS

'[Whatever] she did [or] did not do.'

krə́bli mən-xurásti,' qam-majgərráli ṛàba,' xaráe séla máḥkya ʾə́mmi,' là-qam-samḥanna,' ʾúzla là-ʾuzla,' là-məḥkeli ʾə́mma.'

I was angry with my friend, she made me very angry, afterwards she came to speak with me, I did not forgive her, [whatever] she did [or] did not do, I did not speak to her.

xási ṭlə́bla ʾán ʾə́mma ʾəl-šùqa,' là-g-banwa,' ʾúzla lá-ʾuzla là zə́lli ʾə́mma.'

My sister asked me to go with her to the market. I did not want to. [Whatever] she did [or] did not do, I did not go with her.

(124) kás-a   qam-mamərʾà-la.'
belly.F-POSS.3FS PAST-cause_pain.3FS-ACC.3FS

'She made her [own] belly hurt.'

Cf. proverb no. (128) below.

ṭlə́bli mən-básso zonáli xapča-bandóra dammǝd-hóya go-šùqa,' harám-hakan xzéli xà-bandora,' kása gǝ-mamǝrʾàla,' lébi ṭálban mánna čù-məndi.'

I asked Basso to buy some tomatoes for me when she is in the market. But I have not seen a single tomato [lit. it is forbidden if I saw one tomato]! She made her [own] belly hurt [to avoid the task], I cannot ask her for anything.

See also the context situation for proverb no. (128) below.

(125) našé-lax márʾa u-mòsa.'
forget.IPFV-ACC.2FS pain.M and-death.M
'May pain and death forget you.'

'wi-nšéli zonánnax tarpe-sǝ̀lqe.'[116] 'lə́bbax la-pàeš,' našélax márʾa u-mòsa,' bráti zùnna-li.'"

'Oh I forgot to buy you [some] chards.'[116] 'Your heart should not stay [=do not worry], may pain and death forget you, my daughter bought [some for] me.'

(126) ʾamóma u-yóm-e kòma.'
scarecrow[117].M and-day.M-POSS.3MS black
'A scarecrow[117] and his day is black.'

ʾo qaṣaba mǝrute raʿ-ile. la-g-maḥke, kake xriče pǝmme sṭima, ʾamoma u-yome koma.'

This butcher, his face is bad. He does not speak, his teeth are gnashed, his mouth is sealed, a scarecrow[117] and his day is black.

(127) barbáṭ-ǝd núra fǝr-ru mǝn-ʾén-e.'
spark.PL-GEN fire.M fly.PFV-3PL from-eye.PL-POSS.3MS
'Sparks of fire flew from his eyes.'

Cf. Sabar (2002a, 114), under bɪrbāṭe.

---

[116] An important ingredient of the soup known as xamuṣta; see ch. 2, fns 36–37.
[117] The translation of ʾamoma is according to Khan (2008b, 1215).

See the context situation for proverb no. (132) below.

(128) *gárm-ox   là mayqər-ə́t-tu.*'
bone.PL-POSS.2MS NEG make_heavy.IPFV-2MS-ACC.3PL

'Do not make your bones heavy.'

Var.: *gárm-e   yaqùre.*'
bone.PL-POSS.3MS heavy.PL

'His bones are heavy.'

Cf. Sabar (2002a, 124), under *garma*; proverb no. (124) above.

šábti mšaqʿàna,' gárme kma-yaqùre,' hay-tré šabása peláve-didi hílu kə̀sle,' xà bəzmára lázəm čáyək ʾə̀bbu,' káse g-mamrèʾla[118] *u-lá qam-ʾawə̀zlu.*'

Shabti the cobbler, his bones are so heavy, it's three weeks [that] my shoes are with him, he has to knock in them [only] the one nail, he made his belly ache[118] and he did not fix [lit. do/make] them.

(129) *šmóʾ   la-šamʾə́t   xrìwa.*'
hear.IMP.2S NEG-hear.IPFV.2MS bad.m

'Listen, [may] you not hear [any] evil.'

See the context situations for proverbs no. (60) and no. (104) above.

(130) *k-taqə́l-la   gyàn-e.*'
IND-weigh.IPFV.3MS-ACC.3FS self.F-POSS.3MS

'He weighs himself.'

bə́sso mə̀rra,' b-án maṣiḥànna xmási,' b-nablánna xápča šòrba,'—bə́noke qam-xazyánna b-izála ṣax-salìm,'—k-ĭʾan ṣax-

Basso said, "I shall go visit my mother-in-law, I'll take her some soup, this morning I saw her walking healthy and well—I know that she is healthy and well, but every

---

[118] See proverb no. (124) above.

salìm hı́la,' bắle kúd-kma šabása là-k-əsya kəsléni,' k-taqlàla gyána,' xázya kalása maṣihı́la yan-là,' ʾə́dyo ṭòri-le b-an maṣəḥànna,' réša marwànne.'

several weeks she does not come to us, she weighs herself, [in order to] see whether her daughters-in-law visit her or not. Today is my turn to go visit her, I shall make her head grow [= make her feel important; flatter her]."

(131) *k-íʾa tér gyàn-a.'*
IND-know.IPFV.3FS sufficient_for self.F-POSS.3FS

'She knows sufficiently for herself.'

Var.: *ʾíba tér gyàna.'*

'She is sufficient for herself.'

Cf. Sabar (2002a, 308), under *tēr*.

yalúnkət xási mjoḥə́dlu xá məddaw-xə̀t.' xá mxéla xábre bəd-d-ay-xə̀t.' séla yə̀mmu,' u-mə́rra ta-d-ay-zùrta,' qṭóʾ qàlax.' mə́rri ta-xàsi,' ʾáhat lè-wajax,' ʾay-rábsa k-íʾa tér gyána,' lè[w]a xamə́skin,' ʾíba kúd ṭláha xaswása mayʾilálu go-jèba.'

The children of my sister quarrelled one with the other. One struck words in the other [= they argued; insulted one another]. Their mother came and told the little one, "Cut your voice [= be silent]!" I told my sister, "You should not care, the eldest can get along [lit. knows sufficiently for herself], she is not poor [= helpless], she can put [lit. insert] all her three sisters into her pocket [= she is strong enough to manage them]."

(132) *dín-i g-él m-rèš-i.'*
religion/judgement[119].M-POSS.1S IND-go.IPFV.3MS from-head.M-POSS.1S

'I lose my senses. [lit. my religion/judgement goes away from my head.]'

---

[119] The word *dìn* is borrowed into NENA from both Hebrew, where it means 'Jewish law, judgement', and from Arabic, where it means 'religion'. See Sabar (2002a: 141).

ʾo-náša hàyya g-jágər,ˈ pappúke bàxte,ˈ sela m-šuqa, heš-lá mutúla sálle dìda,ˈ škálle ṣárəx ʾə̀lla,ˈ barbátəd núra fə́rru mən-ʾèna,ˈ[120] g-emrá-le hawa-mà ʾúzli,ˈ mə́rre k-íʾat dammət-k-ésən ʾəl-bésa u-la-k-xazə̀nnax,ˈ díni g-él mən-rèši.ˈ

This man gets angry quickly. [How] poor is his wife! She came from the market, she had not put down her baskets yet, he started yelling at her, sparks of fire flew from his eyes,[120] she tells him, "But what did I do?!" He says, "You know [that] when I come home and do not see you my judgement goes away from my head [=I lose my senses]."

(133) ġné-li u-lá rʾə̀š-li.ˈ
be_suddenly_happy/lucky.PFV-1S and-NEG feel.PFV-1S
'I was so lucky [but] I didn't realise it.'

Can be used either ironically or not.

kálsi škálla pàlxa,ˈ nahagóna zálle ʾəl-màlxa,ˈ[121] mə̀rra,ˈ yalónke masyálu kə́sli ʾozán-bu xudàni.ˈ ġnéli u-là rʾə́šli.ˈ ʾána la-k-ṣayə́ḥli rèši xekánne,ˈ ʾátta lázəm ʾón xudáni bəd-yalónke zòre.ˈ ʾáya u-yə́mma-šik ġnèlu.ˈ

My daughter-in-law started working, the calf went to [bring] salt.[121] She said she would bring the children to [stay with] me, [so that] I [could] take care of them. I was so happy I did not feel it. Me, I do not have free time to scratch my head, now I have to take care of little children. She and her mother also are happy!

(134) dúk-sox lá màrʾa.ˈ
place.F-POSS.2MS NEG hurt.IPFV.3FS
'[May] your place not hurt.'

hár-dammǝd g-maṣiḥə́nna sóti g-mbarxàli,ˈ bróni dalála u-ʿazíza dúkox là márʾa.ˈ

Always when I visit my grandmother she used to bless me: "My dear and darling son, may your place not hurt [= may you will not experience pain]."

---

[120] See proverb no. (127) above.
[121] See proverb no. (54) above.

(135) *pə́š-le   xà-ḷappa.*'
    become.PFV-3MS one-small_lump.M

   'He became [as small as] a lump [= he became frightened].'

Cf. Sabar (2002a, 207), under *lappa*. See the context situation for proverb no. (60) above.

(136) *lə́bb-a   pə́š-le   xa-màsta.*'
    heart.M-POSS.3FS become.PFV-3MS one-hair.F

   'Her heart became [like] a hair [that is, her heart 'shrank' because of fear, sorrow, hard work, or illness].'

See the context situation for proverb no. (60) above.

15.0. Appendix: Additional Proverbs (with No Glossing or Context Situation)

(137) *ʾé tərnìni[122]-la,*' *ternàna*' *wéla pə̀šta.*'

   'This is *tərnìni*,[122] *ternàna* is still left.'

   ʾé tərnìni-la,' *ternàna*' *heš b-àsya.*'

   'This is *tərnìni*, *ternàna* will come.'

   ʾé tərnìni-la,' *ternàna*' *wela bàsra.*'

   'This is *tərnìni*, *ternàna* is behind it.'

Troubles come in bundles. Cf. SA:13 (a synonym), proverb no. (37) above.

(138) *kúd-xa gárəš núra xe/qam-qóqa dìde.*'

   'Everyone pulls the fire [towards] under/in front of his one clay pot.'

---

[122] See fn. 66 above.

Var.: *kúd kabaníye gárəša...*

'Each cook pulls...' Cf. SA:85.

(139) *xáṭra bəd kàlba,' léba znàya.'*

'[The stroke of a] rod in a dog, there is no prostitution [=shame] in it.'

Hitting a dog is permissible. Also used metaphorically: insulting a bad person is allowed (he who acts like a dog will be treated like a dog). Cf. SA:114.

(140) *qú-m-rèši,' lá marčənnox.'*

'Get off me so that I will not crush you.'

Cf. SA:108; proverbs no. (4) and no. (38) above (synonyms).

(141) *rə́sqet kálbe ʾəl šəzàne.'*

'The livelihood of dogs is upon [=provided by] the mad.'

Dishonest or cunning people (or underdogs) achieve their needs at the expense of the naïve. Cf. SE:120.

(142) *réša dəd la-mằreʾ,' lá yasrə̀tte.'*

'A head that does not hurt, do not tie it.'

Var.: *réš [GEN] la-g-mằreʾ, lá yasrə̀tte.'*

'A head that does not hurt, do not tie it.' Cf. SE:14.

(143) *rùvi' u-šùqa.'*

'The fox...and the market...'

Said in order to emphasise the lack of connection between two things.

(144) *ríx pəšyàsa k-ése mən mahkóye díde.'*

'The smell of farts comes from what he says.'

(145) *túrran ʾó jalìda,' ta-šátyax ʾán màya.'*

'We broke this ice in order to drink this water.'

Said when a great effort is done to achieve something.

> Var.: ...*máya qarìra.*'
>
> '...cold water.'

(146) *ʿáqel léwe bəd-rúwwa u-zòra.*[123]

> 'Intelligence is not in big and small [=not dependent on size or age].'

(147) *ʾíyo íle bə-qzàya,' u-kəz-làbbe' xòre wéna.'*

> 'ʾIyo is preparing, and in his heart [=he thinks that] I am his friend [=cooperating].'

(148) *pə́šli pìre,' ʿúmri pèva.*'[124]

> 'I became an old woman, my life is from now on.'

Cf. [...] אַחֲרֵי בְלֹתִי הָיְתָה לִּי עֶדְנָה [...] '[...] Now that I am withered, am I to have enjoyment [...]' (Gen. 18.12)

(149) *yə́mmi dúqla tə̀rši,' heš-lá mtèle.'*

> 'My mother prepared pickles, it[s time] has not yet arrived [=it is not ready yet].'

Said when someone is delaying a favour which has been asked.

(150) *kpìna' k-éxəl tìna.'*

> 'The hungry eat [even] mud.'

Anyone who is hungry would eat anything. Cf. the Prov. 27.7.

(151) *návyan kálsa u-xmàsa,' zá'lu ʾéra u-ʾəškàsa.'*

> 'Between the daughter-in-law and the mother-in-law [=amidst their arguments and struggles], the penis and testicles got lost.'

---

[123] I thank Ahuva Baruch for this proverb.
[124] I thank Ahuva Baruch for this proverb.

Cf. R:55 (a synonymous proverb).

(152) *xáyi ta-gyàni!¹ júlle dəd-kúd-yom ʾə̀lli,¹ ʾə́dyo bə̀š k-šaklì-li.*¹²⁵

'My life is for me![126] I wear clothes of every day [=normal clothes] [lit. clothes of every day are on me], today they suit me better.'

An expression of good mood, satisfaction.

(153) *qóqəd ʾarása g-ṛàsəx¹ qóqəd ʾizamyása là g-ṛásəx.*¹

'The clay pot of the rival wives[127] boils, the clay pot of the sisters-in-law does not boil.'

Rival wives, living in the same home, must find a way to get along (in the proverb they cook together), sisters-in-law do not get along and they do not have to collaborate.

(154) *dámməd šə́mša g-nàpqa¹ ʾéwa g-él kə̀sla¹ ʾáp-awa g-ə́be šàxən.*¹

'When the sun comes out [=appears], the cloud goes to her, it also wants to warm up.'

Var.: *dámməd ʾéwa k-xáze šə́mša mpə̀qla¹ ʾéwa g-él k-ə̀sla¹ áp-awa g-ə́be šàxən.*¹

'When the cloud sees that the sun came out [=appeared], the cloud goes to her, it also wants to warm up.'

(155) *xréle go zàya.*¹

'He defecated in the issue.'

---

[125] Contraction of *k-šákli ʾə̀li.*

[126] An expression of love, but usually addressed to or about another person, predominantly to children: *xáyi ṭàlox! / ṭàle!* 'My life is for you! / for him!'

[127] In polygamy.

He spoiled the business.

(156) *ʾíza la g-mátya ʾəl šə̀rma.*'

'Her hand does not reach her buttocks.'

She is a miser. Also a curse: may she not be able to serve herself.

(157) *ʾə́l xa čáŋga máya, k-ṭèpa.*

'She [can] float on a handful of water.'

She knows how to get along.

(158) *ʾo mìsaʾ la k-ṭawéle ʾé ʿazàya.*'

'This dead is not worth this mourning/lamentation.'

Said about an exaggerated response to something. Or saying that something is unworthy.

(159) *hìye hìye labanìye.*'

'This and this [are both] yogurt.' (Ar.)

It's all the same, it's nothing new.

(160) *zaharóke dʾə́rra la-gwàra.*'

'Zaharoke returned without getting married.'

Said when someone returns without achieving what he or she had intended.

(161) *zóʾəd zamàre.*'

'A pair of singers.'

Said, often dismissively, about inseparable friends or about two people who collaborate in something.

(162) *ḥále ḥále kúd-xa ʾəl maḥàlle.*'

'His situation his situation, everyone [goes] to his neighbourhood.'

At the end of the day everyone should mind their own business.

(163) là ṭrə́sli,' drə̀zli,' là nə́xli,' nùxli.'

'I did not heal, I cracked; I did not rest, I barked [=howled].'

Life is hard.

(164) kúlla dúnye šud-péša ʾèra,' lá ʿálqa ʾə̀bbi.'

'May the entire world be a penis [but] do not stumble upon / touch me.'

Vars.: ...la náḥqa ʾə̀lli.'

'...do no touch me.'

...la qàrwa ʾə́lli.'

'...do not come close to me.'

Cf. proverb no. (29) above which has a synonymous message.

(165) xmáre g-él b-ʾùrxa.'

'His donkey is walking on the road.'

Things are going well for him.

(166) ma-də́qnox bə́d máyəd dòʾe qam-maxurə́tta?'[128]

'What, did you dye your beard white with a yogurt drink?!'

Said to an older man who says something unwise.

(167) ʾelíko b-xà nása.'

'ʾEliko with one ear.'

Used to describe someone or something with some defect, lacking something, incompetent. Or said about a task which was performed only partially. Cf. R:64.

(168) xá xábra nùra,' xá xábra bàrud.'

'One word [of] fire, one word [of] gunpowder.'

---

[128] I thank Ahuva Baruch for this proverb.

Used of someone speaking angrily.

(169) *mə́ndi dəd-lá-ʾáse ʾəmməd-kàlo,*' *lá-kese bàsra.*'[129]

'What does not come with the bride, shall not come after her.'

Past promises are irrelevant. If one promises something, one should deliver now.

(170) *kúd lá šxə́nne bəd-šə́mšəd bə̀noke.*' *la-g-šáxən bəd-šə́mšəd ʿaṣə̀rṭa.*'[130]

'He who did not warm up in the morning's sun, will not warm up in the evening's sun.'

Something done too late is useless. Cf. R:11, SE:124 (explained with various messages).

(171) *šaláqtəd bèʾe.*'

'[She who] boils the eggs.'

Said of someone who knows how to get along in life. Also: a fomenter of quarrels.

(172) *xábrox qṭéʾli bəd-šàkar.*'

'I cut your word[s] with sugar.'

Said as an apology when interrupting someone's speech.

(173) *g-yáʾla go-ʾèni.*'

'She goes into my eye.'

She argues with me, contradicts what I say.

(174) *ʾéna qáṭʾa qam-gyàna.*'

'Her eye cuts in front of her.'

---

[129] I thank Naftali Mizraḥi for this proverb.
[130] I thank Mordechai Yona for this proverb.

She thinks highly of herself; makes a big deal out of the respect she thinks is due to her.

(175) *'áxəl réše páyəš mə̀nne.*¹

'May it eat his head, and [still] stay from him.'

May the object that he did not agree to give me harm him and exist after him.

(176) *pə́sra b-axlàle,' gárme mṭašyàlu.*¹³¹

'She would eat the meat [and] hide the bones.'

She won't reveal my dirty laundry.

(177) *fáqir zə́lle l-tə̀ksa,' u-zángin 'riqále l-bə̀dra.*¹³²

'The poor went to his belt [=euphemism for intercourse?] and the rich ran to the threshing floor.'

The only pastime of the poor is sexual intercourse (?). Cf. proverb no. (9) above.

(178) *mən-jamà'a' là-g-'eqa dúksa.*¹³³

'From [=because of] the congregation, space does not become narrow'.

Var.: *mən-naše...*

'From [=because of] people...'

They feel the space is sufficient because they love each other. Cf. כי רחימתין הוה עזיזא אפותיא דספסירא שכיבן השתא דלא עזיזא רחימתין פוריא בר שיתין גרמידי לא סגי לן 'When our love was strong, we could lay on the blade of a sword, now our love is not strong, a bed sixty ells wide is not enough for us' (BT Sanhedrin 7a; my translation).

---

¹³¹ I thank Ḥabuba Messusani for this proverb.

¹³² I thank Boʻaz Sando for this proverb.

¹³³ I thank Naftali Mizraḥi for this proverb.

(179) *cúxxa látle kafíl u-damàn.*[134]

'No one has a guarantor and protection-tax/bail.'

Everyone is mortal. Cf. proverb no. (11) above.

(180) *kárti u-ṭèʾni' wélu š-xàṣi,' u-xóri k-čáhe ʾə̀bbu.*[135]

'My load and my burden are on my back, and [=but] my friend is getting tired because of [lit. in] them.'

Cf. proverbs no. (7) and no. (26) above.

(181) *də́qən qáša qam-ʾozále kanə̀šta.'*

'She made the beard of the priest a broom.'

She used something in a disrespectful way.

Var.: *...ʾozále sponjədòr.'*

'...she made it a rag.'

Synonymous message to that of proverb no. (182) below.

(182) *mxélu tambúr b-ʾér bàbu.'*

'They struck the drum with the penis of their father.'

Said when someone is showing disrespect while thinking they are, or trying to be, respectful. Synonymous message to that of proverb no. (181) above.

(183) *ymút al-dìk' u-ʿéno ʿala-naxàla.'*

'The rooster dies and [=but] his eye is on the waste [or: bran].' (Ar.)

Desires never die. Cf. Aramaic version in SE:33; proverb no. (191) below, a synonym.

---

[134] I thank Naftali Mizraḥi for this proverb.
[135] I thank Naftali Mizraḥi for this proverb.

(184) *ʾáw d-čáyək réše go-tanùra' q-qáyəz bəd-nùra.*[136]
'He who sticks his head into the oven gets burnt by the fire.'

Synonymous message to that of proverb no. (40) above.

(185) *g-yáʾəl go-xa-u-xə̀t.'*
'He enters one into the other.'

He is starting to get angry.

(186) *ʾiláha šqilále mə̀nne.'*
'God has taken it from him.'

He lost his senses. He became angry.

(187) *mən-qóma ta-ʿaqlùsa.'*
'From stature to wit.'

May you lose some of your stature and gain it in intelligence. Cf. proverb no. (116) above.

(188) *kúd šqə́lle ʿaqə̀llax' là mtáhne ʾə́bbe.'*
'Whoever took your wits, may he not enjoy it!'

Cf. SA:9.

(189) *kúd g-máxe šud-màmreʾ,' kúd g-máxəl šud-màswe.'*
'He who hits should hurt, he who feeds should satiate.'

Cf. SE:11.

(190) *kusís ʿàlo' dréle b-érš jàllo.'*
'He put the hat of ʿAlo on the head of Jallo.'

He confused two matters.

---

[136] Sabar (2002a, 131), under *č-y-k*.

(191) *kása kpə́nta k-sò'a,* ' *'éna kpə́nta là k-só'a.* [137]

'A hungry belly [can be] satiated, a hungry eye [can]not [be] satiated.'

Cf. the synonymous proverb no. (183) above.

(192) *'áza qál'a qala'ìsa* ' *párya kása béb kulìsa.* '

'[May] she go away [to hell, and may] her belly burst and overflow together with her kidney.'

A curse.

(193) *šám'a 'ár'a, lá 'amràla.* '

'[May] the earth hear [it, and] not tell it to her.'

Said about a deceased person, when mentioning a negative fact about them.

(194) *'ə́ba gyàna.* '

'[May] she love herself.'

Said about a deceased person, after saying that she had loved the speaker, or that the speaker had loved her, in order that the deceased person shall not cause the speaker to join her.

(195) *xábra xé pelàvax.* '

'A word under your slippers.'

Keep a secret. See the context situation at proverb no. (27) above.

(196) *pə́mmi twíra qàme.*

'My mouth is broken in front of Him.'

Said to God, when saying something which may be construed as resentful towards Him. Cf. Jer. 12.1.

---

[137] Sabar (2002a, 188), under *kpìna*.

(197) *'amórka 'amə̀rra' zamórka zamə̀rra.'*
   'May the sayer say it, may the singer sing it.'
Let people say whatever they want.

CHAPTER 2: ENRICHED BIBLICAL NARRATIVES

1.0. The Enriched Biblical Narrative

The topic of this chapter is a central genre in the oral culture[1] of the Jews of Zakho, and indeed of all Kurdistan: the enriched biblical narrative (EBN). The EBN is the retelling and re-composition of a biblical story, usually one of heroic or epic nature. The core, skeletal, biblical narrative is enriched with numerous additions which are woven into it in an organic manner, producing an smooth, even story that does not reveal its composite nature. The fact that it draws on elements from various sources which often originated in different historical periods and in different cultural realms is not evident to the listener, nor is its history of change and growth.

The chapter will consider the EBN through the prism of a concept taken from the study of thematology, the *motifeme*, and it will propose a new concept, the *transposed motifeme*. The chapter claims that the transposed motifeme is a phenomenon central to the EBN and its related genres, and that it is important for their understanding and analysis.

An example of an EBN will be discussed and analysed in this chapter. It consists of two related, and consecutive, stories: the story of Ruth and Naomi and the story of king David. It was told by Samra Zaqen, and recorded in her home on 19 April

---

[1] On this term see Ong (1982).

2012.² The complete narrative, with a translation, is presented in §7.0.

2.0. Related Genres³

The EBN shares certain characteristics with other prevalent genres of the oral as well as the written culture of the Jews of Kurdistan. These characteristics, predominantly the mechanism of transposed motifemes and the mediatory function (both discussed below),⁴ may therefore be regarded as meta-generic characteristics in the culture of the Jews of Kurdistan (that is, characteristics which encompass several genres).⁵ The genres which are related to the EBN may be divided into two categories:

> 1. Synchronically related genres: the living genres native to the culture of the Jews of Kurdistan. These are epic songs (traditionally referred to as *tafsir* or *qəṣta*); oral translations of the Hebrew Bible; older NENA translations of the Hebrew Bible; NENA Midrashim; expositions of the *hafṭarot* and of the Megillot; and Jewish NENA *piyyuṭ* (liturgical poetry).

---

[2] I have published another EBN told by Samra Zaqen, the story of Joseph and his brothers, elsewhere; see Aloni (2014a, 26–60). For another recording of a NENA text recounted by Samra, where she talks about her arrival in Israel in 1951 and her first encounter with Modern Hebrew, see Aloni (2015).

[3] For a comprehensive overview of the literature of the Jews of Kurdistan, see Sabar (1982a; 1982c, xxxii–xxxvi).

[4] In §§4.0 and 2.2.1, respectively.

[5] For discussions of the centrality of genre as a category in the study of folklore, see Ben-Amos (1969; 1976b); Seitel (1999).

2. Diachronically related genres: genres belonging to earlier layers of Jewish culture to which the origins of the EBN phenomenon may be traced. These genres are the *Targum* in various configurations; the *Midrash* in various configurations; *piyyuṭ*; and post-antiquity Rewritten Bible texts.

The geographical isolation of the Jewish communities of Kurdistan—as well as the social structure and their material culture, which greatly resembled those known to us from the rabbinic period—enabled the Jewish communities of Kurdistan to preserve ancient literary traditions and practices, and thus the deep connection between the literary genres of the Jews of Kurdistan and the world of classical Midrash: ancient literary and exegetical genres were kept alive in the Jewish communities of Kurdistan well into modern times.[6]

---

[6] Rivlin (1942, 183) commented: "It is indeed possible that Midrashim otherwise lost, were preserved in the Aggadah of the Jews of Kurdistan" (my translation). For examples of that type, see Rivlin (1942, 183–84; 1959, 106–8). Gerson-Kiwi (1971, 59) similarly stated that "Kurdistan is known as a territory... where... archaic languages and... archaic singing and playing have survived the vicissitudes of history.... Here we seem to have some samples of a living antiquity, doubly interesting in that it is to a considerable extent connected with Jewish history of the biblical period." According to Brauer (1947, 12), translated as Brauer (1993, 27), "one gains the impression that a great many ancient (Talmudic) Jewish usages and beliefs, both religious and secular, have been preserved and kept alive among the Jews of Kurdistan."

2.1. Synchronically Related Genres

2.1.1. Epic Songs

Epic songs recount biblical or Midrashic narratives, rich in heroic and dramatic elements. These songs were a popular pastime in Kurdistan, and also served as an educational medium for those members of the community who did not have access to the written sources (Sabar 1982a, 63). The songs are usually rhymed and have a clear strophic structure, and each of the songs was performed with a unique melody (Gerson-Kiwi 1971). Similar to the case of the EBN, as we will see below, motifemes added to the skeletal narrative of an epic poem are woven into it in an organic manner.

A term commonly used for these epic songs is *tafsir* (pl. *tafsirim*). The word is borrowed from Arabic, where it means "elucidation, interpretation," or "commentary on the Qurʾan" (Wehr and Cowan 1976, 713). Another term used interchangeably with this is *qəṣta*, meaning "story" (Sabar 2002a, 282). Sabar described the *tafsirim* as "the foremost literary product of the *ḥaxamim* of Kurdistan" (Sabar 1982c, xxxvi).

Rivlin collected many of the epic songs and published them with an elaborate introduction (Rivlin 1959). Naʿim Shalom, a *hazzan* 'cantor' at Šaʿarey Tora, a synagogue of the Jewish community of Zakho in Jerusalem, has recorded and published his performance of two of these epic songs: the story of Joseph and his brothers and the story of the binding of Isaac (Shalom 1986).

Naʿim Shalom's renditions differ in many details from the equivalent songs in Rivlin's book, though they follow the same structure.

Other recordings of NENA epic songs are kept in the National Sound Archive in the National Library of Israel, notably: David and Goliath, performed by Ḥakham Ḥabib ʿAlwan in the Zakho dialect, recorded by Johanna Spector (class mark Y 00039); David and Goliath, performed by Eliyahu Gabbay, Naḥum ʿAdiqa, and Salem Gabbay in the Zakho dialect, recorded by Avigdor Herzog (class mark Y 03627); Joseph and Benjamin, performed by Eliyahu Gabbay, Naḥum ʿAdiqa, and Salem Gabbay in the Zakho dialect, recorded by Avigdor Herzog (class mark Y 03627); the story of Joseph performed by Nehemya Hoča in the Zakho dialect, recorded by Edith Gerson-Kiwi (class mark CD 04871 F424-425 item 5351-5366); David and Goliath, performed by Raḥamim Ḥodeda in the dialect of ʿAmidya, recorded by Jacqueline Alon (class mark Y 02719); and the binding of Isaac performed by David Salman in the dialect of Ḥalabja, recorded by the performer (class mark Y 04514).

2.1.2. Translations of the Hebrew Bible

The Jews of Kurdistan kept a living tradition of translations into their NENA dialects of the entire Hebrew Bible.[7] These translations were handed down orally,[8] and committed to writing at the

---

[7] With the exception of the book of Psalms.

[8] There are recordings of oral performances in the National Sound Archive of the National Library of Israel, for example ʿAlwan (1974),

request of scholars only in the 20th century.[9] The term often used by the Jews of Kurdistan to describe these translations is *šarḥ* or *šarʿ*, from Arabic, meaning "expounding, explanation, elucidation" (Wehr and Cowan 1976, 463).

These translations of the Hebrew Bible are often very literal—"the general tendency is to translate the biblical formulation word by word as much as possible, and therefore the result is a frozen and unnatural language" (Sabar 1983, 27, quoted in Avinery 1984, 138; my translation). However, they were "often based on the traditional commentaries, such as Rashi and the classical Aramaic Targum… [and] in certain cases… a more homiletic translation or allegorical translation was preferred" (Sabar 1982c, xxxv). It is precisely in these instances that the translations show a family resemblance to the EBN.

2.1.3. NENA Midrashim

NENA Midrashim were preserved in manuscripts originating from the 17th century, copied in Nerwa and ʿAmidya. It seems that these NENA Midrashim, in their edited form, were the product of the school of Ḥakham Shemuʾel Barazani (Sabar 1982a, 60). They contain homilies and lessons on three portions of the

---

which consists of the book of Ruth performed by Ḥakham Ḥabib ʿAlwan, recorded by Jacqueline Alon (class mark Y 01790).

[9] See Rivlin (1959, 68–69). Multiple volumes of these translations were published by Sabar (1983; 1988; 1990; 1993; 1995a; 2006; 2014). A translation of the book of Ruth, as read by Zeʾev (Gurgo) Ariel, was published by Goldenberg and Zaken (1990).

Torah: *Wayḥi*, *Bešallaḥ*, and *Yitro*. They were written with the intention of being delivered publicly, and therefore have a captivating, dramatic character (Sabar 1982a, 60).

A large percentage of the Aggadic material in these Midrashim can be traced back to older, classical Midrashim, but has been reworked and given new, elaborate formulation. In many instances, however, the Aggadic material cannot be traced back to earlier sources and it must be regarded as either original work of the Ḥakhamim of Kurdistan or classical Aggadic material that did not survive elsewhere. Whatever the case may be, the reworking of older material and the incorporation of original material are features that unite the Midrashim with the EBN.

The NENA Midrashim were published by Sabar (1976; 1985).

2.1.4. Expositions of the *Hafṭarot* and the Megillot

The NENA expositions of the *hafṭarot* (portions taken from the books of the biblical prophets, read in synagogue after the reading of the Torah) are of *hafṭarot* for special occasions: the afternoon of Yom Kippur (the book of Jonah; Sabar 1982b);[10] the eight days of Passover (Isa. 10.32–12.6); the second day of Shavuot (Hab. 2.20–3.19; Sabar 1966, 381–90); and the Ninth of Ab (Jer.

---

[10] A recording of the book of Jonah performed in the dialect of ʿAmidya by Raḥamim Ḥodeda, recorded by Jacqueline Alon, is kept in the National Sound Archive of the National Library of Israel (class mark Y 02718).

8.13–9.23).[11] They follow the Hebrew text more closely than do the NENA Midrashim, but also contain Aggadic material aimed at interpreting the verses. Similarly to the NENA Midrashim, they are preserved in manuscripts in the Nerwa and ʿAmidya dialects, except for the *haftarah* for the Ninth of Ab, which is preserved in the Zakho dialect and is still used liturgically today by the Jewish community of Zakho in Israel (Sabar 1982a, 61).

The expositions of the Megillot (the Five Scrolls) are similar in character to those of the *haftarot*, although they tend to follow the Hebrew text even more closely. One exception is the exposition of the Song of Songs, which is a translation of the book's classical Aramaic *Targum*, itself an allegorical interpretation of the Hebrew text (Sabar 1991). The exposition of the book of Ruth is preserved in several manuscripts.[12] The exposition of Lamentations is preserved in manuscripts in the dialects of Nerwa and

---

[11] National Library of Israel, Institute of Microfilmed Hebrew Manuscripts no. F74965 copied by Rabbi Shemuʾel Baruch from the author, his father, Rabbi Yosef Binyamin; Michael Krupp Manuscript Collection Ms. 2915 written by Ḥakham Ḥabib ʿAlwan; the National Library of Israel Ms. Heb. 1007 copied by Mordechai Naḥum Zakhariko; Ms. Heb. 494 written by Darwish Ben Shimʿon Shanbiko; Ms. Heb. 695 written by Shabbetai Ben Yaʿaqov. Several recorded performances are kept in the National Sound Archive of the National Library of Israel (class marks Y 00028(8-13), Y 00504(02), Y 00504, YC 02657, CD 05033, CD 05037).

[12] National Library of Israel, Institute of Microfilmed Hebrew Manuscripts nos F26847, F26945, F44919, F73987, Ms.Heb.1012=28, Ms.Heb.7806=28, and MSS-D2233. An exposition of the book of Ruth from a privately owned manuscript by Shimʿon Ben-Michael written in

'Amidya, but is known to the Jews of Zakho in Israel and is recited orally on the Ninth of Ab. No exposition of Ecclesiastes survives, and it is unclear whether it was ever translated into NENA. The exposition of the book of Esther is preserved in a single manuscript.[13] Two recordings of the book of Esther, both in the dialect of 'Amidya, are kept in the National Sound Archive of the National Library of Israel: one is performed by Repha'el ʾEliyahu, and recorded by Nurit Ben-Zvi (class mark Y 05750); the other is performed by Raḥamim Ḥodeda, and recorded by Jacqueline Alon (class marks Y 02717, Y 02718).

2.1.5. NENA *Piyyuṭ*

Jewish NENA *piyyuṭim* (liturgical poems) in various dialects, which are recorded in manuscripts, have been published by Sabar (2009). Most of these *piyyuṭim* are translations, sometimes very free translations, of earlier Hebrew *piyyuṭim*, but several of them are original works.[14] A number of the *piyyuṭim* recount biblical

---

the dialect of Urmi was published by Ben-Rahamim (2006, 192–215). It contains elaborate Midrashic narrative expansions.

[13] National Library of Israel, Institute of Microfilmed Hebrew Manuscripts no. F44919, pp. 70a–104a. This is a Neo-Aramaic translation of the older Aramaic Targum Sheni of the book of Esther. Sabar (1982a, 61) states that exposition of the book of Esther is preserved only orally.

[14] One of these original works is 'The Binding of Isaac', from a manuscript by Ḥakham Yishay in the Urmi dialect, which was sung on Rosh Hashana and Yom Kippur, published in Sabar (2009, 60–79). Sabar (2009, 60, fn. 149) writes about this *piyyuṭ*:

narratives,[15] which they elaborate in a manner similar to that of the epic songs (see §2.1.1. above). These *piyyuṭim* were sung in synagogues during certain Jewish festivals.

2.2. Diachronically Related Genres

2.2.1. Targum[16]

The tradition of Targum, Jewish translation of the Hebrew Bible into Aramaic, dates back to the pre-rabbinic period. It seems that the many extant Targumim are related to the ancient liturgical practice of public translation of the Torah, whose aim was to make scripture accessible to members of the community who

---

> It seems that the Neo-Aramaic version is not a direct translation of a Hebrew piyyuṭ, but is rather drawn, with considerable elaboration and dramatisation and with a variety of additions taken from the local linguistic reality… from the rabbinic Midrashim about the binding [of Isaac].

There are also four *piyyuṭim* about the passing away of Moses, which were sung on Simḥat Torah after reading the *meʿona* Torah portion (Deut. 33.27–29): the first without dialect specification, in Sabar (2009, 299–302); the second in the dialect of Saqqəz, in Sabar (2009, 302–6); the third from a manuscript by Ḥakham Sason, son of Rabbi Babba Barazani of Arbil, in the dialect of Arbil, in Sabar (2009, 306–9); and the fourth, taken from Ben-Rahamim (2006, 216–21), from a manuscript by Shimʿon Ben-Michael in the dialect of Naghada, republished in Sabar (2009, 309–12).

[15] In one case, *qəṣttət ḥanna* 'The story of Hannah', the *piyyuṭ* is based on a Midrashic narrative. Sabar (2009, 425–43) gives two versions: one in the dialect of Zakho and one in the dialect of Dohok, from a manuscript by Ḥakham Eliyahu Avraham Yitzḥaq Dahoki.

[16] For a comprehensive overview of this topic, see Kasher (2000).

were not able to understand the Hebrew. In antiquity, this simultaneous translation was done extemporaneously (or memorised in advance) during the public reading of the Torah by a designated person, the *meturgeman* (Elbogen 1972 [1913], 140–41). Later in the history of *Halakha*, the study of *Targum* side by side with the study of the Hebrew text of the Torah became an obligation, rooted in a Talmudic decree: "Rav Huna son of Judah said in the name of Rabbi Ammi: 'A man should always complete his portions [of Torah] together with the congregation [reading] twice [the Hebrew] scripture and once [the] Targum'" (BT Brakhot 8a; translation based on the Soncino English edition). According to the rabbis, translating the Hebrew Bible properly is a delicate task with sharp borders on both ends of the literal-paraphrase axis: "Rabbi Yehudah said: 'one who translates a verse literally, he is a liar; one who adds, he is a blasphemer and a libeller'" (BT Qiddushin 49a; Tosefta Megillah 3.41).

The extant Targumim (Targum Onkelos, Targum Pseudo-Jonathan, Targum Neofiti, the Genizah Targum, the Fragments Targum, and the Tosefta Targum of the Pentateuch; Targum Jonathan Ben 'Uzzi'el, and the Tosefta Targum of the Prophets; the Targumim of the Writings) vary in the degree of literalness and the amount of Aggadic material they incorporate into the text.

The Targum tradition is relevant to the EBN genre in two of its aspects. Firstly, in its mediatory function. It serves as a bridge between the biblical text and the people. This is a very important function in a community where many members could not understand the Hebrew in which the Bible is written. The EBN fills this mediatory function, and declares it in formulas such as *de šmoʾun ya kulloxun mḥubbe didi, de mṣitun kullu ʿazize didi* 'Oh hear all of you my loved ones, oh listen all my dear ones' (Rivlin 1959, 228).[17] Secondly, the Targum weaves Aggadic material into the text in a manner that produces a smooth, unified text. It does not indicate when it departs from a literal translation and incorporates Aggadic additions, and this is very similar to the EBN.

An example of a classical Targum which is particularly close to the EBN style is the Tosefta Targum of the Prophets.[18] It is a Targum especially rich in Aggadic additions incorporated into the text. One half of the material of the Tosefta Targum is for chapters that are, or were, used as *hafṭarot*. Thus it also has stylistic ties to the NENA expositions of the *hafṭarot*.[19]

2.2.2. Midrash

Midrashic discourse is a central component of rabbinic literature. Its hermeneutical techniques and style are an important foundation of, and can be found in, all of the works of the relevant literature: both those which are classified as Midrash (e.g., Midrash Rabbah for various books of the Hebrew Bible), and those which are not classified as such (e.g., the two Talmudim). The technique

---

[17] See also the comments of Sabar (1982a, 63). Kasher (2000, 73) describes the Hebrew formula עמי בני ישראל 'my people sons of Israel' used to address the audience, which appears dozens of times in the classical Aramaic *Targumim* for the Torah. Kasher lists this formula as one of the proofs that the *Targumim* were performatively used in the liturgy.

[18] See edition with commentary in Kasher (1996).

[19] See §2.1.4 above.

of elaborative hermeneutics of Midrash, which is so central to Jewish culture, is the direct ancestor of the EBN.

Nonetheless, one point of dissimilarity between the two must be noted: the Midrashic text, in most cases, quotes the original biblical text dealt with within the Midrashic discourse. By doing that it poses a differentiation between the written text, and the oral Aggadic material. Thus an inherent classification system exists within the Midrashic text itself.[20] The EBN, as we shall see, does not do that. In fact, one of the core features of the genre is the unity of the narrative: the teller and the audience are not necessarily aware, nor are they expected to be aware, of the various ingredients—many of them dating back to entirely different periods and cultural realms—that make up the unified EBN text.

2.2.3. Post-antiquity Rewritten Bible Texts

The term 'Rewritten Bible' usually refers to a genre prevalent in Second Temple literature, particularly in the Qumran literature. Here it is intended to describe several medieval works (e.g., *Sefer ha-Yašar*; Dan 1986) as well as several modern works (e.g., *Toqpo šel Yosef* and some of the stories in *'Ose Fele*, both by Rabbi Yosef Shabbetai Farḥi[21] [1867 and 1864–1870,[22] respectively]). These

---

[20] In the Talmud, one of the ways this is achieved is by linguistic differentiation: the biblical text is in Hebrew and the Midrashic interpretation is often in Aramaic.

[21] On Farḥi, his books, and his influence, see Yassif (1982).

[22] On the uncertainty regarding the year of publication, see Yassif (1982, 48, fn. 7).

works are similar in their programme to their better-known Second Temple namesake: they rewrite narratives taken from the Hebrew Bible while adding Aggadic material into the stream of narration. What is common to Rewritten Bible texts and the EBN is that both produce a continuous narrative whose added themes become integral parts of the whole and are not marked as being added material.

Not only is there this theoretical overlap between Rewritten Bible texts and the EBN, one of these works, *Toqpo šel Yosef*, published in 1867 in Livorno, surprisingly shares much of its Aggadic material with a Zakho EBN, the story of Joseph and his brothers (Aloni 2014a, 27–30; 2014b, 339).

2.3. The Christian *Durekta*

Another related Neo-Aramaic genre that should be mentioned in this context is the Christian *durekta* (Mengozzi 2012). This is a genre of rhymed and metred poetry on religious themes sung at public gatherings. The genre has its roots in the Classical Syriac genre of *memra*. Many *durekyata* are based on biblical narratives with added material.

Comparing the Jewish Targum and the Christian *durekta*, Mengozzi writes that both are "presented as bridge-genres from written to oral tradition" (Mengozzi 2012, 335). This bridging function is also shared by Jewish *tafsirim* 'epic songs' (see §2.1.1 above), and indeed the *tafsirim* and the *durekyata* have additional characteristics in common: the *tafsirim* and the *durekyata* both contain religious themes and narratives, but are both performed publicly in non-liturgical circumstances (Mengozzi 2012, 338–

39); they both contain within their verses expressions directed to attract the audience's attention and meta-poetic statements about the act of performing the song and recounting its narrative (Mengozzi 2012, 335); neither is anonymous,[23] as the names of their authors are recorded (Mengozzi 2012, 337). In addition, some *tafsirim* and *durekyaṯa* are based on the same biblical narratives, and in these cases some of the themes of the additional material are shared. A comparative study of the themes in these cases— for example, comparing those of the Jewish *tafsir* of Joseph and his brothers (Aloni 2014a, 26–60; 2014b) with those in the *durekyaṯa* (see, for example, Mengozzi 1999, 477–78, 482 no. 16; Rodrigues Pereira 1989–1990) about the same biblical narrative—would certainly prove fruitful.

3.0. Thematology

Following a discussion of the motif in the analysis of folklore, this section considers the most important concepts of thematology, the methodological approach which will be used in the analysis of the EBN below. The following section then proposes a new concept, the transposed motifeme.

---

[23] This is not always the case for Jewish epic songs. Rivlin (1959) gives traditions about the names of the authors for only some of the songs.

3.1. The Motif as a Fundamental Concept in Folkloristics

The concept of motif, which is defined as a small meaning-bearing element of a text[24] that may recur in other texts, is central to, some say distinctive of (Ben-Amos 1980, 17), the study of folklore. The standard reference work most closely associated with the concept of motif in folklore is the Thompson motif index (Thompson 1955–1958). It offers a systematic classification of motifs—recurring elements—in folk-literature. The ability to use this index has been described as "a skill which is indispensable to the folklorist, and the defining trait that separates him from all other student of culture" (Dorson 1972, 6, quoted in Ben-Amos 1980, 17). However, over the years, many theoretical critiques have been made of both the motif index and the concept of the motif itself.[25]

One such critique is found in Alan Dundes's (1962) article 'From Etic to Emic Units in the Structural Study of Folktales'. Dundes criticises the choice of the motif as a basic unit in the study of folklore. While not denying the value of the motif index

---

[24] In the context of this chapter, a small meaning-bearing element of a narrative. But the concept of motif is relevant to other art forms as well: music, dance, visual art, textile, and more.

[25] For a thorough overview, see Ben-Amos (1980). See also Ben-Amos (1995, 71): "as much as motif-analysis has become the hallmark of folklore research in the first half of the twentieth century, it has failed to yield substantive interpretive insights into the nature of oral literature and the dynamics of tradition." Although Thompson's motif index is the most well-known, it is not the only one—for a list of motif indexes, see Uther (1996). For an annotated bibliography, see Azzolina (1987).

(or that of the Aarne-Thompson tale type index [Aarne and Thompson 1961; Uther 2004), noting that these indexes are "useful... [as] bibliographical aids or as means of symbol shorthand" (Dundes 1962, 96), he deems that the motif unit is inadequate. The root of Dundes's criticism is that the motif is, according to him, not a structural unit.

To explain his argument Dundes uses a pair of concepts coined by the American linguist and anthropologist Kenneth Pike (1967): etic and emic (see ch. 1, §7.0, fn. 25 above). Pike's binary distinction—which originates from the modes of thought of theoretical linguistics and is etymologically derived from the suffixes of the terms 'phonetic' and 'phonemic'—refers to two approaches to the analytical study of any cultural item: language, narrative, literary works, items of art, or folklore. 'Etic' denotes a systematic approach where the concepts and analytical units are external to the object of study and to its cultural context, and do not account for the internal functional relations between the elements of that object. Etic units are objective, predetermined, and measurable independent of the particular context. 'Emic', on the other hand, denotes an approach whose concepts and units are conceived with attention to the internal function and reciprocal relations between the elements of the object. It emphasises the structure that these elements constitute, as well as the cultural context of the object at hand. One may add that such an approach takes into consideration two contexts, the internal one which is formed between the constituents of the cultural item, and the external one which exists between that item and its culture.[26]

According to Dundes, the motif (as well as the tale type)—at least in the way it is used in folklore studies—is an etic unit, in that it pays no attention to the function of the motif in the context in which it appears. Dundes stresses the need for a new *emic* structural unit to serve as the fundamental point of reference for folklore studies. As a possibility, he (Dundes 1962, 100) quotes what he describes as "one of the most revolutionary and important contributions to folklore theory in decades": Vladimir Propp's (1962, 100) definition of the function, the structural unit proposed by him in his famous work about Russian fairy tales, *Morphology of the Folktale*,[27] where he states that "an action cannot be defined apart from its place in the process of narration" (Propp 1958, 19, quoted in Dundes 1962, 100).

---

[26] Another example for the various possible contexts is the acceptance of the item in its culture as an item—i.e., as a 'type'—as well as the relation item-audience in a particular performance—i.e., as a 'token'.

[27] In this work (which first appeared in Russian in 1928), Propp analyses a corpus of 115 Russian folktales. He defines 31 plot events, which he terms 'functions', which may appear in each of the folktales. The functions are generalised and formulated in a reductive manner. In the actual texts, they may take up various different surface realisations. What is striking is that, though any given folktale may have any number of Propp's functions, their order of appearance is fixed and invariable. Propp also defines seven types of characters which undergo the 31-one functions. Thus, the product of Propp's work, which is considered one of the first demonstrations of a structuralist approach towards texts, is a grammar of Russian folktales. For more detail, see Toolan (2005, 167),

The methodological approach known as thematology is an attempt to create tools which overcome these shortcomings of the concept of the motif.

3.2. Thematology: The Concepts

Thematology is a branch of the study of literature whose foundations were laid by scholars such as Trousson (1965) and Weisstein (1988).[28] The basis for the thematological study of Jewish literature, together with a new methodology, was proposed by Elstein and Lipsker (2004). Its central accomplishment is the multi-volume *Encyclopedia of the Jewish Story*, which presents entries on Jewish 'themes' (see §3.2.1 below).

At the core of the thematological study of Jewish narratives stands a system of concepts developed by Elstein and Lipsker. These concepts differ from the parallel concepts used in general thematology and the study of folklore, and aim to meet the requirements that the special characteristics of Jewish literature pose.[29] Some of the concepts were introduced specifically for thematology of Jewish narratives to accommodate their unique features—in particular, the tendency of Jewish narratives to be told and retold in numerous versions over long periods of time and

---

where he writes that "reactions to the *Morphology* [*of the Folktale*] provide striking parallels to some of the critical reception given to transformational-generative grammar in the 1960s.".

[28] In the context of Jewish culture, see also the numerous studies of Christoph Daxelmüller referred to in Elstein, Lipsker, and Kushelevsky (2004, 20–21).

[29] On the problem of terminology, see Elstein amd Lipsker (2004, 34).

wide geographical and cultural spaces, and to leave written documentation of many of these versions over these vast time and space scopes. For example, we find about forty distinct written versions of the famous story of Ḥoni the Circle Maker who prayed for rain,[30] and these are almost evenly distributed over a period of thirteen centuries (Tohar 2013). These different versions, though showing immense variation, all tell the same story: they are constructed on the same structural skeleton, the same chain of motifemes (the same 'constant', see §3.2.2 below). To describe this phenomenon of a series of varied versions of the same narrative, which unfolds over a long period of time and wide geographical areas, the term 'homogenous series' was coined. In what follows, a description of the fundamental concepts of the methodology of thematology of Jewish narratives is given (based on Elstein, Lipsker, and Kushelevsky 2004, 9–21 and Elstein and Lipsker 2004).

3.2.1. The Homogenous Series

As mentioned, a striking feature of the literature of the Jews, which sets it apart from other literatures, is the tendency of Jewish narratives, often first found in the Hebrew Bible or in other classical Jewish sources, to be told and retold over and over again in varying versions, many of which have come down to us in written form. A single story may exhibit several dozens of versions, each of which differs from the rest, but all nevertheless telling the same recognisable story. Each individual version of

---

[30] The most famous of which is in the Mishna, tractate Taʿanit 3.8.

the series may originate from anywhere across a vast geographical and cultural space—from anywhere inhabited by Jews. It may be told in any of the Jewish languages and come from any period of Jewish history.

In the thematological methodology, it is the series itself—rather than any single version of the story—that becomes the object of investigation. Trends in the development of the series as a whole are discovered, and its trajectory may be contextualised in extra-textual observations. The homogenous series, also sometimes simply referred to as a 'theme', is the central object of study in the methodology proposed by Elstein and Lipsker. It is different from what is in many instances the object of other thematological studies, the heterogeneous series, where texts are grouped and studied together based on a looser resemblance, for instance, the use of the same set of motifs.

3.2.2. Levels of Text

In the methodology proposed by Elstein and Lipsker, six levels of text are analysed. The levels are hierarchical: each level contains the previous. In addition, each level is paired with a corresponding concept that describes the elements of which that layer is composed.

> 1. The level of material (*Stoff*)—the concept of motif: the motif (see §3.1 above) is a small unit of narrative syntax. It belongs to the level of the textual material. A motif may be a narrative element, such as a ring, a wedding, rain, or a dance. The motif, when treated as an independent unit, is an abstraction detached from context, and is not sufficient

for the study of its original literary environment. In reality, motifs always appear within given textual contexts, and therefore they perform a function, or participate in performing a function, of narrative syntax. Only when it is looked upon as an organic part of its original context can a motif lend itself to hermeneutic deciphering.

2. The level of function—the concept of motifeme: the motifeme[31] is the smallest functional unit of a narrative. As opposed to the motif, which is accounted for outside of the texts it originated from, the motifeme cannot be considered an abstraction detached from its place in the narrative—it is always a part of that context. Its functional value is manifested in that it is the binding principle of motifs. The motifeme is the element that forms meaningful connections between individual, abstract, meaningless motifs and anchors them in a meaningful narrative sequence. Therefore, it is the prime unit of the narrative. It constitutes the link between the units of the material and their role in the text and gives meaning to both—to the motifs and to the textual sequence. It is the central building block in thematological methodology, and is what replaces the motif (which was given this fundamental role in some other schools of folkloristics and literary study) as the smallest meaningful—that is, meaning-carrying—unit of the text. In a narrative sequence, the motifeme may be either an

---

[31] The term was coined by Pike (1954, 75). Elstein and Lipsker (2004, 38) and Elstein, Lipsker, and Kushelevsky (2004, 11) erroneously ascribe its coining to Dundes (1962).

element of the storyline or an element of poetic function (introduction, epilogue, scenery, description of the non-storyline elements, and so on).

3. The level of structure—the concept of constant: the constant is the chain of motifemes which recur in all versions of a particular narrative. It is formed by the homogenous series, and is what is common to all of its incarnations. Different versions may give more or less emphasis to particular motifemes of the constant. The variation in emphasis given to each motifeme in a particular token of the constant enables the researcher to infer conclusions about the telos (see below). The variety in the ways in which a constant materialises in different versions of a narrative raises the question of the borders of the homogenous series: a version which omits one or two of the motifemes will normally be considered a member of the series, but what about more remote versions on the spectrum of change? Here, the judgement of the researcher plays a role.

4. The level of ideas—the concept of telos: the telos represents the quality related to ideals and values of the homogenous series as a whole, as well as of each individual instantiation of it. Each change from one version to another in the chain of versions, each particular emphasis or unique expression of a motifeme in a version, may be linked to a value or ideal prevalent in the intellectual and social atmosphere in which that version was created. The concept of telos links literary development and literary entities to

social, non-literary, realities. Thus the analysis of a complete homogenous series can point to long-term trends of change in the extra-literary reality of the community to which that series belongs.

5. The two mediatory levels: in addition to these four main levels of the text, there are two mediatory levels, which Elstein and Lipsker call 'teleological mediators'. These are the 'configuration', which mediates between the motif and the motifeme, and the 'substructure', which meditates between the constant and the telos.

a. The configuration: a configuration is a set of motifs that show a tendency to appear together in the same alignment. Examples of this from familiar tales would be a dragon which guards gold or a wolf which is in a forest. As such, the configuration is still detached from the textual connectivity which would give it meaning, and still does not lend itself to hermeneutic deciphering. It is a mediatory stage which organises the motifs before the motifeme grants them their narrative meaning.

b. The substructure: the substructure is similar to the telos, in that it is an extra-literary reality which gives form to the literary object. The substructure is, however, not a formal, well-structured, system of ideas, beliefs, or moral values which are consciously retained by a society, but rather an unconscious, implicit, state of mind which is prevalent in society at the period when a story version originates.[32] The

---

[32] The examples of substructure given by Elstein and Lipsker (2004, 46–47) are the implicit norms of the courtly love of the Middle Ages as the

substructure is thus a mediatory stage between the constant and the telos.

4.0. Transposed Motifemes

As we have seen, Elstein and Lipsker propose a methodology which has a fixed sequence of motifemes, the constant, at its centre. It emphasises the structural similarity between the many versions of each narrative, seen collectively as a set—the homogenous series. This methodological approach relies on a shared structural thread of motifemes, on the homogeneity of the series: its principal object of study is not the narrative itself nor an individual version of it, but rather the homogenous series as a whole, the development of the narrative over time. This approach is particularly fruitful when applied to Jewish literature and folk-literature due to their striking tendency to tell and retell narratives, and to leave traces, i.e., written attestations, of many of the retold versions over very long periods.

What I would like to suggest here is an approach that considers the matter through an equally important feature of Jewish literary folk-traditions, and indeed Jewish literature as a whole, a feature which is very much present in the oral heritage of the Jews of Kurdistan. This is a feature that represents the opposite impulse from the retention of the same motifemic structure that produces the homogeneity of the homogenous series. It is the tendency to mix into a story narrative elements taken from various historical periods and cultural realms in a way which bypasses

---

platform of the medieval romance and the Heavenly City as portrayed in the writings of the 18th century.

the chronological development of the series. A reiteration of a narrative may unexpectedly contain a motifeme 'foreign' to the constant of the series, or more accurately what has been the constant up to this point. In many cases, this newly planted motifeme is taken from another, entirely different, and sometimes traceable, narrative. It is, so to speak, transposed from its 'original' locus and incorporated into a new one by the teller or the community that creates the narrative. I call this phenomenon the 'transposed motifeme'.

4.1. Manners of Transposition

What is interesting in tracing the origin of transposed motifemes is that there seem to be few constraints on what these origins may be: motifemes may be borrowed intra-culturally from narratives originating in the same culture, but of completely different genres, periods, and content, or they may also be borrowed extra-culturally. What is offered here is an analysis that follows the life of the motifeme: its migration from one series to the other and the changes it undergoes.

There are several ways in which a motifeme may be transposed. Here these will be exemplified using the motifemes which will be discussed in more detail in the following section.

A motifeme may be taken from an entirely different narrative or non-narrative text. This other text may be a Jewish one—for example, the motifeme in §5.9, that of the merging of the stones, is taken from a non-narrative portion of a Jewish text, the Zohar, which may itself have derived the idea from the appearance of a motifeme of merging stones in relation to the stones of

Jacob, attested in many places in classical rabbinic literature. Alternatively, the originating text might be one of another culture—for example, the in motifeme §5.10, that of splitting one's opponent into two without him realising this, is taken from the Assyrian folk-epic, Qaṭine.

A motifeme can also be taken from the very same narrative, but transposed into a new location in it. This may be a result of a structural change, or a result of mere stylistic choice of the storyteller. Examples of this can be seen with the motifemes in §§5.17 and 5.18, where in the biblical narrative the episode of Saul and David in the cave appears before the episode of Abigail, whereas in Samra's story the order is reversed. Another example is the motifeme §5.5, where speaking to the crowd at a funeral is transposed from Boaz's wife's funeral to Boaz's own funeral.

A special case of transposition within a narrative is a motifeme which retains its previous location in the narrative sequence, but where the causality structure is altered: the causality nexuses linking the motifeme to previous or subsequent events (motifemes) in the narrative are different from those in earlier versions of the narrative. This is a very subtle transposition. An example of this can be seen in the motifeme in §5.12, where king Saul's illness is explained as resulting from his anger and his realisation that David will become king instead of him. In the biblical text, Saul is not said to have an illness, and the explanation given for his behaviour is "an evil spirit from God" (1 Sam. 16.14).

Naturally, when motifemes are transposed from different sources and fused together in the new narrative, new causality structures appear. An example of this can be seen in the motifeme in §5.13, where Jonathan's recommendation of David as the one to play music for his father king Saul is explained as resulting from Jonathan having seen David playing for the sheep and his compassionate care of them.

A motifeme may be split, and told in portions in non-sequential parts of the narration, as occurs with that in §5.8.

Two previously independent motifemes may be unified into one. An example of this is seen in the motifeme in §5.18, where two separate episodes of the biblical narrative, the episode of the cave and the episode in Saul's camp, are united into one in Samra's story.

The location of a motifeme, or its historical context, may be altered. In the motifeme in §5.4, what takes place in the biblical narrative at the city gate instead takes place in Samra's story at the synagogue; and in the motifeme in §5.8, the biblical location of the Elah Valley is now Jerusalem. Similarly, when it comes to the motifeme in §5.17, in the Bible the episode takes place in biblical Ma'on and Carmel, and in Samra's story it takes place near the modern city of Haifa. The modern neighbourhood of Gilo in Jerusalem is also mentioned.

Another type of manipulation of the motifemic structure, which is not a transposition in the strict sense but nonetheless may be considered in the same category, is what the scholar James Kugel termed "narrative expansion" (Kugel 1994, 3–5,

276).³³ This is the elaboration of a previously existing motifeme in the narrative sequence. This elaboration can be so expansive that, in the new narrative, what was previously one short motifeme has grown into a whole episode, which in and of itself contains several subordinate motifemes. An example is the motifeme in §5.1, where Naomi's righteousness—in itself a motifeme transposed into the narrative from classical rabbinic literature—is described at length, and includes her cooking the Jewish-Kurdish *xamuṣta* soup and giving some to her poor neighbours.³⁴

5.0. Motifemes in Samra's Story

In what follows 19 of the motifemes contained in Samra's story are listed. Each subsection begins with a description of the motifeme³⁵ as told in Samra's story, and continues with a discussion of the sources of the motifeme. The intention is to demonstrate the varied histories and transposition processes of the motifemes.

5.1. Naomi and Elimelech's Wealth, the Charity of Naomi (14)–(35)

Naomi and Elimelech are rich.

---

³³ Kugel (1994, 4), however, defines the narrative expansion as an exegetical device which is "based on something that *is* in the [original] text" (original emphasis).

³⁴ For further discussion of types of motifeme transposition, see §6.0 below.

³⁵ Some of the subsections deal with groups of interconnected motifemes, rather than a single one.

(19) ᴴʿaširìmᴴ wélu,' ʾəswá-lu ᴴsadè,ᴴ' ʾəswá-lu... xə̀ṭṭe,' ʾəswá-lu...'
'They were rich, they had a field, they had... wheat, they had...'

Naomi is a charitable woman, taking care of her needy neighbours and giving them some of the produce that God has given her. For example, whenever she cooks *xamuṣta*[36] soup, she makes sure her needy neighbours have some, too.

(23) ᴴšəxenímᴴ dídi làtlu?!' ʿa[w]òn-ile!' (24) g-daryáwa xápča gə̀rsa,' g-daryáwa xápča...' màd-ʾətla,' xà qárʾa,' hàʾ' ʾúzlu,' kutéle ta-yalúnke dìdax,' lá šoqátte bésax spìqa.'

'"My neighbours do not have [any]?! It's a sin!" She would put some cracked wheat, would put some... whatever she had [lit. has], a zucchini, "Here," [she says to the neighbour,] "make [=cook] [with] these some dumplings[37] for your children, don't leave your home empty [of food]."'

---

[36] A sour soup made with meat-filled dumplings. See following footnote.

[37] The dish *kutèle* 'meat-filled dumplings' is very popular in Jewish-Kurdish cuisine, particularly in a sour green vegetable soup called *xamuṣta*; see Shilo (1986, 80–81, 139, 142–43). The *kutèle* will appear again in the narrative: when they return to Bethlehem, Naomi sends Ruth to glean ears of grain. Naomi says she would make dumplings with whatever Ruth brings: (49) u-ʾóz šəbbólim bàsru,' mèse,' deqànnu garsànnu g-ozànnu,' b-ózax kùtele' b-àxlax.' 'Make ears of grain behind them [=the harvesters, i.e., glean], bring [here what you have gleaned], I will crack [lit. knock (in a mortar)], grind them, prepare them, we shall make dumplings, we shall eat.'

Her husband, Elimelech, is angry with her for giving away their property. In order to prevent her from giving away any more he decides to move to the city of Meʾohav (in the Bible, Moab).

(33) *krǝ̀ble mə́nna,¹ g-érra là g-šoqə́nnax go-bet-lèḥem.¹ g-yáwat ràba...¹ kúlla dawə́lti b-yà[wa]tta.¹* (34) *wàlox¹ g-zèda dwə́ltox!¹ là-g-naqṣa!¹ ʾálḷa d-húlle húlle ṭàli¹ yáwan ta-ġèri šíʾ!¹ là-q-qabǝlwa.¹* (35) *qam-nabə̀lla¹ qam-nabə́lla l-...bážǝr mǝʾohàv,¹*

'He got angry with her, he tells her, "I will not let you stay [lit. leave you] in Bethlehem. You give a lot... you will give [away] all of my property." "Look now, your property will increase! It will not lessen! God, who gave, gave to me [in order that] I should give to others [lit. my other = other than me] also." He didn't accept. He took her. He took her to... the city of Meʾohav.'

In the Bible, the reason that Naomi and Elimelech and their two sons Mahlon and Chilion leave the Judahite city of Bethlehem and move to Moab is famine: "And it came to pass in the days when the judges judged, that there was a famine in the land. And a certain man of Bethlehem in Judah went to sojourn in the field of Moab, he, and his wife, and his two sons" (Ruth 1.1).[38] There is no direct indication of their wealth in the biblical text, nor for Naomi carrying out charitable actions.

---

[38] All translations of biblical verses into English in this chapter are based on JPS (1917) and JPS (1999), with some modifications.

Many rabbinic sources describe Elimelech's family as members of the aristocracy.[39] Targum Ruth translates the phrase אפרתים מבית לחם (Ruth 1.2), otherwise rendered 'Ephrathites of Bethlehem', as 'leaders of Bethlehem', and mentions that Elimelech's family became 'royal adjutants' upon arriving in Moab (Levine 1973, 46–47).

One source of Naomi's description as a good, charitable woman is Midrash Ruth Rabbah 2.5 (Lerner edition): "'And the name of his wife Naomi' since her deeds were worthy (naʾìm) and pleasant (nəʿimìm)." (my translation)

A source for Elimelech's stinginess as the reason of leaving Bethlehem is Midrash Ruth Zuta 1 (Buber edition 1925, 40): "Thus he said: 'Tomorrow the poor gather and I cannot reside among them'" (my translation; see also Yalquṭ Šimʿoni Ruth 598). The following passage of the same Midrash states, however, that stinginess was common to all the members of the family: "Why did scripture mention his wife and his sons? Since they held each other back, out of miserliness that they all had. When the husband wants [to give charity] the wife does not want, or the wife wants but the sons do not want" (Midrash Ruth Zuta 2, Buber edition 1925, 40).[40]

---

[39] BT Bava Batra 91a; Midrash Tanḥuma Shemini 9; Midrash Tanḥuma BeHar 3; Seder ʿOlam Rabbah 12, Ratner edition (1897, 53–54); Midrash Ruth Rabbah 1.9; 2.5; Yalquṭ Šimʿoni Ruth 598.

[40] This Aggadah appears also in Yalquṭ Šimʿoni Ruth 599, and in Rabbi Tobiah Ben Eliʿezer, Midrash Leqaḥ Ṭov on Ruth 1.2, Bamberger edition (1887, 9).

The Jewish ʿAmidya NENA translation of Ruth 1.1 adds 'rich man' (Sabar 2006, 59).[41] The 'Ephrathites' in Ruth 1.2 mentioned above are translated as 'great' or 'heroes' (Sabar 2006, 59, fn. 3). A recorded performance by Ḥakham Ḥabib ʿAlwan of the Jewish Zakho NENA translation of Ruth translates 'Ephrathites' as *maʿaqule* 'noblemen, aristocrats' (ʿAlwan 1974). The Jewish Urmi NENA translation of the same verse states that they became 'high officials' in Moab, similar to Targum Ruth (Sabar 2006, 59, fn. 6).

5.2. Ruth and Orṭa are the Daughters of Meʾohav (40)

Elimelech marries his two sons to Ruth and Orṭa (in the Bible, Orpah), the daughters of Meʾohav (in the Bible, Moab):

(40) *məʾoháv ší ʾə́tle trè bnàsa:ˈ rùt,ˈ u-ʾòrṭa.ˈ qam-ṭaláblu ta-kútru bnóne dìde.ˈ*

'Meʾohav also has two daughters, Ruth and Orṭa. He [=Elimelech] asked for them [=for their hand] for both his sons.'

The book of Ruth does not mention any family relationship between Ruth and Orpah and the king of Moab. Nor does it indicate they are sisters. From the biblical text, it seems that Elimelech and Naomi's two sons, Mahlon and Chilion, were married only after the death of Elimelech (Ruth 1.3–4).

In classical rabbinic literature there is an old, well-established exegetical tradition that Ruth was the daughter, or the

---

[41] Sabar states that this may be taken from Rashi's commentary on v. 1.

granddaughter, of Eglon king of Moab, who was himself, according to the same tradition, the grandson of Balak king of Moab (BT Horayot 10b; BT Nazir 23b; BT Sotah 47a; BT Sanhedrin 105b; see Levine 1973, 48, fn. 6). A later source, Midrash Ruth Rabbah 2.9 (Lerner edition), states that Orpah is a daughter of Eglon as well, and therefore Ruth's sister.

5.3. Naomi's House Remains as She Left It (48)

When Naomi returns with Ruth to her house in Bethlehem, all of her wheat-grinding implements are still there, just as she left them.

(48) *psə́xla dárgət bet-leḥə̀m' tùla.' ...'ə́tla sə̀tta' u-garùsta' u-...' múx qamàe' bésa wéla mə̀l̲ya 'awáe.'*

'She opened the door of [her house in] Bethlehem, she sat [down].... She has a stone mortar and a hand mill and... like [it was] before, her house was full of things.'[42]

This motifeme does not appear in previous sources. Both the Bible and the classical rabbinic literature describe Naomi's return to Bethlehem in a way that may be interpreted as quite the opposite: in Ruth 1.21, Naomi says to the people of Bethlehem, "I went out full, and the Lord has brought me back home empty." Midrash Ruth Rabbah on v. 19 gives the following speech said by the people of Bethlehem:

> Is it she, whose deeds were good and worthy? Once she wore her colourful and woollen clothes and now she is

---

[42] These specific grinding implements reflect the realia in Kurdistan.

wearing rags, once her face was red from eating and drinking and now her face is green from hunger, once she went by sedan chair and now she is walking barefoot.⁴³

The association of Ruth and Naomi's return with grinding implements may be explained by the end of Ruth 1.22, "they came to Bethlehem at the beginning of barley harvest," and by the fact that the entire narrative from that point onwards is set within the period of harvest.

5.4. At the Synagogue (56)–(62)

After Ruth, heeding the advice of Naomi, spends the night at the foot of Boaz's bed, she asks him to marry her in levirate marriage (*yibbum*), since Boaz's father and Elimelech's father were brothers. Boaz tells Ruth to come with Naomi to the synagogue on the following day, where they will resolve the matter.

(56) *g-érra sé l-bèsa,¹ ᴴmaḥá[r]ᴴ bə́nne m-bə́noke sáloxun ʾəl-knə̀šta,¹ masyálax naʿòmi,¹ u-ʾána-šik p-áwən go-knìšta,¹ u-knı́šta m̭lı́sa jamàʿa,¹ b-ózaxni ᴴpšarà.ᴴ¹*
'He tells her, "Go home, tomorrow morning come to the synagogue, Naomi will bring you, and I will also be in the synagogue, and the synagogue is full of people, we shall make a compromise."'

---

⁴³ Midrash Ruth Rabbah 3 (Lerner edition); my translation. Original Hebrew: [ותאמרנה הזאת נעמי] אמרו, [זו] היא שהיו מעשיה נאים ונעימים? לשעבר היתה מתכסה בבגדי צבעונין ומילתין שלה, ועכשיו היא מתכס' בסמרטוטין, לשעבר היו פניה אדומות מכח האכילה והשתיה, ועכשיו פניה ירוקות מכח רעבון. לשעבר היתה מהלכת באסקפסטיות [שלה], ועכשיו היא מתהלכת יחפה.

On the following day, Boaz brings his 89-year-old elder brother to the synagogue, and asks him to perform the *yibbum* and to take Ruth as wife. The brother replies:

(58) ʾàxoni' təlta-ʾsár yalúnke ʾə̀tli,' u-ʾána ᴴməvugárᴴ lébi màḥkən,' lébi ʾəmmed-bàxti máḥkən,' (59) šqúlla ṭàlox' hóya bráxta ʾə̀llox,' wéla ᴴnàʿalᴴ dídi lúšla,' …(61) si-mbàrəx-la.'

"'My brother, I have thirteen children, and I am old, I cannot speak, I cannot [even] speak with my wife. Take her [=Ruth] for you, may she be blessed upon you. Here is my shoe,[44] wear it. …Go wed [lit. bless] her.'"

The congregation agrees. On the following day, Boaz and Ruth are married in the synagogue by performing the ceremony of the seven blessings.

In the Bible, the *yibbum* scene is recounted in Ruth 4.1–12. It does not take place in the synagogue, but rather at the city gate. Ruth and Naomi are not mentioned as being present. The

---

[44] Handing over one's shoe is associated with levirate marriage. In Deut. 25.5–10, it is stated that if a man does not wish to perform levirate marriage with his brother's widow, the ceremony of *ḥaliṣa* 'loosening of the shoe' must be performed: "Then shall his brother's wife go up to him in the presence of the elders, and loose his shoe from off his foot, and spit in his face; and she shall answer and say: 'So shall it be done unto the man that does not build up his brother's house.'" (Deut. 25.9). In Ruth 4.7–8, it is stated: "Now this was the custom in former times in Israel concerning redeeming and concerning exchanging, to confirm all things: a man drew off his shoe, and gave it to his neighbour; and this was the attestation in Israel. So the near kinsman said unto Boaz: 'Acquire for yourself,' and he drew off his shoe." See also BT Gittin 34b–37b.

legal procedure described in the biblical text is defined (in vv. 4 and 7) as *ge'ula*, the re-appropriation of agricultural land by a kinsman, and not *yibbum*, levirate marriage, as it is in Samra's narrative. Indeed, the *ge'ula* procedure as described in Ruth is not identical to the one formulated in Lev. 25.25–34, since the latter describes only re-appropriation of property and does not mention marriage. The inclusion of marriage to Ruth in the legal procedure creates a strong association with the *yibbum* procedure. In addition, one procedural component taken from *yibbum* (or, more accurately, from the renouncement of the *yibbum* obligation), namely *ḥaliṣa*—taking off the shoe of one party and giving it to the other party—does appear in the biblical text. In both the biblical and Samra's texts, the refusal of the more closely related *go'el*, or redeemer, is explained by his reluctance to marry an additional wife, Ruth, though in the biblical narrative, he initially agrees to acquire the land and withdraws his agreement only when he hears of his obligation to marry Ruth as well. The Bible does not reveal the familial relation between Boaz and the closer *go'el*, nor does it give any other identifying details, such as his name, age, or the number of his children. Boaz's taking Ruth as a wife is discussed in Ruth 4.13, but there is no mention of a ceremony of the seven blessings.

When it comes to the locale, Targum Ruth 4.1 translates the 'gate' as 'the gate of the court of the Sanhedrin' (see Levine 1973, 98).[45] Several classical rabbinic literary sources identify the closer redeemer as one of Boaz's paternal uncles and as a brother

---

[45] Targum Ruth translates Ruth 3.11 similarly. The Sanhedrin was the supreme rabbinical court.

of Elimelech (e.g., BT Bava Batra 91a; Midrash Tanḥuma BeHar 3). However, one source maintains that the *goʾel*, whose name is Tob, is indeed Boaz's elder brother (Midrash Ruth Rabbah 6.6 Lerner edition).[46] Boaz is said to have been 80 years old at the time of the marriage (Midrash Ruth Rabbah 6.4 Lerner edition; Yalquṭ Šimʿoni Ruth 606), thus an elder brother aged 89 is plausible.

Both the recorded performance by Ḥakham Ḥabib ʿAlwan for the Jewish Zakho NENA translation of Ruth (ʿAlwan 1974) and the Jewish ʿAmidya NENA translation of Ruth 4.1 (Sabar 2006, 74) name the *goʾel* as Tob, but do not provide details about his age, family relationship, or number of children. The recorded performance renders the 'gate' of Ruth 4.1 as *bes din* 'court of law' (ʿAlwan 1974). The ʿAmidya translation renders it as *darga d-sanhedrin* 'the gate of the Sanhedrin' (Sabar 2006, 74).

5.5. Boaz's Death and Elishay's Birth (64)–(83)

Boaz dies the day after marrying Ruth. Many people come to the funeral and Naomi, being a resourceful woman, publicly declares that the marriage took place, that Ruth spent one night with Boaz, and that if Ruth is pregnant, the child is Boaz's:

(77) ʾilá[ha] sàhəz u-náše sàhzi!ˈ kúllo márru ᴴbəsèder.ᴴˈ ʾilá[ha] hùlleˈ smə̀xla,ˈ máni sèle-la?ˈ k-ʾìtun máni?ˈ

"'God shall [bear] witness and people shall [bear] witness!" Everyone said, "Okay". God gave, she became pregnant,

---

[46] According to this and other sources, the name of the closer redeemer was Tob; this is derived from an interpretation of Ruth 3.13.

who came to her [=who was the child]? Do you know who?'

Ruth gives birth to Elishay.

The biblical text does not say how long Boaz lived after marrying Ruth. The name of their child was Obed, who was the father of Jesse (Hebrew *Yishay*), and Jesse was the father of David (Ruth 4.17–22).

Only one source in classical rabbinic literature mentions Boaz's death immediately after his marriage to Ruth, Midrash Ruth Zuta:[47] "They said, in the same night that he came unto her he died" (Midrash Ruth Zuta on Ruth 4.13, Buber edition 1925, 49; my translation). The motifeme appears in two later rabbinic sources: Yalquṭ Šimʿoni (Ruth 608) and Midrash Leqaḥ Ṭov (Rabbi Tobiah Ben Eliʿezer, Midrash Leqaḥ Ṭov on Ruth 4.17, Bamberger edition 1887, 44).[48] The latter contains a description of the actions which Ruth takes to prevent suspicion with regard to her fidelity:

> When Boaz came to Ruth, on that same night he died. And Ruth held him upon her belly the entire night so that they should not say that she was disloyal to him with another man. And when all came in the morning, they found him dead on her belly and therefore they named him [=the child] after Naomi [since she adopted him]. (Rabbi Tobiah

---

[47] On the problem of dating Ruth Zuta, see Shoshani (2008). Midrash Ruth Zuta was first published by Buber in 1894.

[48] Midrash Leqaḥ Ṭov is a Midrashic collection for the Pentateuch and the Megillot composed by Rabbi Tobiah Ben Eliʿezer in Macedonia during the 11th century. It contains both material derived from ancient sources and original material by the author.

Ben Eli'ezer, Midrash Leqaḥ Ṭov on Ruth 4.17, Bamberger edition 1887, 44; my translation)[49]

While the strategy to prevent suspicion described in this source is not the same as the one in Samra's story, Naomi plays a role in both.

The motifeme of speaking to the crowd gathered for Boaz's funeral found in Samra's story may have originated from the Midrashic description of the funeral for Boaz's wife:

> And some say that the wife of Boaz died on that day, and [the people of] all of the towns congregated in order to pay an act of kindness [= participate in the funeral]. Ruth entered with Naomi, and it came to pass that she [= Boaz's wife] was taken out and she [= Ruth] entered [at the same time]. And all the city was astir concerning them. (Midrash Ruth Rabbah 3.5–6 Lerner edition; my translation)[50]

In both texts, the gathering of a congregation for a funeral is exploited to serve as an event of interaction with the public. However, the two similar motifemes are positioned and integrated at two different points of the narrative sequence; this is an example of the transposition of a motifeme from one point to another within the same narrative.

The Jewish 'Amidya NENA translation of Ruth 4.14 associates the night of Boaz and Ruth's marriage with the death of

---

[49] Original Hebrew: ד"א ילד בן לנעמי ולא לבועז מלמד כשבא בעז אל רות באותו הלילה מת ותפשתו רות על בטנה כל הלילה שלא יאמרו זנתה תחתיו מאיש אחר וכשבאו הכל בבוקר מצאוהו מת על בטנה ולפיכך קראוהו על שם נעמי.

[50] Original Hebrew: ויש אומרים, אשתו של בועז מתה באותו היום, ונתכנסו כל העיירות לגמילות חסד, ועד כל עמה בגמילות חסד, נכנסה רות עם נעמי, והיתה זו יוצאה וזו נכנסת, ותהום כל העיר עליהן.

Boaz's previous wife: *qam do lele mətla bax-boʿaz u-mosele ʾaya, mən-ʾilaha* 'On that night the wife of Boaz died and he brought this one [i.e., he took Ruth], [it was] from God' (Sabar 2006, 76; my translation). This association between the two events may have opened the door for the transposition of the motifeme of the funeral for purposes of providing an opportunity for interaction with the public.

5.6. Elishay Suspects His Wife of Unfaithfulness (85)–(89)

Elishay (in the Bible, Jesse), the father of David, is angry with his wife. He chases her out of the house. She stays at her father's house for one month while pregnant with David.

(85) *krə̀bwale' mən-dè báxta' dammәd-wéla smə́xta bəd-dávid ha-mèlex.'* ...(86) *qam-karə̀dwala' xá yaŕxa zə́lla be-bàba.'*

'He got angry with this woman [i.e., his wife], while she was pregnant with king David.... He chased her out, for one month she went to her father's house.'

When she returns, Elishay does not believe that the child is his.

(86) *sèla' g-əmrà-le' qam-kardə̀tti' u-hə̀nna' u-ʾána báxta smə̀xta.' g-ér là' là!' léwat smə̀xta!'*

'She came, she says to him, "You chased me out, and this and I am a pregnant woman." He says, "No, no! You are not pregnant!"'

The wife calls God as a witness that she had not been touched by other men.

(88) *rəbbonó šel-ʿolàm¹ sáhəz ʾə́lla ʾe-bàxta,¹ báni básar lèwa nḥə́qta,¹ yála dìdox híle.¹*

"'Master of the Universe, bear witness to this woman, she has not been touched by humans, it is your child.'"

God is angry with Elishay for casting doubts upon the morality of his righteous wife and his paternity of the child.

(89) *rəbbonó šel-ʿolàm,¹ kʿə́sle ʾə̀lle.¹ g-er-yála dìdox híle,¹ má g-əmrə̀tta?!¹ bàxta,¹ ᴴnakiyà,¹ u-ṣadikà,ᴴ¹ màni b-náḥəq ʾə́lla?!¹*

'The Master of the Universe got angry with him. He says, "It is your child, what are you saying to her?! [She is a] clean, and righteous, woman, who would touch her?!"'

This motifeme has no trace in the biblical text. In classical rabbinic literature, the prominent trend is to portray Jesse as a person of impeccable behaviour and moral stature. He is mentioned as one of four people who never sinned (BT Shabbat 65b; Targum Ruth 4.22 [=Levine 1973, 41]; Rabbi Menaḥem Ben Rabbi Shelomo, Midrash Sekhel Ṭov on Exod. 6.20, Buber edition 1901, II:35). It is hard to see how this view is compatible with the motifeme in Samra's story.

There is, however, a source in which this motifeme does appear. Curiously, it is a work that did not have as wide a distribution in the Jewish world as other late Midrashic works: *Yalquṭ ha-Makhiri*. This is a compilation of earlier Midrashic material that was composed by Rabbi Makhir Ben Abba Mari, apparently in 14th-century Spain or Provence. In *Yalquṭ ha-Makhiri* on Ps. 118, we read the following story:

Jesse was the head of the Sanhedrin[51]... He had sixty grown sons, and he became celibate with his wife for three years. After three years, he had a beautiful female slave and he desired her. He told her, "My daughter, prepare yourself tonight in order to come to me in exchange for a release document." The slave went and said to her mistress, "Save yourself and myself and the soul of my master from hell." She said to her, "What is the reason for that?" She told her everything. She said to her, "My daughter, what can I do? For he has not touched me for three years now." She said to her, "I will give you some advice, go prepare yourself and so will I, and this evening when he says 'shut the door' you shall enter and I shall go out." And thus she did. In the evening, the slave stood and extinguished the candle, she came to shut the door, her mistress entered and she went out. She spent the entire night with him and was impregnated with David. And out of his love for that slave, David turned out redder than his brothers... after nine months, her sons wanted to kill her and her son David, since they saw he was red. Jesse told them, "Let him be and he will be enslaved to us and a shepherd." This was concealed for 28 years, until God said to Samuel, "Go, I will send you to the house of Jesse the Bethlehemite." (Rabbi Makhir Ben Abba Mari, Buber edition 1899, II:214)[52]

---

[51] The supreme rabbinical court.

[52] Original Hebrew: ...פליגי בה תרי אמוראי במערבא, חד אמר דוד בן אהובה היה וחד אמר דוד בן שנואה היה, כיצד ישי ראש לסנהדרין היה, ולא היה יוצא ונכנס אלא באוכלוסא בס׳ רבוא, והיו לו ס׳ בנים גדולים ופירש מאשתו ג׳ שנים, לאחר ג׳ שנים היתה לו שפחה נאה ונתאווה לה. א״ל בתי תקני עצמך הלילה כדי שתכנסי אלי בגט שחרור, הלכה השפחה ואמרה לגברתה הצילי עצמך ונפשי ואדוני מגיהנם, א״ל מה טעם, שחה לה את הכל, א״ל בתי מה אעשה שהיום ג׳ שנים לא נגע בי, א״ל אתן ליך עצה, לכי תקיני עצמך ואף אני כך, ולערב כשיאמר סגרי הדלת תכנסי את ואצא אני, וכך עשתה. לערב

Yalquṭ ha-Makhiri remained in manuscript form until it was published in six volumes by five scholars over four decades, starting in 1893. The volume that contains this passage was published by Shelomo Buber in 1899. Rabbi Makhir lists his source for each of the passages of his book, but the source given for this particular passage is simply "a Midrash." It is not to be found in any earlier extant rabbinic work.[53] However, the story does appear, in a different formulation, in another work from the same period and region, *Torat ha-Mminḥa*, by the 14th-century Spanish Rabbi Yaʿaqov Ben Ḥananʾel Sikili (or, of Sicily), which remained in manuscript form until 1991 (Sikili 1991, homily no. 23; referred to by Azulay 1957, 72). The story is then mentioned in several later sources, each giving a different formulation as well as different reasoning for Jesse's actions, and citing different biblical verses as support. It appears in *Keli Yaqar* (Laniado 1992, 416, on 1 Sam. 16.11),[54] a commentary on the books of the prophets,

---

עמדה השפחה וכבת את הנר, באת לסגור את הדלת נכנסה גברתה ויצאה היא, עשתה עמו כל הלילה נתעברה מדוד, ומתוך אהבתו על אותה שפחה, יצא דוד אדום מבין אחיו, מכאן אמרו חכמים צריך אדם לקשט עצמו ולעמוד כנגד אשתו בשעה שהיא עולה מבית הטבילה לט' חדשים בקשו בניה להרגה ואת בנה דוד, כיון שראו שהוא אדום, אמר להם ישי הניחו לו ויהיה לנו משועבד ורועה צאן, והיה הדבר טמון עד כ"ח שנה, כיון שא"ל הקב"ה לשמואל לך אשלחך אל בית ישי הלחמי... On the tension between David and his siblings in the Bible and in classical rabbinic literature, see Grossman (1995).

[53] Though, as Ginzberg (1909–1938, VI:247, fn. 13) states, BT Pesaḥim 119a gives a dialogue between David, Jesse, David's brothers, and Samuel, composed of the verses of Ps. 118.21–28. Three of these verses appear in the dialogue between David's mother and brothers in the passage in Yalquṭ Ha-Makhiri.

[54] This is referred to by Ginzberg (1909–1938, VI:246, fn. 11).

by Rabbi Shemu'el Ben Avraham Laniado (16th–17th century, Aleppo). Rabbi Menaḥem Azariah da Fano (1548–1620, Mantova, Italy) gives a long version of the story, considerably different from the *Yalquṭ ha-Makhiri* version and containing Kabbalistic interpretation, in his *Ma'amar Ḥiqqur ha-Din* (printed in 1597).[55] This passage by Fano is quoted in a responsum (printed in 1723) by Rabbi Ya'aqov Alfandari (17th century), which deals with a Halakhic question concerning the possibility of marriage between someone who may perhaps be a *mamzer*[56] and a released slave.[57] Rabbi Ḥayyim Yosef David Azulay (the Ḥida, 1724–1806) has the story in his *Sefer Midbar Qedemot* (Azulay 1957, 72) and in several other places in his writings.[58] Rabbi Eliyahu of Vilna (known as the Vilna Gaon, 1720–1797) gives a commentary on Rabbi Yosef Caro's *Yore De'a* 157:24 (Ginzberg 1909–1938, VI:246, fn. 11), where he simply adds the comment *ke-'uvda de-yišay* 'as the deed of Yishay' to a decree of Rabbi Moshe Isserles (the Rema) dealing with a disguised wife.

---

[55] Part 3, ch. 10. *Ma'amar Ḥiqqur ha-Ddin* was printed as part of Fano's *Sefer 'Asara Ma'amarot* (Fano 1649, 60a), referred to by Azulay (1957, 72).

[56] A child born from forbidden relations between a married woman and a man who is not her husband.

[57] Responsum 68 in Part A of *Sefer Muṣal me-'Eš*, a collection of Alfandari's writings that survived a fire; see Alfandari (1998, 95). This responsum was referred to by Azulay (1957, 72).

[58] For the various other places the story appears in Azulay's writings, see fn. 5 there. Azulay's version of the story is referred to by Ginzberg (1909–1938, VI:246, fn. 11).

Shinan (1996) notes that the *Yalquṭ ha-Makhiri* passage deals with but one case of a series of women in king David's ancestry who disguised themselves in an intimate situation: Leah and Jacob (Gen. 29), Tamar and Judah (Gen. 38), Ruth and Boaz (Ruth 3), and the daughters of Lot (Gen. 19). Shinan (1996) also claims that although the purposes of this tradition are not entirely clear, it must have a connection to Ps. 51. 7: "Behold, I was brought forth in iniquity, and in sin did my mother conceive me."

Curiously, a similar story is told by Josephus in his Antiquities of the Jews (book 12, ch. 4.6; referred to by Ginzberg 1909–1938, VI:246, fn. 11); in this case the story is about Joseph the son of Tobias who had a son, Hyrcanus, with his niece, who had been disguised by her father as an actress and with whom Joseph fell in love.

The fact that Elishay's wife stays at her father's house for a month in Samra's story represents the realia of marital life in Kurdistan. It was common for a woman, who would be living with her husband's extended family,[59] to take shelter at her parents' house for a period of time after a quarrel with her husband or her mother-in-law—there is a verb to describe this, *moxšəmla*.[60]

---

[59] On the patrilocal pattern of marriage in the Jewish communities of Kurdistan, see Aloni (2014a, 85–101); also Feitelson (1959, 207); Starr Sered (1992, 13).

[60] See Sabar (2002a, 201) on *x-š-m*: "(K[urdish]/P[ersian]) to feel alienated (daughter-in-law who after a quarrel goes back to live temporarily with her parents)."

5.7. David's Anointment (90)–(119)

God sends the prophet Samuel to anoint a son of Elishay as king. Elishay has six sons, and he presents them to Samuel by age. God had told Samuel to anoint the son that had a pillar of fire, the *Shekhinah* 'divine presence', upon his head. But Samuel does not see the pillar of fire upon any of the sons' heads.

(109) *maséle ʾaw-xət| stún núra lá xəzyàle.| (110) šmúʾəl hannavì,| márrele rəbbonó šel-ʿolàm| dámməd ḥmálla,| šəxína b-rèše,| ʾòha-le!|*

'He brought the other one, he didn't see the pillar of fire. Samuel the prophet, the Master of the Universe [had] told him, "When the Shekhinah stood [=dwells] upon his head, this is he."'

Samuel asks Elishay:

(111) *ʾətlóx xá bròna xə́t?|*

'Do you have another son?'

Elishay says that he has one more son, who is seven years old.

(111) *wéle go-^H sadè^H| ʾə́mməd ʾə̀rba,|*

'He is in the field with the sheep.'

Samuel tells him to fetch that son. He comes from the field wearing a *dəšdàša* 'ankle-length robe' and a white hat.

(113) *g-ér ḥmól ʾàxxa,| monə́xle bəd-rəbbóno šel-ʿolàm| šaxiná ḥmə̀lla.|*

'He [=Samuel the prophet] says, "Stand here," he looked towards the Master of the Universe, the *Shekhinah* stood [i.e., dwelt upon the head of that son, David].'

The prophet Samuel anoints David as king of Israel, using oil from the Temple.

The anointment of king David by Samuel is told in 1 Sam. 16. There God tells Samuel to anoint the son that he points out (16.3), Jesse brings forth his sons in order (16.7–10), and Samuel asks whether there are more sons and then instructs Jesse to fetch David from the field where he was tending the sheep (16.11).

The anointment is referred to, or retold, in numerous rabbinic sources, ranging from early Tannaitic works (e.g., Sifre Devarim 17; Midrash Tannaim on Deut. 1.17) to the late Midrashim.[61]

The motifs of the pillar of fire and *Shekhinah* are well-known from other places in Jewish literature, but both are absent from all sources that recount David's anointment. The biblical text states that "the spirit of the Lord came mightily upon David from that day forward" (1 Sam. 16.13), immediately after the anointment, but not before.[62]

David's age at the time of his anointment is not mentioned in the Bible. He is said to be 28 in *Seder ʿOlam Rabbah* (Ratner edition 1897, 57, ch. 13),[63] an early rabbinic work from the Tannaitic period, as well as in *Yalquṭ ha-Makhiri* (see §5.6 above) and in *Torat ha-Minḥa* (see §5.6 above).

---

[61] For a list of further references, see Ginzberg (1909–1939, VI:247–49, fns 13–23).

[62] Midrash Tannaim on Deut. 1.17 does, however, state that David prophesied as a young child that he would destroy the cities of the Philistines, kill Goliath, and build the Temple.

[63] Ratner notes that although the printed version is '29', the correct version according to manuscripts is '28'.

5.8. *Guri Kunzəri* (128)–(131), (179)–(181)

King Saul had *Guri Kunzəri*,[64] a suit of armour. Only the one chosen to be king, David, would be able to wear it. The suit is described as an object able to test the capability to fight Goliath.

(128) *mád ʾìz,' yalúnkəd yerušalàyim,' ṣróxle ᴴrámkolᴴ ʾàse,' ḥakóme g-ə́be qaṭə̀lle gòlias.' g-emer-ʾáwd lawə́šla ʾè bádla' ʾìbe qaṭə́lle.'*
'All of [lit. whatever there is] the children [i.e., boys] of Jerusalem, a loudspeaker called out that they should come, [since] the king wished to kill Goliath. He says, whoever wears this outfit, he is able to kill him.'

But it does not fit anyone. Only one boy has not tried the suit on, a seven-year-old boy who was left in the fields. King Saul orders him to be fetched.

(131) *qam-malušíla ʾə̀lle,' bə́r šoʾá šə̀nne,' yištabbáḥ šemò' rwéle qam-maḷèla!'*
'They dressed him with it [lit. it on him], [only] seven years old [i.e., therefore small], may His name be praised, he [=David] grew and filled it!'

When king Saul sees this, he is angry, since he feels that this boy, David, will become king instead of him. Later in the story, David refuses to wear the suit of armour, and insists on wearing his own *dašdàša* 'ankle-length robe'.

---

[64] From Kurdish *zirih* 'coat of mail' and *kum* 'helmet'; see Sabar (2002a, 161), where he also refers to occurrences of the word in Rivlin (1959, 233, 241).

(180) *gələləslə léwa ḫáš ṭàli!' lášši qèzla!' ᴴlò lò lò!ᴴ' makušə́nna mə̀nni' 'ána bəd-dəšdáša dídi b-azèna!'*

'Gələlələ it [= the suit] is not good for me! My body has been burnt. No no no! I'll take it off me, I shall go in my ankle-length robe!'

His reason for doing so is that he noticed Saul's anger, and he does not want to draw his animosity.

(181) *g-émer 'éne lá-hoya 'ə̀lli,'*

'He says [= his reasoning was], "His [= Saul's] eye should not be upon me."'[65]

The basis for this motifeme is to be found in 1 Sam. 17.38–39, immediately after king Saul agrees to send David to fight Goliath:

> And Saul clad David with his apparel, and he put a helmet of brass upon his head, and he clad him with a coat of mail. And David girded his sword upon his apparel, and he essayed to go[, but could not]; for he had not tried it. And David said unto Saul: "I cannot go with these; for I have not tried them." And David put them off him.[66]

---

[65] Interestingly, the Hebrew word *'oyen* 'hostile' in 1 Sam. 18.9 is derived from the same root as *'ayin* 'eye'. The (1917) JPS translation for the verse is "And Saul eyed David from that day and forward."

[66] One more exchange of clothes by David which occurs in the biblical narrative is in: "And Jonathan stripped himself of the robe that was upon him, and gave it to David, and his apparel, even to his sword, and to his bow, and to his girdle" (1 Sam. 18.4). The robe in this verse may be the source for the *dašdàša* 'ankle-length robe'.

This motifeme appears in several rabbinic sources (BT Yevamot 76b; Midrash Leviticus Rabbah 26.9; Midrash Tanhuma Emor, 4; Midrash Shemu'el 21, Buber edition 1925, 64).[67] In all these sources, the suit which Saul gives to David miraculously fits his size, Saul's dissatisfaction is visible, and David refuses to wear the suit for the battle, saying "I cannot go with these; for I have not tried them" (1 Sam. 17.39). In some of these sources, the miraculous fitting on David of clothing that belongs to Saul, who was previously described as being "from his shoulders and upward... taller than any of the people" (1 Sam. 9.2), is presented as a sign of David's future kingship:[68] for example, "even if a person is short, once he is appointed king he becomes tall" (Midrash Leviticus Rabbah 26.9; my translation) and "that is proof that David, may peace be upon him, was worthy for kingship" (Midrash Aggadah on Lev. 21.15, Buber edition 1894, 54; my translation). Nonetheless, in none of the sources is the suit presented as a test object, as in Samra's formulation.

Saul giving his coat of mail, helmet, and sword to David is mentioned in the epic song by Hakham Eliyahu Avraham Dahoki Mizrahi of Dohok published by Rivlin (Rivlin 1930, 114; 1959, 241), but there is no mention of a miraculous change in size in the song.

---

[67] Subsequent references to this tradition include: Midrash Aggadah on Lev. 21.15, Buber edition 1894, 53–54); Rashi on 1 Sam. 17.38; Abravanel on 1 Sam. 17.55.

[68] Cf. motif H36.2 "Garment fits only true king" in Thompson (1955–1958).

5.9. The Seven Stones (147)–(150), (162)–(164)

On his way to the battlefield, David collects seven stones to use with his *bardaqaniyye* 'slingshot'. As he picks up the stones, he proclaims:

(148) *bəzxút ʾavrahàm,ˈ [bəzxút] yitsḥàk,ˈ [bəzxút] yaʿaqòvˈ*

"'For the merit of Abraham, [For the merit of] Isaac, [For the merit of] Jacob'"

He continues in this manner to name five patriarchal figures. He puts the stones in his pocket. Before using these stones in battle, David again says:

(162) *yá ʾilàhi,ˈ bəzxút kúd xá u-xà,ˈ šóʾa nàse,ˈ*

"'O my God, for the merit of each and every one [of those] seven [sic] men'"…

He then puts his hand in his pocket and discovers that the seven stones he collected have become one stone.

> The biblical source of this motifeme is 1 Sam. 17.40:
>
>> And he took his staff in his hand, and chose him five smooth stones out of the brook, and put them in the shepherd's bag which he had, even in his scrip; and his sling was in his hand; and he drew near to the Philistine.

The following extract appears in Midrash Shemuʾel:[69]

> "And he took his staff in his hand, and chose for himself five smooth stones out of the brook," one for the name

---

[69] Original Hebrew: ויקח מקלו בידו ויבחר לו חמשה חלוקי אבנים מן הנחל, אחד לשמו של הקדוש ברוך הוא, ואחד לשמו של אהרן, ושלשת לשלשת אבות העולם, אמר אהרן לא אני הוא גואל הדם עלי להיפרע ממנו, [א"ל] [אמר] הקב"ה והלא לפני חירף וגידף, עלי להפרע ממנו…

> [=sake] of the Holy One blessed be He, and one for the name [=sake] of Aaron, and three for the three patriarchs. Said Aaron, "Is it not me who is the blood-avenger? I must take vengeance on him [=Goliath]!" Said the Holy One blessed be He, "But it is before me that he had taunted and cursed! I must take vengeance on him!" (Midrash Shemuʾel 21, Buber edition 1925, 64; my translation)

Here, there is no mention of the separate stones becoming one. The merging of the stones is reminiscent, though, of a famous Aggadah about the stones collected by Jacob, which appears in various formulations in several places in classical rabbinic literature, for example:

> It is written: "And he took of the stones of the place" (Gen. 28.11); but it is also written: "And he took the stone" (Gen. 28.18)! Said Rabbi Yitzḥak: "That teaches us that all of these stones gathered to one place, while each one of them says, 'Upon me shall this righteous man rest his head,'" a Tanna taught: "They were all merged into one." (BT Ḥullin 91b, my translation)[70]

The application of the motifeme of the merger of the stones to the stones of David appears in the Zohar in several places (Zohar III:272a; Tiquney Zohar 62a; Zohar Ḥadash 66b), for example:

---

[70] Original Hebrew: כתיב ויקח מאבני המקום, וכתיב ויקח את האבן! אמר רבי יצחק: מלמד שנתקבצו כל אותן אבנים למקום אחד, וכל אחת ואחת אומרת עלי יניח צדיק זה ראשו; תנא: וכולן נבלעו באחד. Also in: Midrash Genesis Rabbah 68; Midrash Tanḥuma VaYeṣe 1; Midrash Yelammdennu Genesis 128; Midrash Tehillim 91.6; Rabbi Tobiah Ben Eliʿezer, Midrash Leqaḥ Ṭov on Gen. 28.11, Buber edition (1880, 140–41); Midrash Genesis Rabbati 28.11; Rabbi Menaḥem Ben Rabbi Shelomo, Midrash Sekhel Ṭov on Gen. 30.13, Buber edition (1900, I:140–42); Yalquṭ Šimʿoni VaYeṣe 118.

"They were made one, all of the five" (Zohar III:272a; my translation).

In the epic songs published by Rivlin (1959, 246), the motifeme of the merger of the stones appears only in the epic song by Ḥakham Eliyahu Avraham Dahoki Mizraḥi of Dohok.

5.10. The Battle against Goliath (151)–(166)

David goes to fight Goliath. Goliath is surprised to see a child standing in front of him, and disparages him. In the battle, blows will be struck in turn. Goliath says:

(152) *mxí darbàdox [= dárba dìdox],*'

"'Strike your blow.'"

David replies that Goliath should strike first, since he is the one wearing armour and since David does not know how to strike.

(152) *mxí dárba dìdox¹ xázax mà šə́kəl-híle.*'

"'Strike your blow [and] we'll see what sort [of a blow] it is.'"

Goliath strikes his blow and destroys half a mountain. He causes David to go flying. God saves David, cushioning his landing. When David returns to the battlefield, Goliath is surprised that he is still alive.

(156) *g-er-má-wət ṣàx?! má?¹ g-er wən-ṣàx¹ ᴬḥamdu-l-là.ᴬ¹ bés ʾilá[ha] ʾmìra.*¹⁷¹

---

[71] See above, ch. 1, §14.0, proverb no. (79).

'He [=Goliath] says, "What, you're alive?! What?" He [=David] says, "I'm alive, thank God. The house of God is built[71] [=everything is well]."'

Now it is David's turn. First he proclaims:

(162) *yá ʾilàhi,' bəzxút kúd xá u-xà,' šóʾa nàse,'*

"'O my God, for the merit of each and every [of those] seven men'"

Then, using his *bardaqanìyye* 'slingshot', he shoots the single stone into Goliath's forehead.

(164) *ʾúzla gər-gər-gər-gər-gər qam-ʾozále trè qə́ṭʾe.*

'It made gər-gər-gər-gər-gər [and] it made him two pieces [i.e., sliced him].'

Goliath, not being aware that he has been split in two, asks contemptuously 'Is this your blow?', to which David replies by asking Goliath to wiggle a bit.

(166) *šʾə́šle gyàne' xá qə́ṭʾə mpə́lle mànne'*

'He wiggled himself, one piece fell off him.'

The battle between David and Goliath is described in 1 Sam. 17.41–50. Taking turns in striking is not mentioned there, or anywhere in classical rabbinic literature. The sources do not mention Goliath having a chance to strike—indeed, some of the sources state that upon seeing David, Goliath was rooted to the ground, unable to move (Midrash Leviticus Rabbah 21.2; Midrash Shemuʾel 21, Buber edition 1925, 65.

However, such a motifeme of taking turns in battle appears in the well-known folk-epic 'Qaṭine'. This folk-epic describes the adventures of the Assyrian national hero, Qaṭine. The various folk-traditions comprising this tale were shaped into the national Assyrian epic song *Zmīrta D'Qāṭine* by the 20th-century poet William Daniel, and published it in three volumes containing some 6000 verses (see Warda and Odisho 2000; Donabed 2007; Lamassu 2014). One version of the folk-traditions of this epic, known to the Jews of Zakho and told in prose, is attested in Shilo (2014, 148–65). In one episode in Shilo's version, Qaṭine fights against the hero of Armenia. In this episode, like in that recounting the battle of David and Goliath in Samra's story, the motifs of taking turns and cutting the opponent into two without him realising are both present. When Qaṭine's turn to strike comes, he cuts the hero of Armenia, head to toe, with his recently sharpened dagger. The hero is not aware that he has been cut and laughs at Qaṭine. Qaṭine asks him to dance a little before he strikes his third blow. When the hero does, he falls into two pieces.

Taking turns and cutting one's adversary into two also appear in the episode of the David and Goliath battle in the epic song recorded by Rivlin from Ḥakham Eliyahu Avraham Dahoki Mizraḥi of Dohok (Rivlin 1930, 116; 1959, 245–47).

5.11. Goliath's Sword and 'Eliya Ḥəttè and His Condition (167)–(178)

King Saul has ordered that Goliath's head must be cut off and placed before him, so that he knows that Goliath has indeed been killed; no sword but Goliath's own can cut off his head. David asks 'Eliya Ḥəttè (in the Bible, Uriah the Hittite), the bearer of Goliath's armour, to give him Goliath's sword, so that he can cut off Goliath's head and carry it to king Saul.

(172) *g-er-lá-g-yanne-lox [= la-g-yawənne-lox]*' *ʾə́tli šàrṭ ʾə́mmox*' *hákan yawə́tti xà-brat-yəsraʾèl,*' *b-yawə̀nne-lox.*'

'He says, "I will not give it to you. I have a condition for [lit. with] you: if you give me a daughter of Israel [i.e., a girl of Israel to marry], I will give it to you."'

David hesitates, but eventually agrees. As a result, God becomes angry with David:

(175) *g-er-lébox yáwət čù brát yəsraʾél ṭàle*' *ʾə́lla brát,*' *ʾáy d-híla* ^{H}*ba[t]-zzúg*^{H} *dídox bat-šévaʿ mən-*^{H}*šamáyim*^{H} *ksúta ṭàlox,*'*ʾa̋ya b-yawə́tta ta-ʾeliyá ḥəttè.*'

'He says, "You cannot give any daughter of Israel to him but the daughter, the one that is your spouse, Bathsheba, [which is] written [i.e., destined] for you from heaven, you will give **her** to ʾEliya Ḥəttè."'

David cuts off Goliath's head, and takes it and places it in front of king Saul. The Israelites are freed from Goliath and the Philistines.

(178) *zə̀lla,*' *ʾùrra,*' ^{H}*ra*^{cH}*-ʾáfe, mən-yəsraʾèl,*' *ʾilá[ha] b-yá[wə]l* ^{H}*ṭòv*^{H} *ta-ʾəsraʾél,*' *pə́šla šahyàna,*'

'That trouble went [away and] passed from Israel. God will give good to Israel, there was a celebration.'

David appoints ʾEliya Ḥəttè the head of his army.

David's decapitation of Goliath is recounted in 1 Sam. 17.51:

> And David ran, and stood over the Philistine, and took his sword, and drew it out of the sheath thereof, and slew him,

and cut off his head therewith. And when the Philistines saw that their mighty man was dead, they fled.

In v. 54, it is told that David brought Goliath's head to Jerusalem: "And David took the head of the Philistine, and brought it to Jerusalem; but he put his armour in his tent." The condition imposed by ʾEliya Ḥəttè regarding an Israelite woman alludes to the story of David and Bathsheba, told in 2 Sam. 11.

The idea that Bathsheba was David's destined wife appears in the Talmud: "Bathsheba the daughter of Eliam was destined for David from the six days of creation, but she came to him with pain" (BT Sanhedrin 107a). However, the Aggadah that identifies Uriah the Hittite as Goliath's armour-bearer, that says he is given an Israelite woman by David, and that indicates that God punishes David by making this woman David's destined wife Bathsheba, is quoted only by later sources. The earliest attestation thereto is an allusion in a commentary on Chronicles ascribed to a disciple of Saadia Gaon (10th century CE): "And the one who says that Uriah the Hittite was the military servant of Goliath, is wrong" (Kirchhiem 1874, 10; commentary on 1 Chron. 2.17; quoted by Lewin 1940, 189). The two earliest sources in which our Aggadah explicitly appears are Rabbi Shemuʾel Ben Avraham Laniado's *Keli Yaqar* (Laniado 1603, 293a, commentary on 2 Sam. 11.3) and Rabbi Moshe Alsheikh's *Marʾot Ha-Tzovʾot* (Alsheikh 1603–1607, 45a, commentary on 2 Sam. 12.1), which cites it as being from "a Midrash of our rabbis which became known though I have not seen it written [= a copy of it]." Though there is insufficient information to determine the exact years that Rabbi Laniado spent in the city of Safed, it is possible that the two rabbis lived there concurrently, during the latter half of the

16th century CE; it is certainly the case that their two books were printed in the same year and by the same publisher in Venice. Subsequent sources are *Petaḥ Ha-'Ohel*, an alphabetical collection of homilies and Aggadot by Rabbi Avraham Ben Yehudah Leb of Przemysl (1691, 15a); *Pney Yehoshuaʿ*, a Talmudic commentary by Rabbi Yaʿakov Yehoshuaʿ Falk (Falk 1739, commentary on BT Qiddushin 76b); and *Ḥomat 'Anakh*, a biblical commentary by Rabbi Ḥayyim Yosef David Azulay (Azulay 1803, 20b, commentary on Ps. 38.19). Lewin, who lists the two early sources by Laniado and Alsheikh and the later source by Leb (as well as additional sources which state that Bathsheba was indeed predestined for David, but do not relate specifically our Aggadah) in his *'Otzr Ha-Ge'onim* (Lewin 1940, 189–90), writes in the introduction to the volume that these relatively late sources do not seem to be the original source of this Aggadah (Lewin 1940, viii).

Our Aggadah does appear in the epic songs by Ḥakham Eliyahu Avraham Dahoki Mizraḥi of Dohok (Rivlin 1930, 116–17; 1959, 248), by Rabbi Ḥayyim Shalom son of Rabbi Avraham son of Rabbi ʿOvadya of Nerwa and ʿAmidya (Rivlin 1959, 253), and by Ḥakham Yishay of Urmia (Rivlin 1959, 299), all recorded by Rivlin. In the first song, David asks for Goliath's sword, in the second he asks for a key for Goliath's armour which was hidden in Goliath's beard, and in the third he asks Uriah to open the armour around Goliath's neck. In Samra's version both the sword and the key are mentioned. Rivlin writes about this Aggadah:

> As for the use of Aggadah by the authors of the [epic] songs, we should keep in mind that the Jews of Kurdistan also had a tradition and Aggadah, which may originate in lost Midrashim. We should not assume that all Aggadot in

these songs originate with the author. Such is the case with the Aggadah about Uriah the Hittite and Bathsheba in these songs, which is not to be found in the Midrashim, but a source for it was found[72] in the writings of the Geonim. (Rivlin 1959, 104; my translation)

5.12. Saul's Illness (183)–(184)

Realising that David will take his place as king, king Saul becomes angry and ill.

(183) *pášle ràba* ᴴ*ḥolé.*ᴴ' (184) *dúqle rèše,*' *ráḥqa mən-ʾəsraʾèl',* *màrʾa,*' *là-g-baṭəl!*'

'He became very sick. A pain, may it be far from Israel, caught his head, it does not stop!'

The Bible several times links Saul's "evil spirit from God" and David's success. Saul's condition is never described as an illness, let alone a headache. The first mention of the evil spirit occurs immediately after David's anointment by Samuel, as a consequence of it:

> Then Samuel took the horn of oil, and anointed him in the midst of his brethren; and the spirit of the Lord came mightily upon David from that day forward. So Samuel rose up, and went to Ramah. Now the spirit of the Lord had departed from Saul, and an evil spirit from the Lord terrified him. (1 Sam. 16.13–14)

It is the remedy to this evil spirit, the music of the harp, that brings David into the house of Saul for the first time:

---

[72] The source, the aforementioned commentary on Chronicles, was located by Lewin (Lewin 1940, 189; my footnote).

> Let our lord command your servants, that are before you, to seek out a man who is a skilful player on the harp; and it shall be, when the evil spirit from God comes upon you, that he shall play with his hand, and you will be well. (1 Sam. 16.16)

The second mention is after the battle against Goliath, when Saul witnesses the public support for David resulting from the battle:

> And Saul eyed David from that day and forward. And it came to pass on the next day, that an evil spirit from God came mightily upon Saul, and he raved in the house; and David played with his hand, as he did day by day; and Saul had his spear in his hand, and Saul threw the spear, thinking to pin David to the wall. But David eluded him twice. (1 Sam. 18.9–11; see §5.14 below as well)

One more time is again immediately after another of David's victories over the Philistines:

> And there was war again; and David went out, and fought with the Philistines, and slew them with a great slaughter; and they fled before him. And an evil spirit from the Lord was upon Saul, as he sat in his house with his spear in his hand; and David was playing with his hand. (1 Sam. 19.8–9)

It appears that the first time Saul's condition was 'diagnosed' as an illness is quite late. Rabbi Yitzḥak Abravanel writes in the 15th century:

> After the spirit of the Lord departed from him, he did not remain as the rest of men, but rather apprehensions and bad thoughts surrounded him, and his mind was always occupied with his punishment and with how the Lord had rent the kingdom of Israel from him, and how his good spirit departed from him, and due to that his blood burnt

> and the illness of melancholia developed in him, which is developed in men due to the burning of the blood and the burnt red humour, and the physicians have already written that this illness causes the loss of imagination and the faculty of judgement. (Abravanel's commentary to 1 Sam. 16.14; my translation)[73]

This notion that Saul has some kind of mental disorder recurs only very rarely in the history of traditional Jewish biblical exegesis. The passage by Abravanel is cited by Rabbi Meir Leibush Ben Yeḥiel Michel Wisser (the Malbim) in his 19th-century commentary on the same verse. Similarly, Rabbi Naftali Zvi Yehudah Berlin (the Natziv) writes in his commentary on Lev. 2.2 about "an illness of black humour which had come upon Saul" (my translation). Despite the few occurrences of this idea in traditional exegesis, reading a mental disorder into the character of Saul has become very common among modern readers of the text, in both academic and popular culture. However, I have not found any previous source that identifies the illness of king Saul as a 'headache'.

5.13. Jonathan's Friendship with David (185)–(190)

David and Jonathan, Saul's son and heir to the throne, are very good friends.

(185) xà roḥáya-lu' xà nəšáma-lu' xà-^{H}gil^H-ilu.'

---

[73] Original Hebrew: ...אחרי שסרה ממנו רוח השם הנזכר לא נשאר כיתר האנשים, אבל סבבוהו בלהות ומחשבות רעות, והיה תמיד דמיונו מתעסק בענשו ואיך קרע השם את מלכות ישראל מעליו ואיך רוחו הטוב סר מעליו, ומתוך זה נשרף דמו ונתהוה בו חולי המילאנ"קולייא המתהוה באדם משריפת הדם והאדומה השרופה, וכבר כתבו הרופאים שבחולי הזה יפסד הדמיון והכח המחשב...

'They are one spirit, they are one soul, they are the same age.'

Jonathan goes to visit David in the field. He sees that when David plays his *jezuke*,[74] all the sheep gather around him, bow their heads, and listen.

(185) *k-xáze damməd-g-máxe jezùke,' kúlle ʾérba k-èsē,' k-ḥàməl.'*

'He sees that when he plays his *jezuke* all the sheep come, stand.'

Jonathan finds another good quality in David: he treats with compassion the ewes that have given birth. He pets them, washes them, and feeds them with fresh green grass.

(186) *dàre...' go-ʾìze...' gəlla' yarùqa' yarùqa,' raʾìza' raʾìza' g-maxəlla.'*

'He puts... in his hand... green green [and] fresh fresh grass, [and] feeds her.'

It is Jonathan's friendship with David, and his seeing David playing music for the sheep, that causes him to recommend David's playing to his father Saul, as a cure for his headache.

In the biblical text, David and Jonathan's friendship appears in various places, for example:

> The soul of Jonathan was knit with the soul of David, and Jonathan loved him as his own soul.... Then Jonathan made a covenant with David, because he loved him as his own soul. (1 Sam. 18.1–3)

---

[74] A musical instrument. See fn. 131, below, and also ch. 3, fn. 56.

> And Saul spoke to Jonathan his son, and to all his servants, that they should slay David; but Jonathan Saul's son delighted much in David. (1 Sam. 19.1)
>
> David arose out of a place toward the South, and fell on his face to the ground, and bowed down three times; and they kissed one another, and wept one with another, until David exceeded. And Jonathan said to David: Go in peace, forasmuch as we have sworn both of us in the name of the Lord, saying: The Lord shall be between me and you, and between my seed and your seed, for ever. (1 Sam. 20.41–42)
>
> And Jonathan Saul's son arose, and went to David into the wood, and strengthened his hand in God. And he said unto him: Fear not; for the hand of Saul my father shall not find you; and you will be king over Israel, and I shall be second to you; and even my father Saul knows this is so. (1 Sam. 23.16–17)

However, the biblical narrative talks about David playing music for Saul before it mentions David and Jonathan meeting: "David took the harp, and played with his hand; so Saul found relief, and it was well with him, and the evil spirit departed from him" (1 Sam. 16.23). David's playing is thus not presented as a result of Jonathan's friendship.

The motifeme of Jonathan's friendship subsumes, in Samra's story, two additional motifemes: David playing music for the sheep and David feeding the ewes. Both are given as reasons for Jonathan's acknowledgement of David's worth.

A Midrashic tradition about taking care of sheep by giving them soft grass appears in three places in classical rabbinic literature: Midrash Tehillim 78 (edited prior to the 8th century CE in the Land of Israel); Midrash Exodus Rabbah 2.2 (probably edited in the 10th century CE; Shinan 1984); and Yalquṭ Šimʿoni Psalms 823 (edited in the 12th or 13th century CE). In these sources, unlike in Samra's story, David gives the soft grass to the newborn lambs, not to their mothers: "[David] would bring out the small ones to graze first so that they should graze on the soft [grass]" (Midrash Exodus Rabbah 2.2 Vilna edition; my translation). Furthermore, the focus in these sources seems to be David's ability to provide for each of his sheep in accordance with its needs:

> ...and then he would bring out the old [sheep] so that they would graze on the medium grass, and after that he would bring out the youths so that they would graze on the hard grass. The Holy One blessed be He said, whoever knows how to shepherd each sheep according to its strength should come and shepherd my people. (Midrash Exodus Rabbah 2.2 Vilna edition; my translation)[75]

This contrasts with Samra's story, where the focus is David's compassion towards the newborn lambs and their mothers.

In these sources, the fact that David takes care of the sheep is not said to be witnessed by Jonathan, nor is it connected to David's appointment as a musician for king Saul. Rather, it forms part of a tradition of stories about leaders being tested by God for their leadership skills, based on their performance as shepherds. God's response to David's action is to correlate the ability

---

[75] Original Hebrew: ויקחהו ממכלאות צאן, מהו ממכלאות צאן כמו ויכלא הגשם, היה מונע הגדולים מפני הקטנים והיה מוציא הקטנים לרעות כדי שירעו עשב הרך ואחר כך מוציא הזקנים כדי שירעו עשב הבינונית, ואח"כ מוציא הבחורים שיהיו אוכלין עשב הקשה, אמר הקב"ה מי שהוא יודע לרעות הצאן איש לפי כחו יבא וירעה בעמי, הה"ד מאחר עלות הביאו לרעות ביעקב עמו.

to shepherd sheep with the ability to care for people—a tradition that is also recounted in connection to other leaders, such as Moses. Samra indicates that David's behaviour is the reason for Jonathan's esteem towards him, although she does follow this with an element of the divine thereafter:

(187) *ə́tle ᴴlév ṭòvᴴˈ u-[q]urbáne ʾilá[ha] k-iʾè.ˈ ᴴgaluy-yadùaᶜᴴ-ile,ˈ k-iʾeˈ hàdxa-le,ˈ k-iʾe go-ləbbəd náše mà-ʾis.ˈ*

'He has a good heart and God [may I be] His sacrifice knows. It is well known [to Him] [lit. revealed (and) known], He knows it is so, He knows what [there] is inside the heart[s] of people.'

I have not found any attestation of the motifeme of David playing for the sheep in earlier sources.

5.14. King Saul's Sword and the Angel (191)–(193)

After a few days of David playing to king Saul in order to relieve his pain, Saul attacks David with his sword. An angel diverts the sword and causes it to hit the wall above David. Jonathan says:

(193) *qày,ˈ réšox k-ṭàrəṣˈ ʾaz-qáy q-qaṭlə̀tte?ˈ*

"'Why? Your head heals [when he plays for you] so why do you kill him?'"

King Saul replies:

(193) *p-qaṭlə̀nne.ˈ*

"'I shall kill him.'"

Two episodes are found in the Bible where king Saul attempts to smite David with his spear, 1 Sam. 18.10–11 and 19.9–10. Miraculous deliverance by an angel is not described there, nor anywhere else in the exegetical tradition. The only reference that I have found to there being something miraculous about David's evasion of the attack is in the commentary by Rabbi Levi Ben Gershon (the Ralbag, Gersonides) on 1 Sam. 19.10, where he states that David's being able to evade the strike was a miracle, since his attention was focused on playing properly at the same time.

5.15. King Saul's Promise (194)

King Saul makes a promise that whoever kills Goliath will receive half of the kingdom and marry his daughter Michal.

(194) ...*palgɔ́t dawɔ́lta p-póya ṭàle,ˈ u-bràtiˈ mìxalˈ ṭále ᴴmatanà.*ᴴˈ
"'...half of the wealth [or: kingdom] will be his, and my daughter Michal—a gift for him.'"

This motifeme originates from 1 Sam. 17.25: "And it shall be, that the man who kills him, the king will enrich him with great riches, and will give him his daughter, and make his father's house free in Israel."

The promise to give half of the kingdom echoes Est. 5.3: "'What troubles you, Queen Esther?' the king asked her. 'And what is your request? Even to half the kingdom, it shall be granted you'" (see also Est. 5.6; 7.2).

5.16. The Cave of Elijah the Prophet (195)–(200)

David escapes from king Saul and hides in the Cave of Elijah the Prophet in Haifa. He has with him eight hundred men.

The Cave of Elijah the Prophet is a well-known pilgrimage site, located on Mount Carmel in the city of Haifa. The Bible states, one chapter before the episode with Abigail (see the following subsection) that while being pursued by king Saul, David and his men stayed in a cave in the desert of En-Gedi (1 Sam. 24.1–2). The episode with Abigail, in ch. 25, is said to take place in the area of Maʿon and Carmel, two biblical Israelite settlements located in Judah to the south of Hebron. The association of the cave of David and his men with the Cave of Elijah the Prophet on Mount Carmel in Haifa in Samra's story is due to the coincidentally identical names of the biblical settlement and the mountain. In the biblical narrative, the En-Gedi cave is not a part of the Abigail episode, and it is in the desert of Judah, not in the region of Hebron. The cave is incorporated into Samra's story because it appears immediately before the Abigail episode in the biblical text.

5.17. Gila of Haifa (201)–(231)

The festival of Rosh Hashana is approaching, and David needs sustenance for his men. A very rich man, Elimelech, lives in Haifa; he owns flour-mills. His wife, Gila, is also very rich, and she owns the neighbourhood of Gilo (in Jerusalem), which her father had named after her. David sends two soldiers to ask for sustenance for Rosh Hashana, but Elimelech refuses. He replies to Gila's protests:

(206) lá g-ya[wə̀]nne čù-məndi.ˈ fèrat ̍ yàtwat ̍ ha-ʾàsqad šī la-g-ya[wə́]nne.ˈ

'"I will not give him anything. You [can] fly [or] sit, even this much I will not give him."'

Gila goes after the soldiers and gives them a written document permitting them to take anything they might need.

(210) *xamší kəsyása qàmxa,' mən-ṭaḥúnət qàmxa.' xamší bakbùke,' ʾəmmá bakbúke ᴴšèmənᴴ' mən-ṭáḥ-' ᴴšèmənᴴ dídi.'* ... (212) *sáʾun lə-ʾə̀rba,' ʾəmmá réše ʾə̀rba mèsun,' ʾúzule ta-ᴴróš-ha-šanà.*ᴴ'

"'Fifty bags of flour, from the flour-mill. Fifty bottles, a hundred bottles of oil from my mi[ll], oil…. Come to the sheep, bring one hundred heads of sheep, prepare them [lit. it] for Rosh Hashana.'"

When Gila tells her husband she has given David's men all of that, he dies.

(218) *ʾóha mə̀tle,' pqèʾle l-dúke,' mə̀tle l-dúke!'*

'This one [=the husband] died, he exploded [i.e., died from anger] on the spot [lit. his place], he died on the spot [lit. his place]!'

After the mourning period for her husband, Gila invites David to visit. He thanks her for the food she sent, and she proposes giving him all of her property if he marries her. David agrees and marries her.

This episode is told in 1 Sam. 25.2–43. However, Samra's version differs from that one on several points.

The names of the couple in the Bible are Nabal and Abigail. Samra uses Elimelech, the same as the name of the husband of

Naomi at the beginning of Samra's narrative,[76] and Gila, after whom Gilo was said to be named by her rich father. The modern-day neighbourhood of Gilo in Jerusalem is located near the Palestinian town of Beit Jala, thought to be the site of biblical Gilo,[77] which appears later in the biblical narrative: it is the home of Ahitophel the Gilonite (2 Sam. 15.12), David's counsellor and the grandfather of Bathsheba (2 Sam. 11.3; 23.34; cf. 1 Chron. 3.5). I have found no previous source presenting an association between Abigail and Gilo, nor any which states that Abigail was rich in her own right.

As explained with regard to the motifeme in §5.16 above, in Samra's story Gila and Elimelech's home is located in the modern city of Haifa because the biblical settlement of Carmel shares its name with Mount Carmel near Haifa.

In the Bible, Nabal is said to be a wealthy owner of herds of sheep and goats. In Samra's narrative, he is the owner of flour-mills. This is perhaps taken from the realia of Kurdistan, where millers were among the wealthy property owners.

The Bible indicates that this episode took place when Nabal was shearing his sheep. Although shearing, as a family celebration, did not have a fixed time, it most commonly occurs during the spring.[78] In Samra's story, the episode takes place just before

---

[76] A point of similarity between the two characters called Elimelech is that they do not allow their wives to use their wealth to provide goods to those in need.

[77] Though a more probable identification is Ḥirbet Jala in the Hebron area; see Luncz's comment in Schwarz (1900, 126).

[78] On shearing as a familial feast in the Bible, see Haran (1972).

Rosh Hashana, at the beginning of autumn. This originates from BT Rosh HaShana 18a, where Rav Naḥman ascribes to Rabba Bar Abbuha the opinion that the ten days of Nabal's sickness (1 Sam. 25.38) were the ten days between Rosh Hashana and Yom Kippur (see also Yalquṭ Šimʿoni Samuel 134; Rashi on 1 Sam. 25.38). The notion that David needed sustenance for his men for the feast of the eve of Rosh Hashana comes from Rashi's commentary on 1 Sam. 25.8.

In the Bible, it is David who "sent and spoke concerning Abigail, to take her to him to wife" (1 Sam. 25.39), whereas in Samra's story the initiative comes from her. This is possibly due to the interpretation of 1 Sam. 25.31 by the rabbis—after convincing David not to punish Nabal, and referring to his future as king of Israel, Abigail says to David, "then remember your handmaid." The rabbis understood this as a hint for David to marry her after the death of Nabal (BT Bava Qamma 92b; BT Megilla 14b; JT Sanhedrin 2.3;[79] and many other subsequent commentators). Samra's version is also reflective of the independence and assertiveness of the Jewish women of Kurdistan in matters pertaining to marriage.[80] Abigail's independence and assertiveness are also stressed in Samra's story when she issues a written document permitting David's soldiers to take abundant goods from

---

[79] JT = Jerusalem Talmud, Vilna edition.

[80] See Sabar (1982c, xv): "Kurdish women in general enjoy more freedom and a wider participation in public life than do Arab, Persian, and Turkish women. They are also freer in their behavior towards males and rarely wear the veil." On the life of Jewish women in Kurdistan, see Brauer (1947, 147–57; 1993, 175–89).

her and her husband's property, and by emphasising that she was wealthy in her own right and not only due to her husband.

5.18. David Finds King Saul Asleep (233)–(234)

David finds king Saul asleep. He cuts a piece of his coat, takes a bite of his apple, and drinks from his water, but he does not hurt him.

(234) *ksúle ṭàle,' ʾána là' q-qaṭlə̀nnox,' ʾàhət' g-ə́bət qaṭlə̀tti' ʾána lá-g qaṭlə̀nnox,' ʾáhət ᴴmélex yəsraʾèlᴴ-wə́t.'*

'He wrote to him, "I shall not kill you, you want to kill me, I shall not kill you, you are the king of Israel."'

This draws from two separate biblical episodes. The first is in 1 Sam. 24, where, when Saul enters the caves in which David and his men are hiding, David cuts off a corner of Saul's cloak without him noticing. The second is in 1 Sam. 26, in which David and Abishai enter the camp of king Saul while the king and his men are asleep. David does not hurt the king, but rather takes his spear and flask of water. In both cases, the objects taken are used as proof of David's good intentions and reverence for the king of Israel. It is probably this similarity between the two episodes that led to their unification in Samra's story.

The unification of the two biblical episodes also appears in the epic song published by Rivin (1959, 257), where it says that David "ate a little from his plate, drank some water from his jar, cut [a piece] off from Saul's coat."

It seems that the three objects that are taken in Samra's story and in the epic song, instead of the one object in the episode in 1 Sam. 24, or the two objects in the episode in 1 Sam. 26, align better with a general tendency of folktales to use typological numbers.[81] I have found no source referring to king Saul's apple.

5.19. King Saul and Raḥela the Fortune-teller (235)–(242)

King Saul goes to Raḥela the fortune-teller.

(236) *báxta pasxáwa bəd-fàla,' k-iʾáwa má-ʾiz go-^H ʿolàm^H' má lès.'*

'A woman that used to open in fortunes [i.e., she was a fortune-teller], she knew what there is in the world [and] what there is not.'

He asks her to tell his fortune. She refuses, because she swore to king Saul three months ago that she would not tell anyone's fortune. Saul does not reveal himself, but promises her that he will ensure that the king exempts her from her oath. In the process of telling Saul's fortune, the prophet Samuel appears. He says:

(241) *šàʾul,' ṭláṭha] yóme ʾə́tlox piše,' ʾàhət u-kúd ṭláṭha] bnóne dídox ʾásət qṭàla.'*

"'Saul, you have three days [lit. three days you have remained], you and your three sons will be killed [lit. come to killing].'"

---

[81] That is, numbers that bear special symbolic meaning for a particular culture and tend to recur in many of its texts and art forms. For example, Law no. 14, "the law of three and the law of repetition," in Olrik's influential "Epic laws of folk narrative" (Olrik 1965 [1908]) describes the many repetitions of the number three in European folktales (Olrik's study was of folktales of European origin). In the Hebrew Bible, the numbers seven, ten, twelve, and forty often recur.

King Saul gets sick, and Raḥela takes care of him for three days.

(242) ʾúzlale ᴴmaràkimᴴ' šòrḅa' máyət ksèsa,' qam-maxlàle,' qam-maštyàle,'

'She made for him soups, thick [rice] soup, chicken soup [lit. chicken water], she fed him, she gave him to drink.'

The story of the diviner of Endor is told in 1 Sam. 28,[82] although her name is not specified in the biblical text. Yalquṭ Šimʿoni gives the name Zephaniah, and states that she was the mother of Abner (Yalquṭ Šimʿoni Samuel 140).[83] Raḥela's reluctance to tell fortunes is rooted in vv. 3 and 9 of 1 Sam. 28:

> And Saul had put away those that divined by a ghost or a familiar spirit out of the land.... And the woman said unto him: "Behold, you know what Saul has done, how he has cut off those that divine by a ghost or a familiar spirit out of the land; So why are you laying a trap for me, to get me killed?"

The period of three months is not mentioned in the biblical text, nor is her oath not to tell fortunes. In the tragic message given to king Saul by Samuel, Samra's narrative specifies three days, a further period of three, where the biblical text gives only one day (1 Sam. 28.19). The fortune-teller's compassionate care towards Saul after he receives the tragic message is recounted in the Bible in vv. 21–25. However, Samra tells of thick rice soup and chicken soup—known folk remedies—as Raḥela's offerings, in lieu of the biblical fatted calf and unleavened bread.

---

[82] For a literary analysis of the biblical narrative, see Simon (1992).
[83] Another source claims that she was the wife of Zephaniah: Pirqey De-Rabbi Eliʿezer 32, Higger edition (1944–1948).

6.0. Conclusion

We have seen that various motifemes in Samra's story draw from different historical layers of Jewish literature, as well as from other traditions. The way in which the motifemes are amalgamated into a new cohesive narrative 'bypasses' the consecutive historical development of the homogenous series of Elstein and Lipsker's thematology of Jewish narratives, since motifemes are drawn from sources of various periods, and various cultural spaces, regardless of their historical consecutiveness.[84] This process in fact disrupts the homogeneity of the homogenous series. It is this non-linear borrowing of motifemes that I refer to as motifeme transposition.

It should be noted again that in addition to straightforward transposition of motifemes from one source to another there are several other mechanisms of motifeme manipulation:

- altered causality: keeping the motifeme structure of previous versions of the narrative, but tying them

---

[84] This criticism of Elstein and Lipsker's notion of the historical development of the homogenous series resembles Moshe Idel's criticism of Gershom Scholem's historical picture, expressed, for instance, in Scholem (1941). Idel (1990, xxiii) states: "Thus I am hesitant to conceive the history of Kabbalah as it appears in the written documents as a 'progressive' evolution alone. It seems that alongside this category we shall better be aware of the possibility that later strata of Kabbalistic literature may contain also older elements or structures, not so visible in the earlier bodies of literature. In other words, I allow a greater role to the subterranean transmission than Scholem and his followers did." See also Idel (1988, 20–22).

together with a new causal nexus (e.g., the motifeme in §5.12);
- unification: combining previously separate motifemes into one unified motifeme (e.g., the motifeme in §5.18);
- reorganisation of narrative time: the relocation of a motifeme in the narrative time sequence (e.g., the case of the motifeme in §5.5);
- subsuming: one motifeme subsumes under it several other motifemes in a hierarchical structure (e.g., the motifemes in §5.13);
- temporal transposition: the re-setting of a motifeme in a new historical period, or milder forms of anachronism (e.g., the motifeme in §5.16; the use of a 'loudspeaker' in the motifeme in §5.8).

7.0. The NENA Text and Its Translation

The text was recorded at the home of Samra Zaqen on 19 April 2012. Present at the recording session were Samra Zaqen (SZ),

Batia Aloni (BA), and myself (OA). The recording ID is SZ120419T1 9:30–37:29.[85]

(1)	BA: *k-taxrát mə́rrax b-sapràttan e...*ˈ	BA: Do you remember you said you will tell us eh...
(2)	SZ: *hè hé,*ˈ *ᴴsəppùrᴴˈ dəd hə́nna*[86] *g-əbètun...*ˈ	SZ: Yes yes, do you want [to hear] the story of *this*...[86]
(3)	BA: *mád g-əbàt.*ˈ	BA: Whatever you want.
(4)	SZ:...*dəd naʿòmi?*ˈ	SZ: ...of Naomi?
(5)	BA: *naʿómi u-rùt.*ˈ *ᴴʾavalᴴ mád g-ə̀bat màḥke.*ˈ *hakan-g-ə̀bat gèr-məndi*ˈ *gèr-məndi.*ˈ	BA: Naomi and Ruth. But tell [us] whatever you want. If you want [= prefer] something else [then tell] something else.
(6)	SZ: *ᴴlò-xašúvᴴˈ ʾátta wàʿdu-hile.*ˈ *séle ᴴzmàn.ᴴˈ*	SZ: Never mind, now it is its [= this story's] time. The time has arrived.
(7)	BA: *ᴴnaxòn.ᴴˈ*	BA: Right.
(8)	SZ: *séle ᴴzmàn.ᴴˈ*	SZ: Time has arrived.
(9)	BA: *séle wàʿdu,*ˈ *ᴴnaxòn.ᴴˈ*	BA: Their time has arrived, correct.
(10)	SZ:...*hé, g-emə́rwa—ʾiláha nàtə*[87]...*manə̀xle*ˈ *ʾaxòni*ˈ *go-gan-ʿèzen.*ˈ	SZ:... Yes, he used to say—may God sa[ve][87]... give rest unto him, my brother, in heaven.

---

[85] The recording is available for listening on the North-Eastern Neo-Aramaic Database Project site at https://nena.ames.cam.ac.uk/dialects/78/.

[86] See note on *hènna* in Introduction, §5.0.

[87] Samra started the word *natə̀rre* of the expression *ʾiláha natə̀rre* 'may God protect him', but changed it to the expression *ʾiláha manə̀xle* 'may God grant him rest'.

(11) g-emə́rwa naʿòmi...' u- e... šə́mmed góre hə̀nna wéle' ᴴrègaᶜᴴ'... ʾelimèlex!'
He used to say [=tell] Naomi... and eh... the name of her husband was *this*, [wait a] moment... Elimelech!

(12) BA: ʾelimelèx.'
BA: Elimelech.

(13) SZ: ʾélimelèx.'
SZ: Elimelech.

(14) skíne-welu go-bet-lèḥem.' ʾə́swa-lu ᴴbáyit gadòl,' parnasà ṭóvā,'
They lived in Bethlehem. They had a large house, good livelihood,

(15) háya-lahem sàde' ve-ḥə̀tta...ᴴ'
they had a field, and wheat...

(16) BA: wéalu ᴴʿaširìm.ᴴ'
BA: They were rich.

(17) SZ: máḥkax ᴴʿəvrìt' ʾóᴴ kùrdi?' là k-íʾan,'
SZ: Shall we speak Hebrew or Kurdish [=Neo-Aramaic]? I don't know

(18) BA: ᴴkùrdit!ᴴ'
BA: Kurdish [=Neo-Aramaic]!

(19) SZ: ʾə,' ʾəswá-lu,' ᴴʿaširìmᴴ wélu,' ʾəswá-lu ᴴsadè,ᴴ' ʾəswá-lu... xə̀ṭṭe,' ʾəswá-lu...'
SZ: OK, they had, they were rich, they had a field, they had... wheat, they had...

(20) BA: zangìn wéalu' ṛàba.'
BA: They were very rich.

(21) SZ: hè.'
SZ: Yes.

(22) ᴴʾazᴴ-ʾàya ʾə́swa-la trè bnóne.' ᴴʾazᴴ-ʾaya ᴴʾišà,' ʾáxi' tovàᴴ wéla.' ᴴʾišà' ʿim-lèv' patùaḥ.ᴴ' g-ə́ba yàwa.'
So she had two sons. So she was a very good [lit. the best] woman. A woman with an open heart. She wants to give.

(23) ʾəròta-la.ˈ ʾána mbášlan xamùṣta,¹⁸⁸ ᴴšəxenímᴴ dídi làtlu?!ˈ ʿa[w]òn-ile!ˈ

It's Friday. "Shall I cook *xamuṣta*,⁸⁸ [while] my neighbours do not have [any]?! It's a sin!"

(24) g-daryáwa xápča gə̀rsa,ˈ g-daryáwa xápča...ˈ màd-ʾə́tla,ˈ xà qárʾa,ˈ hàʾˈ ʾúzlu,ˈ kutéle⁸⁹ ta-yalúnke dìdax,ˈ lá šoqátte bésax spìqa.ˈ

She would put some cracked wheat, would put some... whatever she had [lit. has], a zucchini, "Here," [she says to the neighbour,] "make [=cook] [with] these some dumplings⁸⁹ for your children, don't leave your home empty [of food]."

(25) ta-dèˈ b-nàblaˈ xápča sayìhe,ˈ ʾúzlu mabòse⁹⁰ ta-yalúnke dìdax.ˈ la-šoqátte qanúnax spìqa.ˈ g-ozàwa.ˈ

To this [woman] she takes some crushed wheat, "Make [=cook] *mabose*⁹⁰ [with] these for your children. Don't leave your stove empty." She [that woman] would do [so=cook the crushed wheat].

(26) ʾàwaˈ ᴴləfʿamim̀ᴴˈ k-esèwaˈ k-xazèwa,ˈ ᴴʾoᴴ-wéla nabòle,ˈ ᴴʾoᴴ-wéla b-isàya,ˈ méka kàsyat?ˈ k-karə̀bwaˈ ràḅa.ˈ

He [Naomi's husband Elimelech] would sometimes come [and] see her, either while she was taking [produce to her neighbours] or while she was coming [back], "Where are you coming from?" He would get very angry.

(27) wàlox,ˈ là-karbət,ˈ ʾàḷḷa g-yáwəl ṭàluˈ yáwəl ṭàli,ˈ yáwan ta-xa-

"Look now, don't get angry, God gives to them, [He] gives to me, I shall give to someone

---

⁸⁸ A sour soup made with meat-filled dumplings. See fns 36 and 37 earlier in this chapter.

⁸⁹ See previous footnote.

⁹⁰ Sabar (2002a, 210) on *mabose*: "(< ב-י-ת)... Sabbath-food cooked overnight." Sabar (2002a: 110) on *b-y-t*: "ב-י-ת... to spend the night... to cook overnight... to keep overnight."

xə̀t.' ʾə̀tli,' g-ə́be yàwan!' xer-ʾalla!' là qabə́lwa.' k-karə̀bwa mə́nna.'

else! I have, [therefore] I should give! [It's the] benevolence of God! [i.e., it is not ours]" He did not accept that. He would get angry with her.

(28) kúllu gorgiát ḥə̀t' [= grásət xə̀ṭ[ṭe] ?]. ʾəswá-la dànga.' ʾəswá-la sə̀tta.' g-deqáwa mnòša.'

All of the grinding [implements] of wheat. She had a wooden mallet. She had a stone mortar. She would grind [lit. knock] by herself.

(29) g-deqáwa xə̀ṭṭe,' ʾəswá-la garə̀sta.' g-garsáwa gə̀rsa,' garsáwa kəškə̀ri.' kùlle geb-g-ozáwa.'

She would grind wheat, she had [manual] millstones. She would mill groats. She would mill semolina. She would do all of the things.

(30) naʿòmi,' kùllu geb-gozáwa,' u-g-yawàwa.' [gə-m]palʾàwa ta-náše ší.' g-ə́ba ʾàxla u-màxla.'

Naomi, she does all of the things, and she gives. She would also give away [lit. divide, distribute] to people. She wants to eat and to feed [as well].

(31) BA: brát ḥalàl.'

BA: A worthy woman [lit. daughter of kosher].

(32) SZ: hè.'

SZ: Yes.

(33) ᴴʾázᴴ ʾèha wéla.' krə̀ble mə́nna,' g-érra là g-šoqə́nnax go-bet-lèḥem.' g-yáwat ràba...' kúlla dawə́lti b-yà[wa]tta.'

So that's what's happened [lit. so this (FS) was]. He got angry with her, he tells her, "I will not let you stay [lit. leave you] in Bethlehem. You give a lot... you will give [away] all of my property."

(34) wàlox' g-zèda dwə́ltox!' là-g-náqṣa!' ʾálla d-húlle húlle ṭàli' yáwan ta-ġèri ší!' là-q-qabəlwa.'

"Look now, your property will increase! It will not lessen! God who gave, gave to me [in order that] I shall give to others [lit. my other = other than me] also." He didn't accept.

(35) qam-nabə̀lla¹ qam-nabə́lla l-...¹ məʾo...¹ bážər məʾohàv,¹ ʾèka wéla¹ bážər məʾohàv?¹

He took her. He took her to... Meo... the city of Meʾohav.[91] Where was the city of Meʾohav?

(36) BA: go-məšəlmàne,¹

BA: In [the country of] the Muslims,

(37) SZ: qam-nabə̀lla.¹ məʾoháv k-iʾə̀tule maní-le? k-ʾə̀tule máni-le¹ mekàle?¹ ᴴmakórᴴ dìde,¹ k-ʾə̀tule ᴴmákorᴴ díde mekàle?...¹

He took her. Meʾohav, do you know who he is? Do you know who he is, where he is from? His source, do you know where his source is from?...

(38) OA: ᴴlò,ᴴ¹

OA: No,

(39) BA: ᴴlò,ᴴ¹

BA: No,

(40) SZ:... məʾohav?...ʾàz e...¹ g-émer nablə́nnax bážər məʾohàv,¹ ʾána ʾə́tli, g-bàre mə́nni.¹ məʾoháv ší ʾə́tle trè bnàsa:¹ rùt,¹ u-ʾòrṭa.¹ qam-ṭaləblu ta-kútru bnóne dìde.¹

SZ:... Meʾohav?... So eh... he says, "I'll take you to the city of Meʾohav, I have [means], I can afford it." Meʾohav also has two daughters, Ruth and Orṭa.[92] He asked for them [= for their hand] for both his sons.

(41) qam-nabə̀lla,¹ zə́lla ʾə̀mme,¹ ʾúzlu ᴴḥatonàᴴ¹ qam-gorìlu kútru bnása díde.¹ ràḥqa m-bát[ət] ʾəsraʾèl¹ ʾáwwa mə̀tle,¹ gòra.¹

He took her [= Naomi], she went with him, they made a wedding, they married both of his daughters. [May it be] far from the houses of Israel,[93] he died, her husband.

(42) BA: ʾelimèlex,¹

BA: Elimelech.

---

[91] In the Bible: Moab.
[92] In the Bible: Orpah.
[93] An expression said when mentioning a bad event.

(43) SZ: hè,ˈ ʾelimélex màtle.ˈ zólla xa-šáta go-pàlga,ˈ

SZ: Yes, Elimelech died. One year had passed [lit. one year went in the middle (i.e., in the midst of the story)],

(44) ʾàz e,ˈ zə́lla xápča xə́t go-pàlga,ˈ u-kútru bnòne-ši mə́tlu,ˈ màni píšen?ˈ ṭlá[ha] baxtàsa.ˈ

So eh, some more time passed [lit. some more went in the middle], and both sons also died, who remained [alive]? The three women.

(45) g-ə́mra brà ti,ˈ lá-g-samxan másyan bnóne magurànnax,ˈ sàʾun ˈ gòrun ˈ mésun yalùnke,ˈ ʾána zə̀llu xlə̀ṣlu,ˈ ʾànya-tre wélu.ˈ

She [= Naomi] says, "My daughter, I will not become pregnant [and] bear [lit. bring] sons that will marry you. Go [PL] get married [and] have [lit. bring] children, I, they've gone, they're finished [= for my part, I will not bear any more children], there were [only] these two [lit. these two were]."

(46) rùtˈ g-ə̀mra,ˈ mèsatˈ mèsan,ˈ pèšat pèšan,ˈ ᴴhayím šə̀lliˈ ʿal-hayím šə̀llàx.ˈ ʾaní lò ʾaʿazóv ʾotáxˈ bə-šúm ʾòfen!ˈ hayím šə̀llí v-šə̀llàxˈ—ʾeḥàd!ᴴˈ ʾá[h]at mèsatˈ ʾána mèsan,ˈ ʾá[h]at ʾàxlatˈ ʾána b-àxlan,ˈ ʾá[h]at…ˈ g-ə́mra ᴴbəsèder.ᴴ94

Ruth says, "[If] you die, I die, [if] you live, I live [lit. you remain, I remain], my life is on [= for] your life. I will not leave you under any circumstances! My life and yours—are one. [If] you die, I die, [if] you eat, I eat, [if] you…" She [= Naomi] says, "Fine."94

(47) ʾòrta g-əmrá-laˈ sé l-be-bàbax.ˈ zə̀lla,ˈ zə́lla ᴴberaxàᴴ [or: b-ʾùrxa].ˈ rút séla ʾə̀mma.ˈ

Orṭa, she tells her, "Go [back] to your father's house." She went [away, may a] blessing [be with her] [or: she went her way]. Ruth came with her [= with Naomi].

---

94 See Ruth 1.16–18.

(48) sèla,' sèla,' psə́xla dárgət bet-leḥèm' tùla.' ᴴyéš láᴴ xə̀ṭṭe' u-ʾə́tla e... xə̀ṭṭe lát-la,' ʾə́tla sə̀tta' u-garùsta' u-...' múx qamàe' bésa wéla mə̀lya ʾawáe.'

She came, she came, she opened the door of [her house in] Bethlehem, she sat [down]. She has wheat and she has eh... wheat she doesn't have, she has a stone mortar and a hand mill and... like [it was] before, her house was full of things.

(49) g-ə́mra bràti,' sè,' bòʿaz' g-mápəq xə̀ṭṭe,' sè,' u-ʾóz šəbbólim⁹⁵ bàsru,' mèse,' deqànnu garsànnu⁹⁶ g-ozànnu,' b-ózax kùtele' b-àxlax.' b-ózax qámxa b-àxlax,' b-ózax gə́rsa b-àxlax!' k-iʾax ʾózax.'

She says "My daughter, go, Boaz brings out [=harvests?] wheat, go, and make ears of grain⁹⁵ behind them [=the harvesters, i.e., glean],⁹⁷ bring [here what you have gleaned], I will crack [lit. knock (in a mortar)] them, grind them,⁹⁶ prepare them, we shall make dumplings, we shall eat. We shall make flour [and] eat. We shall make groats [and] eat! We know [how] to make [them]."

(50) zə̀lla,' xà yóma' trè' ṭlàha,' zə́lla bàsru,' sèle,' bòʿaz,' xá yóma qam-xazèla' mə́rre-le wày!' ᴴézeᴴ báxta ᴴyafàᴴ' màṭo k-šáqla...?'

She [=Ruth] went, one day, two, three, she went behind them [=the harvesters]. He came, Boaz saw her one day, he said to himself [or: to his harvester], "Way! What a beautiful woman, how [is it possible that] she takes... [=collects ears]?"

---

⁹⁵ From Hebrew šibbolìm 'ears of grain' (borrowed before contact with Modern Hebrew).

⁹⁶ Two separate stages of the grinding process.

⁹⁷ The Jewish law of lèqet (Lev. 19.9; 23.22) states that harvesters must not collect the ears of grain that fall to the ground during the process of harvesting. They should leave them for the poor to glean.

(51) màndu-la,ˈ mčančəlun⁹⁸ [or: mčămčumun⁹⁹] ṭála.ˈ ᴴʾèn-davár.ˈ ʾimᴴ-sèlaˈ ʾé-baxta ᴴyafàᴴˈ u-ˈ màʿqulˈ ʾóza šəbbòləṭ,ˈ¹⁰⁰ hàllu-la.ˈ

[He said to his harvesters:] "Throw to her [some extra ears], tear [some ears]⁹⁸ for her [or: pretend you don't see for her sake⁹⁹]. [There's] no harm [lit. thing] [in that]. If [such] a beautiful and noble woman came to glean [lit. make ear¹⁰⁰], give [or: let] her."

(52) zə́lla márra ta-xmàsaˈ g-ə́mra k-ĭʾatˈ márre bóʿaz hádxa, qam-baqránnu màni-leˈ márru bòʿaz hìle.ˈ

She went and told her mother-in-law, she says, "You know, Boaz said so-and-so. I asked them who he is, they said, 'It is Boaz.'"

(53) g-ə́mra ʾàwa…ˈ mpə́llax yabúm¹⁰¹ ʾə̀lle.ˈ g-əmrà-laˈ ṭòv,ˈ sè,ˈ xòp,ˈ u-msèˈ [or: u-mšè],ˈ sé dmòxˈ qam-ʾàqle.ˈ

She [=Naomi] says, "He… you fell yibbum¹⁰¹ on him." She says to her, "Good, come, bathe, and wash your clothes [or: dab yourself (maybe with perfume, etc.)], go sleep near his feet."

(54) zə́lla dmə́xla qam-ʾàqle,ˈ sèleˈ qam-xazéla šṭə̀ḥta qam-… ᴴmìṭaᴴ díde.ˈ

She went [and] slept near his feet, he came [and] saw her lying down near… his bed.

---

⁹⁸ See Ruth 2.16.
⁹⁹ From č-m-č-m 'have bleary eyes' (Sabar 2002a, 132), to avoid embarrassing her. This would parallel the biblical "…and you shall not put her to shame" (Ruth 2.15).
¹⁰⁰ From Hebrew šibbòlet 'ear of grain' (borrowed before contact with Modern Hebrew).
¹⁰¹ That is, he is obliged to fulfil yibbum (levirate marriage) with you. See §5.4 and fn. 44 earlier in this chapter.

(55) g-er-qày' bràti,' ᴴláma,ᴴ g-ə̀mra,' xmási mə̀rra,' g-náplan ʾə̀llox,' hàdxa wéla ḥəkkòsa' mə́tle bròna u-...,' ᴴze naxon,ᴴ bábe u-bábe ʾaxwàsa-lu.'

He says, "Why, my daughter, why?" She says, "I fall on you [yibbum]." The story was like that [=she told him the whole matter], her [=Naomi's] son died and..., that [=the story] is true, his [=Boaz's] father and his [=Elimelech's] father are brothers.

(56) g-érra sé l-bèsa,' ᴴmaḥá[r]ᴴ bə́nne m-bə́noke sáloxun ʾəl-knə̀šta,' masyálax naʿòmi,' u-ʾána-šik p-áwən go-knə̀šta,' u-knə̀šta ml̥ísa jamàʿa,' b-ózaxni ᴴpšarà.' psèder.ᴴ'

He tells her, "Go home, tomorrow morning come to the synagogue, Naomi will bring you, and I will also be in the synagogue, and the synagogue is full of people, we shall make a compromise." Fine.

(57) ᴴle-məhràtᴴ' zə́llu l-knə̀šta,' zə́llu l-knə̀šta,'¹⁰² m-əséle ʾaxòne,' ʾə́tle ʾaxóna bə́š rúwwa mə̀nne,' bərtmáne u-ʾə́č̣ʾa šə̀nne-le.' g-ə̀'márre ʾaxòni,' g-nápla ʾə̀llox,' ʾè báxta.'¹⁰³

The following day they went to the synagogue, they went to the synagogue,¹⁰² he brought his brother, he has a brother older than he, 89 years old. He says, "My brother, she falls on you,¹⁰³ this woman.

(58) hàdaxa-la ḥál u-qə́ṣṭa.' g-ér ʾàxoni' təlta-ʾsár yalúnke ʾə̀tli,' u-ʾána ᴴməvugárᴴ lébi màḥkən,' lébi ʾəmmed-bàxti máḥkən,'

This [lit. thus] is the situation and the story." He [=the brother] says, "My brother, I have thirteen children, and I am old, I cannot speak, I cannot [even] speak with my wife.

---

¹⁰² This repetition of a word or phrase with this intonation is a typical stylistic feature of Jewish Zakho NENA narration. It usually appears at the beginning of an episode in the narrative. See also ch. 3, fn. 29.
¹⁰³ That is, you are obliged to perform levirate marriage (or ḥaliṣa). See fn. 101 above.

(59) šqúlla ṭàlox' hóya bráxta ʾəllox,' wéla ᴴnàʿalᴴ dídi lúšla,'¹⁰⁴ — Take her [= Ruth] for you, may she be blessed upon you [= be blessed together, *mazal tov!*]. Here is my shoe, wear it.

(60) BA: hè...' — BA: Yes...

(61) SZ: si-mbàrəx-la.' — SZ: Go wed [lit. bless] her."

(62) jamáʿa kúllu məskùmlu¹⁰⁵...' g-ér ᴴmaḥàr' taxíni...ᴴ' bəne' máxən¹⁰⁶ gyànax,' lòš,' u-ʾána b-lòšən' b-áx ʾəl-knə̀šta,' b-ozáx ᴴšévaʿ braxòt!ᴴ¹⁰⁷ — The congregation all agreed.... He says, "Tomorrow, prepare... tomorrow prepare yourself [= get ready], wear [wedding garments] and I will wear [wedding garments], we shall go to the synagogue, [and] we shall do [= perform the ceremony of the] seven blessings!"¹⁰⁷

(63) ᴴle-maḥrátᴴ sélu ʾúzlu ᴴšévaʿ braxòt,ᴴ' qam-gawə̀rra.' ᴴ[yi]štabáḥ šəmò!ᴴ' ʾáwwa ʾəmmèt' ᴴṭóra šeló ʾəmmèt.ᴴ' — The following day they came [and] did [= performed the ceremony of the] seven blessings, he married her. May His name be praised! He [= God] is true [= lit. truth], [and] His Torah is true [= lit. truth].

(64) ᴴle-moḥorátᴴ ʾomrím ba-bóker humèt.' bóʿaz mèt!ᴴ' — The following day, they say, he died, Boaz died!

(65) BA: e bòʿaz?' ʾāa...!' — BA: Boaz? Oh...!

(66) OA: ᴴkèn?!ᴴ' — OA: Really [lit. yes]?!

---

¹⁰⁴ See Ruth 4.7–8.

¹⁰⁵ The Modern Hebrew root *skm* is used here with NENA morphology.

¹⁰⁶ The Modern Hebrew root *kwn* is used here with NENA morphology. The equivalent NENA root is *ḥzr*.

¹⁰⁷ A ceremony marking the *qiddušin*, the second and final stage of a Jewish wedding, in which seven benedictions are said.

(67)	SZ: ^{H}bó'az mèt!,' láyla 'exàd nəš'ár 'ita.^{H_1}	SZ: Boaz died! He stayed with her [only] one night.
(68)	BA: wī!...'	BA: Wi!
(69)	OA: ^{H}'á kèn?!' zé ló yadàti.^{H_1}	OA: Really [lit. yes]?! I didn't know that.
(70)	BA: pappùke!...'	BA: Poor man!...
(71)	SZ: ^{H}bó'az mèt...^{H}	SZ: Boaz died...
(72)	zə́lle xábra 'əllù' bó'az mə̀tle,' bó'az mə̀tle,' xmàsa' šàṭər-ila.'	The word went to them [=they were informed, they learned the news that] Boaz died, Boaz died. Her [=Ruth's] mother-in-law is [a] resourceful [woman].
(73)	sélu jmə́'lu nàše' kúlla 'àlam jmə́'la ^{H}la-ləvayà.^{H_1}	People came and gathered, the entire world [=many people, the entire community] gathered, for the funeral.
(74)	ḥmə̀lla u-ṣrə̀xla,' g-əmrá rəbbóno šel-'olàm,' xzàwun,' kúlloxon sahzètun,' tə́mmal 'úzle ^{H}ḥatùna,^{H_1}	She [=Naomi] stood up and cried out, "[In the name of the] Master of the Universe, see, all of you, testify, yesterday he made the wedding,"
(75)	'é báxta[108] kàlsa híla,' 'é báxta qam-barxála 'ə̀lle,' lál-xəl wəl-	this woman[108] is her daughter-in-law, this woman [=Ruth], she [=Naomi] blessed her to him [=married her off to

---

[108] Samra switches here to third person. Switching from first to third person within direct speech is a common feature of Samra's narration, especially in instances where the narrator does not wish to take upon herself an utterance which is perceived as negative. In relation to that, see Kasher (2000, 74, feature B) where one of the features he mentions as indicative of Targum liturgical use is switches from second to third person in order to avoid giving offence to the audience.

dmáxle kə̀sla,ˈ ʾakán smáxla ᴴʾò̀ᴴ bróna ᴴʾò̀ᴴ bráta dəd-bòʿaz-ilu.ˈ | Boaz], last night he indeed slept with [lit. at] her. If she got pregnant, a son or a daughter, they are of Boaz.

(76) BA: ᴴnaxò̀n.ᴴˈ | BA: Correct.

(77) SZ: ʾilá[ha] sàhəz u-náše sàhzi!ˈ kúllo márru ᴴbəsèder.ᴴˈ ʾilá[ha] hùlleˈ smə̀xla,ˈ máni sèle-la?ˈ k-ʾìtun máni?ˈ | SZ: "God shall [bear] witness and people shall [bear] witness!" Everyone said, "Okay." God gave, she became pregnant, who came to her [= who was the child]? Do you know who?

(78) BA: là̀ʾ.ˈ | BA: No.

(79) SZ: bróna màni,ˈ má-yle šèmme?ˈ bər-rùti?ˈ | SZ: Her son, who [is he], what is his name? The son of Ruthie?

(80) BA: là-k-iyan.ˈ | BA: I don't know.

(81) SZ: ʾelišàу!ˈ | SZ: Elishay!

(82) BA: ʾà̀!ˈ ʾelišà̀y.ˈ | BA: Ah! Elishay!

(83) SZ: hwéle-la ʾelišày!…ˈ hwéle-la ʾelišày,ˈ¹⁰⁹ naʿómi qam-ṭaʾanàle,ˈ qam-ʾozábe-xudàni,ˈ ʾelišày,ˈ ʾilá[ha] hùlle-leˈ šoʾá bnòne,ˈ u-xá bràta.ˈ rùt,ˈ ᴴsáftaᴴ dìde híla.ˈ rùtˈ héš wéla pə̀šta,ˈ | SZ: She gave birth to Elishay [lit. Elishay was born to her]! She gave birth to Elishay [lit. Elishay was born to her],¹⁰⁹ Naomi reared him, she took care of him. Elishay, God gave him seven sons, and one daughter. Ruth was his grandmother. Ruth was still alive,

(84) BA: hè,ˈ | BA: Yes,

(85) SZ: ʾə̀z e,ˈ xà yóma,ˈ hə̀nna,ˈ ʾelišày,ˈ krə̀bwaleˈ mən-dè báxtaˈ dammə̀d-wéla smáxta bəd-dávid | SZ: So eh, one day, this, Elishay, he got angry with this woman [i.e., his wife], while she was pregnant with king

---

¹⁰⁹ See fn. 102 above.

	ha-mèlex.ˈ ᴴʾaharònᴴ sé[le]ˈ ᴴyéled ševiʿᴵᴴ.ˈ	David. He came last, the seventh child.
(86)	ʾàz e...ˈ qam-karədwalaˈ xá yaŕxa zólla be-bàba.ˈ sèlaˈ g-əmrà-leˈ qam-kardə̀ttiˈ u-hə̀nnaˈ u-ʾána báxta smə̀xta.ˈ g-ér làˈ là!ˈ léwat smə̀xta!ˈ	So eh, he chased her out, for one month she went to her father's house. She came, she says to him, "You chased me out, and *this* and I am a pregnant woman." He says, "No no! You are not pregnant!"
(87)	BA: léwe mə̀nni,ˈ	BA: "It is not from me,"
(88)	SZ: lèwe mánni!ˈ g-èrra,ˈ g-əmrà-le,ˈ rəbbonó šel-ʿolàmˈ sáhəz ʾóllaˈ ʾe-bàxta,ˈ¹¹⁰ báni básar lèwa nḥóqta,ˈ yála dìdox híle.ˈ smə́xta zə̀lla.ˈ¹¹⁰	SZ: "It is not from me!" She says, she tells him, "Master of the Universe, bear witness to this woman,¹¹⁰ she has not been touched by humans, it is your child. She¹¹⁰ went pregnant [= she was pregnant when she left]."
(89)	ᴴtòvᴴ!ˈ lá-wele ᴴkol-káx meruṣè,ᴴˈ rəbbonó šel-ʿolàm,ˈ kʿə́sle¹¹¹ ʾə̀lle.ˈ g-er-yála dìdox híle,ˈ má g-əmrə̀tta?!ˈ bàxta,ˈ ᴴnakiyà,ˈ u-ṣadikà,ᴴˈ màni b-náḥəq ʾə́lla?!ˈ	Good! He [= Elishay] was not so satisfied. The Master of the Universe got angry with him. He says, "It is your child, what are you saying to her?! [She is a] clean, and righteous, woman, who would touch her?!"
(90)	g-émer ta-šamúʾel ha-nnàvi,ˈ g-émer sí mbárəx xá yála dəd-ʾelišày,ˈ páeš ḥakómədˈ yisraʾèl!ˈ	He says to Samuel the prophet, "Go bless [i.e., anoint] one child of Elishay, so that he shall become the king of Israel!"

---

¹¹⁰ See fn. 108 above.

¹¹¹ The Modern Hebrew root *kʿs* is used here with NENA morphology.

(91) zə̀lle' dámməd zə̀lle' šmú'el hannávi šárəf 'əl-kúllu bátəd yisra'él 'əl-dó bésa u-'əllòxun!'

He went, when he went, Samuel the prophet, may [his blessing] shine on [or: may he watch over] all the houses of Israel [and] on this house and on you!

(92) BA: 'amèn!

BA: Amen!

(93) SZ: 'ilá[ha] ya[wə́]lox ᴴ'éšet ḥàyil,ᴴ'

SZ: May God give you [=OA] a woman of valour

(94) OA: 'amè̀n!'

OA: Amen!

(95) BA: 'amèn!',

BA: Amen!,

(96) SZ: u-bánət bésa go-rušaláyim xazyálu yalónke dìdox,'

SZ: and build a house in Jerusalem, may she [=BA] see your children,

(97) OA: 'amèn 'amèn 'amèn!'

OA: Amen amen amen!

(98) BA: 'amèn,' 'amèn, 'amèn!',

BA: Amen, amen, amen!,

(99) SZ: u-'in-šá'-'alla muxwàsi fárḥat 'əbbu

SZ: and God willing you [=BA] will be happy with them like myself [i.e., like I am happy with my own grandchildren]

(100) BA: 'amèn, 'amèn,' 'amèn!'

BA: Amen, amen, amen!

(101) OA: 'amèn' 'amèn!'

OA: Amen amen!

(102) SZ: 'ána kmà kéfi séle!' 'ilàha k-î'e!'

SZ: Me, I am so happy [lit. how much my joy came]! God knows!

(103) BA: 'amèn!'

BA: Amen!

(104) SZ: 'àz e,...' ᴴha-'emèt' e' bàᴴ' g-érre bròni' rùwwa' dalàla,' məsélu bróne rùwwa,' šamú'el hannaví monə̀xle' là ḥmálla stún...'

SZ: So uh,... The truth, uh, he [=Samuel the prophet] came, he [Elishay] says to him, "My son, the eldest, [my] dear one," they brought his eldest son, Samuel the prophet looked, the pillar [of

(105) ʾaz-è,' g-emárre léwe ʾó bróna,'— ʾàtta' mà' g-àban' ᴴyotér mədday̌ᴴˡ g-máḥkiyan ᴴᶜə̀vritᴴˡ kúlle wáʿada lišáni g-éza ᴴʾəvrìt,ᴴˡ g-əbánna ᴴʾəvrítᴴ ṛàba,'

So, he says, "It is not this son"—now, what, I like to speak Hebrew too much, I speak Hebrew, all the time my tongue goes [to] Hebrew, I love Hebrew very much,

(106) BA: ᴴkèn' naxòn' naxònᴴˡ

BA: Yes, right, right,

(107) SZ: hè,'

SZ: Yes.

(108) BA: ʾaz-lá qam-šaqə́lle ʾaw-bróna,'

BA: So he didn't take that son,

(109) SZ: g-emárre ᴴlò,' lò raʾúy.ᴴˡ məséle ʾaw-xə́t g-ér ᴴlò,ᴴˡ məséle ʾaw-xə̀t' stún núra lá xəzyàle.'

SZ: He says to him, "No, [he is] not worthy." He brought the second one, he says "No," he brought the other one, he didn't see the pillar of fire.

(110) šmúʾəl hannavì,' márrele rəbbonó šel-ʿolàm' dámməd ḥmə́lla,' šəxína b-rèše,' ʾòha-le!'

Samuel the prophet, the Master of the Universe [had] told him, "When the Shekhinah stood [=dwells] upon his head, this is he [i.e., that is the son who will be king]."

(111) g-er-lè¹¹² ʾóha' g-er-lè¹¹² ʾóha,' kùd ʾaštá ḥmàllu' g-ér ᴴlò!ᴴˡ ʾətlóx xá bróna xát?' g-ér ʾə̀tli xa-bróna xát' ᴴʾaválᴴ bár šoʾà šə́nne-le.' wéle go-ᴴsadèᴴˡ ʾə́mməd ʾə̀rba,' g-érre mà-g-ot..., ʾáni mxalpì-le' mesèle.'

He [=Samuel the prophet] says, "It's not him," he says, "It's not him," all of the six stood [in front of him], he says, "No!" "Do you have another son?" He says, "I have one more son, but he is [only] seven years old. He is in the field with the sheep." He says, "What are you doing... [=why are you making an issue out of it?], they [=the other sons] will substitute for him [lit. switch him] [and] will bring him."

---

¹¹² Contraction of lèwe.

(112) *séle məd-xa-dəšdàša,*¹¹³ *xa-kusísa xwàrta b-rèše.' g-emér ʾòha-le' g-ér ʾòha-le.'*
He came with [i.e., wearing] an ankle-length robe,¹¹³ a white hat on his head. He [=Samuel the prophet] says, "This is he?" he [Elishay] says, "This is he."

(113) *ḥməlle' g-ér ḥmól ʾàxxa,' monáxle bəd-rəbbóno šel-ʿolàm' šaxiná ḥməlla.'*
He [David] stood, he [=Samuel the prophet] says, "Stand here," he looked towards the Master of the Universe, the Shekhinah stood [i.e., dwelt upon David].

(114) *g-er-ʾòha brònox' màyle šə́mme?' dàwid-hile' g-er-ʾó p-pà[y]əš' ᴴdàvid mèlex yəsraʾèl!ᴴ' ʾò brònox!'*
He says, "This son of yours, what is his name?" "It is David." He says, "This [one] will be David, the king of Israel! This son of yours!"

(115) *hawéle ᴴməšḥàᴴ' də́d məséle ᴴšémenᴴ mən-bét məqdàš,' qam-dahə̀nle' u-qàm-' ʾa[wə̀]zle' u-ʾál' káffəd-ʾìze' u-ləbbe' u-xàṣe' u-ʾàqle' u-ʾəqər-ʾaqle,*
Here is the ointment that he had brought, oil from the Temple, he anointed him, and made [i.e., applied it] towards [lit. the side of] his palms and his heart and his back and his legs and his feet,

(116) *g-ér ᴴʾəlohím yišmòr ʾotxá,ᴴ' dúkšət ʾàzət,' háwət ᴴbarì.ᴴ' kúlle yalúnkət yəsraʾèl.'*
he says, "May God protect you, [every] place that you go, may you be healthy." [And] all the children of Israel [as well].

(117) BA: *ʾamen.'* BA: Amen.

(118) OA: *ʾamen.'* OA: Amen.

(119) SZ: *qam-, xàḷaṣ,' pə́šle bár...' qam-mašə̀ḥle.'*¹¹⁴
That's it, he became, the son of..., he anointed him.

---

¹¹³ Translation of *dəšdaša* according to Sabar (2002a, 145).
¹¹⁴ The Hebrew root *mšḥ* is used here with NENA morphology.

(120) básər ʔòt̯o,ˈ xaràye,…ˈ ᴴšáʔul ha-mmèlexᴴ ṣráxle…ˈ e…ˈ ᴴgám-kenᴴ šáʔul ha-mmèlexˈ séle gólyas paləštàya,ˈ ə g-ə́be nàṣe ʔəmmed-yəsraʔèl.ˈ

After that, later on… king Saul called… eh… also king Saul, Goliath the Philistine, eh he wants to fight with Israel.

(121) máni mšàdriˈ máni là-mšadri?ˈ šáʔul ha-mèlex ʔə̀tle,ˈ xá ᴴḥalifàᴴˈ zigúri kunzə̀ri,[115] čùxxa lèbeˈ lawə̀šla,ˈ ᴴrákᴴ ta-dávid ha-mélex hila-ʔùzta.ˈ bás mèlex,ˈ ʔaw-dəd-páyəš mèlex…ˈ

Whom shall they [=Israel] send [and] whom shall they not send? King Saul has, one suit, Ziguri Kunzəri,[115] no one can wear it, it is made only for king David. Only a king, the one who will become king…

(122) BA: máyla kúri kunzə̀ri?ˈ

BA: What is Kuri Kunzəri?

(123) SZ: gúri kunzə́ri-le šə̀mma.ˈ

SZ: Its name is Guri Kunzəri.

(124) BA: ʔá gúri kunzə̀ri,ˈ ᴴyàfeᴴ,ˈ

BA: Oh Guri Kunzəri, nice,

(125) SZ: gúri kunzə́ri bəd-kùrdi,ˈ bəd-hə̀nnaˈ lá-kyan bəd-ᴴʕvrítᴴ mày-le,ˈ

SZ: Guri Kunzəri in Kurdish [=Neo-Aramaic], in this I don't know, in Hebrew, what it is.

(126) BA: ᴴʔávalᴴ ʔə́tla ᴴperùšᴴ?ˈ yáʕane mày-la gúri kunzə́ri,ˈ šə̀mma?ˈ

BA: But does it have a meaning [lit. interpretation]? Meaning, what is Guri Kunzəri, its name?

(127) SZ: é šə̀mma,ˈ ᴴḥalifáᴴ dəd-ᴴmélexᴴ hìla,ˈ kúlla ʔə́mməd ᴴbarzalìmᴴˈ u-ʔə́mməd éˈ ṣanéʔta

SZ: Uh, its name, it is the suit of the king, all of it with irons [i.e., made out of pieces of iron], and with uh, it is made by craftsmanship, not just a simple thing. It's valuable [lit.

---

[115] Sabar (2002a, 161): "zɪri(-kunzɪri) coat of mail (=H[ebrew] תחרא B[ible] T[ranslations]), armour." In Rivlin (1959, 233, 241): "ziri ukum ziri." Sabar (2002a, 161) explains: "kum = helmet, K[urdish]."

ʾùzta¹ lá ᴴstàm.ᴴ¹ ʾə̀tlā...¹ ʾə́tla ᴴʿèrex!ᴴ¹ čúxxa lèbe lawə́šla.¹ — it has value]. No one is able to wear it.

(128) mád ʾìz,¹ yalúnkəd yerušalàyim,¹ ṣróxle ᴴrámkolᴴ ʾàse,¹ ḥakóma g-óbe qaṭə̀lle gòlias.¹ g-emer-ʾáwd lawə́šla ʾè bádla¹ ʾìbe qaṭə́lle.¹ — All of [lit. whatever there is] the children [i.e., boys] of Jerusalem, a loudspeaker[116] called out that they should come, [since] the king wished to kill Goliath. He says, whoever wears this outfit, he is able to kill him.

(129) ...là...¹ xá d-làwəšla¹ xá ràbsa-la ṭále¹ xá zùrta-la ṭále,¹ lá g-ʾóra qáme u-xà...¹ — ... not... whoever [lit. one who] wears it, for one it's [too] large, for one it's [too] small, it doesn't fit him [lit. it doesn't enter in front of him], and one...

(130) g-ə́mri ʾíz xà píša,¹ bár šoʾà šə̀nne-le¹ wéle gó ᴴsadè,ᴴ¹ ʾàw-gora-le píša!¹ qu-sáʾun mèsu-le.¹ — They say, there's one [boy] left, he is seven years old, he is in the field, only this man is left [i.e., only he did not try the suit yet]! "Go fetch him."

(131) qam-malušíla ʾə̀lle,¹ bár šoʾá šə̀nne,¹ yištabbáḥ šemò¹ rwéle qam-maḷèla!¹ — They dressed him with it [lit. it on him], [only] seven years old [i.e., therefore small], may His name be praised, he [=David] grew and filled it!

(132) šáʾul ha-mélex krə̀ble,¹ g-er-ʾò̀...¹ p-páyəš šwìni,¹ p-šaqə̀lla...¹ — King Saul got angry, he says [to himself] "This one... will be instead of me, he will take it... [i.e., the kingship]"

(133) ᴴṭòv,ᴴ¹ g-óbe ʾázət qaṭlə́tte góliyas palištàya,¹ g-émer ᴴṭòv,ᴴ¹ ʾéyn beʿayà.ᴴ¹ lùšle¹ dəsdàša díde,¹ ᴴkóvaᶜᴴ díde b-rèše,¹ kafìya díde,¹ — "Good, you need to go and kill Goliath the Philistine," he [=David] says, "Very well, no problem." He wore his ankle-length robe, his hat is on his head, his keffiyeh, and he has,

---

[116] Clearly, an anachronism.

u-[ʾə]tle,ˈ ʾə́tle hə̀nna,ˈ ʾáy-dəd e...ˈ	he has *this*, that [thing] which uh...
(134) BA: tfàkke,ˈ	BA: a gun,
(135) SZ: là,ˈ dəd-g-màxeˈ kèpaˈ ʾəbbaˈ tràq,ˈ hə̀nna,ˈ lá-k-yan šə́mme máy-le b-kùrdi,ˈ e...ˈ	SZ: No, [the thing] that you throw a stone with, *traq! this*, I don't know what its name is in Kurdish [=Neo-Aramaic], uh...
(136) BA: e wì!ˈ ʾòtoˈ hè,ˈ	BA: Uh *wi!* Like that, yes,
(137) SZ: lá tfàkke,ˈ e...ˈ ᴴhèvelᴴ...ˈ	SZ: Not a gun, uh... a rope...
(138) BA: ᴴhèvelᴴˈ ʾòtoˈ	BA: A rope, like that...
(139) SZ: u-hə̀nna,ˈ g-e[wə́]z tsràq!ˈ hə̀nna,ˈ šə́mma mày-le?ˈ	SZ: And *this*, it does *tsraq! this*, what is its name?
(140) BA: ᴴhéts va-kèšetᴴˈ	BA: An arrow and a bow,
(141) SZ: hé ᴴhéts va-hèts,ˈ héts va-kèšet.ᴴˈ	SZ: Yes, an arrow and an arrow, an arrow and a bow.
(142) BA: ᴴhéts va-kèšet.ᴴˈ u-bəd-ᴴkúrditᴴ mày-la?ˈ	BA: An arrow and a bow, and in Kurdish [=Neo-Aramaic] what is it?
(143) SZ: ʾà?ˈ	SZ: Eh?
(144) BA: bəd-ᴴkurdìt?ᴴˈ	BA: In Kurdish [=Neo-Aramaic]?
(145) SZ: bəd-kùrdi?ˈ šə́mma nšèliˈ g-əmrànnax,ˈ šə́mma nšèli.ˈ šə́m[ma] ʾát[ta]-táxr[an] b-amrànnax.ˈ[117]	SZ: In Kurdish [=Neo-Aramaic]? I forgot its name, I tell you, I forgot its name. I'll remember its name now and tell you.[117]
(146) BA: ᴴtòv.ᴴˈ	BA: Good.

---

[117] Samra will remember the word *bardaqaniye* 'slingshot' in (164).

(147) SZ: ʾóha zəlle,ˈ qam-šaqə́lla ʾə́mme u-zəlle. zə́lle rə́š-...ˈ qrúle ʾəl-hə̀nna,¹¹¹⁸ šqə́lle xa-kèpa,ˈ

SZ: This one [=David] went [away], he took it with him and went. He went to [lit. upon]... he came close to the *this*,¹¹⁸ he took a stone,

(148) g-ér [declaiming:] bəzxùtˈ ʾavrahàm,ˈ šqə́lle xa-képa xə̀t g-érˈ bəzxút yaʿaqòv,ˈ bəzxút ʾavrahàm,ˈ yitsḥàk,ˈ yaʿaqòvˈ haytḷàha.ˈ

he says, "For the merit of Abraham," he took another stone, he says, "For the merit of Jacob, for the merit of Abraham, Isaac, Jacob." Here this is three [of them].

(149) sqə́lle tré kèpe-xətˈ g-ə́r bəzxùtˈ mòšeˈ ve-haròn.ˈ kúd xámša drέle go-jèbe,ˈ zəlle.ˈ

He took two more stones, he says, "For the merit of Moses and Aaron." The five of them he put in his pocket, [and] he went [away].

(150) qam-darέlu go-hə̀nna dìde,ˈ nəšèliˈ šə́mma bassìma-le bədkùrdi.ˈ¹¹¹⁹

He put them in his *this*, I forgot, its name is [very] pleasing [=beautiful] in Kurdish [=Neo-Aramaic].¹¹⁹

(151) zə́lle g-èmerˈ màni séleˈ qaṭə̀lli?ˈ kèlu,ˈ pošùlkanˈ mošùlkat?ˈ¹²⁰ g-èmrī...ˈ k-xàzeˈ xa-yàla-le,ˈ ḥmìla,ˈ¹²¹

He [=Goliath] went [and] he says "Who [is it that] came to kill me? Where are the *pošùlkan mošùlkat*?"¹²⁰ They say... He sees it is a child, standing.¹²¹

(152) g-ér mxí darbàdox [=dárba dìdox],ˈ¹²² g-ér ʾàna mã́?...ˈ

He says "Strike your blow,"¹²² he [=David] says, "What I...? You are wearing clothes of

---

¹¹⁸ Maybe to a river, to collect pebbles, or to the battlefield. See 1 Sam. 17.40.

¹¹⁹ See fn. 117 above.

¹²⁰ Unclear. Perhaps Goliath is mocking Hebrew names?

¹²¹ See 1 Sam. 17.42.

¹²² David and Goliath take turns in striking. See §5.10 above.

ʾàhətˈ lwìšaˈ júlllət kúde kunzə̀ri,ˈ ʾíbox máxət dàrbe,ˈ ʾána mà-k-iʾən máxən.ˈ mxí dárba dìdoxˈ xázax mà šə́kəl-hile.ˈ	Kude Kunzəri [=armour], you are able to strike a blow, I, what do I know [how] to strike. Strike your blow [and] we'll see what sort [of a blow] it is."
(153) mxéle xá hə̀nna,ˈ xàʾˈ palgə́d,ˈ e…ˈ ʾáy dùka,ˈ xrùla.ˈ hə̀nna,ˈ ᴴhàr.ᴴ	He struck a *this*. A half of uh… that place was destroyed. *This*, mountain.
(154) BA: hè,ˈ	BA: Yes,
(155) SZ: kúlle ᴴhàrᴴ kúšle,ˈ bəd-dé bəd-hə́nna dìde.ˈ	SZ: The entire mountain went down, with that with his *this*.
(156) ʾó fə̀rre,ˈ qam-mafə̀rre,ˈ ʾilá[ha] qam-matùle,ˈ séle ḥmə́lle xá-ga xə́t barqùle.ˈ g-er-má-wət ṣàx?! má?ˈ g-er wən-ṣàxˈ ᴬḥamdu-l-là.ᴬˈ bés ʾilá[ha] ʾmìra.ˈ¹²³	This one [=David] flew [away], he [Goliath] made him fly [away], God made him land safely [lit. sat him down], he came [and] stood again in front of him [=Goliath]. He [=Goliath] says, "What, you're alive?! What?" He [=David] says, "I'm alive, thank God. The house of God is built¹²³ [=everything is well]."
(157) g-er-de mxí dàrbox,ˈ g-ér ʾo-màni-le?ˈ ehh.ˈ hàdxa ʾúzle,ˈ morə̀mle hə́nna ʾə́sw[a]ˈ ʾíne [=ʾene ?] dwìqe wélu,ˈ	He [=Goliath] says, "Well strike your blow," he [Goliath] says, "Who is this [guy]?" Uh… He did like that, he lifted *this*—there was—his eyes were held [i.e., covered],
(158) BA: he,	BA: Yes,

---

¹²³ See ch. 1, §14.0, proverb no. (79).

(159) SZ: *bád-e...*ˡ ᴴ*barzèl.*ˡ *kóvaʿ barzèl.*ᴴˡ *gúri kunzəri* ᴴ*barzèl*ᴴ *híla,*ˡ *kùlla.*ˡ

SZ: ... in uh... iron. Iron helmet. The *Guri Kunzəri* is [made of] iron, all of it.

(160) BA: *he he,*

BA: Yes yes,

(161) SZ: *kúlle* ᴴ*kòvaʿ barzél.*ᴴˡ *u-...*ˡ *hənna* ᴴ*barzél.*ᴴˡ *morámle hádxa ʾène,*ˡ *gōbʾène gléle,*ˡ *g-ér mxí dárba dìdox,*ˡ

SZ: All of it is an iron hat. And... iron *this*. He lifted his eyes like that, his forehead was uncovered, he says, "Strike your blow,"

(162) *g-ér yá ʾilàhi,*ˡ *bəzxút kúd xá u-xà,*ˡ *šóʾa nàse,*ˡ *ʾiḍe* [or: *déˡ²⁴*] *m[ən]dèle go-jébe,*ˡ *šoʾà*ˡ *hánna šqəlle,*ˡ *xàʾ pášlu!*ˡ *pášlu xà képa.*ˡ

he says, "O my God, for the merit of each and every one [of those] seven men," he put [lit. threw] his hand in his pocket, he had taken seven *this*, they became one! They [all] became one stone.

(163) BA: *əmhəm,*ˡ

BA: Hmmm,

(164) SZ: *qam-daréle go-barda-qanìye.*ˡ¹²⁵ *qam-daréle go-barda-qanìye dìde*ˡ¹²⁶ *ʾúzle tràq!!*ˡ *ʾúrra go-gobʾène*ˡ *ʾúzla gər-gər-gər-gər-gər qam-ʾozále trè qə̀ṭʾe.*

SZ: He put it in [his] slingshot.¹²⁵ He put it in his slingshot.¹²⁶ He made *traq!!* It penetrated his [= Goliath's] forehead, it made *gər-gər-gər-gər-gər* [and] it made him two pieces [i.e., sliced him].

(165) BA: ᴴ*yòfi,*ˡ *yòfi!*ᴴˡ

BA: Nice, nice!

(166) SZ: *qam-ʾozále trè qə̀ṭʾə.*ˡ *ʾoà!*ˡ *g-emàrre,*ˡ *ʾòha-le dárba dídox,*ˡ

It [= the stone] made him two pieces. *Oa!* He [= Goliath] says [dismissively], "Is this your blow?" He says, "Well,

---

¹²⁴ Interjection expressing encouragement.

¹²⁵ Samra remembers the word she had forgotten, thus the strong intonation. See fn. 117 above.

¹²⁶ See fn. 102 above.

g-er-dé šʾùšla gyánox.ˈ šʾə́šle gyàneˈ xá qə́ṭʾə mpə́lle mənne.ˈ	wiggle yourself a little." He wiggled himself, one piece fell off him.
(167) ᴴʾával màᴴˈ wéle míra ta-dàw,ˈ tà...ˈ ta-šáʾul ha-mèlex,ˈ lázəm réše qaṭéʾle matúle qàme,ˈ dəd-yáʾe qam-qaṭə̀lle,ˈ làxwa...ˈ	But what [more], he had told to that, to... to king Saul, he needs to cut his [= Goliath's] head and put it in front of him [= king Saul], in order that he knows that he had killed him, otherwise...
(168) BA: hè,ˈ	BA: Yes,
(169) SZ: là-g-bar[e],ˈ lát-le ᴴbrerà.ᴴˈ ʾə́lla g-èrre,ˈ màni-leˈ ᴴʾaḥraʾṭ̂ᴴ dìde?ˈ ʾeliyá ḥəttè.ˈ ʾelyá ḥəttà.ˈ	SZ: It [i.e., this action] cannot be, he does not have a choice. So he tells him... Who is his [= Goliath's] responsible person [i.e., his armour-bearer]? ʾEliya Ḥəttè. ʾEliya Ḥəttà.
(170) BA: hè,ˈ	BA: Yes,
(171) SZ: ʾàwaˈ g-emə́rre hàllileˈ qzìla,ˈ hàllile sépa dìde,ˈ čù-sepa lébe qaṭéʾle réšˈ d-gólyas paləštàya,ˈ láh[aw]e sépa dìde.ˈ	SZ: He tells him, "Give me the key, give me his sword," no sword can cut the head of Goliath the Philistine, if it is not his [own] sword.
(172) g-er-hàllile sépa dìde,ˈ qaṭʾə̀nne réšeˈ nablə̀nne.ˈ g-er-lá-g-yanne-lox¹²⁷ˈ ʾə́tli šàrṭ ʾə́mmoxˈ hákan yawə́tti xà-brat-yəsraʾèl,ˈ b-yawə̀nne-lox.ˈ	He [= David] says, "Give me his sword [so that] I shall cut his head off and bring it [to king Saul]." He says, "I will not give it to you. I have a condition for [lit. with] you: if you give me a daughter of Israel [i.e., a girl of Israel to marry], I will give it to you."

---

[127] Contraction of *la-g-yawə̀nne-lox*.

(173) ḥmə́lle dáwəd ha-mmèlex, mā́ṭo b-yawə́nne brát yəsraʾèl?ˈ u-là g-bárya šī́kˈ g-əbe-réše nabə́lle ta...ˈ

King[128] David waited [and thought], "How will I give him a daughter of Israel?" and it is also not possible [not to take the head], he must carry his head to...

(174) ḥmə́lle xá-gar xèta ˈ g-emə́rre ᴴtòvᴴˈ b-yawə́nnox xa brát yəsraʾèl,ˈ hàllile,ˈ sèpa díde.ˈ

He waited [and thought] once again, he tells him, "Very well, I will give you a daughter of Israel, give it to me, his sword."

(175) qurbáne ʾílaha ʾày-damma,ˈ kʿə́sle[129] ʾəl dàwid,ˈ g-er-lébox yáwət čù brát yəsraʾél ṭàleˈ ʾə́lla brát,ˈ ʾáy d-hı́la ᴴba[t]-zzúgᴴ dídox bat-šévaʿ mən-ᴴšamáyimᴴ ksúta ṭàlox,ˈ ʾáya b-yawə́tta ta-ʾeliyá ḥəttè.ˈ lébox yáwətˈ čù brát yəsraʾèl.ˈ

Then God [may I be] His sacrifice, got angry with David, He says, "You cannot give any daughter of Israel to him but the daughter, the one that is your spouse, Bathsheba, [which is] written [i.e., destined] for you from heaven, you will give **her** to ʾEliya Ḥəttè. You cannot give any [other] daughter of Israel."

(176) BA: ᴴnaxòn.ᴴˈ

BA: Right.

(177) SZ: waḷḷà,ˈ ʾàya...ˈ šqə́lle sèpa,ˈ qṭèʾle,ˈ dréle go-čànṭaˈ zə́lle m[o]túle qám e...ˈ šáʾul ha-mmèlex.ˈ

Waḷḷah, that [happened]... He took the sword, he cut, he put it in a bag, he went and laid [lit. sat] it in front of uh... king Saul.

(178) zə̀lla,ˈ ʾùrra,ˈ ᴴraᶜᴴ-ʾáfe,[130] mən-yəsraʾèl,ˈ ʾilá[ha] b-yá[wə]l

That trouble [i.e., Goliath or the Philistines] went [away

---

[128] At this point in the narrative, David is not yet king (though he is already anointed).

[129] The Modern Hebrew root kʿs is used here with NENA morphology.

[130] Sabar (2002a, 89): "(Ar[abic]) f. ʾāfe misfortune, mishap; pl. ʾāfityāṯa."

^Htòv^H ta-ʾəsraʾél,ˈ pə́šla šahyàna,ˈ qam-qaṭlìle xằlaṣ,ˈ ʾeliyá ḥə̀tte sí̂ g-ábe mesèle,ˈ b-awázle ^Hṣár ṣavá^H dìde ʾe-náqla.ˈ

and] passed from Israel. God will give good to Israel, there was a celebration, they had killed him, that was it. ʾEliya Həttè, he [=David] wants to bring him [or: it is necessary to bring him], he will make him his general [lit. minister of the army] now.

(179) ʾaz-dámməd qam-malùšla ^Hḥalífa^H ʾə̀lle,ˈ šáʾul rába krə̀ble,ˈ dáwid monáxle bəd-ʾén šáʾul,ˈ ʾen-šáʾulˈ ġèr-šəkəl-ilu,ˈ ġèr-šəkəl pə́šleˈ ^Hpartsúf^H dìde.ˈ

So when he dressed him in the suit [lit. dressed the suit on him], Saul became very angry, David looked at the eyes of Saul, the eyes of Saul became different [lit. are of different colour/form], his face became different [lit. is of different colour/form].

(180) gələləlàlà léwa ḅáš ṭàli!ˈ lášši qə̀zla!ˈ ^Hlò lò lò!^Hˈ makušə́nna mə̀nniˈ ʾána bəd-dəšdáša dídi b-azèna!ˈ qam-makušíla mánne.ˈ

Gələləlàlà it [=the suit] is not good for me! My body has burnt. No no no! I'll take it off me, I shall go in my ankle-length robe! They took it off him.

(181) g-émer ʾéne lá-hoya ʾə̀lli,ˈ pə̀šla,ˈ pə́šla tère!ˈ

He says [=his reasoning was], "His [=Saul's] eye should not be upon me [i.e., I do not want him to become hostile to me]." It [=the suit] became, it became his size!

(182) BA: hèˈ ^Hbètaḥ,^Hˈ

BA: Yes, sure,

(183) SZ: ʾèh,ˈ zə́lle u-sèle,ˈ ʾaz-šáʾul,ˈ pə́šleˈ ^Hholè,^Hˈ qhə̀rre,ˈ g-əmer-ʾó p-pá[y]əš šwìni.ˈ pə́šle ràba ^Hholé.^Hˈ

SZ: Uh, he went and came [back, from the battle against Goliath], so Saul, became sick, he became angry, he says, "This one [=David] will be [king] instead of me." He became very sick.

(184) dúqle rèše,' ráḥqa mən-ʾəsraʾèl',
    màrʾa,' là-g-baṭəl!'

A pain, may it be far from Israel, caught his head, it does not stop!

(185) yonàtan bróne,' ràbəd rába'
    ᴴḥáverᴴ dəd-dàwid-hile.' xà
    roḥáya-lu' xà nəšáma-lu' xà-
    ᴴgilᴴ-ilu,' g-él kášle go-ᴴsadèᴴ' u-
    kèse,' u-k...' k-xáze dammad-
    g-máxe jezùke,'¹³¹ kúlle ʾérba
    k-èse,' k-ḥàməl.' k-épi rèšu,'
    k-šàmʾi jezúke díde.'

His son Jonathan, he's very much a friend of David. They are one spirit, they are one soul, they are the same age, he [=Jonathan] goes to him [=David] to the field, and he... he sees that when he plays his *jezuke*¹³¹ all the sheep come, stand. They bow their heads, they hear [=listen to] his *jezuke*.

(186) u-ʾə́tle xa-mə́ndi xét ši-ᴴṭòvᴴ'
    dáwid ha-mmèlex,' kud-g-másya
    yàla,' bròna,' bràta,' ʾéma
    ʾiwánta g-hawèla,' g-él k-šaqə̀lla'
    u-g-mašmə̀šla' k-xayə̀pla,'
    dàre...' go-ʾize...' gə̀lla' yarùqa'
    yarùqa,' raʾìza raʾìza'
    g-maxə̀lla.' u-[g-]màštela máya.'

And he has another thing that is good, king David: whoever brings a child [=gives birth], a boy, a girl, whichever ewe gives birth, he goes [and] takes her, and pets her, he washes her, he puts... in his hand... green green [and] fresh fresh grass, [and] feeds her.

(187) ʾə́tle ᴴlév ṭòvᴴ' u-[q]urbáne
    ʾilá[ha] k-îʾè.' ᴴgaluy-yadùaᶜᴴ-
    ile,'¹³² k-îʾe' hàdxa-le,' k-îʾe go-

He has a good heart and God [may I be] His sacrifice knows. It is well known [to Him] [lit. revealed (and) known],¹³² He

---

¹³¹ Evidently Samra refers here to a musical instrument. According to Sabar (2002a, 127), a *jəzunke/čəzuke* is a "booklet (of religious or magic nature)." According to another informant, Ḥabuba Messusani, the correct name of the intended musical instrument is *suzuka*. Perhaps it is the plucked string instrument *saz*, common in Kurdistan. See also ch. 3, fn. 56.

¹³² A loan from (pre-Modern) Hebrew *galùy ve-yadùaᶜ*. The connective *vav* is omitted to fit the common asyndetic hendiadys pattern in NENA.

ləbbəd náše mà-ʾis.' kúd-xa u-xá
k-îʾe má-ʾiz go-ləbbe.'

knows it is so, He knows what [there] is inside the heart[s] of people. Each and every one, He knows what is in their hearts [lit. his heart].

(188) ʾáud ʾətle ṭòv,' ʾáud látle k-îʾe.'
márre, qày' g-əmri ᴴparšánᴴ
kóda u-kùlisa-le,' k-îʾe!'

Whoever has good[ness] [in his heart], whoever does not have, He knows. He said, why do they say, "He is the interpreter of the liver and the kidney"? He [=God] knows!

(189) ʾáz ẽ,' g-emárre bàbi b-án
mesónnox,' ʾətli xà' dàwid e...'
g-máxe b-jezùk'¹³³ ta-ʾárba,' šud-ʾàse.'

So uh, he [=Jonathan] says, "My father, I'll go bring you, I have one, David uh... he plays the *jezuke*¹³³ for the sheep." "Let him come."

(190) zəlle mxélele b-jezùke' réše
ṭràsle.' kud-dàmməd' ṭlá[ha]
sàʿe,' g-ewázle maxéle jezùke'
ʾáwa g-nà[y]əx.' ṭrásle rèše,'
dámməd g-èzel' ʾáwa réše
g-màreʾ.'

He went [and] played the *jezuke* for him, his head healed. Every three hours he used to do for him, to play the *jezuke* for him, he [=Saul] would rest. His head healed, whenever he [=David] goes away, his [Saul's] head hurts.

(191) xá yòma,' trè,' ʾàrba,' xá yòma'
g-šaqàlle sépa díde,' g-ábe
maxèle ʾálle,' qaṭálle,' qaṭálle
[or: p-qaṭálle,' p-qaṭálle] dáwəd.'

One day, two, four, one day he takes his sword, he wants to strike him with it, in order to kill him, to kill David [or: he will kill him, he will kill David].

(192) malàx qam-šaqálle sèpa,' qam-
daréle mən-ʾél dáwəd go-gùda.'

An angel took the sword [and] put it above David in the wall.

---

¹³³ See fn. 131 above.

(193) sèle yonatán' g-emárre qày,' réšox k-ṭàrəṣ' ʾaz-qáy q-qaṭlətte?' g-émer p-qaṭlənne.'

Jonathan came, he tells him, "Why? Your head heals [when he plays for you] so why do you kill him?" He says, "I shall kill him."

(194) wéle mìra šíne' máni dəd-qaṭólle gòlyat,' palgót dawólta p-póya ṭàle,' u-bràti' mìxal' ṭále ᴴmatanà.ᴴᴵ ʾaz-ʾé náq[la] hám p-pá[y]əš xətne' u-hám p-pá[y]əš...' k-sáyən mànne.'

He had said also, "Whoever kills Goliath, half of the wealth [or: kingdom] will be his, and my daughter Michal—a gift for him." So now, he will also become his son-in-law, and also become... he hates him.

(195) sə́mle mànne,' ʾè wéla.' ᴴbə-sóf šel-davàr,...ᴴᴵ séla ᴴmalḥamà,ᴴᴵ ʾərə́qle bàsre,' ʾərə́qle bàsre'[134] dáwəd ha-mmélex zə̀lle,' zə́lle l-ᴴmaʿarátᴴᴵ ʾelyáhu naví ᴴbeḥèfa.ᴴᴵ

He hated him, that was that [=all of that happened]. Eventually, war came, he chased after him, he chased after him,[134] king David went, he went to the cave of Eliyahu the prophet in Haifa.

(196) nobə̀llele' tmanyá ʾəmmáe ᴴbaḥurìm,ᴴᴵ ʾə̀mme,' túle go-ᴴmaʿarà,ᴴᴵ mṭošéle gyàne' mən-qam-šàʾul' g-ʾərə̀qla.'

He took with him eight hundred men, he sat in the cave, he hid himself from Saul, he ran away.

(197) ʾay-rút u-naʿómi moḥkyàli?' xlə̀ṣla?' rút [u-]naʿòmi,' hè.' sélan ʾàxxa.'

The one of Ruth and Naomi I've [already] told? It's finished? Ruth and Naomi, yes. We came here [in the story].

(198) BA: hè,' hè,' hè.'

BA: Yes, yes, yes.

---

[134] See fn. 102 above.

(199) SZ: ʾaz-dáwəd ha-mmélex sèle,' sèle,' ᴴróš ha-šanà,ᴴ' wéle go-ᴴmaʿarátᴴ ʾelyáhu navì.' | So [with regard to] king David, Rosh Hashana came, he was in the cave of Eliyahu the prophet.

(200) tmanyá ʾəmmáe ᴴḥayalímᴴ ʾə̀tle,' g-ə́be ʾàxli' g-ə́be šàte,' làt-le.' màni b-ya[wə́]le?' ḥukúma lèwa ʾə́mme,' ḥukúma wéla ʾə́mməd šàʾul.' | He has eight hundred soldiers, they need to eat, they need to drink, he does not have [anything to give them]. Who will give him? [= no one will give him] The government [or: reign] is not with him, the government [or: reign] is with Saul.

(201) ʾìsen' xàʾ,' ʾelimèlex.' wéle go-ḥèfa,' ᴴʿašîrᴴ' dəd-kùlla,' kúlla yəsraʾèl-ile.' ᴴgilóᴴ135 ʾe ᴴgilò,ᴴ' dìde-ila. kúlla ᴴgilóᴴ dìde-ila.' | There is one, Elimelech. He was in Haifa, a rich [person] of all of Israel [i.e., very rich, the richest]. Gilo,[135] this Gilo, is his. All of Gilo is his.

(202) ʾə̀tle,' bàxta,' ʾàya' bába ᴴʿašîrᴴ-ile,' ᴴgilóᴴ dìda-ila,' šə́mma-ile dárya díde gìla,' ᴴgilóᴴ kúlla wéla ksúta bəd-šə́mma.' u-góra ᴴʿašîrᴴ-ile,' ʾə́tle...' ʾə̀rxe' u-ʾə́tle ṭaḥùne' u-ʾə́tle qàmxa.' | He has, a wife, she, her father is rich. Gilo is hers, she was named after it Gila [lit. her name was put Gila; or: he put her name Gila], all of Gilo belongs to her [lit. is written in her name]. And her husband is rich, he has... a mill and he has a mill [Ar.], and he has flour.

(203) mšodárre tré ᴴḥayyalímᴴ kə̀sle' g-émer séla ᴴroš-ha-šanàᴴ' g-əbéli ʾə̀rba,' g-ə́be' pəsər-rèša'136 g-ə́be ʾó-məndi ʾò-məndi.' | He sent two soldiers to him he says, "Rosh Hashana came, I need sheep, need head-flesh,[136] need this and that."

---

[135] A modern neighbourhood in the south of Jerusalem, near the site of biblical Gilo (Josh. 15.41; 2 Sam. 15.12). See §5.17 above.

[136] It is a custom to eat the flesh of the head of an animal or a fish in the festive meal of Rosh Hashana eve.

(204) g-ər-lá g-ya[wə́]nne čù-məndi.ˈ

He says, "I will not give him anything."

(205) g-ərrále gìla,ˈ m̓àṭo lá g-yawáxle?!ˈ tmanya-ʾəmáe ᴴḥayyalímᴴ ʾə̀tleˈ tíwa go-ᴴmaʿaràᴴˈ bắla ʾixàla,ˈ štàya,ˈ ʾə̀rba,ˈ qàmxa,ˈ rə̀zza,ˈ šàkar.ˈ

Gila tells him, "How will you not give to him?! He has eight hundred soldiers sitting [=staying] in a cave with him, without food, drink, sheep, flour, rice, sugar."

(206) g-émer lá g-ya[wə̀]nne čù-məndi.ˈ fèratˈ yàtwatˈ ha-ʾàsqad šı́ la-g-ya[wə́]nne.ˈ

He says, "I will not give him anything. You [can] fly [or] sit, even this much I will not give him."

(207) g-əmrá de-tú ʾəl-dùkox.

She says, "Well sit at your place."

(208) [m]pə́qla básər ᴴḥayyalìm,ᴴˈ g-ə́mra ᴴbòʾu,ᴴˈ g-ə́mra sáʾun màruleˈ márun ta-dàwid,ˈ ʾàna,ˈ—

She went out after the soldiers, she says, "Come," she says, "Go [and] say to him, say to David, that I—

(209) wəl-šqúlloxun xá waràqa,ˈ—sáʾun šqòlunˈ ʾə̀s[ra]ˈ t̤làṣiˈ ʾə́m[ma] a xamšı́ kəsyása rə̀zza,ˈ mən-ṭaḥúne dìdi.ˈ

here, take a piece of paper [=confirmation]—come take ten, thirty, a hundred um fifty bags of rice, from my mill.

(210) mʾošə̀ri.ˈ¹³⁷ xamšı́ kəsyása qàmxa,ˈ mən-ṭaḥúnət qàmxa.ˈ xamšı́ bakbùke,ˈ¹³⁸ ʾəmmá bakbúke ᴴšèmənᴴˈ mən-ṭáḥ-ˈ ᴴšèmənᴴ dídi.ˈ

I've authorised [that]. Fifty bags of flour, from the flour-mill. Fifty bottles, a hundred bottles of oil from my mi[ll], oil."

---

¹³⁷ The Modern Hebrew root ʾšr is used here with NENA morphology.
¹³⁸ The Modern Hebrew word baqbùq is here given a NENA plural form. The corresponding NENA words are bə̀ṭle, baqbaqìyat.

(211) hùlla,ˈ màd ʾɔ́tla,ˈ húlla waràqaˈ xtəmla¹³⁹ ʾálla,ˈ sáʾun šqólun xòlun.ˈ

She gave, whatever she has, she gave a piece of paper [and] signed it, "Come take [and] eat.

(212) sáʾun lə-ʾə̀rba,ˈ ʾəmmá réše ʾɔ́rba mèsun,ˈ ʾúzule ta-ᴴroš-ha-šanà.ᴴˈ

Come to the sheep, bring one hundred heads of sheep, prepare them [lit. it] for Rosh Hashana."

(213) ṭòv,ˈ ʾilá[ha] máʾmər bèsax,ˈ¹⁴⁰ gilá hùlla.ˈ

Good. May God build your house,¹⁴⁰ Gila gave.

(214) séla dʾɔ́ra, wéle tə̀kyā,ˈ gòra.ˈ

She came [and] returned, he was reclined [and] relaxed], her husband.

(215) g-əmrà-le,ˈ là húllox čù-məndi,ˈ ta-dàwid.ˈ tmanyàˈ ʾəmmàyaˈ ᴴḥayylìmᴴ ʾɔ́tleˈ u-látle maxə̀llu,ˈ séle ᴴroš-ha-šanáᴴ u-ʾə̀za,ˈ ʾáxnan ʾàxlaxˈ ʾáwa là ʾáxəl?!ˈ

She says to him, "You did not give anything, to David. Eight hundred soldiers he has and he does not have [anything] to feed them, Rosh Hashana came and the festival, we shall eat [and] he shall not eat?!"

(216) g-er-lá g-yawə̀nne,ˈ ʾɔ́tli ṭaḥùnaˈ u-ʾɔ́tli kùllu-geb.ˈ

He says, "I shall not give him, I have a mill and I have everything."

(217) g-əmrá xud-rèšoxˈ ʾàsqad húlliˈ u-ʾàsqadˈ u-ʾàsqadˈ u-ʾàsqadˈ u-

She says, "[By the] life of your head, I gave this much, and this much, and this much, and

---

¹³⁹ The NENA root *xtm* 'to seal, to end, to obscure, to overfill or to be overfull' (Sabar 2002a, 202) is used here with the meaning of its Hebrew cognate, 'to sign'.

¹⁴⁰ A blessing expressing gratitude.

qam-xatmánnu¹⁴¹ ᴴxatímaᴴ¹⁴² dìdox,ˈ u-mṭelu ʾə́lle ʾawáe.ˈ

I signed them [with] your signature, and the things have [already] arrived to him."

(218) ʾóha màtle,ˈ pqèʾle l-dúke,ˈ màtle l-dúke!ˈ

This one [= the husband] died, he exploded [i.e., died from anger] on the spot [lit. his place], he died on the spot [lit. his place]!

(219) BA: pqèʾle!ˈ

BA: He exploded!

(220) SZ: pqèʾle!ˈ g-ə́mra pqòʾˈ sì.ˈ

SZ: He exploded! She says, "Explode, go ahead."

(221) básər xlə́šla mən-ᴴšəvʿáᴴ¹⁴³ díde yàrxa,ˈ¹⁴⁴ mšodə̀rra,ˈ g-ə́mra ṣrùxuleˈ dàwidˈ ʾáse ʾàxxa.ˈ

After she had finished with his shivʿa,¹⁴³ month,¹⁴⁴ she sent [word], she says, "Call David to come [or: he should come] here."

(222) séle dàwidˈ túla ʾə̀mme,ˈ mə̀rra-le,ˈ g-emə́rra ṛàba,ˈ ᴴtodá rəbbáᴴ ṭàlax,ˈ hullàx-lan,ˈ u-ʾə̀šlanˈ u-xə̀llan,ˈ u-mosèlan u-,ˈ ᴴkol-tòvᴴ.ˈ

David came, she sat with him, she told him, he tells her, "Many thanks to you, you gave us, and we ate [lit. ate dinner], and we ate, and we brought and, all the good [of the earth, i.e., an abundance of high-quality foods]."

---

¹⁴¹ See fn. 139 above.
¹⁴² The Modern Hebrew lexeme ḥatimà is given NENA phonology here: ḥ > x, penultimate stress.
¹⁴³ The mourning period of seven days.
¹⁴⁴ The mourning period of a month.

(223) g-ə́mra mènex,' xá ḥál u-qə́sta ʾèha-la,' ʾé báxta¹⁴⁵ pə́šla yàbbum,'¹⁴⁶ ʾàna' kúllu ʾánya ʾarxàsa' u-ʾánya kùllu kaswánnu b-šə̀mmox,'

She says, "Look, that is the situation [lit. one situation and story is that], this woman¹⁴⁵ became *yibbum*,¹⁴⁶ and all these mills, and all these, I will write them in your name [i.e., I will make you the owner],

(224) ᴴʾavàl,ᴴ hwí ᴴfèr,ᴴ|¹⁴⁷ ʾàp-aya nábəlla¹⁴⁵ dámməd péšət ᴴmèlex,ᴴ| šqùlla' péša bàxtox.'

but be fair, take also her¹⁴⁵ when you become king, take her [and] she will be your wife."

(225) g-ér go-ʾèni.' húlle ʾízu d-xa-u-xə̀t.'

He says, "In my eye [=I agree completely]." They gave their hands of each other [=they shook hands].

(226) BA: mát̩o mpə́lla yábbum ʾə̀lle,' xolá ʾaxón...'

BA: How [do you mean] she fell *yibbum* on him, after all [is he] the brother of...

(227) SZ: là yábbum!' g-əmrále pə́šla ʾarmə̀lsa,'

SZ: Not *yibbum*! She tells him she became a widow,

(228) BA: ʾà' ʾarmə̀lsa,'

BA: Oh, a widow,

(229) SZ: u-ᴴtseʿiràᴴ-la,' u-ʾə́tla màl,' u-ʾə́tla...'

SZ: And she is young, and she has property [or: wealth], and she has...

(230) ʾó mál ta-máni b-yawànne?' ᴴgilòᴴ|¹⁴⁸ b-šə̀mmòx,' ʾərxawása

"This wealth, to whom will I give [it]? Gilo¹⁴⁸ is in your name [=yours], the mills are

---

¹⁴⁵ See fn. 108 above. The switch from first to third person here produces 'combined speech'; see Golomb (1968).

¹⁴⁶ Levirate marriage. See §5.4 and fns 44 and 101 earlier in this chapter. Unlike Ruth, Gila did not need *yibbum*, and Samra corrects herself in (227) below.

¹⁴⁷ Borrowed into Hebrew from English 'fair'.

¹⁴⁸ The neighbourhood. See fn. 135 above.

ṭàlox,' ˀá[hə]t ᴴmagíaᶜᴴ ṭálox ᴴha-kòl.ᴴ'	for you, you are entitled to everything."
(231) g-ér ᴴmagiˁáᴴ ˀà[ha]t ší táli.' šqə́lle ˀìza.' zə́lle ˀàya mséla ˀàya' pə́šle dáwid ha-mmèlex.'	He says, "I am also entitled to you." He took her hand. Some time has passed [lit. this one went this one brought], he became king David.
(232) BA: ᴴyòfiᴴ!'	BA: Great!
(233) SZ: zə̀lle...' šáˀul ṭˁéle ˀə̀lle' qam-xazèle,' ˀàwa,' xzéle šáˀul dmìxa,' qṭéˀle ˀásqad m-ˁabáyye dìde,' šqə́lle xá laqqá m-xabúša dìde' štéle máya dìde' là nḥə́qle ˀə̀lle.'	SZ: He went... Saul searched for him. [It was] he [=David] [who] found him, he found him asleep, he cut this much of his cloak, he took a bite of his apple, he drank his water, [but] he did not touch him.
(234) ksúle ṭàle,' ˀána là' q-qaṭlə̀nnox,' ˀàhət' g-ə́bət qaṭlə̀tti' ˀána lá g-qaṭlə̀nnox,' ˀáhət ᴴmélex yəsraˀèlᴴ-wət.'	He wrote to him, "I shall not kill you, you want to kill me, I shall not kill you, you are the king of Israel."
(235) SZ: xaráe ᴴba-sòfᴴ e' šáˀul ha-mmélex básər ṭlà[ha] yóme,' zə́lle kə́z e...' bàxta,' e ᴴkor[ˀ]ím-laᴴ raḥèla.'	SZ: After that in the end, uh, king Saul after three days, went to uh... a woman, uh, her name is Raḥela.
(236) g-emə́rra psóx ṭàli' báxta pasxáwa bəd-fàla,' k-iˀáwa má-ˀiz go-ᴴˁolàmᴴ' má lès.'	He tells her, "Open [my fortune] for me [= tell me my fortune]," a woman that used to open fortunes [i.e., she was a fortune-teller], she knew what there is in the world [and] what there is not.
(237) g-ə́mra-wan...' šáˀul ha-mmèlex' wéle ˀə̀sya qábəl' ṭlá[ha]-yárxe	She says, "I'm... king Saul came to me three months ago, I swore to him [lit. I am sworn

kàsli,| wan-yəmísa ž-ˀíze là pasxán ta-čù-xxa.| là zéˀla šáˀul ha-mmèlex híle.|

(238) ˀána lá g-naḥqàna ˀəl-^Hséfer^H la-g-pàsxan,| čə́kkən wan-márta xá xábra ta-šáˀul ha-mmèlex ^Hlò,| lò!^H|

"on his hand] that I shall not open [the fortune] for anyone." She did not know that it is king Saul.

"I shall not touch the book [and] not open, because I have said [lit. I am said] [this] one thing [or: word] to king Saul, no—no!"

(239) g-ér psòx,| là kšáfle gyàne| ^Hˀával^H g-émer ˀàna... e| paṭrə̀nnax,[149] šóqən paṭèrrax šáˀul ha-mmélex mɔ́n,| mən-momàsa dídax.| psə̀xla,| xzèla,| šamúˀel ha-nnàvi-le.

He says, "Open," he did not reveal himself, but, he says, "I will... exempt you, I will see that king Saul exempts you from your oath." She opened, she saw, it is Samuel the prophet.

(240) xzéla dámməd séle šamúˀel ha-nnàvi,| k-ı̀ˀa,| šáˀul mayə̀s,| xàḷaṣ.| là-məḥkela,| g-ə̀mra,| sa-xzì.| má ˀíz gó...|

She saw when Samuel the prophet came, she knows, Saul shall die, that's it. She did not speak, she says, "Come see, what there is in the..."

(241) psə̀xla,| u-xzéle šamúˀel ha-nnàvi.| šamúˀel ha-nnàvi g-ére,| šáˀul,| ṭlá[ha] yóme ˀə́tlox piše,| ˀàhət u-kúd ṭlá[ha] bnóne dídox ˀásət qṭàla.| zèˀle.|

She opened, and he saw Samuel the prophet. Samuel the prophet tells him, "Saul, you have three days [lit. three days you have remained], you and your three sons will be killed [lit. come to killing]." He knew.

(242) pášle ^Hholè.^H| ˀày báxta,| ˀúzlale ^Hmaràkim^H| šòrḅa| máyət ksèsa,| qam-maxlàle,| qam-maštyàle,|

He became sick. That woman, she made for him soups, thick [rice] soup, chicken soup [lit. chicken water], she fed him, she gave him to drink, he slept

---

[149] The Modern Hebrew root *ptr* is used here with NENA morphology.

dmáxle kásla ṭlá[ha] yòme,¹ pə́šla ᴴməlḥamàᴴ¹ kúd ṭlàhun...¹

there [lit. at hers] three days, a war started, all three of them...

(243) xzéle kúd¹ ṭláhun yalúnke díde qṭìlin.¹ ʾáwa šìn pṣíʿa¹⁵⁰ wèle,¹ dréle sépa dìde,¹ məndéle gyàne¹ ʾápawa zə̀lle.¹ ʾaz-máni pìšən?¹ dáwid ha-mmélex pə́šle ᴴmélex yəsraʾèl.ᴴ¹

He saw all his three children getting killed. He [himself] also was wounded, he put his sword, he threw himself, he also went [away, i.e., died]. So who became [king] [or: who remained (alive)]? King David became the king of Israel.

(244) BA: ʾəmhə̀m,¹

BA: mmmm...

(245) SZ: mád qṭə́lle qṭə̀lle,¹ u-mád ʾə́mme ysə̀qle¹ ʾəl-ᴴšəltòn,¹ bárux ha-šèm,ᴴ¹ ḥkə̀mle.

SZ: Whatever he killed he killed, whatever [=whoever] was with him ascended to the rule, blessed be the Lord, he reigned.

---

[150] The Modern Hebrew root *pṣʿ* is used here with NENA morphology.

CHAPTER 3: A FOLKTALE

At the centre of this chapter is a folktale told in the Jewish Zakho NENA dialect. This is a rather unusual folktale, since it is built around a relatively uncommon motif in folk-literature, that of magical gender transformation. The folktale, 'The King and the Wazir', was told by Ḥabuba Messusani.

1.0. The Folktales of the Jews of Zakho

An essential part of the rich oral heritage of the Jewish community of Zakho is the large and complex corpus of folktales. This draws on both Jewish and Kurdish folklore: many of the tales bear distinctive Jewish characteristics, while others belong to the general regional repertoire. Recounting folktales, and listening to them, was a very common and popular shared pastime of the communities of Kurdistan. The very same folktales, in different versions, with additions, omissions or creative embellishments—all depending on the taste (and talent) of the tellers and their audience—could be told throughout Kurdistan, and in all of its different languages and dialects. The practice of storytelling continued in the Jewish-Kurdish communities in Israel: the senior members of the Zakho community in Jerusalem tell of the regular gatherings in a *diwan*, a drawing room of a home of one of the elders of the community, for the purpose of telling and listening to stories. Zakho folktales vary in length from relatively short ones, like the one presented here, to very long ones capable of filling several long consecutive winter evenings—oral novels, one may call them. Folktales are a social institution that plays a role in the forming and maintaining of Zakho communal identity. They also perform a function in intergenerational communication: in a society that experienced a deep intergenerational gap brought about by the sharp transition to modern Israel (see Sabar 1975),[1] folktales (and other oral genres) are a mode of contact between the generation of the grandparents and their grandchildren.[2]

2.0. 'The King and the Wazir': Synopsis

A king and his wazir go out to explore their town, wearing ordinary clothes. After crossing a bridge, the wazir's horse breaks into a gallop, leaving the king alone. The king arrives at a river, and

---

[1] About the social changes within the community caused by the migration, see Gavish (2010, 316–36).

[2] For published Jewish Zakho folktales see: Socin (1882, 159–68, 219–23); Polotsky (1967), two episodes from a 'novel'; Alon and Meehan (1979); Avinery (1978; 1988, 48–65); Zaken (1997); Shilo (2014), a collection of 14 folktales written originally in NENA (not transcribed from a recording), which I edited; Aloni (2014a, 65–79). An important collection of oral literature of the Jews of Kurdistan, though only in English, is Sabar (1982). The most important collection of folktales in the Jewish NENA dialect of Zakho remains unpublished. It is a corpus of 33 stories recorded from Mamo ('uncle') Yona Gabbay Zaqen, father of the teller of our present folktale, Ḥabuba Messusani. Mamo Yona (Zakho 1867–Jerusalem 1970), an exceptional bearer and performer of the rich tradition of the Jews of Kurdistan and a well-known storyteller throughout Iraqi Kurdistan, was recorded during 1964 by Prof. Yona Sabar for the Hebrew University's Jewish Language Traditions Project (*Mifʿal Masorot ha-Lašon*; see Fellman 1978). Only a small portion of this material has been published, in Sabar (2005): Mamo Yona's own life story, narrated by him.

he sits down in order to eat and rest. He plays with his ring, and it falls into the water. The king dives into the water in order to recover his ring, and when he gets out, *yímmed máya* 'the mother of the water' (a water spirit) hits him on the head, and he is transformed into a woman. As he sees his reflection in the water, he realises that he is now a very beautiful woman. Some fishermen who pass by take the beautiful woman, with the intention of marrying her to the son of their own king. The king and queen are astounded by the woman's beauty, and their son the prince falls in love with her. The woman and the prince get married and have three children. To celebrate the third birth, the king throws a *seherane* 'an outdoor celebration' for all his people. The woman goes to the riverside in order to look again for her lost ring (the king's ring). She sees the ring in the water, and gets into the river to take it. The mother of the water comes again, hits her on the head, and the woman becomes a man once more, the king. He does not know what to do next.

In the meantime, the wazir, who had fallen from his horse, is found by some hunters, who, seeing his beautiful clothes and horse, realise that he is an important man. He does not remember who he is, as he has lost his memory. The hunters take him to a hospital, where he is given care for one year. A professor takes him home to be his servant, and eventually the wazir becomes like a son to him. One day while the wazir is riding his horse, the horse again gallops, and the wazir falls off at the same place where he had fallen before. He regains his memory. The wazir and his adoptive father go to the wazir's home, but his wife does not recognise him. She suggests that they should go to the imam, and he will decide whether the wazir is her husband or not.

The king also comes back to his home. His wife does not believe that he is her husband, so he also waits for the imam to come on Friday. The imam, who turns out to be Bahlul, the king's brother, decrees that the king is the king and that the wazir is the wazir, and he sends them back to their homes.

The prince, who had been married to the woman whom the king became, searches for his wife everywhere. Eventually he arrives in the town of the king and the wazir. He goes to the imam and tells him about his lost wife. The imam tells the prince that his wife is not lost, but is a king. The king demands that the prince give him the children that he bore as a woman, and tells the whole story of his transformation. The imam decrees that the prince should keep those children, since the king has other children whom he had earlier fathered as a man. The king and the prince both return to their homes.

3.0. The Motif of Gender Transformation

Many of the motifs[3] that appear in our story are known from other literary and folk traditions. To list but a few: the king and his wazir go out wearing ordinary clothes (motif K1812.17 'king in disguise to spy out his kingdom'); the king drops his ring in water and then recovers it (K1812.17 'Solomon's power to hold

---

[3] As classified by Thompson (1955–1958). Motif numbers and titles discussed here are taken from Thompson's classification. For the concept of motif in folklore, and critiques thereof, see Dundes (1962); Ben-Amos (1980); Ben-Amos (1995). See also ch. 2, §3.1.

kingdom dependent on ring; drops it in water'); *yímmed máya* 'the mother of the water' (motif F420 'water spirits');[4] the king looks at his reflection in the water after having been transformed and sees an extraordinarily beautiful woman (motif T11.5.1 'falling in love with one's own reflection in water. (Narcissus.)').[5] But the most surprising motif in our folktale, and one which plays a fundamental role in its structure, is certainly motif D10 'transformation to person of different sex'.[6]

Motif D10 is relatively uncommon in literary and folk traditions cross-culturally. In both written and oral literature, it is predominantly found in narratives from the Indian cultural space,[7] though it is not restricted to it. Some of its other occurrences in oral folk-literature come from the Middle-East–Egypt (El-Shamy 1980, 33–38), Turkey (Walker and Uysal 1992, 241–

---

[4] In his index, Noy (Neuman 1954, 395) refers to Ginzberg (1909–1938, V:87, 204), who lists several occurrences of water spirits in Jewish literature. Ginzberg mentions the belief, also found in Greek literature, that "water is the abode of demons."

[5] See also motif J1791.6.1.

[6] Similar relevant motifs are: D10.2 'change of sex after crossing water'; D12 'transformation: man to woman'; D695 'man transformed to woman has children'; T578 'pregnant man'.

[7] For a thorough overview of the sources, see Brown (1927); Penzer (1927).

43), the Jews of Iraqi Kurdistan,[8] and the Jews of Yemen[9]—although it appears in non–Middle Eastern traditions as well.[10]

Only one occurrence of motif D10 is to be found in classical Jewish literature. It is found in a story about a poor widower whose wife left him a nursing baby. The widower could not afford a wet nurse, and by way of miracle gained breasts and fed his son himself (Babylonian Talmud, Shabbat 53b).[11]

Perhaps the most well-known occurrence of D10 in Western culture is the Greek myth of Tiresias, the blind prophet who, as a punishment from Hera for hurting a pair of copulating snakes, spends seven years as a woman and gives birth to children. After encountering another pair of copulating snakes and sparing them, he is released from his punishment. Having the experience of being both a man and a woman, Tiresias is asked to judge in an argument between Zeus and his wife Hera: who has more pleasure in sexual relations, men or women? Tiresias agrees with Zeus, and says that women's enjoyment is ten times greater.

An Indian story from the Mahabharata, the story of King Bhangaswana (Ganguli ca. 1900, 35–38, book 13, §12), shares

---

[8] In addition to our folktale, tales number 3932, 13471, and 16376 at the Israel Folktale Archives Named in Honor of Dov Noy (IFA), University of Haifa.

[9] Tale number 1235 at IFA.

[10] For instance, it is found in Benin, China, the French-speaking region of Canada, Inuit regions, and Ireland. See Thompson (1955–1958, II:8–9); Thompson and Balys (1958, 97).

[11] Noy (Neuman 1954, 281) gives several cases of male embryos transformed into females in the womb.

many plot elements with our folktale. King Bhangaswana is punished by Indra for not including him in a sacrificial ceremony. He is transformed into a woman while bathing in a lake. Bhangaswana had one hundred sons as a man and one hundred sons as a woman. They all slew one another in a battle incited by Indra. When Indra pardons Bhangaswana, now living as an ascetic woman, he asks which of the children should be resurrected. Bhangaswana replies that those he had as a woman should be resurrected, since the affection of a woman for her children is greater than that of a man for his. Highly pleased by the woman's truthfulness, Indra resurrects all two hundred children. He then gives Bhangaswana the choice of being a man or a woman, but Bhangaswana chooses to remain a woman, since the pleasure a woman finds in sexual relations is greater than that of a man.

The many print and manuscript versions of the *Arabian Nights* include four stories which contain the motif of a change of gender: 'The Enchanted Spring', 'Hasan the King of Egypt', 'Warlock and the Young Cook of Baghdad', and 'Shahab al-Din' (stories number 191, 545, 412, and 435 in Marzolph, Leeuwen and Wassouf 2004). The latter two correspond to international tale-type ATU 681 'relativity of time' (Uther 2004, I:373; Marzolph, Leeuwen, and Wassouf 2004, 797), previously known as tale-type AT 681 'king in a bath; years of experience in a moment' (Aarne and Thompson 1961, 238). 'Hasan the King of Egypt' is reminiscent of an Egyptian oral tale (El-Shamy 1980, 33–38). In 'Warlock and the Young Cook of Baghdad' a transformed vizier gets married and gives birth to seven children; the transformed vizier of 'Hasan the King of Egypt' gives birth to only a single child. In all four stories the change of sex is by means of dipping in water.

The oldest of the Middle-Eastern manifestation of the motif is the one of the tale of Khurafa (*Ḥadith Khurafa*).[12] In its most elaborate version, in the book *Al-Fākhir* by 9th-century writer Al-Mufaḍḍal ibn Salama, Khurafa, taken prisoner by three *jinns*, hears the following story told by a man: the man was transformed into a woman after being trapped in a particular well; he then got married and gave birth to two children; after some time he went back to the same well, was transformed back into a man, got married again and had two more children.[13]

The final story that will be mentioned here is possibly the earliest recorded folktale of the Jews of Zakho. It also includes the transformation of men into women in proximity to water—in this case, the transformation of two men. This is a Jewish Zakho NENA text recorded by Socin as early as 1870 from Pineḥas of Zakho,[14] which recounts the story of the two brothers ʿAli and ʿAmar (Socin 1882). Sabar (2002b) has published an updated version of this story, written in language as if it were told in the 1950s, together with a commentary on the linguistic differences between the two versions. In this story, the son of ʿAmar and his friend go hunting. They chase after a gazelle for three days, and

---

[12] See Drory (1994), where she claims that *Ḥadith Khurafa* was one of the earliest "attempts to legitimize fiction in classical Arabic literature". See also Marzolph, Leeuwen, and Wassouf (2004, 616).

[13] This story is classified by El-Shamy (2004, 378, as tale-type 705B "'I have begotten children from my loins, and from my womb!': Khurâfah's experience," where he lists more of its occurrences.

[14] Sabar (2002b, 613), suggests that this is Pineḥas Čilmèro.

on the third day they reach a river. The gazelle leaps over it and says to them, "Stop following me. God will, if you are men, you will become women; if you are women, you will become men!" (Sabar 2002b, 625). They marry men and live as women for seven years. One of them gives birth to a triplet of boys, and the other to a triplet of girls. One day they dress as men, take their horses, and ride to find the gazelle. Again they chase after her for three days, and then reach a river. The Gazelle leaps again and says the same words, and the two are transformed back into men and return to their homes.

Almost all of the stories mentioned here present a curious coupling: the proximity of motif D10 to water. Indeed, in his article about the motif in Indian literature, Brown (1927, 4) lists "bathing in an enchanted pool or stream" as the first of five means by which a change of sex is effected,[15] and Penzer, after providing an overview of cases of sex transformation "by a magic pill, seal or plant, or merely by mutual agreement with a superhuman being" (Penzer 1927, 224), writes that "as the *motif* travelled westward it seems that water became the more usual medium" (Penzer 1927, 224).

One more element of our story deserves comment: the name of the imam, Bahlul. The character of Bahlul, or Behlül Dane—the clever brother, or son, of caliph Harun Al-Rashid—is well-known from many folktales, especially those originating in

---

[15] The other four are curse or blessing of a deity; exchanging sex with a Yakṣa, "a creature that is unique in possessing the power to make this remarkable exchange"; by magic; by the power of righteousness or in consequence of wickedness. See Brown (1927, 4–5).

eastern Turkey (Walker and Uysal 1966, 296). A whole sub-genre of folktales features him. In all of them he seems at first like a simpleton, or pretends to be one, but eventually proves his mental and moral superiority over everyone, including the caliph. One of the many Behlül Dane stories is particularly relevant to our folktale. In the story 'Behlül Dane Teaches God's Time versus Human Time' (told by Hacı Mehmet Sivri in 1974; see Walker and Uysal 1992, 241–43), the caliph Harun Reşit is sceptical when he hears Behlül Dane saying, "I have a God whose one hour is equivalent to a thousand of our hours." When entering the bathroom with a kettle of water, Harun Reşit has a vision in which he lives as a woman for years, gets married, and has children. He then wakes up to discover himself still in his bathroom.

4.0. *Baxtox ḥakoma-la* 'your wife is a king': Gender Boundaries and Perplexity

Many scholars have commented on the cultural and social unrest and anxiety that undermining gender boundaries may create.[16] In

---

[16] For example, "Cross-dressing is about gender confusion." About this sentence, taken from Marjorie Garber's book *Vested Interests: Cross-Dressing and Cultural Anxiety* (1992, 390), Tova Rosen (2003, 149–50), writes: "If clothing is a language, then cross-dressing poses a gender riddle. Clothes are intended both to cover and to reveal; they hide the body's sexual signs and, at the same time, signify the binarism of the sexes. The concealed anatomical differences are replaced by a culturally determined gendered symbolism of clothing. Thus, in texts, as well as in life, clothing functions as a code for sexual (and other) differences. Moreover, the language of clothing does not only encode 'masculinity' or 'femininity', but rather points to the very constructedness of gender

our folktale, confusion generated by the focal point of motif D10—the notion that breaking genders boundaries is possible, even by magic—permeates many of the narrative elements. There is a latent sense of confusion everywhere: in the plot and the reasoning of its events, in the words and the actions of the characters, in the narration, even in the language of the folktale. From the very first event in the storyline, obscurity is present. The wazir's horse breaks into a gallop for no apparent reason. He then falls from it, loses his memory, and spends several years under another identity. The king is transformed into a woman by a water spirit, gets married, and has children. He has not done anything to enrage the water spirit to merit this unwelcome transformation.[17]

What is the reason for or purpose of these ordeals? Do they come as a punishment, or in order to teach some lesson? In many of the other stories built around these motifs, some rationale for the tormenting adventures undergone by the characters is given: they are either punished by enraged gods or spirits, or taught a lesson after showing disbelief. Not in our folktale. The king and the wazir's long and harsh ordeals come and then go away with

---

categories. Cross-dressing, on the other hand, manifests the discontinuity between the sexual body and the cultural gender and, thus, offers a challenge to easy notions of binarism." Also, Meiri (2011, 164–65): "Transsexuality evokes categorical and epistemic crises more than any other form of crossing of gender.... [T]ranssexuality, in its visibility, holds in itself the various anxieties evoked by different forms of crossing of gender" (my translation).

[17] On gender transformation as unexpected and unwelcome, see Brown (1927, 6–9).

no apparent motive or benefit of a lesson learned. Even when their period of transformation is done and they regain their original identity, there are hardships involved—the disbelief of the wives, the king torn away from the children he gave birth to as a woman, the prince losing his beloved wife—and no greater power, position, wealth or wisdom—no compensation—is gained. This is a Kafkaesque folktale, almost as Kafkaesque as Kafka's own *Metamorphosis*, where the suffering of the protagonists is left unexplained and unresolved.

The words of the king after being transformed back into a man in his second encounter with the mother of the water, where we would expect him to rejoice at having recovered his identity, are

(45) wi-má-b-ozən ʾə-nàqla?ˈ... lá-k-iʾən ma-ʾòzən.ˈ
 'Oh, what shall I do now?... I do not know what to do.'

His confusion is evident, and is growing:

(46) la-k-îʾa ma-ʾòza,ˈ ta-máni ʾáza ʾámra ʾána ḥakòma-wan.ˈ ta-máni ʾámra ʾána bax-ḥakòma-wan.ˈ
 'She does not know what to do, to whom would she go [and] say "I am the king"? To whom would she say "I am the wife of the king"?'

This reaction of the king, his manhood restored, seems even more helpless than his reaction to his first transformation, where he simply wore his original man's clothing and was taken away by the fishermen.

The peak of confusion and loss of identity in the story is found in the secondary character, the wazir. When he is found by the hunters after he has fallen from his horse, the following short dialogue takes place:

(51) là-g-maḥke,ˈ la-hè la-lá,ˈ g-əmríle màni-wət?ˈ g-émer là-k-iʾen, wéle pṣìˁa.ˈ m-èka wét? g-émer là-k-iʾen.ˈ

'He does not speak, not "yes" [and] not "no," they say to him "who are you?" He says, "I don't know," he is wounded. "Where are you from?" He says, "I don't know."'

The wazir's words are at variance with his appearance, a tension between his external identity markers and his own lack of identity: he is recognised by the hunters as being an important person by his clothing and horse, but the external aspects of his identity do not help him when he loses his sense of self.

The atmosphere of confusion is not created by the events of the storyline alone; stylistic features of the narrative contribute to it as well. For instance, the characters are nameless. Only one character, who appears towards the end of the story, has a name: the imam Bahlul. It is interesting to note that the named imam Bahlul plays a role of clarifying the events and restoring order. Indeed, also the children of the wazir, who play no role in the story as characters, are given names: Mirza-Maḥamad, Aḥmad, and Fatma. Their only function is to be named. The knowledge of their names is used as proof of identity. That is, once again, names and naming take part in restoring order. The lack of names of characters, which is a well-known characteristic of fairy-tales in itself, contributes to the confusion of the listener due to the identity transformations in our folktale. Furthermore, the confusion is aggravated. Our folktale contains three kings (the main character; the father of the prince; and the prince, who is also referred to as king), three queens (the wife of the main character; the mother of the prince; and the woman who used to be king, who is referred to as queen after marrying the prince), and three women (the main character; the wazir's wife; the main character's wife). These sets of characters are referred to as 'the king', 'the queen', and 'the woman' respectively, without specification.

It seems that even the teller of the story herself partakes in the general bafflement. The following episode occurs just before the wazir goes out for the ride which will bring about the regaining of his memory:

(55) ʾáwaˈ qə́mle xà-yoma,ˈ g-ə́mri wéle ḥakòma,ˈ ʾə́tle ṭèra.ˈ ḥakóma dóhun màtle.ˈ ʾə́tle ṭéra g-mandèle.ˈ
'He rose one day, they say there's a king, who has a bird. Their king died. He has a bird which they throw.'

This episode, which seems incoherent and has no clear ties to preceding or subsequent events, is located at a crucial point of the storyline, just before all the entanglements of the story begin to be resolved.

Gender transformation spreads confusion and chaos even in the grammatical structure of the language of the folktale: at the points of transformation, as well as when the king later recounts his experiences, the use of referential elements with specified gender—pronouns and conjugations—becomes unclear. Grammatical elements of the 'wrong' gender are used both before and after a transformation takes place. For example, in (44)–(46):[18]

(44) pə́š-la gòra.'...
become.PFV-3FS man.M
'She became a man...'

(46) qə́m-la lwiš-í-la júlle dìd-a'...
rise.PFV-3FS dress.PFV-ACC.3PL-3FS clothes.PL GEN-3FS
'She rose [and] wore her clothes...'

(46) ...mxé-la l-ʾúrxa
hit.PFV-3FS on-way.F
'...and started walking.'

And also, (79)–(81):

(79) báxt-ox ḥakòma-la.'...
wife.F-POSS.2MS king.M-COP.3FS
'Your wife is a king';

(80) k-xáze gòr-a híle,'...
ind-see.IPFV.3M.SG husabnd.M-POSS.3FS COP.3MS
'He [= the king] sees it is her [= the king's] husband';

(81) g-émer yalúnkəd mà?' ʾa[he]t-gòra wə́t!'
ind-say.IPFV.3MS children-GEN what you.MS-man.M COP.2MS
'He [= the husband] says [to the king]: "Children of what? You are a man!"'

(81) ṃạ̀ṭo' yalúnke mes-ən-nu-lax?'
how children bring.IPFV-1MS-ACC.3PL-DAT.2FS
'"How will I bring you [feminine] the children?"'

---

[18] For the purpose of clarifying the grammatical gender discrepancies, the following examples are glossed. For explanation of the abbreviations used see ch. 1, fn. 42.

The same grammatical confusion occurs in other places in our folktale as well.[19]

5.0. 'The King and the Wazir': The Text

This folktale,[20] 'The King and the Wazir', told by Ḥabuba Messusani, was recorded on 7 January 2013 at Ḥabuba's home in Jerusalem's Katamonim neighbourhood, where many of the Jewish immigrants from Kurdistan settled when arriving in 1951. Ḥabuba was born in Zakho in 1936 and came to Jerusalem in 1951. As mentioned, she is the daughter of the famous storyteller Mamo Yona Gabbay.[21] Present in the recording session were Ḥabuba Messusani (HM), Batia Aloni (BA), Prof. Geoffrey Khan (GK), and myself. The recording ID is HM130107T4 00:04–12:16.[22]

---

[19] This linguistic abnormality appears also in the story of the brothers ʿAli and ʿAmar; see Socin (1882, 164, ln. 6; Sabar 2002b, 621, no. 51).
[20] This folktale clearly belongs to the genre of fairy-tale (*Märchen*). It presents the genre's distinctive characteristics: unknown time and place of happening, nameless protagonists, archetypical characters, miraculous incidents, and supernatural beings. That being said, keep in mind Dundes's assertion (1964, 252): "…thus far in the illustrious history of the discipline [=folkloristics], not so much as one genre has been completely defined."
[21] See fn. 2 above.
[22] The recording is available for listening on the North-Eastern Neo-Aramaic Database Project site at https://nena.ames.cam.ac.uk/dialects/78/.

(1) HM: ᴴhayá mélexᴴ xá ḥakòma' u-wazìra.'

HM: There was a king, a king, and a wazir.

(2) ḥakóma g-émer ta-wazíra dìde,' d²³-áx xàzax' má hìle' ᴴmaṣàvᴴ' bážer dèni.'

The king says to his wazir, "Let us see what is the situation of our town.

(3) b-lóšax júlle dád ᴴragìl,ᴴ' hàdxa,' júlləd dàrwiše,' b-áx zàvrax.'

We shall wear these ordinary clothes [lit. clothes of regular], like that, beggars' clothes, we shall go [and] wander around."

(4) g-émer[r]e go-ʾèni.'²⁴

He says to him, "upon my eyes."²⁴

(5) g-émer náblax xa-ġolàma ʾə́mman,' g-émer là.'

He says, "Shall we take a servant with us?" he says, "No."

(6) ṭón xápča ʾawàye,' ʾixàla,' u-drí go-kə́sta dìdox,'

Carry some things, food, and put [them] in your bag,

(7) ʾá[hə]t go-mahíne dídox, ʾàna go-mahíne dídi' kútran b-áx.

you on [lit. in] your horse, I on [lit. in] my horse. Both of us will go.

(8) [m]pə́qlu básər gə̀šra,'

They went out, [and right] after the bridge,

(9) mahíne dəd wàzir' dhə̀rra.'²⁵ ʾí u-dì²⁶ u-ʾrə́qla u-ʾrə́qla u-ʾrə́qla u-ʾrə́qla u-qam-nablále ʾèmma,' hìl' ʾúrxət-ᴴʾezeᴴ xamšá ᴴkelométerᴴ qam-mamp[ə]làle.'

the wazir's horse broke into gallop. I and di²⁶ she ran and ran and ran and ran and took him [= the wazir] with her, until a distance [lit. way] of some five kilometres [where] she dropped him.

---

²³ Contraction of the interjection *de*.
²⁴ Idiomatic expression meaning 'I will fulfill your request'.
²⁵ The Modern Hebrew root *dhr* is used here with NENA morphology.
²⁶ Sabar (2002a, 141): "*day-day-day*: sounds describing speed of racing animals."

(10) *pə́šle ḥákoma* ᴴ*levàd,*ᴴ¹ *lá-k-i'e 'éka 'àl,*¹ *'éka lá 'àzəl.*¹²⁷

The king was left [lit. became] alone, he does not know where he should go, where he should not go.[28]

(11) *zə̀lle.*¹

He started walking [lit. he went].

(12) *zə́lle*²⁹ *xzéle xá,*¹ *xawòra.*¹ *xawóra k-î'ət mà-yle?*¹

He went[29] [and] saw a river. Do you know what is *xawóra*?

(13) GK: ... he...

GK: ... Yes...

(14) HM: *xawòra,*¹ ᴴ*nàhar.*ᴴ¹

HM: *xawóra*, a river.

(15) *xzéle-xa xawòra,*¹ *rùwwa.*¹

He saw a river, [a] big [one].

(16) *qə́mle túle ž̌*³⁰*-dáw... tàma.*¹

He rose [and] sat down upon that... there.

(17) *šláxle ḥášak dídox*³¹ ᴴ*na'alà...*ᴴ¹ *qundáre dìde,*¹ *dréle 'áqle go-ṃàya,*¹ *mopə́qle xápča 'ixála xə̀lle,*¹ *mopə́qle józi díde 'úzlele xa-qàhwa,*¹ *mto'ə́lle bə́d*¹ *'asə́qsa díde hàdxa.*¹ *'asə́qsa díde mpélla go-ṃàya.*¹

He took off, excuse my language,[31] his shoes..., [and] put his feet in the water. He took out some food [and] ate, took out his coffee kettle [and] made himself a coffee, he played with his ring, like that. His ring fell into the water.

---

[27] Note the use of two allomorphic forms of the same verb within one sentence: *'àl, 'àzəl*.

[28] Idiomatic expression meaning 'he did not know where to go, he was utterly perplexed'.

[29] This repetition of a word or phrase with this intonation is a typical stylistic feature of Jewish Zakho NENA narration. It usually appears at the beginning of an episode in the narrative. See also ch. 2, fn. 102.

[30] Contraction of *rəš-*.

[31] Sabar (2002a, 169) on *ḥàšak dōxun*: "All present/of you excluded (said after saying a dirty word)."

(18) wày g-émer¹ mpə̀lla¹ ʾátta lá-k-iʾən ʾéka má b-òzen,¹ d-lá ʾasə̀qsa.¹ qə̀mle,¹ šláxle júlle dìde¹ u-g-émer b-àn,¹ kóšən go-ṃàya,¹ zéʾli ʾéka mpə̀lla.¹ mapqə̀nna.¹

"Oh!" he says, "It fell, now I do not know where, what I shall do, without a ring." He rose, took off his clothes, and he says, "I shall go, go down into the water, [since] I know where it fell. I shall bring it out."

(19) mpə́qle, yímmed ṃáya³² sèla.¹ mxéla-[ʾəl]le xá… hə̀nna¹³³ rašóma³⁴ go-rèše,¹ qam-ʾozále xà ᴴbaḥorà,ᴴ¹ lá g-hanélox ʾə̀bba men[xət].¹ ḥakòma pášle ᴴbaḥurà.ᴴ¹

[When] he went out [of the water], the Mother of the Water³² came. She struck him with one… this,³³ rašòma³⁴ upon his head. She turned him into such a girl, you could not stare enough at [lit. you would not enjoy (i.e., be satisfied) to stare at her]. The king became a young woman.

(20) k-xáze gyàne,¹ bràta-le!¹ xà sqélta! lá g-hanèlox ʾə̀bba.¹

He sees himself [= his reflection in the river], he is a woman! So beautiful! You could not enjoy [staring enough] at.

(21) [m]pə́qle l-wàrya,¹ júllet gùre-lu táma. lúšle júlle dìde¹ túle l-tàma.¹³⁵

He went out [of the water], men's clothes were there. He wore his clothes. He sat there.³⁵

(22) sèlu,¹ ʾánya¹ də́d g-dóqi hə̀nna¹ šabakvàne¹ g-ə́be dóqi g-doqí

Came, these, who catch *this*, fishermen, they want to catch, they catch fish. They see this

---

³² Sabar (2002a, 177): "a female ghost that dwells in the river."

³³ See note on *hə̀nna* in §5.0 of the Introduction.

³⁴ Sabar (2002a, 292): "vertical hand used as cursing sign; a blow with open hand on top of the head (to indicate disdain, disapproval…)." Also appears in Rivlin (1959, 226, 240).

³⁵ Verbal forms and pronouns in this sentence are masculine. The woman is still referred to as a man here.

nunyàsa.' k-xáze ʾé ᴴbaḥuráᴴ hádxa sqə̀lta,' g-ə́mri wálḷa bə́r ḥakóma dèni,' hay-ṭlá[ha] šə́nne wélu bə-zvára xa-ᴴbaḥuráᴴ ṭàḷe,' xa-sqə̀lta,' xa-bràta u-là' g-ráẓe bəd-čù-xa.'	so beautiful girl, they say, "Indeed the son of our king, for three years they have been seeking [lit. turning around] for a girl for him, a beautiful [girl] [or: a beauty], a girl, and he is not satisfied with anyone."
(23) BA: ʿaqə́le la-qṭéʾle ʾəl-čù-xa.'	BA: His mind was not cut on anyone [=He was not satisfied with anyone].
(24) HM: ʾéha b-nabláxla ᴴʾulàyᴴ raẓe-ʾə́bba.'	HM: "This one [=the girl], we shall take her [to him], perhaps he would be satisfied with her."
(25) qə́mlu sèlu,' sèlu,'³⁶ qam-nablíla qămáye kəz-ḥakòma, yímme u-bàbe,' qam-... g-ə́mri,' ʾéha ġe[r]... ʾé ġèr-məndi-la' go-ᴴkól ha-ʿolámᴴ lez-moxwà[sa]' bəs³⁷-sqə́lta-la məń ráḥel ʾəmmènu ʾafə́llu.'	They rose [and] came, they came,³⁶ they took her first to the king, his mother and father, they... say, "That [girl is something] different... she is something different, in the entire world there is not [a girl] like her, she is even more beautiful than Rachel our Mother."³⁸
(26) ᴴtòv.ᴴ' məsélu ᴴyèled,ᴴ ʾéne...' qam-xazèla,' ʿə́šqle ʾə̀lla,' qam-ʾebèla.'	Good. They brought the child [=the prince]. His eyes... he saw her, he fell in love with her, he loved [or: wanted] her.
(27) zə́llu məsélu qam-barxíla ʾə̀lle,' u-ʾáy šàta,' smə̀xla.' [h]wélela xa-bròna.' šátəd...' pə̀šla,' báser	They went [and] brought [and] married them [lit. they blessed her to him], and in that year she became pregnant.

---

³⁶ See fn. 29 above.
³⁷ The shift š > s is due to the following consonant.
³⁸ Rachel the Matriarch.

tré šǝ̀nne,' smɔ̀xla, hwélela xa-bróna xɔ̀t.' báser tré tḷá[ha] šǝ̀nne' smɔ̀xla hwélela xa-bróna xɔ̀t hay-tḷàha.'

She gave birth to a son [lit. a son was born to her]. A year... she stayed [=she did not become pregnant for one year, and then] after two years she became pregnant [again] and gave birth to another son. After two [or] three years she became pregnant [again and] gave birth to another son, that's three.

(28) qǝ́mlu [H]anšey[H]-bàžer,' ʾo ḥakóma mɔ̀rre,' g-émer b-ózen' seheràne.[39] k-ĭʾǝt má-yla seheràne?'

They rose, the people of the city, the king said, he says, "I shall do a *seheràne*."[39] Do you know what is a *seheràne*?

(29) GK: mm

GK: Mm.

(30) HM: mà-yla?'

HM: What is it?

(31) GK: [H]mesibà.[H]'

GK: A party.

(32) BA: [H]naxon.[H]

BA: Right.

(33) HM: seheráne nápqax ʾǝ́l-e...'

HM: *Seheràne*, we go out to the...

(34) BA: [H]mesibà.[H]'

BA: A party.

(35) GK: [H]pìknik.[H]'

GK: A picnic.

(36) HM: ...[H]pǝ̀knǝk.[H]'

HM: ...picnic.

(37) [m]pǝ́qlu b-seheràne,' u-b-nablǝ́nna báxti u-yalúnke dìdi, kúlle ʾixàla' ʾána b-yáwǝn ta-nɔ́š bàžer,' bàlaš.' ʾáse ʾǝl-xǝšbòni,'

They went out for the *seheràne*, "and I shall take my wife and my children, I will give all of the food to the people of the city, for free. They should come at my expense, because

---

[39] Sabar (2002a), 237: "communal procession and picnic in the country side (during Passover or Succoth Holidays)."

čukun-kálsi [h]wélela haytlà[ha] bnóne.'	my daughter-in-law gave birth to three boys."
(38) [m]pə̀qlu.'	They went out.
(39) kàlse-ši,' ᴴmalkà ᴴ-la,'...wéle ᴴkétér ᴴ b-rèša.'	His daughter-in-law, she is also a queen,... [she has] a crown on her head.
(40) zə̀llu,' wélu, ʾaw-yòma' xə̀llu,' štèlu,' kùllu' welu bə-rqàza' u-ḍòla' u-zə̀rne⁴⁰ u' u-mád' g-ə́be' b-ʾ[w]ázat' farà ḥe.'	They went, they were, on that day they ate, they drank, everyone was dancing, and ḍola and zurne,⁴⁰ and whatever is necessary for a celebration [lit. whatever is needed in making celebrations].
(41) ʾéha séla xa-hə́nna b-rèša,' g-ə́mra wàḷḷa' b-azána kəz-gəván ᴴnàhar.ᴴ ʾasə́qsa dídi mpə́lwala tàma.' u-ʾasə́qsa lá xəzyàli.' qam-ʾozáli ʾe-yə́mməd máya ᴴbaḥurà ᴴ'.	That one [= the woman], some *this* came into her head, she says [to herself], "Indeed, I shall go to the riverside. My ring fell there. And I did not find [lit. see] the ring. That Mother of the Water made [= turned] me into a girl."
(42) zə́lla l-tàma,' zə́lla l-táma⁴¹ ʾèna,' báz monə́xla bəd-màya' ʾéna nzə́rra bə[d]-ʾasə̀qsa.' qam-xazyàla.'	She went there, she went there,⁴¹ her eye, she only looked at the water, her eye caught a glance of her ring. She saw it.
(43) wáy! g-ə̀mra' wáḷḷa wéla ʾasə́qsa ʾasə́qsət ḥakòme-la.' p-košàna.'	Oh! She says, "Indeed here is the ring!" It is the ring of the king. "I shall go down [there]."

---

⁴⁰ The *zurne*, a conical wind instrument with a double reed (similar to the Western oboe), is played together with a large double-headed bass drum, the *ḍola*, during weddings and other happy occasions.

⁴¹ See fn. 29 above.

(44) šlixíla júlle dìda, šlixíla júlle dìda,ˈ kùšla.ˈ kùšla,¹⁴² g-ə́ba šáqla ᴴtabàʕat,ᴴˈ séla yímmed màya,ˈ mxéla-la xáˈ rašòma,¹⁴³ pə́šla ḥakòma.ˈ pə́šla gòra.ˈ

She took off her clothes, she took off her clothes, she went down [into the water]. She went down [into the water],⁴² she wants to take the ring, the Mother of the Water came, she hit her with a rašoma⁴³ she became the king. She became a man.

(45) wi-má b-ozə́n ʾə-nàqla?ˈ júlləd baxtàsa ʾísən!ˈ lá-k-iʾən ma-ʾòzən.¹⁴⁴

"Oh what shall I do now [lit. this time]? There are women's clothes! I do not know what to do."⁴⁴

(46) qə́mla lwišíla júlle dìdaˈ mxéla l-ʾúrxa b-[ʾ]àqle u-dí u-dí u-dí u-sèla.ˈ la-k-iʾa ma-ʾòza,ˈ ta-máni ʾáza ʾámra ʾána ḥakòma-wán.ˈ ta-máni ʾámra ʾána bax-ḥakòma-wán.ˈ

She rose [and] wore her clothes and started walking [lit. hit the road by legs] and onwards she came. She does not know what to do, to whom would she go [and] say "I am the king"? To whom would she say "I am the wife of the king"?

(47) lá-k-iʾa mà-[ʾ]oza,ˈ ʾə́tla tḷá[ha] bnóne mànne.¹⁴⁵ ᴴtóvᴴ mṭèla,ˈ ᴴʕaxšávᴴ ʾáya b-šoqànna,ˈ sélan kəz-wàzir.ˈ

She does not know what to do. She has three sons from him.⁴⁵ Good, she arrived, now we shall leave her, we come [lit. came] to the wazir.

(48) wázir sèlu, ʾànyaˈ də̀dˈ g-èzi,ˈ g-dóqiˈ hə̀nnaˈ ṭère.ˈ nəšàre.ˈ

The wazir, they came, those [people] that go [and] catch *this*, birds. Hunters.

---

⁴² See fn. 29 above.

⁴³ See fn. 34 above.

⁴⁴ The verbal forms with which the king refers to himself in (45) are masculine.

⁴⁵ Unlike in (45), where the king is referred to using masculine forms, in (46)–(47) he is referred to using feminine forms.

(49) BA: *nəčàre.*ˈ

BA: Hunters.

(50) HM: *g-él g-mènxi,*ˈ *ʾòˈ xá nàša,*ˈ *mux-ḥakòma-le wázir,*ˈ *xá-kma júlle sqìle-ʾəlle,*ˈ *ʾe mahíne, wele-mpíla l-tàm.*ˈ

HM: He walks, they look. [They see] this, one man, he is like [= he looks like] a king, the wazir, some beautiful clothes he has, and a horse [lit. that horse], he [the wazir] had fallen there [lit. he is fallen there].

(51) *là-g-maḥke,*ˈ *la-hè la-lá,*ˈ *g-əmríle màni-wət?*ˈ *g-émer là-k-iʾen, wéle pṣìʿa.*[46] *m-èka wét? g-émer là-k-iʾen.*ˈ ᴴ*zikarón*ᴴ *díde zəlla.*[47] *la-k-táxer ču-məndi.*

He does not speak, not "yes" [and] not "no," they say to him, "who are you?" He says, "I don't know," he is wounded. "Where are you from?" He says, "I don't know." His memory was gone [lit. went]. He does not remember anything.

(52) *qəmlu qam-nablìle,*ˈ *qam-daréle gó,*ˈ *ʾe hə̀nna,*ˈ *gó xastaxàna,*ˈ *márru ta-dáw...*ˈ *e dóktor g-émer ʾòh! ʾó xà náša rúwwa-le,*ˈ *qam-xazáxle wele-mpíla mən-mahìne,*ˈ *msàdərre,*ˈ *mtàpəl*[48] *ʾə́bbe.*ˈ

They rose and took him, they put him in a, *this*, in a hospital, they said to that... eh doctor, he [= one of the hunters] says, "Oh! This is a great [= important] man, we saw him [he had] fallen down from a horse, fix him, treat him."

(53) *mtopə̀lle*[63] *pə́šle gó...*ˈ *xastaxàna*ˈ ᴴ*éze*ᴴ *xá, xá šàta.*ˈ *g-mbaqríle m-èka wét,*ˈ *g-émer là-k-iʾən,*ˈ

He treated him... he stayed in the hospital for about one year. They ask him "where are you from?" He says "I don't know."

---

[46] The Modern Hebrew root *pṣʿ* is used here with NENA morphology.

[47] Verb in the feminine form, although ᴴ*zikarón*ᴴ is masculine. See fn. 55 below.

[48] The Modern Hebrew root *ṭpl* is used here with NENA morphology. Since the historical emphatic quality of the consonant *ṭ* is not retained in Modern Hebrew, it is pronounced as *t* by Ḥabuba.

ʾéka b-àt?ˈ là-k-iʾən,ˈ pášle l-tàma.ˈ

"Where will you go?" "I don't know." He stayed there.

(54) xà,ˈ muxwàsoxˈ profèsorˈ[49] g-émer ysáloxˈ[50] kə̀sliˈ b-yà[wə]nnoxˈ ʾixàlaˈ štàya,ˈ ʾə́tli šùla,ˈ ʾúzli xápča šùla,ˈ mád g-ə́bət ʾòz.ˈ g-émer hàwwa.ˈ là-k-iʾe čù-məndi.ˈ

One, like yourself, a professor,[49] says, "Come stay with me, I will give you food [and] drink, I have work [for you], do some work for me, do whatever you like." He says, "all right." He does not know anything.

(55) ʾáwaˈ qə́mle xà-yoma,ˈ g-ə́mri wéle ḥakòma,ˈ ʾə́tle ṭèra.ˈ ḥakóma dóhun mə̀tle.ˈ ʾə́tle ṭéra g-mandèle.ˈ

He rose one day, they say there's a king, who has a bird. Their king died. He has a bird which they throw.

(56) ʾóha rkúle mahíne dìde,ˈ mahíne díde dhə̀rra,ˈ dhə̀rra,ˈ dhə̀rra,ˈ[51] ʾə́ka mpə̀lleˈ mpə́lle xa-gar-xét ʾəl-tàm.ˈ ᴴʾavalᴴ-mpə̀lle,ˈ labrélele čù-məndi,ˈ txə̀rre.ˈ

He [the wazir] rode his horse, his horse galloped, galloped, galloped. Where he had fallen, he fell there again. But [when] he fell, nothing happened to him, he remembered.

(57) wáy! g-èmerˈ ʾána wàzir wéliˈ kéle ḥakòma? ʾéka zə̀lle? ʾána pášli ᴴkvàrˈ mevugàr,ˈ zakèn,ᴴˈ mà-b-amrən?ˈ ʾéka p-šaqláli bàxti? la-k-šaqlàli,ˈ ᴴkvárᴴ la-g-bàli!ˈ ʾána wə́l pə̀šli...ˈ la-g-mhémənə ʾə̀bbiˈ díwən ʾána wàzir!ˈ

"Wow!" he says, "I was a wazir! Where is the king? Where has he gone? I became already old, what will I say? Would [lit. where would] my wife take me [back]? She wouldn't take me [back], she doesn't love [or: want] me anymore. Indeed I became... She won't believe me that I am the wazir!"

---

[49] Directed to Prof. Khan.

[50] *Dativus ethicus.*

[51] The Modern Hebrew root *dhr* is used here with NENA morphology.

(58) séle ʾəl-bèsa,' kəz-bàbe,' kəz-daw-bábe d-qam-hənnəlle,¹⁵² g-emə̀rre,' mà qə́ṣṭa?' g-émer hàl' u-qə́ṣṭa dídi hàdxa wèla.' dídi u-dəd-ḥakòma.' ḥakóma zə́lle b-xá ʾàl,' lá-k-iʾen ʾèka zə̀lle,' u-ʾána zə́lli b-xà-ʾal.'

He came home, to his father, to that father of his that did such and such for him,⁵² he says to him, "What is the story?" he says, "My story [lit. situation and story] is thus. Of mine and of the king. The king went to one side, I do not know where he went, and I went to another [lit. one] side [=we separated]."

(59) g-émer de-qú sà bròni,' k-taxréten ʾèka-wət,' go-d-éma bàžer?' g-émer hè.' k-taxrə́tte šə́mmed bèsox,' k-iʾə̀tte?' g-émer hè.' qu-d-àx' b-ásən ʾə̀mmox.'

He [the father] says, "So go ahead [lit. rise come] my son, do you remember where you were?" He says, "Yes." "Do you remember the name of your home, do you know it?" He says "Yes." "So let's go [lit. rise that we shall go], I'll come with you."

(60) šqə́lle ʾáwa u-báxte, làtle yalúnke,' ʾó pə́šle mux-bròne.' se-d-áx b-ásən ʾə̀mmox,' zə́lle ʾə̀mme.'

He took his wife [lit. he took himself and his wife], he doesn't have children, he [the wazir] was [lit. became] like a son to him [lit. his son]. "Let's go [lit. go that we shall go], I'll come with you." He went with him.

(61) zə́lle ʾə̀mme,¹⁵³ mtoqtə́qlu [b-]dàrga,' [m]pə́qla xa-xəddàmta,'—ʾə́tle pàre,' wàzir

He went with him,⁵³ they knocked on the door, a maid opened—he has money, he is a wazir, he receives [lit. take] a salary, his wife receives [lit.

---

⁵² The irregular root *hnl*, with gemination of the second root letter, is derived from *hə̀nna*; see fn. 33 above and §5.0 of the Introduction. Sabar (2002a, 151): "to say this and that; to do this and that, have intercourse...."

⁵³ See fn. 29 above.

hîle,¹ k-šáqəl mà'aš,¹ báxte k-šáqla mà'aš,¹—g-əmrále màni-wət ʾàhət?¹ g-émer ʾána wàzir wə́n,¹ ʾó bésa dìdi-le.¹

(62) g-ə́mra wày!¹ zə́lla məfra ta-báxte g-əmra-xa-šəzàna wəl-sèle,¹ g-émer¹ ʾána wàzir wə́n,¹ ʾó bésa dìdi-le.¹

(63) g-ə́mra màʾurre,¹ máʾurre xázyan ʾèma šəzàna.¹ k-xazyá-le la-g-yaʾàle.¹

(64) g-emə́rra ʾáhat bàxti wát,¹ šə́mmed bróni, mirza-maḥàmad-íle,¹ šə́mmed bróni xèt,¹ ʾàḥmad-íle,¹ šə́mmed bràti¹ fàṭma-le.¹ ʾàna¹ ḥàl¹ u-qə́sta dìdi hádxa-la.¹

(65) g-ə́mrale ḥmòl,¹ tú tamà,¹ xà ʾála.¹ nablánnox kəz-ʾìmam.¹ hăkan-ʾìmam mə̀rre də[d]¹ ᴴbeʾemétᴴ ʾá[hə]t gòri wét,¹ góri, láʾ làʾ¹ lèwət góri.¹

(66) g-emə́rra ᴴbəssèder.ᴴ¹

(67) ḥákoma šíne ṭréle ṭréle ʾáw ḥakòma,¹ séle ʾáp-awa.¹ séle, séle⁵⁴ mṭéle ʾəl bèsa.¹ séle g-pásxa take] the [=his] salary—she [=the maid] tells him "Who are you?" he says, "I am the wazir, this house is mine."

She says, 'Huh?!' She went [and] said to his wife, she says, "A madman indeed came, he is saying 'I am the wazir, this house is mine.'"

She [the wife] says, "Show him in, show him in [and] I'll see what madman [this is]." She sees him [and] she doesn't know [=recognise] him.

He tells her, "You are my wife, the name of my son is Mirza-Maḥamad, the name of my other son is Aḥmad, the name of my daughter is Fatma. I, this is my story [lit. my situation and story is thus]."

She tells him, "Wait, sit over there, aside. I'll take you to the imam. If the imam says that you are my husband, [you are my] husband, [if] not, [then] not, you are not my husband."

He tells her, "Okay."

The king also, he rode and rode that king. He also came. He came, he came⁵⁴ he arrived home. He came, the maid opened the door, he says, "I

---

⁵⁴ See fn. 29 above.

dárga xəddàmta,' g-émer ʾána ḥakóma wə̀n.' ʾána... ʾáya bàxti-la.'

am the king, I... that is my wife."

(68) ʾə́lla g-əmrá, lèwan ʾána báxtox,' ʾáhət wət-pìša ġèr šəkə́l,' lá-welox hàdxa!' ʾátta-wal pə́šlox ġèr hə̀nna!' ʾána là gə-mhémənan ʾə́bbox.' g-émerra ᴴtòv.ᴴ'

On the contrary she replies [lit. says], "I am not your wife, you changed [lit. you became a different shape], you were not like that! Now you indeed became [of] different *this*! I do not believe you." He tells her, "Okay."

(69) ʾáp-awa zə́lle qam-matùle, ʾéka wàzir,' qam-matwíle xàzre.'

He also went, [someone] sat him down where the wazir [was], they sat him down next to him.

(70) yóm ʾəròta,' yóm ʾəròta-g-əmri b-áse ʾímam dèni.' ímam déni ʾáwa b-qàṭeʾ.' k-ìʾe.' ʾə́tle ᴴnevuʾà.ᴴ k-xáza ʾákan d-íle ᴴbe-ʾemèt ᴴ ḥakóma.'

"Friday, [on] Friday our imam will come. Our imam he will decree. He knows. He has [the gift of] prophecy. He sees whether he is really the king."

(71) wálla k-èse,' ʾímam dóhun yóm ʾərròta,' k-xáze bàhlul-íle,' ʾaxón ḥakóm,' k-xàze ʾàwa-le.'

Indeed, their imam comes [on] Friday, he [= the king] sees it is Bahlul, the king's brother. He [= the king] sees it is him.

(72) g-əmríle wálla k-iʾèt,' ʾé hə̀nna' dèni,...' ᴴmišpátᴴ déni qam-mesáxla⁵⁵ kə̀slox.' ᴴkt̂ᴴ là-mṣax.' ʾòha,' ḥakòma-le,' ʾó wàzir-ile.'

They tell him, "Indeed, you know, our *this*... our case [lit. trial] we brought to you. Because we are not able [to decide whether] that [man] is the king [and] this [is the] wa-

---

⁵⁵ Verb in the feminine form, although ᴴmišpátᴴ is masculine. This may be because NENA šarìʾta/šərʿata 'trial, judgment' is feminine. See fn. 47 above.

ʾàhət' màr,' psóx jəzúka⁵⁶ b-qúrˤan dìdox' kan-díle wàzir' kan-díle ḥakòma.'

zir. You, say [= tell us the answer], open a booklet⁵⁶ in your Quran, whether he is the wazir [and] whether he is the king."

(73) g-émer ʾó wázir-ile u-ʾó ḥakòma-le,' dʾórun l-bés gyanòxun.'

He says, "That is the wazir and that is the king, go back to your homes."

(74) qam-nabə́lle ʾáwa l-bèse' u-ʾáwa l-bèse.'

He led them, him to his home and him to his home [= he led each one of them to his home].

(75) ʾó bár ḥakòma,' dód wéla bàxte,' kúlla ʾáy seheràne' pə́šla ˤázaya ʾèlle.' g-ṭáʾe báxte zə̀lla,' u-zə̀ˤla' u-zə̀ˤla' u-...,' la šúqle xá dùksa,' híl ʾamèrika zə́lle!'

That son of the king, that she⁵⁷ was his wife, that entire seheràne⁵⁸ turned into mourning upon him. He is looking for his wife [but] she is gone, and she has disappeared and disappeared and..., He did not leave [out even] one place, he went all the way to America!

(76) čú dúkka lá šúqle híle bə-ṭʾáya ʾə̀lla.' čú-xxa lá k-ìʾe' lé⁵⁹ xə́zya bàxta.'

He did not leave [out even] one place, he is searching for her. No one knows, [no one] had seen a woman.

(77) xzélu xá góra ḥakòma' zə̀lle.' mṭèle l-d-áy bážer,' mṭéle l-d-áy bàžer,' ʾéka b-àl?' zə́lle ʾə́l hə̀nna,' kəz-ʾìmam,' kəz-jèmaˤ.'

They had seen a man, a king. He [already] went [away]. He [= the husband] arrived in that city, where should he go? He went to this, to the imam, to the mosque.

---

⁵⁶ Sabar (2002a, 127): "booklet (of religious or magic nature)." See also ch. 2, fn. 131.

⁵⁷ Meaning, the king who turned into a woman.

⁵⁸ See fn. 39 above.

⁵⁹ Contraction of léwe.

(78) g-emárre bròni' mà' ᴴbakašáᴴ dìdox híla?' g-émer ḥàl' u-qə̀sta' dìdi' hàdxa wéla.' qam-xazéla xá ᴴbaḥuráᴴ rə́š,' bastád ᴴnàhar,ᴴ' qam-meséla ṭàli' u-qam-gorə̀nna' u-[ʾə]tlí ṭlá[ha] bnóne mə̀nna,' u-zàʿla báxti!'

He tells him, "My son, what is your request?" He says, "This is my story [lit. my situation and story was thus]. They [=the fishermen] saw a girl on the river bank, they brought her to me, and I married her, and I have three sons from her, and my wife has disappeared!"

(79) g-émer là záʿla báxtox,' báxtox ḥàl' u-qə́sta hàdxa-la,' báxtox ḥakòma-la.' ʾátta mnablə́nnox kə̀sle,' u-, ʾàwa' b-qaṭéʾla šarʿə́ta dìdox.'

He says, "Your wife has not disappeared, your wife this is her story [lit. the situation and story is thus], your wife is a king, now I shall take you to him, and, he will decree [lit. cut] your judgement."

(80) g-émərre d-àx.' zə́lle qam-nabə́lle.' k-xáze gòra⁶⁰ híle,' ʾáwa k-îʿe, wéle báxta gòra⁶⁰ híle.' g-əmrále⁶¹ kèlu yalúnke dídi?' g-əbànnu!'⁶²

He tells him, "Let's go." He went and led him. He [=the king] sees it is her [=the king's] husband. He [=the king] knows, he was a woman, this is [=was] her husband. She [=the king] tells him, "Where are my children? I want⁶² them!"

(81) g-émer yalúnkəd mà?' ʾa[he]t-gòra wát!' mầṭo' yalúnke mesə́nnu-làx?'⁶³

He [=the husband] says, "Children of what? You are a man! How will I bring you⁶³ the children?"

(82) g-ə́mra ḥàl' u-qə́sta dídi hàdxa-la.' ʾána' mpə̀lla' ʾasə̀qsa' dìdi,'

She [=the king] says, "This is my story [lit. my situation and story is thus]. I, my ring fell, I

---

⁶⁰ The feminine possessive pronoun -a refers to the king.
⁶¹ Feminine verbal form.
⁶² This verb, uttered by the king, is in the feminine form.
⁶³ Feminine pronoun.

hádxa qam-mazvərànna¹ mpə́la go-m̩àya,¹ séla yímmed m̩àya¹ mxélali xá rašòma¹ qam-ʾózali ᴴbahùraᴴ.¹ qam-gorànnox,¹ ʾiláha wə́lleli¹ tlà[ha] bnóne mə́nnox.¹⁶⁴

twisted it [around my finger] like that, it fell into the water, the Mother of the Water came, struck me with a rašòma⁶⁵ [and] turned [lit. made] me into a girl. I married you, God gave me three sons from you.⁶⁴

(83) ʾúzlox seheràne,¹ sèli,¹ ʾéni nzə́rra-[ʾe]l ʾasə́qsa dìdi,¹ ʾasə́qsa dəd-ᴴyahalòmᴴ hîla,¹ də́d,¹ jawàhar.¹

You made a seheràne,⁶⁶ I came, my eye caught a glance of my ring, it is a ring of diamond, of, diamond.

(84) kə́pli g-ə́ban šaqlànna,¹ séla ʾày yímmed m̩áya¹ mxélali xá rašòma¹ qam-ʾozáli xá-gar xə́t gòra.¹⁶⁷

I bent down in order [lit. I want] to take it, that Mother of the Water came, struck me with a rašòma [and] turned [lit. made] me again into a man.⁶⁷

(85) ʾána hakòma-wən,¹ k-xázət ʾàxxa.¹ ʾe-náqla g-ébanⁿ⁶⁸ yalúnke dìdi,¹ mád mə́rre ʾìman,¹ mə́rre tə́li-ilu,¹ ᴴʾoᴴ-tàlox hílu.¹

I am a king, you see here. Now, I want⁶⁸ my children, whatever the imam says [lit. said]. He says [lit. said] they are for me or they are for you [= he will decree either]."

(86) g-emə́rra ᴴgamᴴ-ʾà[h]at zə́llax¹ ᴴgamᴴ-yalùnke yawə̀nnu-lax?¹ ʾilà[ha]-la qabə́lla mə́nnax.¹

He tells her [= the king], "First [lit. also] you went away, and [now you want that] I will give you the children as well?! God will not permit this! [lit. God will not accept it from you;

---

⁶⁴ All forms in (82) referring to the king are feminine.
⁶⁵ See fn. 34 above.
⁶⁶ See fn. 39 above.
⁶⁷ All forms in (84) referring to the king are feminine.
⁶⁸ Feminine verbal form.

= this is a violation of the divine justice]."

(87) sèle-kəz ʾímamˈ ʾímam g-èmer,ˈ ʾá[h]at ʾə́tlax yalùnke,ˈ ʾàwaˈ— yalúnke dìde hílu.ˈ ʾàniˈ yálunke díde ṭàle,ˈ yalúnke dídax ṭàlax,ˈ sí bròni,ˈ ʾílaha-ha[w]e ʾəmmox,ˈ sí gór xa-xèta.ˈ⁶⁹

He came to the imam, the imam says, "You [= the king] [already] have children, he [= the prince]—those are his children. They, his children are for him [= should stay with him], your children are for you. Go my son, may God be with you, go and marry another."⁶⁹

(88) há ʾèha wéla,ˈ ʾáwa zə́lle l-bèse,ˈ ʾó séle l-bèse.ˈ ᴴzéhuᴴ g-ə́bet xa-xèt?ˈ

Here, this is it, he went to his home, [and the other] one went to his home. That's it, would you like another one [= story]?

(89) BA: kúd šmiʾále xà[y]e…ˈ

BA: [May] whoever has heard it live…

(90) HM: …xà[y]e,ˈ kud-là šmiʾále…ˈ⁷⁰ g-ə́bet xa-xèt?ˈ

HM: …live, whoever has not heard it… [also live].⁷⁰ Would you like another one?

---

⁶⁹ All forms in (86)–(87) referring to the king are feminine.
⁷⁰ A common ending formula in NENA folktales.

CLOSING REMARKS

It is my hope that this book has shown the potential inherent in the folkloristic and literary study of Jewish NENA material. As stated in the Introduction, this book is but a first step. Many genres that are represented in the audio-recorded database but do not appear in this book, as well as many additional examples of genres that are represented here, await subsequent studies. Furthermore, content-based approaches to the study of previously published NENA material will surely prove fruitful.

The three chapters of this book have dealt with three oral genres, whose analytical units progressed from smallest to largest. The first chapter dealt with proverbs, the second with the motifemes of an enriched biblical narrative, and the third with a folktale. Each of the themes of these three chapters deserves future attention. The first chapter dealt with only one member of the family of gnomic genres, the proverb. Other members that are represented in the recorded database were not included: jokes, riddles, aphorisms, anecdotes, idiomatic expressions,[1] and more. The second chapter contains an analysis of only a single example of the several enriched biblical narratives recorded in the audio database. These, as well as related published texts, in

---

[1] Though idioms and idiomatic expressions are usually not considered a genre of folklore, but rather a linguistic category, they also belong in the gnomic category.

particular the Jewish NENA Midrashim,[2] await a study uncovering their sources and their ties to previous and contemporary works and traditions. The folktale featured in the third chapter is, as mentioned, one of the shortest of the many folktales recorded in the database. Additionally, the most important collection, both folkloristically and linguistically, of Jewish NENA folktales—the Mamo Yona stories[3]—remains unpublished and unstudied.

The abundance of Neo-Aramaic material presented by recent scholarship and the relative neglect of content-oriented study focused thereupon bring to mind the words of the anthropologist Alfred I. Hallowell, which though directed to anthropologists are relevant also to us:

> So far as the anthropologists are concerned, I believe it is fair to say that while it has been customary over a long period to collect a representative sample of the oral narratives of the people they happen to be studying, it is an open secret that, once recorded, very little subsequent use may be made of such material. Indeed, these archival collections, once published, often moulder on our shelves waiting for the professional folklorist, or someone else, to make use of them in a dim and uncertain future....
>
> This marginal position which oral narratives have occupied in anthropological studies is not due to the inherent nature of the material but to a failure to exploit fully the potentialities of such data. (Hallowell 1947, 544–45, quoted by folklorist William Bascom 1954, 333)

---

[2] Sabar (1985).
[3] See ch. 3, fn. 2. See also Sabar (2005).

It is my hope that we shall not let the uniquely fascinating and varied Neo-Aramaic material "moulder on our shelves," nor that we treat it merely as raw material, inorganic deposit, for grammatical analysis.

REFERENCES

Aarne, Antti Amatus, and Stith Thompson. 1961. *The Types of the Folktale: A Classification and Bibliography*. 2nd edition. Helsinki: Suomalainen Tiedeakatemia.

Abrahams, Roger D., and Barbara A. Babcock. 1977. 'The Literary Use of Proverbs'. *Journal of American Folklore* 90: 414–29.

Alfandari, Rabbi Yaʿaqov. 1998. *Sefer Mutsal Me-ʾEš*. Edited by Naftali Hayyim Sofer. Jerusalem: Mishor.

Alon, Jacqueline, and Charles Meehan. 1979. 'The Boy Whose Tunic Stuck to Him: A Folktale in the Jewish Neo-Aramaic Dialect of Zakho (Iraqi Kurdistan)'. *Israel Oriental Studies* 9: 174–203.

Aloni, Oz. 2014a. *The Neo-Aramaic Speaking Jewish Community of Zakho: A Survey of the Oral Culture*. Saarbrücken: Lambert.

———. 2014b. 'Folk-Narratives in the Jewish Neo-Aramaic Dialect of Zakho: The Case of *Yosef Ve-ʾEḥav*'. In *Neo-Aramaic and Its Linguistic Context*, edited by Geoffrey Khan and Lidia Napiorkowska, 331–44. Piscataway, NJ: Gorgias Press.

———. 2015. 'The Encounter of Neo-Aramaic with Modern Hebrew: The Personal Experience of a Neo-Aramaic Speaker'. *Carmillim* 11: 99–119.

Alsheikh, Rabbi Moshe. 1603–1607. *Marʾot Ha-Tsoveʾot: Peruš ʿal Neviʾim Rišonim*. Venice: Zuan (=Giovanni) Di Gara Press.

ʿAlwan, Ḥabib. 1974. Recorded Performance of the Jewish Zakho NENA Translation of the Book of Ruth, National Library of Israel, National Sound Archive, reel number Y 01790.

Arama, Rabbi Yitzḥak Ben Moshe. 1573. ʿAqedat Yiṣḥaq. Venice: Zuan (=Giovanni) Di Gara Press.

Arewa, E. Ojo, and Alan Dundes. 1964. 'Proverbs and the Ethnography of Speaking Folklore'. *American Anthropologist* 66: 70–85.

Arnold, Werner. 1989–1991. *Das Neuwestaramäische*. Wiesbaden: Harrassowitz.

Arnold, Werner, and Hartmut Bobzin (eds.). 2002. *'Sprich doch mit deinen Knechten aramäische, wir verstehen es!': 60 Beiträge zur Semitistik—Festschrift für Otto Jastrow zum 60. Geburtstag*. Wiesbaden: Harrassowitz.

Arora, Shirley. 1994. 'The Perception of Proverbiality'. In *Wise Words: Essays on the Proverb*, edited by Wolfgang Mieder, 3–29. New York: Garland. Reprinted from *Proverbium* 1 (1984): 1–38.

Avinery, Iddo. 1978. 'Folktale in the Neo-Aramaic Dialect of the Jews of Zakho'. *Journal of the American Oriental Society* 98: 92–96.

———. 1984. 'Sefer Berešit ba-ʾAramit-Yehudit Ḥadaša' [A Review of Sabar (1983)], *Peʿamim* 20: 137–38.

———. 1988. *Ha-Niv ha-ʾArami šel Yehude Zakho: Teqstim be-Ṣeruf Targum ʿIvri, Mavo u-Milon*. Jerusalem: The Israel Academy of Sciences and Humanities.

Avraham Ben Yehudah Leb of Przemysl, Rabbi. 1691. *Petaḥ ha-ʾOhel*. Sulzbach: Moshe Ben ʾUri Shraga Bloch Press.

Azulay, Rabbi Hayyim Yosef David. 1803. *ʾArbaʿa ve-ʿEsrim ʿim Peruš Ḥomat ʾAnakh*. Pisa: Shemuʾel Molkho Press.

———. 1957. *Sefer Midbar Qedemot*. Edited by Avraham Yosef Wertheimer. Jerusalem: Maʿyan Ha-Ḥokhma.

Azzolina, David S. 1987. *Tale Type- and Motif-Indexes: An Annotated Bibliography*. New York: Garland.

Bar-Adon, Pesaḥ. 1930. 'Me-Haʾaramit ha-Mdubberet ʾeṣel ha-Yhudim ha-Kkurdiyyim'. *Ṣiyon: Yediʿot ha-Ḥevra ha-ʾEreṣ ha-Yisraʾelit le-Historya ve-ʾEtnografya* (Zion: Reports of the Land-of-Israel Society for History and Ethnography) 1: 12–13.

Bascom, William R. 1954. 'Four Functions of Folklore'. *The Journal of American Folklore* 67/266: 333–49.

Bauman, Richard, and Charles Briggs. 2003. *Voices of Modernity: Language Ideologies and the Politics of Inequality*. Cambridge: Cambridge University Press.

Ben-Amos, Dan. 1969. 'Analytical Categories and Ethnic Genres'. *Genre* 2/3: 275–301.

———. 1976a. 'Analytical Categories and Ethnic Genres'. In *Folklore Genres*, 215–42. Austin: University of Texas Press. Reprinted from *Genre* 2 (1969): 275–301.

——— (ed.). 1976b. *Folklore Genres*. American Folklore Society Bibliographical and Special Series 26. Austin: University of Texas Press.

———.1980. 'The Concept of Motif in Folklore'. In *Folklore Studies in the Twentieth Century: Proceedings of the Centenary Conference of the Folklore Society*, edited by Venetia J. Newall, 17–36. Woodbridge, UK: Brewer and Totowa, NJ: Rowman and Littlefield.

———. 1982. *Folklore in Context: Essays*. New Delhi: South Asian Publishers.

———. 1995. 'Are There Any Motifs in Folklore?'. In *Thematics Reconsidered: Essays in Honor of Horst S. Daemmrich*, edited by F. Trommler, 71–85. Amsterdam: Rodopi.

Ben-Dor Benite, Zvi. 2009. *The Ten Lost Tribes: A World History*. Oxford: Oxford University Press.

Ben-Rahamim, Yosef. 2006. *One Language and One Speech: Texts in the Jewish Neo-Aramaic Dialect of Azerbaijan*. Jerusalem: Ben-Zvi Institute. [Hebrew]

Ben Sira. 1544. *Sefer ʾAlfa Beta De-Ven Sira*. Venice: Giovanni di Farri and Brothers.

Ben-Yaacob, Avraham. 1981. *Qehilot Yehude Kurdistan*. 2nd edition. Jerusalem: Qiryat Sefer.

Bendix, Regina. 1997. *In Search of Authenticity: The Formation of Folklore Studies*. Madison: University of Wisconsin Press.

Bendix, Regina F., and Galit Hasan-Rokem. 2012. 'Introduction'. In *A Companion to Folklore*, 1–6. Chichester, UK: Wiley-Blackwell.

Benjamin, Israël Ben Joseph. 1859. *Masʿe Yisraʾel*. Translated by David Gordon, Lyck: R' Zvi Hirsch Petzall New Press.

Brauer, Erich. 1947. *Yehude Kurdistan*. Edited by Raphael Patai. Jerusalem: The Israeli Institute for Folklore and Ethnology.

———. 1993. *The Jews of Kurdistan*. Edited by Raphael Patai. Detroit, MI: Wayne State University Press.

Brown, William Norman. 1927. 'Change of Sex as a Hindu Story Motif'. *Journal of the American Oriental Society* 47: 3–24.

Chomsky, Noam. 1965. *Aspects of the Theory of Syntax*. Cambridge: MIT Press.

Coghill, Eleanor. 2016. *The Rise and Fall of Ergativity in Aramaic: Cycles of Alignment Change*. Oxford Studies in Diachronic and Historical Linguistics 21. Oxford: Oxford University Press.

Cohen, Eran. 2012. *The Syntax of Neo-Aramaic: The Jewish Dialect of Zakho*. Piscataway, NJ: Gorgias Press.

Cover, Robert. 1993. 'Nomos and Narrative'. In *Narrative, Violence, and the Law: The Essays of Robert Cover*, edited by Martha Minow, Michael Ryan, and Austin Sarat, 95–172. Ann Arbor: University of Michigan Press.

Dan, Yosef (ed.). 1986. *Sefer Ha-Yyašar*. Jerusalem: Mosad Bialik.

Donabed, Sargon. 2007. 'The Assyrian Heroic Epic of Qaṭīne Gabbara: A Modern Poem in the Ancient Bardic Tradition'. *Folklore* 118: 342–55.

Doron, Edit, and Geoffrey Khan. 2010. 'The Debate on Ergativity in Neo-Aramaic'. *Proceedings of IATL* 26: 1–16.

———. 2012. 'The Typology of Morphological Ergativity in Neo-Aramaic', *Lingua* 122: 225–40.

Dorson, Richard M. 1972. 'Introduction: Concepts of Folklore and Folklife Studies'. In *Folklore and Folklife: An Introduction*, 1–50. Chicago: University of Chicago Press.

Drory, Rina. 1994. 'Three Attempts to Legitimize Fiction in Classical Arabic Literature'. *Jerusalem Studies in Arabic and Islam* 18: 146–64.

Dundes, Alan. 1962. 'From Etic to Emic Units in the Structural Study of Folktales'. *The Journal of American Folklore* 75: 95–105.

———. 1964. 'Texture, Text, and Context'. *Southern Folklore Quarterly* 28: 251–65.

——— (ed.). 1965. *The Study of Folklore*. Englewood Cliffs, NJ: Prentice-Hall.

———. 1981. 'On the Structure of the Proverb'. In Mieder and Dundes, *The Wisdom of Many*, 43–64. New York: Garland. Reprinted from *Proverbium* 25 (1975): 961–73.

Duval, Rubens .1883. *Les dialectes néo-araméens de Salamas: Textes sur l'état actuel de la Perse et contes populaires, publiés avec une traduction française*. Paris: F. Vieweg.

El-Shamy, Hasan M. 1980. *Folktales of Egypt*. Chicago: University of Chicago Press.

———. 2004. *Types of the Folktale in the Arab World: A Demographically Oriented Tale-Type Index*. Bloomington: Indiana University Press.

Elbogen, Ismar. (1913) 1972. *Ha-Tṭfilla be-Yisraʾel be-Hitpatḥutah ha-Historit*. Translated by Yehoshuaʿ Amir, edited by Joseph Heinemann. Tel-Aviv: Dvir.

Elstein, Yoav, and Avidov Lipsker. 2004. 'Qave Yesod ba-Tematologya šel Sifrut ʿAm Yisraʾel'. In *Sippur ʿOqev Sippur: Encyclopedia of the Jewish Story*, vol. I. Edited by Yoav Elstein, Avidov Lipsker, and Rella Kushelevsky, 25–51. Ramat-Gan: Bar-Ilan University Press.

Elstein, Yoav, Avidov Lipsker, and Rella Kushelevsky. 2004. *Sippur ʿOqev Sippur: Encyclopedia of the Jewish Story*, vol. I. Ramat-Gan: Bar-Ilan University Press.

Falk, Rabbi Jacob Joshua Ben Zvi Hirsch. 1739. *Sefer Pney Yehoshuaʿ*, part 2. Frankfurt am Main: David Jakob Kranau.

da Fano, Rabbi Menaḥem Azarya. 1649. *Sefer ʿAsara Maʾamarot*. Venice: Zuan (=Giovanni) Di Gara Press.

Farḥi, Yosef Šabetay. 1864–1870. *Sefer ʿOse Fele*. Livorno: Rabbi Yisrael Qushta and Associates, Moshe Yeshuʿa Toviana Press.

———. 1867. *Toqpo šel Yosef*. Livorno: Rabbi Yisrael Qushta and Associates, Moshe Yeshuʿa Toviana Press.

Fassberg, Steven E. 2010. *The Jewish Neo-Aramaic Dialect of Challa*. Leiden: Brill.

Feitelson, Dina. 1959. 'Aspects of the Social Life of Kurdish Jews'. *Jewish Journal of Sociology* 1 (Maurice Freedman Research Trust, London): 201–16.

Fellman, Kadia. 1978. *Qaṭalog ha-Tiʿud ha-Muqlat*. Jerusalem: The Hebrew University of Jerusalem.

Finnegan, Ruth. 1977. *Oral Poetry: Its Nature, Significance, and Social Context*. Cambridge: Cambridge University Press.

Fischel, Walter Joseph. 1939. *Masaʿ le-Kurdistan, Paras u-Vavel: mi-tokh Sefer ha-Masaʿot šel R' David De-Bet Hillel*. Sinai 5. Jerusalem: Mossad Harav Kook.

Ganguli, Kisari Mohan (trans.). ca. 1900. *The Mahabharata of Krishna-Dwaipayana Vyasa Translated into English Prose from the Original Sanskrit Text*. Calcutta: Oriental.

Garber, Marjorie. 1992. *Vested Interests: Cross-Dressing and Cultural Anxiety*. New York: Routledge.

Gavish, Haya. 2004. *Hayinu Tzionim: Qehilat Yehude Zakho be-Kurdistan, Sipur u-Mismakh*, Jerusalem: Ben-Zvi Institute.

———. 2010. *Unwitting Zionists: The Jewish Community of Zakho in Iraqi Kurdistan*. Detroit, MI: Wayne State University Press.

Gerson-Kiwi, Edith. 1971. 'The Music of the Kurdistan Jews: A Synopsis of their Musical Styles'. *Yuval* 2: 59–72.

Ginzberg, Louis. 1909–1938. *The Legends of the Jews*. 6 vols. Philadelphia, PA: Jewish Publication Society of America.

Goldenberg, Gideon, and Mordekhay Zaken. 1990. 'The Book of Ruth in Neo-Aramaic'. In *Studies in Neo-Aramaic*, edited by Wolfhart Heinrichs, 151–57. Atlanta, GA: Scholars Press.

Golomb, Harai. 1968. 'Combined Speech: A Major Technique in the Prose of S. Y. Agnon—Its Use in the Story "A Different Face"'. *Ha-Sifrut* 1: 251–62. [Hebrew]

Gottheil, Richard James Horatio. 1893. 'The Judæo-Aramæan Dialect of Salamās'. *Journal of the American Oriental Society* 15: 297–310.

Grossman, Avraham. 1995. 'Taḥat ʾAhavati Yistenuni: Ha-ʾEva le-David u-Meniʿeha'. *Mayim mi-Dlayav* 75: 17–32.

Greenblatt, Jared. 2010. *The Jewish Neo-Aramaic Dialect of Amədiya*. Leiden: Brill.

Häberl, Charles G. 2009. *The Neo-Mandaic Dialect of Khorramshahr*. Wiesbaden: Harrassowitz.

Haig, Geoffrey, and Geoffrey Khan (eds.). 2018. *The Languages and Linguistics of Western Asia: An Areal Perspective*. The World of Linguistics 6. Berlin: De Gruyter.

Hallowell, Alfred I. 1947. 'Myth, Culture and Personality'. *American Anthropologist* 49: 544–45.

Haran, Menahem. 1972. 'Ḥagim, Zivḥe Mišpaḥa va-Ḥagigot: Ḥagigat ha-Gez'. In *Tqufot u-Mosadot ba-Miqra: ʿIyyunim Historiyim*, 102–5. Tel-Aviv: Am Oved.

Hasan-Rokem, Galit. 1982a. *Proverbs in Israeli Folk Narratives: A Structural Semantic Analysis*. Helsinki: Suomalainen Tiedeakatemia, Academia Scientiarum Fennica.

———. 1982b. 'Le-Ḥeqer ha-Pitgam ha-ʿAmami ha-Yehudi'. *Tarbiz* 51: 292–81.

———. 1993. *Adam le-Adam Gešer: Pitgamim šel Yehude Geʾorgya be-Yisraʾel (The Proverbs of Georgian Jews in Israel)*. Jerusalem: Ben-Zvi Institute.

Hoberman, Robert D. 1988. 'The History of Modern Aramaic Pronouns and Pronominal Suffixes'. *Journal of the American Oriental Society* 108: 557–75.

———. 1989. *The Syntax and Semantics of Verb Morphology in Modern Aramaic: A Jewish Dialect of Iraqi Kurdistan*. New Haven, CT: American Oriental Society.

———. 1993. 'Chaldean Aramaic of Zakho'. In *Semitica: Serta Philologica Constantino Tsereteli Dicata*, edited by Ricardo Contini, Fabrizio A. Pennacchietti, and Mauro Tosco, 115–26. Turin: Silvio Zamorani Editore.

Honko, Lauri. 2013. *Theoretical Milestones: Selected Writings of Lauri Honko*. Helsinki: Suomalainen Tiedeakatemia, Academia Scientiarum Fennica.

Hopkins, Simon. 1993. 'Yehude Kurdistan be-ʾErets Yisraʾel u-Lšonam'. *Peʿamim* 56: 50–74.

———. 2000. "ʿEdut Qduma la-ʾAramit ha-Ḥadaša be-Maqor ʿAravi-Yehudi'. In *Masoret ve-Šinuy ba-Tarbut ha-ʿAravit-ha-Yehudit šel Yeme-ha-Benayim*, edited by Joshua Blau and David Doron, 119–25. Ramat-Gan: Bar-Ilan University Press.

———. 2002. 'Preterite and Perfect in the Jewish Neo-Aramaic of Kerend (Southern Iranian Kurdistan)'. In Arnold and Bobzin, *'Sprich doch mit deinen Knechten aramäische, wir verstehen es!'*, 281–98. Wiesbaden: Harrassowitz.

Horowitz, Rabbi Yešaʿayah Ben Avraham Ha-Levi. 1649. *Sefer Šene Luḥot ha-Berit*. Amsterdam: Emmanuel Benveniste Press.

Idel, Moshe. 1988. *Kabbalah: New Perspectives*. New Haven, CT: Yale University Press.

———. 1990. *Golem: Jewish Magical and Mystical Traditions on the Artificial Anthropoid*. Albany: State University of New York Press.

Israeli, Yafa. 1997. 'Targum Sefer be-Rešit la-ʾAramit Ḥadaša be-Lahagam šel Yehude Saqqəz'. *Massorot* 9–11: 455–56.

———. 2003. 'Targume ha-Miqra ba-ʾAramit ha-Ḥadaša: Lahag Saqqəz'. *Ba-Mikhlala* 14–15: 39–53.

———. 2014. "ʿEt Šaʿare Raṣon ba-ʾAramit Yehudit Ḥadaša be-Niv Saqqəz'. *Ḥelqat Lašon* 46: 39–57.

Jakobson, Roman, and Petr Bogatyrev. (1929) 1980. 'Folklore as a Special Form of Creation'. Translated by John M. O'Hara, with an introduction by Felix J. Oinas. *Folklore Forum* 13 (Folklore Publications Group, Bloomington): 1–21.

———. (1929) 1982. 'Folklore as a Special Form of Creativity, Translated by Manfred Jacobson'. In *The Prague School: Selected Writings, 1929–1946*, edited by Peter Steiner, 33–46. Austin: University of Texas Press.

Jastrow, Otto. 1992. *Lehrbuch der Turoyo-Sprache*. Wiesbaden: Harrassowitz.

JPS. 1917. *Torah Neviʾim u-Khtuvim, The Holy Scriptures According to the Masoretic Text*. Philadelphia: Jewish Publication Society of America. Accessed online at https://www.mechon-mamre.org/p/pt/pt0.htm.

JPS. 1999. *JPS Hebrew-English Tanakh, the Traditional Hebrew Text and the New JPS Translation*, Philadelphia: Jewish Publication Society of America. Accessed online at http://taggedtanakh.org.

Kapeliuk, Olga. 2011. 'Language Contact between Aramaic Dialects and Iranian'. In *The Semitic Languages: An International Handbook*, edited by Stefan Weninger, Geoffrey Khan, Michael P. Streck, and Janet C. E. Watson, 738–47. Berlin: De Gruyter Mouton.

Kasher, Rimon. 1996. *Toseftot Targum la-Neviʾim*, Jerusalem: Ha-ʾIggud ha-ʿOlami le-Maddeʿe ha-Yahadut.

———. 2000. 'Targume ha-Miqra ha-ʾAramiyim'. *Peʿamim* 13: 70–107.

Khan, Geoffrey. 1999. *A Grammar of Neo-Aramaic: The Dialect of the Jews of Arbel*. Leiden: Brill.

———. 2002. 'The Neo-Aramaic Dialect of the Jews of Rustaqa'. In Arnold and Bobzin, *'Sprich doch mit deinen Knechten aramäische, wir verstehen es!'*, 395–409. Wiesbaden: Harrassowitz.

———. 2004. *The Jewish Neo-Aramaic Dialect of Sulemaniyya and Ḥalabja*. Leiden: Brill.

———. 2005. 'Some Parallels in Linguistic Development between Biblical Hebrew and Neo-Aramaic'. In *Semitic Studies in Honour of Edward Ullendorff*, edited by Geoffrey Khan, 84–108. Leiden: Brill.

———. 2007a. 'The North-Eastern Neo-Aramaic Dialects'. *Journal of Semitic Studies* 52/1: 1–20.

———. 2007b. 'Ergativity in the North Eastern Neo-Aramaic Dialects'. In *Studies in Semitic and General Linguistics in Honor of Gideon Goldenberg*, edited by Tali Bar and Eran Cohen, pp. 147–57. Münster: Ugarit.

———. 2008a. *The Jewish Neo-Aramaic Dialect of Urmi*. Piscataway, NJ: Gorgias Press.

———. 2008b. *The Neo-Aramaic Dialect of Barwar*. Leiden: Brill.

———. 2009. *The Jewish Neo-Aramaic Dialect of Sanandaj*. Piscataway, NJ: Gorgias Press.

———. 2011. 'North-Eastern Neo-Aramaic'. In *The Semitic Languages: An International Handbook*, edited by Stefan Weninger, Geoffrey Khan, Michael P. Streck, and Janet C. E. Watson, 708–24. Berlin: De Gruyter Mouton.

———. 2017. 'Ergativity in Neo-Aramaic'. In *Oxford Handbook of Ergativity*, edited by Jessica Coon, Diane Massam, and Lisa Travis, 873–99. Oxford: Oxford University Press.

Kirchheim, Raphael. 1874. *Peruš ʿal Divre ha-Yamim: Meyoḥas le-ʾEḥad mi-Talmide Seʿadya Gaʾon*. Frankfurt am Main: Brenner.

Kugel, James. 1994. *In Potiphar's House: The Interpretive Life of Biblical Texts*. Cambridge: Harvard University Press.

Kuusi, Matti. 1966. 'Ein Vorschlag für die Terminologie der parömiologischen Strukturanalyse'. *Proverbium* 5: 97–104.

Lamassu, Nineb. 2014. 'Gilgamesh's Plant of Rejuvenation and Qāṭīne's Sīsīsāmbur'. In *Melammu: The Ancient World in an Age of Globalization*, edited by Mark J. Geller, 117–27. Berlin: Max Planck Research Library for the History and Development of Knowledge.

Laniado, Rabbi Shemuʾel Ben Avraham. 1603. *Keli Yaqar: Peruš Neviʾim Rišonim*. Venice: Zuan (=Giovanni) Di Gara Press.

———. 1992. *Keli Yaqar: Peruš Neviʾim Rišonim, Šemuʾel A*, part 2. Edited by Rabbi ʿEzra Baṣri. Jerusalem: Mekhon ha-Ktav.

Levine, Étan. 1973. *The Aramaic Version of Ruth*. Rome: Biblical Institute Press.

Lewin, Benjamin Manasseh. 1940. *ʾOṣar ha-Geʾonim: Thesaurus of the Gaonic Responsa and Commentaries*, vol. IX: Tractate Qidduišin. Jerusalem: Mossad Harav Kook. [Hebrew]

Makhir Ben Abba Mari, Rabbi. 1899. *Yalquṭ ha-Makhiri on the Book of Psalms*. Shelomo (Salomon) Buber edition, 2 vols. Berdychov: Hayyim Jacob Scheftel. [Hebrew]

Malinowski, Bronisław Kaspar. 1926. *Myth in Primitive Psychology*. New York: Norton.

Mann, Jacob. 1931–1935. *Texts and Studies in Jewish History and Literature*. Cincinnati, OH: Hebrew Union College Press.

Marzolph, Ulrich, Richard van Leeuwen, and Hassan Wassouf. 2004. *The Arabian Nights Encyclopedia*. Santa Barbara, CA: ABC-CLIO.

Meiri, Sandra. 2011. *Any Sex You Can Do, I Can Do Better: Cross-Gender in Narrative Cinema*. Tel-Aviv: Hakibbutz Hameuchad.

Menaḥem Ben Rabbi Shelomo, Rabbi. 1900–1901. *Midrash Sekhel Ṭov* (spelled there *Sechel Tob*). Shelomo (Salomon) Buber edition, 2 vols. Berlin: Zvi Hirsch B"R Yitzḥak Itzkowski. [Hebrew]

Mengozzi, Alessandro. 2012. '"That I Might Speak and the Ear Listen to Me!": On Genres in Traditional Modern Aramaic Literature'. *Journal of Semitic Studies* 57: 321–46.

Midrash Aggadah. 1894. Shelomo (Salomon) Buber edition. Vienna: Abraham Fanto. [Hebrew]

Midrash Ruth Rabbah. 1971. Meron Bialik Lerner edition (in unpublished PhD dissertation, The Hebrew University of Jerusalem). [Hebrew] Accessed online at https://www.responsa.co.il/.

Midrash Ruth Zuta. 1925. Shelomo (Salomon) Buber edition, 2nd edition. Vilnius: Romm.

Midrash Shemu'el. 1925. Shelomo (Salomon) Buber edition. Vilnius: Romm.

Mieder, Wolfgang. 1997. 'Modern Paremiology in Retrospect and Prospect'. *Paremia* 6: 399–416.

Mieder, Wolfgang, and Alan Dundes (eds.). 1981. *The Wisdom of Many: Essays on the Proverb*. New York: Garland.

Mole, Kristine. 2002. 'The Chaldean Dialect of Zakho'. MPhil thesis, University of Cambridge.

Morawski, Stefan. 1970. 'The Basic Functions of Quotation'. In *Sign, Language, Culture*, edited by Algirdas Julien Greimas, 690–705. The Hague: Mouton.

Mutzafi, Hezy. 2002a. 'On the Jewish Neo-Aramaic Dialect of Aradhin and Its Dialectal Affinities'. In Arnold and Bobzin, '*Sprich doch mit deinen Knechten aramäische, wir verstehen es!*', 479–88.

———. 2002b. 'Barzani Jewish Neo-Aramaic and Its Dialects'. *Mediterranean Language Review* 14: 41–70.

———. 2004a. *The Jewish Neo-Aramaic Dialect of Koy Sanjaq (Iraqi Kurdistan)*. Wiesbaden: Harrassowitz.

———. 2004b. 'Two Texts in Barzani Jewish Neo-Aramaic'. *Bulletin of SOAS* 67/1: 1–13.

———. 2008a. *The Jewish Neo-Aramaic Dialect of Betanure (Province of Dihok)*. Wiesbaden: Harrassowitz.

———. 2008b. 'Trans-Zab Jewish Neo-Aramaic'. *Bulletin of SOAS* 71/3: 409–431.

———. 2014. *Comparative Lexical Studies in Neo-Mandaic*. Studies in Semitic Languages and Linguistics 73. Leiden: Brill.

Nakano, Aki'o. 1970. 'Texts of Gzira Dialect of Neo-Aramaic'. *Journal of Asian and African Studies* 3: 166–203.

———. 1973. *Conversational Texts in Eastern Neo-Aramaic (Gzira Dialect)*. Tokyo: Institute for the Study of Languages and Cultures of Asia and Africa.

Neuman (Noy), Dov. 1954. 'Motif-Index of Talmudic-Midrashic Literature'. PhD dissertation, Indiana University.

Noorlander, Paul M. 2021. *Ergativity and Other Alignment Types in Neo-Aramaic*. Leiden: Brill.

Noy, Dov. 1971. 'The Jewish Versions of the "Animal Languages" Folktale (AT 670), A Typological-Structural Study'. In *Studies in Aggadah and Folk-Literature*, edited by Joseph Heinemann and Dov Noy, 171–208. Scripta Hierosolymitana 22. Jerusalem: Magnes Press.

Noyes, Dorothy. 2016. *Humble Theory: Folklore's Grasp on Social Life*. Bloomington: Indiana University Press.

Olrik, Axel. (1908) 1965. 'Epic Laws of Folk Narrative'. In *The Study of Folklore*, edited by Alan Dundes, 129–41. Englewood Cliffs, NJ: Prentice-Hall.

Ong, Walter. 1982. *Orality and Literacy*. London: Methuen.

Penzer, Norman Mosley. 1927. *The Ocean of Story: Being C. H. Tawney's Translation of Somadeva's Kathā Sarit Sāgara*, vol. VII. London: Chas. J. Sawyer.

Permiakov, Grigorii L'vovich. 1985. *300 Obshcheupotrebitel'nykh Msskikh Poslovits i Pogovorok*. Moscow: Russkii Iazyk.

Pike, Kenneth L. 1954. *Language in Relation to a Unified Theory of the Structure of Human Behavior*, preliminary edition, part 1. Glendale, CA: Summer Institute of Linguistics.

———. 1967. *Language in Relation to a Unified Theory of the Structure of Human Behavior*. The Hague: Mouton.

Pirqe De-Rabbi Eliʿezer. 1944–1948. Michael Higger edition. Accessed online at https://www.responsa.co.il/.

Polotsky, Hans Jakob. 1967. 'Eastern Neo-Aramaic: Urmia and Zakho'. In *An Aramaic Handbook*, edited by Franz Rosenthal, part II/1, 69–77, part II/2, 97–111. Wiesbaden: Harrassowitz.

Propp, Vladimir. 1958. *Morphology of the Folktale*. Translated by Laurence Scott. Edited by Svatava Pirkova-Jakobson. Bloomington: Research Center, Indiana University.

Rivlin, Yosef Yoʾel (Joseph Joel). 1930. 'Sipur David ve-Golyat bi-Lšon Targum'. *Meʾasef Ṣion* 1: 109–20.

———. 1942. 'Sifrutam šel Yehude Zakho'. In *Sefer Zikaron le-ʾAšer Gulaq ve-li-Šmuʾel Qlayn*, edited by Baruch Shochetman and Alexander Scheiber, 171–86. Jerusalem: Hebrew University Press Association.

———. 1945. 'Pitgamim bi-Lšon Ha-Targum'. *Rešumot: Meʾasef le-Divre Zikhronot le-ʾEtnografya u-l-Folqlor be-Yisraʾel* (new series) 1: 207–15.

———. 1946. 'Pitgamim bi-Lšon Ha-Targum'. *Rešumot: Meʾasef le-Divre Zikhronot le-ʾEtnografya u-l-Folqlor be-Yisraʾel* (new series) 2: 209–14.

———. 1959. *Širat Yehude ha-Targum: Pirkqe ʿAlila u-Gevura be-Fi Yehude Kurdistan*. Jerusalem: Mosad Bialik.

Rodrigues Pereira, Alphons Samuel. 1989–1990. 'Two Syriac Verse Homilies on Joseph'. *Journal of the Ancient Near Eastern Society Ex Oriente Lux (JEOL)*: 95–120.

Rosen, Tova. 2003. *Unveiling Eve: Reading Gender in Medieval Hebrew Literature*. Philadelphia: University of Pennsylvania Press.

Sabar, Yona. 1966. 'Tafsirim la-Miqra u-Fiyutim bi-Lšonam ha-ʾAramit šel Yehude Kurdistan'. *Sefunot* 10: 337–412.

———. 1974. 'Nursery Rhymes and Baby Words in the Jewish Neo-Aramaic Dialect of Zakho (Iraq)'. *Journal of the American Oriental Society* 94: 329–336.

———. 1975. 'The Impact of Israeli Hebrew on the Neo-Aramaic Dialect of the Kurdish Jews of Zakho: A Case of Language Shift'. *Hebrew Union College Annual* 46: 489–508.

———. 1976. *Pešat Wayhi Bešallaḥ: A Neo-Aramaic Midrash on Bešallaḥ*. Wiesbaden: Harrassowitz.

———. 1978. 'Multilingual Proverbs in the Neo-Aramaic Speech of the Jews of Zakho, Iraqi Kurdistan'. *International Journal of Middle East Studies* 9/2: 215–235.

———. 1982a. 'Ha-Yeṣira ha-Sifrutit šel Yehude Kurdistan li-Thumeha'. *Peʿamim* 13: 57–70.

———. 1982b. 'Peruš Daršani le-Sefer Yona ba-ʾAramit Ḥadaša šel Yehude Kurdistan'. In *Hagut ʿIvrit be-ʾArtsot ha-ʾIslam*, edited by Menahem Zohori et al., 130–43. Jerusalem: Brit ʿIvrit ʿOlamit.

———. 1982c. *The Folk Literature of the Kurdistani Jews: An Anthology*. New Haven, CT: Yale University Press.

———. 1983. *Sefer Berešit ba-ʾAramit Ḥadaša be-Nivam šel Yehude Zakho*. Jerusalem: Magnes Press.

———. 1985. *Midrašim ba-ʾAramit Yehude Kurdistan: Le-Paršiyyot Vayḥi, Bešallaḥ ve-Yitro*. Jerusalem: The Israel Academy of Sciences and Humanities.

———, 1988. *Sefer Šemot ba-ʾAramit Ḥadaša be-Nivam šel Yehude Zakho*. Jerusalem: Magnes Press.

———. 1990. *Sefer Wayyiqra ba-ʾAramit Ḥadaša be-Nivam šel Yehude Zakho*. Jerusalem: Magnes Press.

———. 1991. *Targum de-Targum: An Old Neo-Aramaic Version of the Targum on Song of Songs*. Wiesbaden: Harassowitz.

———. 1993. *Sefer Bamidbar ba-ʾAramit Ḥadaša be-Nivam šel Yehude Zakho*. Jerusalem: Magnes Press.

———. 1995a. *Sefer Devarim ba-ʾAramit Ḥadaša be-Nivam šel Yehude Zakho*. Jerusalem: Magnes Press.

———. 1995b. 'The Christian Neo-Aramaic Dialects of Zakho and Dihok: Two Text Samples'. *Journal of the American Oriental Society* 115/1: 33–51.

———. 2002a. *A Jewish Neo-Aramaic Dictionary, Dialects of Amidya, Dihok, Nerwa and Zakho, Northeastern Iraq*. Wiesbaden: Harrassowitz.

———. 2002b. 'The Story of the Brothers Ali and Amar in the Jewish Dialect of Zakho, Based on Albert Socin's Text from 1870, Transcribed Anew as If It Were Told ca. 1950, and Emphasizing the Linguistic Changes that Occurred in the Dialect since Socin's Time'. In Arnold and Bobzin, *'Sprich doch mit deinen Knechten aramäische, wir verstehen es!'*, 613–27. Wiesbaden: Harrassowitz.

———. 2005. 'Yona Gabbay, a Jewish Peddler's Life Story from Iraqi Kurdistan: As Narrated by Him in His Jewish Neo-Aramaic Dialect of Zakho (Four Episodes)'. *Mediterranean Language Review* 16: 167–220.

———. 2006. *Ḥameš ha-Megilot be-Targumehen la-ʾAramit Ḥadaša Yehudit*. Jerusalem: Magnes Press.

———. 2009. *Tafsirim šel Piyyuṭim, Qinot ve-ʾAzharot, be-Nive ʾAramit Ḥadaša šel Yehude Kurdistan*. Jerusalem: Magnes Press.

———. 2014. *Sefer Daniyel be-Targum la-ʾAramit Ḥadaša be-Niv Yehude ʿAməḏya*. Jerusalem: Magnes Press.

Salzer, Felix. 1962. *Structural Hearing: Tonal Coherence in Music*. New York: Dover.

Schenker, Heinrich. 1977. *Free Composition: Der freie Satz—Volume III of New Musical Theories and Fantasies*. Translated by Ernst Oster. Edited by Ernst Oster and Oswald Jonas. New York: Schirmer Books.

Scholem, Gershom. 1941. *Major Trends in Jewish Mysticism*. Jerusalem: Schocken.

Schwarz, Yehosef (Joseph) Ben Menaḥem. 1900. *Sefer Tevuʾot ha-ʾAreṣ*. Edited and expanded by Avraham Moshe Luncz. Jerusalem: Avraham Moshe Luncz.

Searle, John. 1979. 'Literal Meaning'. In *Expression and Meaning: Studies in the Theory of Speech Acts*, 117–36. Cambridge: Cambridge University Press.

Seder ʿOlam Rabbah. 1897. Baer Ratner edition. Vilnius: Romm.

Segal, Judah Benzion. 1955. 'Neo-Aramaic Proverbs of the Jews of Zakho'. *Journal of Near Eastern Studies* 14/4: 251–70.

Seitel, Peter. 1969. 'Proverbs: A Social Use of Metaphor'. *Genre* 2/2: 143–61.

———. 1999. *The Powers of Genre: Interpreting Haya Oral Literature*. New York: Oxford University Press.

Shalom, Naʿim. 1986. *Naʿim Šalom bi-Qriʾa be-Targum Qurdi: Yosef ve-ʾEḥav, ʿAqedat Yiṣḥaq* [CD]. Jerusalem: Naʿim Shalom. Catalogued in the National Library of Israel as *Širim ʾEpiyim ba-ʾAramit Ḥadaša*, CD 07534, Naʿim Shalom (singer); Avraham Bero (oud); Merad Salman (violin).

Shapiro, Rabbi Pinḥas of Koretz. 1911. *Sefer Nofet Tsufim*. Pietrikow: R. Heynekh Ben Rabbi Yešaʿayah Wolf Folman Press.

Shilo, Varda. 1986. *Ha-Bišul ha-Kurdi*. Jerusalem: Varda Shilo.

———. 2014. *Lishana Deni: A Bilingual Anthology of Folktales of the Jewish Community of Zakho*. Edited by Oz Aloni. Jerusalem: Minerva Press. [Hebrew]

Shinan, Avigdor. 1984. *Midraš Šemot Rabba: Parašot 1–14—Yoṣe la-ʾOr ʿal-pi Ketav-Yad še-bi-Yrušalayim u-v-Ṣiddo Ḥilufe-Nusḥaʾot, Peruš u-Mavo me-ʾet ʾAvigdor Šinʾan*, Tel-Aviv: Dvir.

———. 1996. 'ʾIša, Masekha ve-Taḥposet be-Sifrut Ha-ʾAgada šel Ḥazaˮl'. In *Migvan Deʿot ve-Hašqafot be-Tarbut Yisraʾel* 6, 29–52. Jerusalem: Ministry of Education and Culture.

Shoshani, Ronit. 2008. "ʿIyun bi-Šne Sipurim be-Midraš Rut Zuta u-ve-ʿIbudam be-Ḥibur Yafe me-ha-Yešuʿa'. *Jewish Studies (JSIJ)* 7: 81–103.

Shuman, Amy, and Galit Hasan-Rokem. 2012. 'The Poetics of Folklore'. In Bendix and Hasan-Rokem, *A Companion to Folklore*, 55–74. Chichester, UK: Wiley-Blackwell.

Sikili, Rabbi Yaʿakov Ben Ḥananʾel. 1991. *Torat ha-Minḥa: Derašot ʿal ha-Tora u-Moʿadim*. Edited by Barukh ʾAvigdor Ḥefeṣ. Safed: Barukh ʾAvigdor Ḥefeṣ.

Silverman-Weinreich, Beatrice. 1981. 'Toward a Structural Analysis of Yiddish Proverbs'. In Mieder and Dundes, *The Wisdom of Many*, 68–85. Reprinted from *Yivo Annual of Jewish Social Science* 17 (1978): 1–20.

Simon, Uriel. 1992. 'Šaʾul be-ʿEn Dor: ʾIzun Sipuri ben ha-Navi ha-Doḥe u-Vaʿalat ha-ʾOv ha-Meqarevet'. In *Sefer ha-Yovel la-Rav Mordekhay Broyer (Mordechai Breuer)*, edited by Moshe Bar-Asher, vol. I, 113–24. Jerusalem: Academon.

Socin, Albert. 1882. *Die neuaramäischen Dialekte von Urmia bis Mosul: Texte und Übersetzung*. Tübingen: Laupp.

Sokolov, Yuri M. 1950. *Russian Folklore*. New York: Macmillan.

Starr Sered, Susan. 1992. *Women as Ritual Experts*. New York: Oxford University Press.

Stein, Dina. 2015. 'Ha-Zivug ha-Košel ben Temani le-Mošiʿa me-ʿAseret ha-Švatim'. *Peʿamim* 144: 81–121.

Stein Kokin, Daniel. 2013. 'Toward the Source of the Sambatyon: Shabbat Discourse and the Origins of the Sabbatical River Legend'. *Association for Jewish Studies Review* 37: 1–28.

Taylor, Archer. 1981. 'The Wisdom of Many and the Wit of One'. In Mieder and Dundes, *The Wisdom of Many*, 3–9. Reprinted from *Swarthmore College Bulletin* 54 (1962): 4–7.

———. 1985. *The Proverb and An Index to 'The Proverb'*. With an introduction and bibliography by Wolfgang Mieder. Bern: Peter Lang.

Thompson, Stith. 1955–1958. *Motif-Index of Folk-Literature: A Classification of Narrative Elements in Folktales, Ballads, Myths, Fables, Mediaeval Romances, Exempla, Fabliaux, Jest-Books, and Local Legends*. Bloomington: Indiana University Press.

Thompson, Stith, and Jonas Balys. 1958. *The Oral Tales of India*. Bloomington: Indiana University Press.

Tobiah Ben Eliᶜezer, Rabbi. 1880. *Midrash Leqaḥ Ṭov on Genesis and Exodus*. Shelomo (Salomon) Buber edition. Vilnius: Romm. [Hebrew]

———. 1887. *Midrash Leqaḥ Ṭov on Ruth* (spelled there *Lekach Tob*). Seckel Bamberger edition. Aschaffenburg: Druck von Oscar Lehmann, Mainz. [Hebrew]

Tohar, Vered. 2013. 'Ḥoni ha-Meᶜagel Morid Gešamim'. In *Encyclopedia of the Jewish Story*, edited by Yoav Elstein and Avidov Lipsker-Albeck, vol. III, 29–63. Ramat-Gan: Bar-Ilan University Press.

Toolan, Michael. 2005. 'Propp, Vladimir Iakovlevich (1895–1970)'. In *Encyclopedia of Language and Linguistics*, 2nd edition, edited by Keith Brown, 167. Burlington: Elsevier Science.

Trousson, Raymond. 1965. *Un problème de littérature comparée, les études de thèmes: Essai de méthodologie*, Paris: M. J. Minard.

Tsimhoni, Daphne. 1989. 'Memšelet ᶜIraq ve-ha-ᶜAliyya ha-Gdola šel ha-Yehudim le-Yisraʾel'. *Peᶜamim* 39: 64–102.

Uther, Hans-Jörg. 1996. 'Type- and Motif-Indices 1980–1995: An Inventory'. *Asian Folklore Studies* 55/2: 299–317.

———. 2004. *The Types of International Folktales: A Classification and Bibliography*. Helsinki: Suomalainen Tiedeakatemia.

Walker, Warren S., and Ahmet E. Uysal. 1966. *Tales Alive in Turkey*. Cambridge, MA: Harvard University Press.

———. 1992. *More Tales Alive in Turkey*. Lubbock: Texas Tech University Press.

Warda, William, and Edward Odisho. 2000. 'Qateeni Gabbara: A William Daniel's Legacy'. *Journal of Assyrian Academic Studies* 14/1: 6–22.

Wehr, Hans, and J. Milton Cowan. 1976. *Arabic-English Dictionary: The Hans Wehr Dictionary of Modern Written Arabic*. Ithaca, NY: Spoken Language Services.

Weissberg, Isaac Jacob. 1900. *Mišle Qadmonim: ʾO Haynu de-ʾAmre ʾInše, Mahadura Tinyana*. Nizhyn: M. V. Glezer Press.

Weisstein, Ulrich. 1988. *Comparative Literature and Literary Theory: Survey and Introduction*. Translated by William Riggan. Taipei: Bookman Books.

Werses, Shmuel. 1986. 'Ha-ʾAgadot ʿal ʿAseret ha-Švatim ve-ha-Sambatyon ve-Darkhe Qliṭatan be-Sifrutenu ha-Ḥadaša'. *Jerusalem Studies in Jewish Folklore* 9: 38–66.

Whiting, Bartlett Jere. 1952. 'Proverbs and Proverbial Sayings: Introduction'. In *The Frank C. Brown Collection of North Carolina Folklore*, edited by Newman Ivery White, vol. I, 331–59. Durham, NC: Duke University Press.

Yassif, Eli. 1982. 'Terumato šel S. ʿOse Fele la-Siporet ha-ʿAmamit ha-Yehudit'. *Jerusalem Studies in Jewish Folklore* 3: 47–66.

Zaken, Mordechai (Moti). 1997. 'The Fate of Inventors: A Folktale in the Neo-Aramaic of the Jews of Zakho'. In *Massorot* 9–11: *Studies in Language Traditions and Jewish Languages, Volume in Honor of Gideon Goldenberg*, edited by Moshe Bar-Asher, 383–95. Jerusalem: Department of Hebrew Language, The Hebrew University of Jerusalem. [Hebrew]

———. 2007. *Jewish Subjects and Their Tribal Chieftains in Kurdistan: A Study in Survival*. Leiden: Brill.

Zlotnik Avida, Yehuda Leib. 1938. *Midraš ha-Meliṣa ha-ʿIvrit*. Jerusalem: Darom.

INDEX

Aarne-Thompson tale type index, 185, 186
Aaron, 221, 264
Abigail, (Gila of Haifa), 195, 236, 238, 239
Abishai, 240
Abner, 242
Abraham, 137, 220, 264
Abravanel, Rabbi Yitzḥak, 219, 229, 230
ʿAdiqa, Naḥum, 173
Aggadic Midrashim, 8
ʿaguna, 3
Ahwaz, 11
Akkadian, 9, 14
Aleppo, 213
Alfandari, Rabbi Yaʿaqov, 213
Al-Ḥarizi, Rabbi Yehudah, 2
ʿAli Khan Bag, 5
Al-Mufaḍḍal ibn Salama, 289
Alsheikh, Rabbi Moshe, 226
ʿAlwan, Ḥakham Ḥabib, 33, 124, 173, 174, 176, 201, 206
ʿAlwani, Ḥakham Mordekhai, 33
Amadiya, 13

Ammi, Rabbi, 179
Amos, 21, 26, 75, 170, 184, 284
Anti-Lebanon Mountains, 11
Arabian Nights, 287
Arabic, 10, 16, 33, 71, 104, 107, 119, 155, 172, 174, 288
Arama, Rabbi Yitzḥak Ben Moshe, 110
Aramaean tribes, 9
Arbil, 13, 178
Armenia, 224
ʿArodan (Aradhin), 11, 13
Assyrian Empire, 3, 4, 9
Assyrians (Christian Neo-Aramaic people), 9, 196, 224
ʾAtrush, 13
Avraham Ben Yehudah Leb of Przemysl, Rabbi, 227
Azulay, Rabbi Hayyim Yosef David (the Ḥida), 213, 227
Babylonian Talmud
Bava Batra, 200, 205
Bava Qamma, 239
Brakhot, 179

ʿEruvin, 124
Gittin, 204
Horayot, 202
Ḥullin, 221
Megilla, 239
Nazir, 202
Pesaḥim, 212
Qiddushin, 179, 227
Rosh HaShana, 239
Sanhedrin, 164, 202, 205, 206, 211, 226
Shabbat, 91, 93, 98, 104, 210, 286
Sotah, 202
Yevamot, 219
Bahlul, 284, 289, 293, 308
Bakhʿa, 11
Balak king of Moab, 110, 202
Barashe, 13, 23
Baruch, Rabbi Shemuʾel, 176
Barwar, 12
Barzan, 13
Bathsheba, 225, 226, 228, 238, 268
Beit Jala, 238
Benjamin of Tudela, 2
Benjamin, Israël Ben Joseph ('Benjamin the Second'), 3
Berlin, Rabbi Naftali Zvi Yehudah (The Natziv), 230
Betanure, 12, 13

Bethlehem, 198, 199, 200, 202, 203, 246, 248, 251
bgdkpt consonants, 16
Bhangaswana, King, 286
Binding of Isaac, 177
Binyamin, Rabbi Yosef, 176
Bishmiyaye, 12
Boaz, 195, 203, 204, 205, 206, 207, 208, 214, 251, 252, 253, 254, 255, 256
British mandate over Iraq and Palestine, 5
Buridan, Jean, 31
Buridan's ass, 31
Carmel, 196, 236, 238
Caro, Rabbi Yosef, 213
Challa, 13, 23
Chilion, 199, 201
Chronicles, 226, 228
Dahoki, Ḥakham Eliyahu Avraham Yitzḥaq, 178, 219, 222, 224, 227
Damascus, 11
Daniel (Book of), 9
David, King, 27, 280
David D'Beth Hillel, Rabbi, 3
Diviner of Endor, (Raḥela the fortune-teller), 241
Dohok, 12, 13, 92, 178, 219, 222, 224, 227
Ecclesiastes, 177

Eglon king of Moab, 202
Egypt, 4, 10, 285, 287
Elijah the Prophet, 236
Elimelech, 197, 199, 200, 201, 203, 205, 236, 238, 246, 247, 249, 253, 273
Eliyahu of Vilna, Rabbi (the Gaon of Vilna), 213
'Eliyahu, Repha'el, 177
En-Gedi, 236
ergativity, 14, 15
Esau, 83
Esther, 115, 177, 235
etic and emic, 185
Euphrates, River, 4
Exodus, 233
Exodus Rabbah, 233
Ezra (Book of), 9
Falk, Rabbi Yaʻakov Yehoshuaʻ (Jacob Joshua) Ben Zvi Hirsch, 9
da Fano, Rabbi Menaḥem Azarya, 213
Farḥi, Rabbi Yosef Shabbetai, 20, 181
Five Scrolls (Megillot), 170, 176
folkloristics and the study of folklore, 1, 18, 19, 20, 21, 22, 26, 27, 29, 36, 170, 183, 184, 185, 186, 187, 190, 281, 284, 296, 313
Gabbay, (Mamo) Yona, 282, 296, 314
Gabbay, Eliyahu, 173
Gabbay, Salem, 173
Genesis, 9, 83, 221
Genesis Rabbah, 83, 221
genre, 26, 27, 38, 68, 73, 81, 169, 170, 179, 181, 182, 290, 296, 313
Geonim, 228
glossing, morpheme-by-morpheme, 25, 42
gnomic genres, 26, 29, 313
Goliath the Philistine, 261, 263, 267
Gozan, River, 3
Great Synagogue of Zakho, 4, 5
Great Zab, River, 4, 11, 12, 13
Greek literature, 285
gzira, 13
Habor, River, 3
Ḥadith Khurafa, 288
Haifa, 3, 196, 236, 238, 272, 273, 286
Ḥalabja, 173
Halah, 3
ḥaliṣa, 204, 253
Harun Al-Rashid, Caliph, 290

Hera, 286
historical dialectology, 17
Ḥoča, Neḥemya, 173
Ḥodeda, Raḥamim, 173, 175, 177
Ḥomat ʾAnakh, 227
Ḥoni the Circle Maker, 188
Hoshea, King, 3
Huna, Rav, 179
India, 10
Indian literature, 289
Indra, 287
Iran, 11
Iraq, 5, 6
Iraqi Nationality Laws, 6
Isaac, 172, 173, 178, 220, 264
Isaiah, 4
Islamic countries, 6
Israel, State of, 6
Italy, 213
Jacob, 83, 195, 214, 220, 221, 264
Jeremiah, 9
Jerusalem, 4, 5, 6, 7, 23, 89, 105, 113, 120, 149, 172, 196, 217, 226, 236, 238, 239, 258, 262, 273, 281, 282, 296
Jerusalem Talmud Sanhedrin, 239
Jesse (Elishay), 206, 207, 209, 210, 211, 212, 214, 215, 216, 256, 257, 258, 260
Jonah, 175
Jonathan son of king Saul, 196, 218, 231, 232, 233, 234, 270, 271, 272
Joseph, 3, 20, 170, 172, 173, 182, 183, 214
Josephus, 214
Jubbʿadin, 11
Judah, 30, 179, 199, 214, 236
Kabbalah, 243
Kara, 13, 23
Katamonim (neighbourhood in Jerusalem), 7, 296
Keli Yaqar, 212, 226
Kerend, 13
Khabur, River, 2, 4
Koy Sanjaq, 13
Lamentations, 176
language contact, 1, 16
langue and *parole*, 19
Laniado, Rabbi Shemuʾel Ben Avraham, 213, 226
Leah, 214
Lebanon, 6, 11
Leviticus, 219, 223
Leviticus Rabbah, 219, 223
lišana deni, 13, 152

literature of the Jews of Kurdistan, 170, 282
Livorno, 182
Mahabharata, 286
Mahlon, 199, 201
Makhir Ben Abba Mari, Rabbi, 210, 211
Maʿlula, 11
Mandaic, 11, 14
Mantova, 213
Maʿon, 196, 236
Maʿoz Tsion, 7
Mardin, 11
Marʾot Ha-Tzovʾot, 226
marriage, 3, 87, 109, 203, 204, 205, 206, 207, 208, 213, 214, 239, 252, 253, 277
Media (region), 3
Menaḥem Ben Rabbi Shelomo, Rabbi, 210, 221
Midrash Leqaḥ Ṭov (on Genesis and Exodus, Buber edition), 221
Midrash Leqaḥ Ṭov (on Ruth, Bamberger edition), 200, 207, 208
Midrash Ruth Rabbah (Lerner edition), 200, 202, 203, 206, 208
Midrash Ruth Zuta (Buber edition), 200, 207

Midrash Sekhel Ṭov, 210, 221
Midrash Shemuʾel (Buber edition), 219, 220, 221, 223
Midrash Tanḥuma, 110, 131, 200, 205, 219, 221
Midrash Tannaim, 216
Midrash Tehillim, 221, 233
Midrash Yelammdennu, 221
Mlaḥso, 11, 15
Moab (Meʾohav), 199, 200, 201, 202, 249
Moses, 89, 178, 234, 264
Moshe Isserles, Rabbi (Rema), 213
Mosul, 2, 136
motif, 27, 183, 184, 186, 187, 189, 190, 192, 219, 281, 284, 285, 286, 287, 288, 289, 291
motifeme, 26, 27, 169, 183, 190, 191, 192, 194, 195, 196, 197, 202, 207, 208, 209, 210, 218, 219, 220, 221, 222, 223, 232, 234, 235, 238, 243, 244
Nabal, 238, 239
Nachmanides, 4
Naḥman, Rav, 239
Naomi, 27, 169, 197, 198, 199, 200, 201, 202, 203, 204, 206, 207, 208, 238,

245, 246, 247, 248, 249,
250, 252, 253, 255, 256,
272
Narcissus, 285
Neo-Babylonian empire, 9
Neo-Mandaic, 11
Nerwa, 12, 13, 174, 176, 227
Ninth of Ab, 175, 177
Orpah (Orṭa), 201, 202, 249,
250
paremiography, 29
paremiological minimum, 29
paremiology, 26, 29, 37
Passover, 85, 87, 102, 128,
175, 301
Persian Achaemenid empire, 9
Petaḥyah of Regensburg, 2
Pirqey De-Rabbi Eliʿezer (Higger
edition), 242
processes of change in the
Semitic family of languages,
10, 16, 22
proverbs
formula, 41
image, 41, 42, 51
message, 41
synonymy, 41, 42
Psalms, 173, 233
Pushkin, Alexander, 20
Qumran literature, 181
Qurʾan, 172

Rabba Bar Abbuha, 239
Rachel, 300
Ramah, 228
Rashi, 174, 201, 219, 239
responsa, 2
Rewritten Bible, 171, 181, 182
Rosh Hashana, 177, 236, 237,
239, 273, 274, 275
Russian, 20, 29, 81, 186
Rustaqa, 13
Ruwanduz, 13
Saadia Gaon, Rav, 226
Safed, 227
Salamas, 13
Salman, David, 173
Samuel, 211, 212, 215, 216,
228, 239, 241, 242, 257,
258, 259, 260, 279
Sanandaj, 12, 13
Saqqəz, 13, 178
Saul, King, 217, 224, 234, 235,
240, 241, 242, 261, 262
Scholem, Gershom, 243
Sefer ʿAsara Maʾamarot, 213
Sefer Midbar Qedemot, 213
Shabbat, 91, 93, 98, 104, 210,
286
Shabbetai Ben Yaʿaqov, 176
Shalmaneser V, 3
Shalom, Naʿim, 172

Shanbiko, Darwish Ben Shimʿon, 176
Shavuot, 114, 175
Shekhinah, 215, 216, 259, 260
Shukho, 13
Song of Songs, 176
Succoth, 301
Sulemaniyya, 12, 13
Syria, 9
Syriac, 14, 182
Tamar, 214
Targum, 31, 171, 174, 176, 177, 178, 179, 180, 182, 200, 201, 205, 210, 255
Tel-Aviv, 144
Tigris, River, 4, 11
Tiresias, 286
Tobiah Ben Eliʿezer, Rabbi, 200, 207, 208, 221
Tosefta Megillah, 179
transcription system, 24, 30
Trans-Zab dialects, 12
Ṭur ʿAbdin, 11
Turkey, 11, 285, 290
Turkish, 2, 13, 16, 33, 71, 112, 141, 239
Ṭuroyo, 11, 15

Uriah the Hittite (ʾEliya Ḥəttè), 224, 225, 226, 228, 268, 269
Urmi, 12, 13, 177, 201
Urmia, 227
Venice, 227
Western Neo-Aramaic, 10
Wisser, Rabbi Meir Leibush Ben Yeḥiel Michel (Malbim), 231
Yalquṭ ha-Makhiri, 213
Yalquṭ Šimʿoni, 131, 200, 221, 233, 239, 242
Yehudah, Rabbi, 179
Yemen, 286
Yitzḥak, Rabbi, 221, 229
Yom Kippur, 175, 177, 239
Zakho, 1, 2, 3, 4, 12, 13, 23, 25, 26, 27, 29, 30, 32, 33, 34, 42, 44, 45, 60, 61, 62, 63, 66, 71, 92, 105, 109, 130, 136, 149, 169, 172, 173, 176, 177, 178, 182, 201, 206, 224, 253, 281, 282, 288, 296, 298
Zephaniah, 242
Zeus, 286
Zohar, Book of, 194, 221, 222

Cambridge Semitic Languages and Cultures

General Editor Geoffrey Khan

Cambridge Semitic Languages and Cultures

About the series

This series is published by Open Book Publishers in collaboration with the Faculty of Asian and Middle Eastern Studies of the University of Cambridge. The aim of the series is to publish in open-access form monographs in the field of Semitic languages and the cultures associated with speakers of Semitic languages. It is hoped that this will help disseminate research in this field to academic researchers around the world and also open up this research to the communities whose languages and cultures the volumes concern. This series includes philological and linguistic studies of Semitic languages, editions of Semitic texts, and studies of Semitic cultures. Titles in the series will cover all periods, traditions and methodological approaches to the field. The editorial board comprises Geoffrey Khan, Aaron Hornkohl, and Esther-Miriam Wagner.

This is the first Open Access book series in the field; it combines the high peer-review and editorial standards with the fair Open Access model offered by OBP. Open Access (that is, making texts free to read and reuse) helps spread research results and other educational materials to everyone everywhere, not just to those who can afford it or have access to well-endowed university libraries.

Copyrights stay where they belong, with the authors. Authors are encouraged to secure funding to offset the publication costs and thereby sustain the publishing model, but if no institutional funding is available, authors are not charged for publication. Any grant secured covers the actual costs of publishing and is not taken as profit. In short: we support publishing that respects the authors and serves the public interest.

UNIVERSITY OF CAMBRIDGE
Faculty of Asian and Middle Eastern Studies

You can find more information about this serie at:
http://www.openbookpublishers.com/section/107/1

Other titles in the series

Points of Contact
The Shared Intellectual History of Vocalisation in Syriac, Arabic, and Hebrew

Nick Posegay

https://https://doi.org/10.11647/OBP.0271

A Handbook and Reader of Ottoman Arabic
Esther-Miriam Wagner (ed.)

https://doi.org/10.11647/OBP.0208

Diversity and Rabbinization
Jewish Texts and Societies between 400 and 1000 CE

Gavin McDowell, Ron Naiweld, Daniel Stökl Ben Ezra (eds)

https://doi.org/10.11647/OBP.0219

New Perspectives in Biblical and Rabbinic Hebrew
Aaron D. Hornkohl and Geoffrey Khan (eds)

https://doi.org/10.11647/OBP.0250

The Marvels Found in the Great Cities and in the Seas and on the Islands
A Representative of 'Ağā'ib Literature in Syriac

Sergey Minov

https://doi.org/10.11647/OBP.0237

Studies in the Grammar and Lexicon of Neo-Aramaic
Geoffrey Khan and Paul M. Noorlander (eds)

https://doi.org/10.11647/OBP.0209

Jewish-Muslim Intellectual History Entangled
Textual Materials from the Firkovitch Collection, Saint Petersburg

Camilla Adang, Bruno Chiesa, Omar Hamdan, Wilferd Madelung, Sabine Schmidtke and Jan Thiele (eds)

https://doi.org/10.11647/OBP.0214

Studies in Semitic Vocalisation and Reading Traditions
Aaron Hornkohl and Geoffrey Khan (eds)

https://doi.org/10.11647/OBP.0207

Studies in Rabbinic Hebrew
Shai Heijmans (ed.)

https://doi.org/10.11647/OBP.0164

The Tiberian Pronunciation Tradition of Biblical Hebrew
Volume 1

Geoffrey Khan

https://doi.org/10.11647/OBP.0163

The Tiberian Pronunciation Tradition of Biblical Hebrew
Volume 2

Geoffrey Khan

https://doi.org/10.11647/OBP.0194

www.ingramcontent.com/pod-product-compliance
Lightning Source LLC
Chambersburg PA
CBHW051535230426
43669CB00015B/2608